THE ECONOMIC LESSONS
OF THE NINETEEN-THIRTIES

THE
ECONOMIC LESSONS
OF THE
NINETEEN-THIRTIES

A Report Drafted by
H. W. ARNDT

FRANK CASS : LONDON

Published by
FRANK CASS AND COMPANY LIMITED
67 Great Russell Street, London WC1B 3BT

*First issued under the auspices of the
Royal Institute of International Affairs*

This reprint has been authorized by the Oxford University Press

First edition	1944
Second impression	1963
Third impression	1972

ISBN 0 7146 1204 9

Printed in Great Britain by
Lewis Reprints Ltd.
member of Brown Knight & Truscott Group
London and Tonbridge

FOREWORD TO FIRST EDITION

In undertaking a series of studies on post-war economic problems, the Economic Group of the Chatham House Reconstruction Committee decided to prepare a Report on the economic lessons of the nineteen-thirties. The drafting of this report was confided to their Research Assistant, Mr. H. W. Arndt. In his task Mr. Arndt was assisted by discussion with the members of the Group to whom the various chapters were submitted. The subject is obviously controversial, and though there was a large measure of agreement in regard to all the chapters except the last, the Group decided not to attempt an agreed text, but to publish the document, together with such dissenting notes as were submitted by some of those consulted. Mr. Arndt assumes responsibility for the text of the report itself.

ASTOR
Chairman of the Council

Chatham House,
St. James's Square,
London, S.W.1

8 December 1943

CONTENTS

Chapter One

THE NINETEEN-TWENTIES

I. THE WORLD ECONOMIC SITUATION IN THE NINETEEN-TWENTIES

THE great depression ended a period of short but rapid and in many respects unexampled economic progress. By 1925 most of the immediate problems of post-war reconstruction appeared to be solved. Most of the advanced industrial countries had recovered from a brief but severe post-war slump. The political problems which had prevented economic progress during the first five years after the war seemed settled. The frontiers of the European countries seemed at last stabilized; the reparation problem, which had been the immediate cause of the Ruhr invasion and monetary chaos in Germany, was temporarily solved by the Dawes Plan. By 1925 order had been restored in the internal monetary systems of most countries, and, with the exception of France, all the major countries of the world had returned to the gold standard, which seemed to have resumed its function as the automatic mechanism for the adjustment of the international economic system. Between 1925 and 1929 world production of primary products rose by 11 per cent, industrial production by something between 23 per cent and 27 per cent, and the quantum of world trade rose by about 20 per cent.[1] At the same time, there was considerable progress during the decade in industrial productivity, national incomes, and standards of living, though the rate of progress varied greatly in different countries.

However, the equilibrium of the world economic situation throughout the first post-war decade was unstable. While the immediate causes of the depression must be sought primarily in the *internal* economic development of the countries concerned—and especially in the internal development of the U.S.A., from where the crisis and depression spread throughout the world—the fact that the depression did spread to every country, its severity, and the obstacles to recovery during the nineteen-thirties are largely accounted for by three outstanding factors in the economic conditions of the world during the post-war decade which were all to some extent but different aspects of the same problem.

The world war had meant a violent breach in the continuity of

[1] League of Nations, *Review of World Production 1925-31* (Geneva, 1932), p. 9.

A*

economic change. For four years and more the production and distribution of goods, and the mechanism of trade and exchange, had been governed in the belligerent countries primarily by the exigencies of war, and in the neutral countries by the abnormal conditions of blockade, shipping shortage, greatly extended or vanished markets, and freedom from powerful competitors. The territorial changes and reparations conditions of the peace treaties had added to the dislocation caused by the war. These upheavals alone would have given rise to difficult problems of economic adjustment. They were greatly aggravated by the fact that war conditions had prevented the normal piecemeal adjustments of production and trade in different countries to long-term trends of economic development, such as changes in population trends, in consumers' tastes, or in the rate of economic progress of different countries or industries. These changes, which in the absence of war would have led, through the free play of market forces, to a series of small adjustments, had now in some instances resulted in major maladjustments of production and trade. Some of these problems were solved during the years of post-war reconstruction. But some others had grown too large to be corrected by market forces, supplemented occasionally by uncoordinated and often misguided efforts of national Governments. They could be covered up by international credits and were temporarily concealed by the prosperity of the decade. But they re-emerged after 1929 and became at any rate part causes of the great depression.

a. One of these problems was the development of relative over-production in some branches of world agriculture. War conditions and remarkable improvements in agricultural technique had led to an immense expansion of agricultural production during the years of the war. A constant demand for their products at steadily rising prices had encouraged overseas agricultural producers to take new land under the plough, and to increase production per acre by the application of new techniques. At the same time, European countries, shut off from some of their normal peacetime supplies had also expanded and intensified agricultural production. With the removal of the exceptionally favourable conditions of the war this unprecedented growth of productive capacity might in any circumstances have presented a serious problem. It was aggravated by the fact that after the war the demand for some of the most important agricultural products, especially cereals, ceased to expand at the pre-war rate, owing primarily to changes in nutritional tastes (in turn the symptom of rising standards of living), but also to the beginnings of the trend towards stationary populations in north-west Europe and North America, and to measures of agricultural protection.

The result was a relative surplus productive capacity of the large primary producing countries and a tendency for agricultural prices to fall relatively to those of manufactured goods. The relative cheapening of food and raw materials benefited the industrial countries. It stimulated their production and the volume of trade in materials and led to a rapid rise in their standard of living. But, since it meant that a smaller volume of manufactures could be bought in exchange for a given weight of primary products, the export trades of the manufacturing countries suffered some relative reduction in quantity. The share of manufactures in world trade decreased throughout the years of prosperity and would have decreased very much more if it had not been maintained by international loans which enabled primary producing countries to import finished goods on credit. The fall in agricultural prices which, after the first collapse during the immediate post-war depression, had been held up for several years by improved demand, and in 1927 and 1928 by the accumulation of stocks, resumed its course after the bumper harvest of 1928 and was further accelerated by the American slump and the release of stocks. It was one of the contributing factors in the world depression. It upset the balances of payments of the primary producing countries, forcing them to protect their currencies or default (or both), and led some of the industrial countries to protect their domestic agriculture by tariffs and their balances of payments by exchange control or devaluation.

b. Even more important in the long run was the tendency, which began during the war and continued during the post-war decade, towards a reversal of the process of increasing international specialization. It is customary to refer to this tendency by the convenient, but inadequate term of 'economic nationalism'. The term ignores the fact that, to some extent, the changes in world trade and the measures of protectionism that were adopted in most countries were the natural, and not always harmful, reactions to profound long-term trends which had been accelerated by the war. The war marked the beginning of the end of the process by which the advanced industrial countries of Europe, under the leadership of Great Britain, had for most of the nineteenth century invested vast amounts of capital in the development of large new territories in the Southern and Western Hemispheres for the production of their food and raw material supplies. Investment opportunities in this field had begun to slacken before the war. During the war secondary industries had been developed in all the overseas primary producing countries under the stimulus of the need to replace imports from Europe and of the freedom from European competition. After the war this policy was continued and infant industries were protected by tariffs. The increased difficulties of the primary producers in finding markets for their products merely encouraged the tendency in the new countries, especially the British Dominions, India, and South America, to replace specialization by a better internal balance of production.

At the same time, technological changes lessened the advantages of rigid international specialization between the European industrial countries and the overseas agricultural territories. The development and diffusion of new power resources (oil and hydro-electric power) lessened the need for rigid localization of industry on the basis of coal supplies. The gradual replacement of steel by light metals altered the relative advantages of various countries as the producers of the most important industrial raw material. Mechanization widened the scope of industry based on cheap rather than skilled labour, and the growing importance of tertiary industry implicit in rising standards of living, coupled with decreasing transport costs, reinforced the tendency towards the localization of consumers' goods industries near their markets rather than near the supply of basic raw materials.

These long-term trends largely account for the 'economic nationalism' of the new *non*-European territories, and the difficulties of the export trades of the European industrial countries during the immediate post-war years. But economic nationalism in the usual meaning of the term had some additional effect in hampering international trade and disturbing the international economic system. It was due partly to the peace treaties which had multiplied national frontiers and broken up larger economic units. The policies of the majority of the small newly-created states of central and south-eastern Europe that tried, not altogether unjustifiably, to foster industrial development almost regardless of considerations of relative costs were the outstanding examples of 'economic nationalism' during the nineteen-twenties. At the same time, Germany and other industrial countries of Europe began to adopt or increase measures of agrarian protection, which in turn heightened the difficulties of the overseas primary producer. Lastly, the U.S.A. continued its protectionist policy in circumstances which had changed profoundly since 1914.

c. This leads us to the third and most important cause of the economic instability of the world before 1929. War debts and reparations, the sale of external capital assets during the war by the United Kingdom, and changes in world trade had completely altered the equilibrium of international payments. The U.S.A. had replaced Great Britain as the leading creditor country. Even without the war the U.S.A. would probably have achieved a favourable balance of payments by 1920; as a result of the war the U.S.A. was owed $10 milliard of 'political debts' in addition to some $2—4 milliard on private account.[1] At the other end of the scale was Germany, saddled with a burden of reparations which was determined in 1924 at a rate of about £50—125 million a year. The repayment of these colossal debts in the only ∝ form in which international debts can be repaid, that is, in the form of goods, would have involved a profound alteration in the direction of world trade and profound changes in the internal economic structure especially of the ultimate creditor country, the U.S.A. Such a change was never even contemplated in the U.S.A., where the tariff was closely bound up with the internal political situation, and guarded by powerful vested interests. The only alternative to accepting repayment in the form of European exports was to re-lend the money to the European debtors. During the nineteen-twenties, therefore, the U.S.A. increased her tariff walls, but at the same time lent abroad on long-term more than she received in interest and repayment of old debts. By 1929 her net annual capital exports, largely to Germany, reached $5 milliard.[2] While Great Britain, in spite of an increasingly adverse balance of trade, also continued to lend abroad, the debtor countries of Europe and South America immensely increased their long-term and, what was especially dangerous, their short-term indebtedness. Germany in particular enjoyed a period of prosperity and rapid economic progress which was entirely dependent on the continuation of foreign borrowing. While it lasted, this arrangement concealed the disequilibrium and facilitated the task of European reconstruction. But with the depression and the failure of continued credits from the U.S.A. the structure collapsed.

On these conditions of economic and financial maladjustment had been superimposed a rigid, and at the same time delicate, mechanism for the automatic control of international payments. It is more than doubtful whether the gold standard, which had functioned well enough in the pre-war world of *laisser-faire* and relatively unimpeded international trade, was compatible with the rapidly changing relative national price levels and the greatly increased obstacles to automatic adjustment of the nineteen-twenties. Even had it been worked strictly in accordance with the rules of the game it would, in these conditions, have served to transmit economic disturbances from one country to another. In fact, the Governments of the world, while eager to revive the gold standard as a symbol of the return to 'normalcy', did not stick to these rules. Largely for reasons of national policy, currencies were undervalued or overvalued. Nor were Governments pre-

[1] F. W. Fetter, *U.S. Balance of International Payments*, Foreign Policy Reports, 15 May 1936, p. 58, n. 9.
[2] ibid., p. 59.

pared (or able) to take the drastic measures of internal deflation required by the gold standard system in countries with a temporarily or permanently overvalued currency. With the beginning of the depression the maintenance of the gold standard would have become increasingly difficult for some countries. It was wrecked by the large and increasing movements of short-term capital which constituted an altogether new and disturbing phenomenon of the post-war period.

These international movements of 'hot money', as it came to be called, were themselves the result primarily of political and economic instability, though their volume was increased by the adoption in many countries of the so-called gold exchange standard and the increase in Government financing by means of short-term bills and securities. They darted about between the financial centres of the world in search of temporary security or speculative profit and at frequent intervals exerted a dangerous pressure on the gold and foreign exchange reserves of one or the other country. After the collapse of the Wall Street boom and during the depression, one country after another, faced with sudden recalls or flights of short-term funds, was forced to protect its currency either by depreciation or exchange control. The financial crisis greatly accelerated the spread of the depression and contributed to its severity.

II. THE UNITED STATES

IN any account of the economic condition of the world between the two wars the U.S.A. must occupy a central position. In view of the position of the U.S.A. as the leading creditor country, as one of the greatest import markets, and as one of the most important producers and exporters of many agricultural products and raw materials, her economic condition and policy had a more direct effect on world economic conditions than those of any one other country. For the purposes of this report, the U.S.A. is of further interest because from 1933 onwards the American Government under President Roosevelt pursued the most significant experiment in raising a large capitalist economy out of the depths of economic depression.

When President Roosevelt entered on his first term of office on 4 March 1933, the economic life of the U.S.A. was in a state of suspended animation after an almost continuous decline for four years from the peak of prosperity in 1929. In 1920-1 the U.S.A. had passed through a short post-war slump which was the more severe because it had been postponed for two years by a remarkable flow of exports to Europe and by large-scale government expenditure. In 1922, however, the U.S.A. entered on a seven years' period of rapid economic progress and unprecedented prosperity. The national income, expressed in 1929 dollars, rose from $68·5 milliard in 1922 to $93·6 milliard in 1929, a rise of nearly 40 per cent over the short period of seven years.[1] There was a remarkable, though by no means equal, rise in the standard of living of all classes. Industrial productivity increased by 43 per cent between 1919 and 1929.[2] The value of American foreign trade rose by 28 per cent between 1922 and 1929,[3] and the U.S.A. was investing abroad a large surplus of its national product. This period of economic advance came to an abrupt end in 1929. In July of that year the volume of industrial production began to decline. Employment rose slowly till July, remained constant in August and fell in October. The stock market crash in October accelerated the cumulative downward trend of economic activity which continued unchecked until the summer of 1932, and after a brief and slow ascent was pushed still further by the banking and financial crisis of the spring of 1933. During these four years wholesale prices fell by almost one-third (95·3 to 65·9),[4] and industrial production contracted by more than half (125 to 58);[5] the national income fell from $82·7 milliard in 1929 to $40 milliard in 1932,[6] and the value of U.S. merchandise trade decreased by more than two-thirds;[7] in 1931 net investment, in 1929 prices, was negative to the extent of $358 million and this figure fell to minus $5,800 million in 1932;[8] for five years America lived on her capital. Worst of all, the number of employed workers decreased from 48 million in September 1929 to just over 36 million in March 1933, when the total number of unemployed was conservatively estimated at over 14 million.[9]

No attempt can be made here to analyse the causes of this catastrophic collapse. It will suffice to stress some of the outstanding features of the American boom and depression.

a. The main facts underlying the astonishing boom of the nineteen-twenties had been remarkable improvements in industrial technique which coincided with a pronounced building boom. Between 1919 and 1929 production per wage earner in manufacturing industries had increased by no less than 40 per cent.

[1] S. Kuznets, *National Income and Capital Formation,* quoted T. Wilson, *Fluctuations in Income and Employment* (Pitman, 1941), p. 117.
[2] E. A. Radice and E. M. Hugh-Jones, *An American Experiment,* 1936, p. 43.
[3] F. W. Fetter, Foreign Policy Reports, loc. cit., p. 57.
[4] Department of Labour Index, quoted J. Strachey, *A Programme for Progress* (Gollancz, 1940), p. 194.
[5] T. Wilson, op. cit., p. 159.
[6] *Statistical Abstract of the United States, 1939.*
[7] F. W. Fetter, op. cit., p. 57.
[8] T. Wilson, op. cit., p. 159.
[9] J. Strachey, op. cit., p. 195.

Progress had been particularly rapid in a number of new industries, of which the motor-car industry was the most obvious
example. The tendency towards a rapid growth of investment
was underlined by a residential building boom which began soon
after the war, reached its peak in 1925 with $5,000 million and
then declined gradually, though the decline was offset until 1928
by an increase in public construction expenditure. The result was
an even more marked divergence than in other trade cycles, in the
rate of growth of production between capital and durable consumption goods on the one hand, and non-durable consumption
goods on the other. While the output of the former increased at
a rate of 6·4 per cent and 5·9 per cent a year respectively, the
latter increased at a rate of only 2·8 per cent a year.[1] Without
entering upon the controversial question of the causes of the
downward trend in 1929, it is fairly clear that the usual check to
investment resulting from a decline in the rate of growth of
consumption was accentuated in this case by the simultaneous
decline in the building boom and the fact that investment opportunities in some of the new industries had passed their peak.
There were other internal factors which contributed to the
severity of the decline. The stock exchange crash, while it cannot
be blamed for the downturn itself, since the latter preceded it
by several months, undoubtedly accelerated the decline. The
slump in security values which followed it and which was in turn
hastened by the unsound investment policy of the American
banks, led to an ever increasing pressure upon debtors of every
kind. The resulting scramble for liquidity produced the banking
crisis of 1933.

b. One of the outstanding characteristics of the American
slump was the agricultural depression which, though not peculiar
to the U.S.A., was particularly important in its social and economic consequences in that country. American agriculture had
profited enormously by the war. With a constant demand for
foodstuffs at rising prices, production was greatly expanded at
the price of an immense increase in the indebtedness of the
American farmer. This debt burden, which had been easy enough
to bear during the period of artificial prosperity, became a millstone round the neck of American agriculture after the war, when
the American farmers found themselves faced with powerful competitors in the world market and a tendency towards falling prices.
Throughout the nineteen-twenties American agriculture remained depressed, and the farmers failed to share in the rise of
the national income. Instead of adapting itself to the changed
situation by contracting production, agriculture received further
financial assistance from banks and from the government and

[1] Radice and Hugh-Jones, op. cit., p. 49.

increased its debt burden by a further 20 per cent between 1920 and 1929. Until 1928 agricultural prices were maintained. The large harvest of that year initiated a fall in prices which assumed disastrous proportions with the onset of the industrial depression, a rapidly contracting demand facing a rigid and actually increasing supply and accumulated stocks, which were now released. The result was the virtual bankruptcy not only of the American farmers but also of a large proportion of the rural banks which were involved in the failure of their debtors.

c. Government policy, if it did not actually contribute to the economic disaster, did little to stem the tide. Throughout the nineteen-twenties, the U.S.A. was governed by Republican administrations whose policy was dictated by the principle of *laisser-faire*. Until 1929 the rule of big business appeared to be brilliantly vindicated by prosperity and progress. For a long time after the beginning of the slump, President Hoover and his advisers took the view that business enterprise would solve its problems unaided. At first the Administration confined itself to exhortations to business men to go on employing the same labour force so that purchasing power should not be destroyed. The only important step taken before 1931 was the passage of the Hawley-Smoot tariff in 1930, which considerably increased tariffs on imports. Though it may have steadied conditions in some industries its effects on the American economy, counteracted as they were by reprisals the world over, were probably negligible. Government passivity gave free rein to the deflationary forces which arose automatically from the collapse of profitability. As a matter of fact, wage-rates were not cut seriously before 1930, when a sharp cut might conceivably have maintained profit expectations. When in 1930 employers turned to the traditional policy of wage-deflation any favourable effect of the reduction of costs was more than offset by the effect of a sagging wage-level in inducing producers to postpone orders. The Administration did not pursue a deliberately deflationary policy. When the Federal Reserve Banks made efforts early in 1929 to control the stock exchange boom, they took pains to direct their policy of credit restriction solely against speculation, not against industry and trade, and they continued an 'easy money' policy during 1929 and 1930. But until 1931 the Administration did nothing to counteract the enormous decline of effective purchasing power. In 1931 and 1932 the Federal Government did indeed decide to pursue an active policy of reflation by means of public works and financial assistance to agriculture, banking and industry. During 1931 and 1932 the rate of Federal Government spending on public works was more than double what it had been in the years before the depression. The Federal surplus of $746 million for the fiscal year 1930 was replaced by a deficit of $616 million in 1931, and $2,685 million in 1932.[1] Unfortunately, this was more than counterbalanced by a big contraction in the public works expenditure of cities, counties, and states. In 1932 the Reconstruction Finance Corporation was organized to aid in financing agriculture, banking, commerce, and industry. In the first year of its operations it lent $1,000 million to various institutions, mainly banks, trust companies, and railroads.[2] In June 1932 security values began to advance and there was a small revival of business. But, while it is important to remember that this important change in American Government policy began under the Hoover regime, the change came too late to prevent the disaster and was on an entirely inadequate scale to produce a real economic revival.

d. It must be emphasized that the initial causes of the American depression, in contrast to most other countries, were entirely internal. The internal economic conditions of the U.S.A. were not dependent, as were those of, for example, Great Britain, on her foreign trade. Nor was the American internal credit situation affected by an adverse balance of payments and pressure on her gold and foreign exchange reserves. Throughout the nineteen-twenties continuous capital exports on a vast scale enabled the U.S.A. to maintain a large export surplus. This export surplus was maintained even throughout the depression partly because the failure of long-term foreign lending after 1930 was offset by large withdrawals of foreign short-term balances. The decline in the value of U.S. trade by two-thirds during 1929–32 increased the difficulties of American agriculture, but it was not a major factor in the American depression. As a net creditor to the world in 1929 by about $21,000 million, as the owner of gold reserves which in 1929 amounted to 28 per cent of the world stock of gold, and with a continuously favourable balance of payments, the U.S.A was relatively immune from the effects of international monetary disturbances. During the depression large gold exports occurred several times, particularly after the British suspension of gold payments in September 1931, when President Hoover stated that the U.S.A. had been within two weeks of abandoning gold. But these outflows were all soon halted and counteracted by net inflows of gold. The U.S.A. was never really in danger of being driven off the gold standard, and when gold was actually abandoned the action was taken for reasons related to the internal economic position of the country.

e. But if the U.S.A. was practically unaffected by outside influences, the American depression had a profound effect on

[1] T. Wilson, op. cit., p. 160 f.
[2] Radice and Hugh-Jones, op. cit., p. 62.

world economic conditions. The contraction of American demand and the fall of the American price levels, especially of agricultural products, led the way to the decline of world prices and the rapid contraction of international trade. With the American crisis and depression the unstable equilibrium of the international balance of payments, which had been maintained during the nineteen-twenties largely by American capital exports, completely collapsed. Already the stock exchange boom of 1929, by attracting funds to New York, had exerted some pressure on the exchange position of the European debtor countries. During 1930 the scramble for liquidity in the U.S.A. led to even larger recalls of short-term funds from Europe. At the same time the flow of long-term capital exports declined greatly in 1931 and ceased completely in 1932. From the moment that the U.S.A. ceased to export capital the tariff wall which surrounded her, and which was heightened by the Hawley-Smoot Act of 1930, showed its full effect as an obstacle to the adjustment of the balances of payments of the debtor countries. The combined effect of the fall in world prices, the contraction of international trade, the recall of short-term funds and the failure of continued American long-term investment brought about financial and economic crises in almost every country and in most of them set going cumulative processes of decline similar to that which was going on in the U.S.A. The worst hit were the overseas primary producing countries, which were brought to the verge of bankruptcy by the fall in agricultural and commodity prices, and the European debtor states, whose economic prosperity had been built up on continued foreign borrowing. Pressure on its gold and foreign exchange reserves forced one country after another to protect its currency by exchange depreciation or exchange control. At the same time, the efforts of every country to maintain its exports and protect its balance of payments by imposing increasing tariffs and import restrictions still further diminished the flow of international trade and increased the difficulties of every other country. The American slump and depression cannot be said to have *caused* the world depression, but they upset the unstable economic equilibrium of the world and gave the impetus to a similar economic decline in other countries.

III. GREAT BRITAIN

THE British depression of 1931–2 differed in two very important respects from the American depression. First, the slump in Great Britain was much less severe than in the U.S.A., chiefly because Great Britain never fully shared the prosperity of the nineteen-twenties. Secondly, the causes of the great depression in Great

Britain, like those of most of her earlier cyclical depressions during this century, were primarily external; the downward turn was produced chiefly by the decline in British exports.

Once the unsettled conditions of the immediate post-war years, with their reconstruction boom and slump, were over, Great Britain had some share in the general technical progress and the expansion of output, employment, and trade. Between 1924 and 1929 production increased by 12 per cent, profits rose, and there was some rise in the standard of living.[1] But Great Britain's economic progress was not commensurate with that of other advanced industrial countries. Output in other leading countries, the U.S.A., Germany, Japan, U.S.S.R., increased considerably more than in Great Britain and her share of the total exports of manufactures of leading manufacturing countries fell from 26 per cent to 22 per cent.[2] The chief symptom of her *malaise* was unemployment, which stood at 1,200,000 in 1924 (10 per cent of the insured population), and never fell below the million mark throughout the decade of 'prosperity';[3] it was particularly severe in the staple export industries of coal, cotton, woollen and worsted, iron and steel, and shipbuilding, and in the 'depressed areas' of the Clyde, the Tyne, Lancashire and South Wales, where those industries were localized.

Long-term trends of economic development and short-term policy combined to depress British trade and her most important industries. British trade was more severely hit than that of most other industrial countries by the trend towards a reversal of international specialization which has been mentioned before as one of the features of post-war economic conditions. British industrial supremacy during the nineteenth century had been founded largely on her advantageous position as a supplier of the two basic materials of nineteenth-century industry, coal and iron, and of skilled labour. The technological changes since the beginning of this century which have been mentioned all tended to diminish these advantages. The coal industry was faced with increasing rivalry from new power resources, oil and hydro-electric power; the steel industry began to feel the competition of light metals; mechanization had increased the competitive power of countries with ample supplies of cheap unskilled or semi-skilled labour such as Japan. Economic development in the chief British export markets increased the difficulties of the British export trades. During the war, the expense and difficulty of obtaining British goods had stimulated most of the British Dominions and the republics of South America to establish and expand their own

---

[1] F. Benham, *Great Britain under Protection* (Macmillan, 1941), p. 13 f.

[2] Colin Clark, 'Statistical Studies of the Present Economic Position of Great Britain', *Economic Journal*, September 1931, p. 344.

[3] F. Benham, op. cit., p. 14.

industries, and after the war they protected them with tariffs. This applied especially to the textile industries. To take one example, the growth of the Indian cotton industry, protected by high import duties, resulted in a decline of imports of cotton piece-goods from 3,057 million yards in 1913 to 1,705 million in 1924, and 1,439 million in 1928-9. The total exports of British cotton piece-goods fell from 4,436 million square yards in 1925 to 3,672 million in 1929.[1] The development of alternative sources of power in the former British markets was chiefly responsible for a fall of British coal exports from 73,400,000 tons in 1913 to 47,628,000 tons in 1928,[2] and the exporting districts of the British coal industry were almost continuously depressed, with only a short interval of prosperity during the occupation of the Ruhr in 1923-4. The iron and steel industry suffered both from the decline in overseas demand, and from the subsidized competition of other exporting countries.

The root of the trouble, therefore, was that the general trends of world economic and technological development operated against a revival of Britain's staple exports and chief industries. Ultimately, the only remedy was an adjustment of the British economy to the changed condition of the post-war world. But the requisite transfer of capital and workers from the contracting industries of the North and Midlands to the expanding industries of the South foundered on the rigidity of vested interests and the immobility of labour, though some such transfer did take place.[3]

The long-term problems of British industry were reinforced by the return to the gold standard at the old parity in 1925, largely on grounds of prestige and in the interests of the City and British overseas investors. The importance of this factor has often been overemphasized. But there can be little doubt that the resulting overvaluation of the pound greatly increased the price difficulties from which all industrial exporters were suffering, quite apart from the depressing effect on industry and the standard of living of the deflationary policy which it entailed. It increased the adverse balance of trade, and maintained a constant pressure on the gold reserves of the Bank of England.

[1] International Labour Office, *World Textile Industry*, 1937, vol. i, p. 124.
[2] J. H. Jones, G. Cartwright and P. H. Guerault, *The Coal-Mining Industry* (Pitman, 1939), p. 33.
[3] Between 1920 and 1930 the North, Midlands, and Wales lost 782,000 by migration, while the South-East gained 615,000. Between 1923 and 1930 the number of workers attached to the old staple industries contracted from 1,244,000 to 1,070,000 in the coal industry, from 270,000 to 205,000 in ship-building, from 667,000 to 592,000 in general engineering, from 269,000 to 240,000 in the wool and worsted industry. During the same period the numbers attached to the distributive trades rose from 1,254,000 to 1,764,000, to the motor-car industry from 192,000 to 247,000, hotels and boarding houses from 259,000 to 351,000, electrical engineering 61,000 to 90,000, and silk and rayon from 37,000 to 78,000 (cf. F. Benham, op. cit.. p. 19).

The world depression intensified the very difficulties under which Great Britain had been labouring during most of the preceding decade—an increasing import surplus and adverse balance of trade, depression and unemployment in the export industries, and increasing pressure on her gold and foreign exchange reserves. Great Britain suffered from the repercussions of practically anything that went wrong in the world, and she was a chief sufferer from the general process of 'incapsulation', as it has been called. Between 1929 and the third quarter of 1931 British merchandise exports declined by 30 per cent.[1] It was primarily this fall in exports which started the cyclical depression in Great Britain. But, partly because of the relatively depressed state of the British economic system throughout the preceding decade, partly because, in contrast to the United States, state insurance and unemployment relief provided a bottom to the decline in consumers' income and demand in Great Britain, the decline was comparatively gentle, and not nearly as severe as, for example, in the U.S.A. or Germany, as the following table shows:

Percentage Decline in Industrial Production, National Income and Wholesale Prices 1929–32 in U.S.A., Germany, Great Britain.[2]

	U.S.A. per cent	Germany per cent	G. Britain per cent
Industrial Production	54	42	17
National Income	53	39	20
Wholesale Prices (1929–32)	38	35	30

Nonetheless, in Great Britain as in every other country, the great depression marked the lowest level of economic activity in living memory. Unemployment in 1932 reached almost three million,[3] nearly one-quarter of the insured population, and there was acute misery and poverty in many parts of the country.

One of the most important effects of the world depression on Great Britain was the pressure on the pound which led to the financial crisis of 1931. As the only remaining free market of importance, Great Britain became, during 1929 and 1930, the dumping ground for raw materials and foodstuffs from overseas and manufactured goods from the industrial countries of Europe. The volume of British imports rose from 1928 to 1929 by 5·7 per cent, though their cost fell constantly owing to the slump in wholesale prices. British exports, however, declined very much more, and the net result was an increase in the merchandise import surplus between 1930 and 1931 from £386 million to £408

[1] F. Benham, op. cit., p. 11.
[2] Figures based on League of Nations statistics.
[3] *Statistical Abstract for the United Kingdom.*

million.[1] At the same time, the contraction in world trade brought about a fall in 'invisible exports' from £414 million in 1930 to £304 million in 1931.[2] While the British adverse balance of payments constituted no immediate danger to the pound, since it could have been tided over by the recall of British short-term investments, the speculative movements of large accumulated foreign short-term balances in London imposed altogether too great a strain on the existing gold standard. Gloomy forecasts of a considerable budget deficit and the freezing of British short-term loans in the Austrian and German bank crashes in the summer of 1931 started a panic flight of foreign capital from London. By September the gold reserves of the Bank of England were practically exhausted, despite a large last-minute French and American loan; and on 20 September 1931 the newly formed 'National Government' was forced to suspend gold payments and to allow the pound to depreciate.

IV. FRANCE

OF the four countries, France was the last to feel the effects of the world slump. During 1930, while economic activity was declining fast elsewhere, French prosperity continued virtually unimpaired. It was not until after 1931 that the contraction of world trade, the successive depreciations of the pound and the dollar, and a rigid deflationary internal policy combined to depress the French economy. The depression in France, however, did not reach its lowest point until 1935 when most other countries were well on the way to recovery, and even after that date no real revival followed.

During the nineteen-twenties France had managed to achieve a remarkable degree of solid prosperity. The devastation wrought by the war necessitated an immense reconstruction, sometimes of whole industries, which, after a brief slump in 1921, maintained economic activity at full pitch throughout the first half of the decade and provided France with efficient modern equipment. By 1922 unemployment had vanished and France had to make up for lost manpower by large-scale importation of alien labour. A rapidly increasing budget deficit due to Government reconstruction expenditure and an extremely inefficient fiscal system, coupled with the failure of German reparation receipts and the consequent Ruhr invasion, led to inflation and a prolonged financial crisis from 1924 until 1926. But the financial crisis did not involve a general slump, and when the Poincaré Government turned the budget deficit into a regular surplus by a number of

[1] *Statistical Abstract for the United Kingdom.*
[2] ibid.

energetic reforms and finally, in 1928, stabilized the franc at a low level, internal and external confidence returned and France entered upon a period of solid economic advance.

The French prosperity of the late nineteen-twenties was marred neither by the development of the boom conditions of the U.S.A. nor by the unstable foundation in foreign borrowing of Germany. In direct contrast to Great Britain, which suffered from the contraction of her export markets and the overvaluation of the pound, French prosperity was largely due to her favourable foreign trade position and to the undervaluation of the franc. French exports had already recovered their pre-war level by 1922. From about 1925 onwards American and world prosperity specially favoured French exports by increasing the demand for the luxury and semi-luxury goods of which France was the chief supplier, and swelled her 'invisible exports', while at the same time bringing prosperity to one of her most important industries, through the boom in her tourist trade. The depreciation of the franc and its stabilization at a very low parity compared with the dollar, pound, or mark gave an additional stimulus to French exports. In 1928 and 1929 French foreign trade and especially exports increased rapidly, the latter by 14 per cent, and reached unprecedented levels which were practically maintained in 1930. The advantage of an undervalued currency outlasted the first year of the depression and was one of the reasons for the initial immunity of the French economy.

Another reason, closely connected with the first, was the strength of the franc at the beginning of the world depression. An almost regularly active balance of trade and a high surplus on invisible exports enabled France to accumulate a very large gold reserve after 1928 which was second only to that of the U.S.A. For the first years of the depression this reserve was more than sufficient to prevent any undue pressure on the franc. France, in fact, was one of the few European countries which, during the worst years of the world depression, was completely free from balance of payments difficulties. In the long run, this was perhaps a doubtful blessing. For it was one of the factors which induced the French Governments to retain the gold standard after 1931 and to pursue their disastrous policy of deflation during the following years.

Yet another factor softened the depression in France, though it could neither prevent it nor stay its course. For several reasons the decline in economic activity in France was only very partially reflected in rising unemployment figures. Voluntary or enforced emigration during 1931 and 1932 rid France of some 400,000 alien workers who had found work there during the preceding decade. Simultaneously, changes in the age structure of the

French population are estimated to have reduced the working population of France during these critical years by a further 800,000—1,000,000 persons. Thirdly, many unemployed industrial workers were able to move to the country and live on farms of which they were part owners. As a result, industrial unemployment never became as serious a problem in France as in the other three advanced industrial countries, though the export of alien labour did, of course, add to the number of unemployed elsewhere, while the escape to the land aggravated agricultural underemployment.

The first effect on France of the world slump was the decline in the tourist trade which began in 1929. In 1930 French foreign trade contracted slightly. But the index of industrial production did not reach its peak until that year.[1] By 1931 the competitive advantage which French exports had enjoyed had considerably diminished as a result of the fall in world prices. It was wiped out by the departure of Great Britain and the entire sterling bloc from the gold standard. Exports slumped, and the rising tide of bankruptcies testified to the increasing unprofitability of business. No sooner had the country begun to recover from this first shock than the depreciation of the dollar brought a new and more severe setback. As Great Britain, the U.S.A., and other countries slowly began to recover from the depression, France continued to retrogress. From 1930 until 1935 all indices of economic activity continuously declined. Industrial production fell by 33 per cent, wholesale prices by 46 per cent, and the value of foreign trade by 66 per cent.[2] In spite of the above-mentioned factors, the number of unemployed on relief increased from 928 in 1929 to 426,336 in 1935. In contrast to most other countries, the continued depression of France during this period was itself largely the result of the economic policy pursued in that country during the nineteen-thirties.

V. GERMANY

FOR obvious reasons, Germany during the nineteen-twenties bore the brunt of the economic dislocation caused by the war and the peace settlement, and of the economic disequilibrium of the world during the nineteen-twenties. Germany emerged from the war crippled by the loss of all her substantial foreign investments, her colonies, her merchant fleet, and large slices of territory, including a considerable proportion of her mineral resources, heavy industries and markets. These losses alone would have

[1] J. C. de Wilde, *Political Conflict in France*, Foreign Policy Reports, 1 April 1936, p. 21.
[2] ibid.

necessitated readjustments of her economy. Their effects were overshadowed by the reparation burdens which, measured at first in astronomical figures and fixed in 1921 at 132,000 million marks, directly or indirectly determined the economic development of Germany during the first post-war decade.

The reparation burden was primarily responsible for the catastrophic inflation of 1922–3, although the weakness and indecision of the Government were partly to blame for the complete loss of control. Unable to meet the reparations obligation on top of a national debt which had grown thirty-fold since 1913, the government resorted to borrowing and the printing press. During 1922 the slump of the mark increased in pace; the occupation of the Ruhr which followed the German default on her reparation payments led to the complete collapse of the currency, which was reduced to one million-millionth part of its pre-war value. The economic, to say nothing of the social and political, consequences of the inflation were profound. Until its last phase the inflation period was one of hectic activity. The rapid depreciation of the currency lightened and sometimes completely wiped out the real burden of loans; costs, such as wages, lagged behind prices; and the 'flight into goods' caused the investment of large amounts of borrowed money in plant and buildings. Production increased rapidly and by 1922 unemployment had disappeared. But prosperity was abnormal and lop-sided. Consumption lagged behind production, and activity in the consumption goods industries behind activity in the investment sphere. Production never recovered its pre-war level during this period. Technical efficiency diminished and whatever capital construction there was took the form of a 'widening' rather than a 'deepening' of the structure of production. Much of the unsound growth and malinvestment of the period was weeded out by the depression which followed the steady rise in costs and the decline in exports during 1923, and by the healthy crop of bankruptcies which resulted from the stabilization of the mark in 1924 and the consequent shock of deflation. At the end of the inflation Germany could register certain advantages. The national debt had disappeared, industry was rid of fixed charges, wages were low, and there were reasonably sure prospects of profits. On the other hand, the inflation, by completely wiping out the *rentier* class and the liquid reserves of German industry, had produced an acute scarcity of working capital which manifested itself in the absence of liquid funds and exceedingly high rates of interest. At the same time, the German reparation obligations, though scaled down in 1924 under the Dawes Plan, had to be met either by the creation of a large export surplus or by foreign loans.

The former alternative had by 1924 ceased to be a practical

possibility, if ever it was one. Neither Germany's creditors nor any other countries were willing to increase their imports from Germany to anything like the requisite extent; while an attempt to produce the export surplus by a reduction of German imports would have involved a deflationary movement of such severity that the German social structure, already weakened by the inflation, would have collapsed under the strain. Foreign loans provided the remedy. It is estimated that between 1924 and 1930 Germany borrowed from abroad, mainly from the U.S.A., but also from Holland, Great Britain and some other countries, a total of 30,100 million marks, of which probably nearly half were borrowed on short-term.[1] These loans enabled Germany not only to meet her obligations on reparations account, and to build up foreign balances and investments totalling about 9,700 million marks, but in addition to incur a regular deficit on her balance of trade (except in 1926 and 1929), which between 1924 and 1929 amounted to 7,800 million marks (including payments in goods on reparations account), and cover payment of interest on Germany's foreign debts (2,500 million), an increase of her gold stocks to more than 2,000 million marks, and other minor items.[2]

At the same time, these loans more than met the capital scarcity from which Germany was suffering and provided the finance for four years of rapid internal recovery and expansion. Foreign capital was attracted to Germany after 1924 primarily by the high rates of interest which German borrowers had to offer in the absence of domestic liquid resources, and by the lack of equally profitable opportunities of investment of American and other capital elsewhere. A large proportion of these loans were taken up by the Federal Government and its enterprises, and by states, provinces, and municipalities; about one third went to private industry. Private and public investment in capital equipment immensely stimulated economic activity. During the years while Germany borrowed from abroad, all indices—production, consumption, retail sales, wages, state revenue, foreign trade—showed rapid increases. Between 1925 and 1928 the volume of German production increased by 30 per cent;[3] efficiency increased and was consciously stimulated by intensive rationalization. A large proportion of the national income was devoted to expanding or improving capital equipment; new investment amounted to about 30,000 million marks, to which must be added increased stocks and the much larger amount written off for depreciation.[4] Increased home demand stimulated imports, which rose from 77·4 per cent of their 1913 value in

---

[1] J. A. Schumpeter, *Business Cycles*, 1939, vol. ii, p. 719.   [2] ibid.
[3] E. Roll, 'Germany', in H. A. Marquand, *Organized Labour in Four Continents* (Longmans, Green, 1939) p. 73.   [4] ibid.

1925 to 90 per cent in 1928; exports, too, rose from 58·3 per cent to 77·2 per cent.[1] Foreign borrowing temporarily solved, or rather postponed, the reparations problem. As a matter of fact, only a very small proportion of the funds borrowed from abroad were applied directly to meet Germany's foreign obligations. But by providing the basis for expanding economic activity they enabled the German Government to meet its obligations out of increased taxation and also provided the foreign exchange necessary for the transfer of the payments to Germany's creditors. However, both the internal prosperity of the country and its ability to pay its creditors depended entirely on the continuation of the influx of foreign capital.

Foreign borrowing brought the reparations problem no nearer its solution. Though it largely obviated a severe deflationary adjustment of the German economy, Germany could ultimately repay her creditors only in the form of exports. As a matter of fact, the economic recovery of Germany on the basis of foreign money, though it stimulated much 'extravagant' expenditure by public authorities, and led to overinvestment and an increased rigidity of the internal economic structure, might have provided a genuine alternative to a deflationary adjustment. It put Germany in a position in which she could easily have produced all the exports necessary to pay off her debts. The real difficulty was that at no time were her creditors prepared to accept repayment in real terms, that is, in the form of goods. When in 1929 the flow of capital to Germany ceased, the German balance of trade, which had been heavily adverse since 1926, suddenly and easily became favourable. German reparation exports suddenly became a reality. But their sole effect was to add to the difficulties of the international commercial situation and to contribute to the vicious circle of mutual restrictions, tariffs and quotas. The fundamental cause of disequilibrium was that as a result of the imposition of reparations the economic and financial methods of imperial expansion—capital exports—were for the first time applied to a country whose own economic structure made it an inevitable rival in that very expansion. Germany's economic structure was too much akin to that of her creditors and lenders. On the one hand, she could not repay her debts in the form of 'complementary' goods, raw materials and foodstuffs, like India or the South American Republics; on the other hand, industrial pressure groups in the creditor countries did their utmost to prevent her from repaying in the form of manufactured goods. The liquidation of reparations by the Lausanne agreement of 1932 was the logical conclusion to a disastrous error.

Internally, the prosperity built on the influx of foreign funds

[1] E. Roll, loc. cit.

was bound to collapse as soon as that influx ceased, or was reversed. Throughout these years German economic activity fluctuated with the flow of foreign capital. The fact that the downward turn began in Germany in 1928, a year before the onset of the depression in other countries, was partly due to internal reasons, a decline in profitability caused by heavy taxation and government wage policy, but chiefly to the Wall Street boom which attracted all available funds to New York. During 1929 the inflow of capital ebbed. With the American and world slump, and the general scramble for liquidity, it ceased altogether and, during 1930 and 1931, was reversed by a panic withdrawal of short-term funds. Owing partly to the difficulty of obtaining long-term loans abroad, partly to the policy of the German Government which, conscious of the danger of financing prosperity at home by borrowing abroad, had imposed a system of control on long-term borrowing, more than half of Germany's foreign indebtedness consisted of short-term funds. The danger of a vast short-term debt was increased by the fact that the banks which had chiefly been responsible for raising them had re-lent the money to industry and public authorities on what in practice amounted to long-term conditions. Germany's short-term indebtedness greatly aggravated her financial instability and was the immediate cause of the financial crisis of 1931.

By quick stages the withdrawal of short-term funds led to renewed capital scarcity, and internal depression; political uncertainty caused by the slump and the deflationary policy of the government led to new outflows of funds, Germans as well as foreigners sending their money out of the country. Reparation payments which had to be met out of a rapidly disappearing export surplus increased the pressure on the German exchange position. Early in 1931 the attempt to consolidate Germany's economic and political position by a customs union with Austria failed in the face of French, British, and Italian opposition. French pressure on Austria, exerted by the withdrawal of short-term credits, precipitated the failure of the Vienna Credit Anstalt in May, which marked the beginning of the financial crisis. It led to immense new withdrawals of funds from Germany, which was expected to be the next victim of the financial collapse. In June the situation was temporarily eased by the one-year moratorium on all inter-governmental debts proposed by President Hoover, and by a new $100 million credit granted by foreign central banks. But by July 3,000 million marks of a total of 11,000 million German short-term debts had been withdrawn.[1] A severe internal banking crisis was met by an internal moratorium, and a drastic reorganization of the whole banking system;

[1] E. Roll, loc. cit., p. 75.

and further pressure on the country's gold and exchange reserves and the external value of the mark was checked by the imposition of exchange control. In the circumstances, exchange control was the only alternative open to the Government. Even the most severe intensification of deflationary measures would have been useless in the face of the flight of capital. The horror of uncontrolled inflation which the experience of 1922–3 had left in German public opinion made exchange depreciation a political impossibility. The financial crisis thus forced on Germany the system which the Nazi Government after 1933 developed into the pivotal instrument for the control of the whole economy.

In the meantime, the depression in Germany, caused by the failure of continued foreign capital supplies, continued to run its course. The abnormal character of the preceding years of prosperity increased the severity of the slump. Between 1928 and 1932 production fell by 46 per cent, and the fall in the output of capital goods, which amounted to 65 per cent, was even more disproportionate than in other countries.[1] Unemployment which, during the preceding years of rapid technological advance had fluctuated between 1,000,000 and 2,000,000, rose to 6,000,000 in January 1932.[2] The Brüning Government attempted to adjust the German economy to the failure of capital imports from abroad by instituting a policy of rigorous deflation, in spite of the social upheaval which this entailed. Drastic cutting of costs by reduction of wages and social services, together with an effort to mitigate the effects of this reduction by price control, was the technique adopted under the rule by emergency decree. As in every other country, deflation proved unsuccessful in leading the internal economy out of the depression; it only served to intensify the political struggle. In 1932 the last pre-Nazi Governments began to supplement this policy by reflationary measures, such as tax-remission for firms increasing the number of workers employed and the creation of fresh credit facilities for industry. Possibly owing in part to this policy the German economic system began to recover slightly in the second half of 1932. By December 1932 production had risen by 10 per cent from the low level of August of that year; some commodity prices rose by the same amount, and the index of share prices rose in the same period by 20 per cent.[3] But economic chaos, misery and unemployment had brought the social system to the verge of collapse. Frightened by the prospect of revolution from the Left, big business helped to instal Fascism in power.

[1] E. Roll, loc. cit., p. 76.   [2] ibid., p. 81.   [3] ibid., p. 77.

THE grim stories of prosperity, slump, and depression in the U.S.A., Great Britain, France and Germany might be repeated with some variations for every country of the world with the principal exception of the U.S.S.R. No useful purpose would be served by a melancholy catalogue of this kind. But it is important to note some of the general features of the world depression.

By 1929 the world economy, though outwardly prosperous, had developed a thoroughly unstable equilibrium which was liable to be turned into a cumulative decline by any major depressive factors. In each of the advanced capitalist countries the internal economy was in itself unstable and subject to the danger of a disastrous cyclical decline once internal or external factors turned the scales of prosperity. With the development of commodity surplus capacity relative to effective demand the relative prosperity of the primary producing countries depended on the continued accumulation of stocks. Major maladjustments in the balances of international payments, large-scale international indebtedness and the existence of large volatile international short-term funds constituted the third major element of instability. To a large extent the world depression can be explained in terms of the vicious circle which was set going when the internally generated slump in the U.S.A. upset each one of these unstable equilibria, directly or indirectly. The fall in American demand and the release of accumulated stocks immensely accelerated the collapse of agricultural and commodity prices, which were further depressed by the inelasticity of agricultural production. The withdrawal of American capital and the effect on international trade of the diminished purchasing power of the U.S.A. and the primary producing countries, combined with the fall in world prices, in turn, started cumulative depressions in each of the European industrial countries which further decreased the demand for goods produced elsewhere and depressed wholesale prices and world trade. Again, the decline in the volume and value of exports, accentuated in most cases by adverse capital movements, resulted in all countries except the U.S.A. and a few others who retained or increased their favourable balances of payments in ever increasing pressure upon their gold and foreign exchange reserves and upon the external value of their currencies.

The effects of this vicious spiral, however, were immensely aggravated by the measures taken by each country to protect its internal economy and its currency from the consequences of just that vicious spiral. In order to safeguard its industries and agriculture from foreign competition at cut-prices, and to protect its balance of payments by reducing (or preventing a rise in) imports each country imposed or increased tariffs and quantitative restrictions on imports. These in turn led to reprisals, to a further decline in demand and prices and further reductions of international trade. The Hawley-Smoot tariff in the United States (for which, as we have seen, the condition of the U.S. balance of payments provided no excuse) was the signal for an outburst of tariff-making activity in almost every other country. Extensive increases in duties were made almost immediately by Canada, Cuba, Mexico, France, Italy, and Spain. Further countries, including Great Britain, followed in 1931. When currency instability on a wide scale was unloosed after Great Britain abandoned the gold standard in September 1931, tariff increases, as well as other restrictions on trade, began to follow in the most rapid succession. The tariff warfare continued to feed on itself, stimulated by, and in turn accentuating, every further decline of world trade.

Similarly, the effect of depression on the balances of payments of individual countries resulted in the adoption of defensive measures which still further aggravated the situation. Most of the South American Republics were forced by the fall in the value of their exports to depreciate their currency and in some cases to adopt exchange control soon afterwards. Several of the European manufacturing countries, in particular Great Britain, already faced with increasingly adverse balances of trade as a result of the falling industrial exports and stationary or rising imports of cheap foodstuffs, were driven to the same measures by sudden panic flights of capital. The abandonment of the gold standard by Great Britain immediately affected every creditor or debtor in any country who held British or foreign contracts in terms of sterling and all traders in the large British markets. Almost simultaneously a great number of other countries left the gold standard, and this circle widened constantly. Varying and constantly changing measures of exchange depreciation, moreover, resulted in a degree of exchange instability which further hampered international trade and investment.

It is essential to remember that these impediments to free international trade and the breakdown of the international system of exchange were not the initial cause of the depression. They were measures adopted, in most cases unavoidably, in order to safeguard the internal economic system of each country from the effects of cyclical movements in other countries and the breakdown of the international equilibrium. In individual cases they achieved this purpose, though often at the expense of other countries less strongly placed. But during the first years of the great depression, at any rate, the defensive measures of individual countries largely tended to cancel out, and their chief effect was profoundly to aggravate the world depression and to erect bars against the revival, if not of the economic activity of individual countries, certainly of international trade and exchange.

The combined effect of the initial cumulative depression and the protective measures of commercial and currency policy resulted in an unprecedented decline of world economic activity. Production in most industrial countries reached its lowest point in 1932 at levels ranging from about 25 per cent below peak production in the case of Great Britain to about 55 per cent below the peak in the U.S.A.[1] The agricultural countries did not suffer from decreased production in the same way, but were affected the more severely by the fall in the prices of their products. Both factors combined resulted in reductions in the national income of all countries, in many cases by as much as one half. Unemployment of industrial workers by the end of 1932 involved considerably more than twenty-five millions, though exact figures can hardly be given.[2] To the industrial unemployed must be added millions of agricultural workers and farmers, who, if not unemployed were almost universally underemployed. Unemployed workers and factories were matched by unemployed capital. Accumulated short-term credit in the money markets of the world was estimated in 1932 at 50,000 million Swiss francs.[3] At the same time accumulated world stocks of raw materials reached an aggregate approximately double what they had been in 1925.[4] But the worst-hit section of the world economy was international trade. In their efforts to protect their domestic economies from the effects of the world depression all countries had resorted to restrictive measures which, whatever their benefits to the national economic system, diminished still further the flow of international economic exchange. Between 1929 and the third quarter of 1932 the value of international trade shrank by more than 65 per cent, a decline which was made up of a fall in average prices by about 50 per cent and a reduction in the volume of goods exchanged by about 25 per cent.[5] The decline was not evenly distributed, since agricultural prices fell more than those of finished goods. By 1932 the international trade of the non-European countries had fallen below 30 per cent of its 1929 level.[6]

It is against this background that we shall in the following chapters consider the economic policies during the nineteen-thirties of the four countries which have been selected for special study.

---

[1] League of Nations, *World Economic Survey 1932–3*, p. 12.
[2] ibid., p.   [3] ibid., p. 13.   [4] ibid., p. 12.   [5] ibid., p. 16.
[6] ibid., p. 16.

Chapter Two

UNITED STATES: INTERNAL POLICY

I. THE NEW DEAL

The U.S.A. reached the depths of the depression in the spring of 1933. When, on 4 March 1933, the first Roosevelt Administration came into office, the country was suffering from the most extreme prostration which any capitalist economy had ever experienced in peace-time. For the next five years American economic policy, like that of all other capitalist countries during the nineteen-thirties, was largely dominated by the task of lifting the internal economic system out of the depression. The New Deal was the most spectacular attempt that was made after the great depression to promote recovery by means of a deliberate expansionist policy without using rearmament as the chief stimulus of economic activity, and without recourse to totalitarian control of the economic system. The experience of the New Deal is of immense importance because it demonstrates both the merits and the limitations of an expansionist recovery policy within a free capitalist economic system.

Like every cyclical depression, the American depression presented two main aspects each of which could theoretically serve as the starting-point of a recovery policy; the collapse of profitability and private investment and the collapse of purchasing power and effective demand. The Government could attempt to restore profitability to industry and thus hope to stimulate private investment directly and employment and income and purchasing power indirectly. In order to achieve this object, it could endeavour to lower the costs of production by lowering wages (deflation) and/or by lowering the rates of interest (cheap money policy); and/or it could try to increase profitability at the other end by increasing prices. On the other hand, the Government could attempt to revive the economic system by increasing directly the purchasing power of American consumers and thus increase the effective demand for consumer goods and indirectly the demand for capital goods. Here again a number of different methods could be employed. Something could be done by redistributing the national income in favour of the spending classes. Prima facie, the share of the working classes in the national income could be increased by raising wages, and the share of the farmers by raising the relative price level of their products and reducing their debt burden. In addition the Government could

increase total purchasing power either by supplementing private
investment with public investment (public works) or simply by
distributing money directly to consumers through relief expenditure.

In the course of the first two years of the New Deal the Roosevelt Administration employed all these methods except deflation.
Wage deflation had been the orthodox method employed by the
entrepreneurs themselves to restore profitability, and it was
hardly avoidable in a country whose currency was maintained on
a free gold standard. The experience of the U.S.A. and of almost
all other countries during the great depression, however, seemed
to have shown that the policy of wage-deflation had merely
added to the evil of the general deflationary process of the depression. The Roosevelt Administration, therefore, was determined on an expansionist recovery policy which would counteract
the deflationary forces of the depression.

On the other hand, though the general lines of its policy had
been determined, it would be misleading to suggest that when,
in March 1933, the new Government embarked on its recovery
programme it proceeded on any logically constructed and carefully thought-out plan for the execution of that policy. Most of
the measures of the New Deal were taken in response to the
immediate urgency of the situation. From the first day, when the
new Administration had to take prompt measures to deal with the
banking crisis, to the currency experiments, the huge legislative
schemes of the N.R.A. and the A.A.A., and the relief and public
works policies of the later years of the New Deal, the Administration proceeded by trial and error and often followed contradictory
advice and adopted contradictory policies.

Moreover, recovery, though by far the the most important, was
not the sole object of the New Deal. In fact, it is hardly fair to
judge the New Deal at every point as a recovery policy. It tried
to combine recovery with social reform, improvements in the
standard of living, working conditions, and social services, with
regard to which the U.S.A. was in many respects far behind the
advanced countries of Europe. In most cases, especially where it
corrected the maldistribution of the national income and increased
the purchasing power of the American masses, social reform was
exactly what was needed for recovery. But in some respects the
two objects conflicted. Many of the inconsistencies of the New
Deal can be ascribed to this conflict, though it is true that in some
cases social reform might have been given a form which was less
detrimental to recovery.

II. BANKING REFORM

THE first task which faced President Roosevelt, immediately upon his assumption of office, was to deal with the banking crisis which during the preceding week had assumed catastrophic proportions. The peculiarly complex character of the American banking system and unsound banking policy during the years of the boom had resulted in a steadily increasing number of bank failures. In the early months of 1933 the process had led to a run on the banks which by March threatened to wreck the whole exchange mechanism of the country. The prompt declaration of a national bank holiday on 4 March and the passage of an Emergency Banking Act, which empowered the President to require the surrender of gold and foreign exchange and to issue additional currency to provide the business community with means of payment for day-to-day transactions, were effective in dealing with the panic. Confidence returned and the stampede for liquidity ceased. By June the banking system was for the most part revived, although some thousand banks still remained closed.

Prompt measures to deal with the crisis had been essential if the scramble for liquidity was not to bring the economic life of the country to a complete standstill. But in view of the strategic importance of the supply of credit in an expansionist recovery programme, it was essential for the success of the New Deal that the banking system should be placed on a sound footing. In June, therefore, the emergency measures of March were followed up by a number of measures of banking reform, the most important of which were a system of Government insurance for bank deposits and the transfer to the State-controlled Federal Reserve Board of the power of performing open market operations which had previously been in the hands of the private New York Federal Reserve Bank.

These reforms have been widely criticized on the ground that they did not go far enough in submitting the banking system to public control. It has even been suggested that most of the failures of the New Deal can be traced to this original error. It is true that the first of these two reforms was unfortunate in that it freed the banks from some of the risks of unsound policy without submitting them to closer control. It is also true that the submission of the banking system to public control would have made unnecessary the creation of large new public credit institutions, and that it would probably have been politically feasible in the months immediately following the banking crisis. In the long run, public control, if not ownership, of the banking system may be the logical corollary of a trade cycle policy of the New Deal type, the essence of which is the assumption by the State of conscious control of the volume of money in the economy. On the other hand, there seems no reason to suppose that the later difficulties of the New Deal and the recession of 1937 were due to any weakness of the banking system, though the fact that the banking reforms of 1933 left the *political* power of Wall Street completely untouched was possibly not without influence on the later course of events.

III. THE DEVALUATION OF THE DOLLAR

WHILE the liquidation of the banking crisis was still in progress the Administration took another step which, though in the particular circumstances of the U.S.A. it was probably neither essential nor even on balance beneficial to recovery, was certainly intended to assist the execution of the expansionist policy of the New Deal. The government abandoned the gold standard and embarked on a policy of deliberate devaluation of the dollar.

The measures which had been taken to deal with the banking crisis had already involved the first steps in this direction. The closing of the banks on 4 March had automatically ruptured the convertibility of the dollar with gold, and the order requiring the surrender of gold and foreign exchange had paved the way for measures to prevent a flight of capital. With the passing of the banking crisis, however, these emergency measures were not withdrawn. Gold payments were not resumed. On 6 April an order was issued prohibiting the hoarding of gold, and this was followed a fortnight later by an embargo on the export of gold and the abandonment of the gold standard. These measures had the desired effect of a rapid depreciation of the dollar, which in the course of four weeks fell by 17 per cent in the world market. For several months the dollar was allowed to 'find its own level' without any positive action of the Administration. In October, however, still more drastic steps were taken to force up the dollar price of gold. Legislation passed by Congress in May had empowered the President to reduce the gold content of the dollar by not more than 50 per cent. The Administration now took advantage of this power to pursue a policy of purchasing gold at a steadily increasing price. For four months, the American Government, through the Reconstruction Finance Corporation, bought gold newly mined in the U.S.A. and in the world market at a price which was gradually raised from $31·35 per ounce in October to $35·00 in January 1934. In that month the policy of currency depreciation was at last abandoned and the dollar was re-established on a gold basis at a value equivalent to 59 per cent of its former level.

It is clear that the American decision to abandon the gold

standard and to devalue the dollar was not forced upon the Government by outside pressure on its gold and exchange reserves, as had been the case when Great Britain left the gold standard in September 1931. It is true that during the banking crisis of March a large part of the flight capital which had entered the U.S.A. after the 1931 exodus from London was withdrawn. But the banking crisis was liquidated without having led to a fall in the exchange value of the dollar. The U.S.A. had immense stocks of gold which were more than sufficient to withstand any external run on the currency. Moreover, her balance of payments was strongly favourable and, short of a reversal of her tariff policy, there were no signs that this position would change. The decision of the American Government to abandon the gold standard was entirely voluntary. Its object was to assist the recovery of the internal economy.

The curious fact is that, if the depreciation of the dollar assisted the recovery of the U.S.A. at all, it did so for reasons entirely different from those which led the Administration 'to pursue that policy. One of the outstanding features of the depression had been the catastrophic fall in the internal price level. It had led to a general decline of profitability, it had brought American agriculture to the brink of ruin, it had increased the maldistribution of the national income by further reducing the share of the farmers; and the rise in the purchasing power of the dollar had heightened the debt burden on agriculture and industry. After the banking crisis of March it was clear that it was essential to stem the decline in prices. The Roosevelt Administration, therefore, made price reflation the first object of its recovery policy, and the decision to abandon the gold standard and depreciate the dollar was taken as part of this policy of raising the internal price level.

Influenced probably in part by the memory of the great inflations on the European Continent during the nineteen-twenties, which had been characterized by the simultaneous collapse of the internal and external value of the currency, the President believed that there was a direct relation between the price of gold and internal commodity price levels and that, by devaluating the dollar in terms of gold, prices would be raised. Prices did rise during the first months following the abandonment of the gold standard; by September 1933 the wholesale price index averaged 17 per cent above the March level, and the index of agricultural prices had risen by 35 per cent.[1] But this rise in the price level was primarily due to other measures of the New Deal. It is doubtful whether the abandonment of the gold standard and the gold purchase policy in fact raised prices by a single cent, and it

[1] *Statistical Abstract of the United States.*

is difficult to see that they ever could have had that effect. Once the convertibility of the dollar with gold was ruptured, a rise in the price of gold in terms of dollars could have no direct effect on internal price levels. It could have affected all other prices but indirectly, by raising the prices of imports in terms of dollars. Even in Great Britain (where the gold standard was abandoned for different reasons), the depreciation of the pound had not led to any marked rise in the internal price level, despite the considerable dependence of the British economy on foreign trade. The foreign trade of the United States formed a far smaller proportion of its total trade than in the case of Great Britain. It is now generally agreed that the economic theory which led the American Government to embark on its policy of currency depreciation was false.

It might be suggested that the devaluation of the dollar none the less benefited the internal recovery of the U.S.A. in two important respects. In the first place, while the devaluation of the dollar in itself probably did nothing to raise prices, the Administration was at the same time embarking on a large reflationary recovery programme which could and did raise the internal price level and which, if successful, would raise American demand for foreign goods. It was, therefore, almost certain to result in some 'deterioration' of the American balance of trade. Moreover, the knowledge that the Government was going to pursue an 'inflationary' policy might have led to a flight of capital abroad. These two factors together, it might be argued, would have exerted such pressure on the American balance of payments and currency that the maintenance of the gold parity of the dollar would in any case have become impossible. What is more important, heavy gold exports might have made it more difficult to expand the internal credit structure. Devaluation removed any possible danger that balance of payments difficulties would in any way interfere with the internal expansionist policy of the Administration. Secondly, devaluation could be expected to exercise an immediate favourable effect on the level of economic activity and employment at home since it gave, in effect, additional protection to the home market by raising the prices of imports to American consumers and provided an indiscriminate bounty to American exports.

In fact, it is very doubtful whether either of these arguments really justify the devaluation of the dollar, even from the point of view of the economic interests of the U.S.A. The possession of a large export surplus and an immense gold reserve placed the U.S.A. in a very different position from all other countries (with the possible exception of France until 1934 or 1935). With an export surplus of more than $200 million and a gold reserve of more than $5 milliard, the U.S.A. could afford a considerable 'deterioration' in her balance of merchandise trade without having to fear undue pressure on her balance of payments. The danger of capital flight was more serious, as the sporadic attacks on the dollar in 1931 had shown. But the very strength of the dollar makes it most unlikely that capital exports from the U.S.A. would ever have assumed such proportions as to interfere with internal credit expansion. At the worst, there would still have been time to allow the dollar to depreciate if and when actual pressure on the American balance of payments and currency made such a step appear desirable.

The beneficial effects of devaluation on domestic employment are even more dubious. It is undoubtedly true that a successful internal recovery policy would have increased American imports, while rising American prices might have made it more difficult for American exports to compete in international markets. But this merely means that, if the dollar had not been devalued, some of the benefits of the internal expansionist policy and the resulting economic revival would, through the mechanism of foreign trade, have been transmitted to other countries. In view of the immense importance of the U.S.A. as an import market, rising American demand—but for the barriers to world trade that had grown up since 1930—might have been almost as effective in spreading the recovery as the fall in American demand during the previous four years had been in spreading the depression. In the long run, the U.S.A. could only have benefited from the revival of economic prosperity elsewhere. Foreign demand for American goods would, in turn, have increased, and the gain to American exports might well have outweighed the initial price handicap. There is a good deal to be said for the view that, even in the narrowest American interests, any policy which in practice prevented, or at least retarded, the 'spilling-over' of recovery was short-sighted. The effects of the devaluation of the dollar on other countries will be discussed more conveniently in the following chapter.

IV. CHEAP MONEY POLICY

THE reform of the banking system and the accumulation of large gold reserves laid a sound foundation on which a policy of credit expansion could be built. But it was not enough to enable the banking system to supply credit. For as long as profit expectations remained low, private industry would not avail itself of the credit facilities granted by the banks. The efforts of the Administration during the first months of the New Deal to encourage the banks to make loans to private industry were almost completely unsuccessful. The extent, however, to which private producers were prepared to borrow money for new investment could be expected to depend partly on the rate of interest they were charged. One method, therefore, by which it was hoped to stimulate production was that of Government lending to producers at low rates of interest.

Apart from the policy of budgetary deficits, this policy of 'cheap money' was the only method with regard to which the Hoover Administration had anticipated the expansionist policy of the New Deal. In January 1932 the Hoover Administration had founded the Reconstruction Finance Corporation, which was authorized to lend money to banks, insurance and mortgage companies, and railroads, and which did make loans on a substantial scale. Under President Hoover, however, the R.F.C. was not allowed to interfere with or replace the work of the banks, and its loans were made and used almost exclusively to pay off debts of large corporations and of bankers which they were no longer able to meet. The resulting liquidation of frozen assets of the banks was useful in that it improved their ability to grant new credits; but the money which flowed back to the banks could have no direct effect in stimulating new investment and production.

Under the New Deal the scope of the R.F.C. was immensely extended. The banks which were unable to find private borrowers lent money to the Government by purchasing Government securities. The Government, in turn, through the R.F.C. and a number of other agencies, re-lent the money at lower interest rates to private enterprises which, for one reason or another, could not get bank credit or could not get it cheaply enough. Banks, railways, and agriculture were still the most important borrowers, but loans were also granted to small industries and to local Governments. These loans to private enterprise accounted for a large proportion of the increase in the Federal debt during the first two years of the New Deal. They meant in fact that public credit was largely replacing private credit to producers. By the end of 1937, 46 per cent of the whole Federal debt was held in the form of Government securities by banks and trust companies,[1] whose place as active lenders was being taken by various Federal agencies, of which the R.F.C. alone had made loans amounting to more than $5,000 million.[2]

These figures, however, cannot in any way be taken to indicate the success of the 'cheap money' policy in stimulating private investment. The extension by the Government of cheap credit facilities was extremely important in that it removed any possible obstacle to recovery arising out of credit scarcity; and it is probable that a certain amount of new investment was encouraged by low interest rates which would otherwise not have taken place.

[1] Radice and Hugh-Jones, *An American Experiment*, p. 89.   [2] ibid., p. 90.

B*

But the mere fact that the banks were reduced to lending almost exclusively to the Government shows that 'cheap money' alone could do little to revive economic activity in the capital goods industries. Without new investment opportunities or a rising demand for consumption goods, lower interest rates in themselves could not stimulate production. There can be little doubt that most of the Government loans to private industry which were not used to repay debts were taken up only when the other measures of the New Deal had begun to increase purchasing power and stimulate effective demand for consumption goods. The 'cheap money' policy of the New Deal was really effective in stimulating recovery where, as in the case of the loans of the Federal Farm Mortgage Corporation and the Home Owners Loan Corporation, it reduced the burden of interest and thus indirectly raised the income and purchasing power of large sections of consumers. Its direct effect in stimulating private investment was probably negligible.

V. THE N.R.A.

THE most determined effort of the New Deal to revive the economic system by stimulating private investment was embodied in the National Industrial Recovery Act which was signed by the President on 18 June 1933. Part I of this monumental piece of legislation, which was announced and put into effect by the Roosevelt Administration as its most important and promising effort towards economic recovery, gave power to the President to establish a system for the regulation of the whole of American industrial production. The procedure was for the employers, mostly organized in Trade Associations, and such representatives of labour and consumers as could be found, to submit to a special Government organization a 'code' laying down the conditions within which alone each industry could be conducted in future. Once approved by the Government, this code assumed the force of law. The Administration concentrated immense efforts on the realization of the programme of the N.R.A. and, despite considerable difficulties, succeeded in the end in passing a total of 557 codes with 188 supplementary codes, covering 95 per cent of all industrial employers in the U.S.A. The goals of this codification of industry were defined by the President as 'the assurance of a reasonable profit to industry and living wages for labour with the elimination of the piratical methods and practices which have not only harassed honest business but also contributed to the ills of labour'.[1] What was not realized at the time was that these objects implied two different recovery policies which

[1] Quoted J. Strachey, *A Programme for Progress*, p. 190 f.

not only contradicted each other but each of which was up to a point self-defeating.

The primary object of the N.R.A. was to stabilize or raise industrial prices in the hope that by assuring a 'reasonable profit to industry' private entrepreneurs would be induced to resume investment. The method employed for this end in the codes was to lay down minimum prices or, alternatively, to arrange for the limitation of production. In effect it encouraged or even compelled the elimination of competition and the cartellization of American industry. Behind the price-raising policy of the N.R.A. lay the undoubtedly correct view that recovery of private industry was impossible unless steps were taken to stem the disastrous decline of prices. But the cause of this decline, in the case of manufactures, had been primarily the shrinkage of demand with the fall in income and employment. Legal minimum prices could at best have a brief beneficial psychological effect. But unless they were sustained by the creation of new consumers' income and effective demand they could merely lead to monopolistic restriction of production, and the attempt to produce recovery, that is to say an *expansion* of industrial production, by forcing or inducing industries to *restrict* production was patently absurd. Even the highest prices were not likely to stimulate new investment in an industry in which production was curtailed by law.

The other half of the N.R.A. policy was also self-defeating, though not to quite the same extent. It consisted of measures to raise wage rates, encourage trade union organization and collective bargaining, reduce hours of work, and improve labour conditions. The object of these measures was partly political and social. Politically they served as a compensation to Labour for the benefits conferred by the N.R.A. on Capital; socially, they constituted a courageous programme of social reform in spheres where the U.S.A. still lagged behind most European industrial countries. At the same time, however, they were designed as a direct stimulus to economic recovery. They constituted one of the methods by which the Administration hoped to increase purchasing power and effective demand and thus stimulate the consumption goods industry directly and investment indirectly. Now this was in principle sound recovery policy. In fact, as we shall see presently, it was this policy, pursued by means of budgetary deficits and Government lending and spending, which more than any other part of the New Deal contributed to economic recovery. The most certain method of inducing industry to resume production was to assure it of an effective demand for its products by increasing the purchasing power of the masses of American consumers. There can be little doubt, however, that the particular method which was employed for this end in the N.R.A. codes was mistaken. For while higher wage rates meant larger money earnings of the industrial workers, higher wages, shorter hours, and improved labour conditions also meant higher costs of production. Since increased costs would either push up prices or increase unemployment, the chances were that a wage-raising policy would add little if anything to the real income and effective purchasing power of the industrial workers.[1] In the N.R.A., moreover, the two objectives, wage-raising and price-raising, completely defeated each other. To the extent to which the cartellization of industry succeeded in raising prices it tended to increase the cost of living and thus reduce the pur-chasing power of any given incomes. To the extent to which the 'codes' succeeded in raising wages and reducing hours they tended to raise the costs of production, diminish profitability, and discourage production and investment.

In the light of this analysis it is clear that the high hopes which were set on the N.R.A. by the New Deal authorities were bound to be disappointed. Its initial effects on business activity were probably favourable. Though hailed by progressives and un-doubtedly thought of by its authors as a liberal or even radical measure, the Act was favourably received by big business because the proposal to raise prices by the elimination of competition within each industry meant in effect the reversal of forty years of American anti-trust legislation. The mere psychological effect of the price-raising policy was to encourage business activity, and it was probably largely the anticipation of rising prices as a result of the N.R.A. which led to a brief boom in the summer of 1933. The index of industrial production rose from 60 in March to 85 in September (1933) (1923–5 =100),[2] and unemployment fell

[1] The Administration, of course, was not unaware of the effect of wage in-creases on prices. It was believed, however, that, since wages constitute only part of the costs of production, the increase in prices would reflect only the increase in that part of total costs and would be proportionately smaller, so that the net result would be a substantial increase in the real incomes and effective demand of the industrial workers. The argument ignored the facts that, since entrepreneurs fix prices—where they are in a position to do so—not on a basis of absolute but of proportionate profit margins, profits would in most industries increase in proportion, and that, given an all-round increase in wages throughout the economy, raw material costs were also bound to rise. Even this did not pre-clude the possibility of an increase in real wages since fixed costs, such as rent and interest, would remain stable and might thus account for some difference between the rise in prices and money wages. It is in fact probable that, if it had not been for the deliberate price-raising policy which was carried on simul-taneously, the general increase in money wages would have raised the share in the national income of wage earners and entrepreneurs at the expense of fixed income groups. This might conceivably have been considered desirable on social or political grounds. But there is little reason to assume that such a redistribution of the national income would in any way have increased the nation's 'propensity to consume' and thus have benefited recovery.

[2] *Survey of Current Business*, Department of Commerce, quoted Radice and Hugh-Jones, op. cit., appendix.

during the same period by nearly four million,[1] though this fall cannot be wholly ascribed to the effects of the N.R.A. The boom, however, had no solid foundation in new investment or increased demand. It was an inventory boom due mainly to an increase of stocks, and collapsed in the autumn of 1933. The N.R.A. succeeded in its policy of raising industrial prices; by September wholesale prices had increased by 17 per cent over the March level, and the prices of finished goods also rose, though not to the same degree. But this rise was due at least as much to rising costs as to the price-raising provisions of the 'codes' and was, *a fortiori*, ineffective in encouraging private investment. The effect of the N.R.A. in promoting recovery by stimulating new investment was, therefore, probably negligible.

It was equally unsuccessful in increasing purchasing power. The efforts to promote trade union organization under the famous 'Section 7a' of the Act were only partially successful and, in the absence of strong labour representation, the code-making authorities were dominated by the employers. Moreover, the vague terminology of the codes and inadequate provisions for enforcement gave ample opportunities to employers for 'chiselling'. As a result, wage rates, according to the figures given by Mr. Richberg, the N.R.A. Administrator, increased during the first year of the operation of the N.R.A. by 8·6 per cent, while the cost of living rose by 9·6 per cent.[2] In other words, the purchasing power of an employed worker had been reduced by 1·1 per cent. These figures, of course, do not tell the whole story. The chief cause of the fall in income of the working classes during the depression had not been the fall in real wages of the employed workers (real wages in most industries had increased as a result of the fall in prices), but the decline in the number of workers who earned any wages at all. The reduction in unemployment which resulted from the N.R.A. was, therefore, a more important contribution to the purchasing power of the working classes than the increase in wage rates. Since the total industrial pay roll increased by about 38 per cent between June 1933 and June 1934,[3] compared with an increase of the cost of living over the same period of less than 10 per cent, the rise in the real income of the working classes was considerable, and some of this rise was no doubt due to the N.R.A. But the fact remains that the gains of the workers from increased wage-rates were largely wiped out by rising prices and that the policy of increasing wage-rates and costs on balance retarded the reduction of unemployment. Moreover, while the social effects of some of its provisions, such as those for

[1] A. F. of L. estimates, quoted ibid.
[2] J. Strachey, op. cit., p. 196.
[3] Based on figures quoted by Radice and Hugh-Jones from the *Monthly Labour Review* of the Bureau of Labour Statistics.

the abolition of child labour and the improvement of working conditions, were admirable, the provisions for fixed prices and production quotas were used by the large business interests in control to strengthen their monopoly position on the lines of the German 'cartel' and increased the rigidity of the structure of the economic system.

The administration of the system of industrial codes proved extremely difficult. The attempts of organized labour to improve its position under the sanction of 'Section 7a' met with increasing opposition from the employers. As prices rose consumers' complaints increased. It was found almost impossible to enforce the observation of the codes in those trades which were still carried on on a relatively small scale. As the depression lifted and production again became more profitable, restrictions on production which had at first been welcomed as a protection against the collapse of prices came now to be resented as burdensome restraints. It is generally agreed that, when in May 1935 the Supreme Court declared the N.R.A. unconstitutional, the Act had already become widely discredited.[1]

VI. THE A.A.A.

THE programme for the recovery of American industry of Part I of the N.R.A. had its counterpart in Part I of the Agricultural Adjustment Act, the other pillar of early New Deal legislation, which was to solve the problem of American agriculture. But, although superficially the objects of both Acts were similar, namely to raise prices by regulating production, the function of the A.A.A. in the recovery programme of the New Deal differed from that of the price-raising provisions of the N.R.A. codes. Like the wage-raising policy of the N.R.A. it had as its main object the redistribution of the national income in favour of an important section of American consumers.

Agriculture in 1933 was the most depressed section of the American economy. The catastrophic and disproportionate fall of agricultural prices, which had begun even before the 1929 crisis and had been accelerated during the years of the depression by a constantly contracting internal and external demand for agricultural products and constantly expanding agricultural production, had not only greatly reduced the money income of the American farmers but had also led to a still further reduction of their share of the national income. Their purchasing power had been diminished in addition by the increase in the real burden of their vast

---

[1] Most of the social reforms of the N.R.A., however, survived it, and were further extended in the subsequent Social Security, Wages and Hours, and Labour Relations Acts.

debt which had followed automatically from the rise in the internal value of the dollar. By 1933 the majority of American farmers were reduced to bankruptcy and over wide areas to virtual starvation. Now this was in itself an economic, social and political problem of colossal dimensions, and it was as such that it presented itself to the Roosevelt Administration in March 1933. It meant that nearly one-quarter of the American people were rendered destitute. Politically the agricultural areas had traditionally held the balance between the two parties and their grievances were of special importance to any Administration. In addition, however, the agricultural depression was of special significance for the state of the American economy as a whole. For the farmers, who with their families constituted one-quarter of the population, represented a substantial proportion of the consumers of the products of American industry. While it would be wrong to ignore the intrinsic social importance of the agricultural problem in the U.S.A. in 1933, from the point of view of the recovery of the American economic system from the depression any measures for the relief of the farmer were primarily significant because they raised the purchasing power of a large section of the consuming public.

The simplest method of relieving the plight of the farmers and at the same time increasing their purchasing power and effective demand for the products of industry would have been direct financial assistance financed out of the Federal budget deficit. This was in effect the method adopted in the Emergency Farm Mortgage Act which formed the second part of the A.A.A. But just because the disproportionate fall of agricultural prices had resulted in a disastrous maldistribution of the national income at the expense of the farmers, any measures which would increase their share even at the expense of the rest of the population would not only correct this social injustice and relieve their plight but in all likelihood in itself do something to increase the nation's propensity to consume. It was this redistribution of the national income in favour of the farmers which was the object of Part I of the Agricultural Adjustment Act.

The immediate goal of the Act was to raise agricultural prices. The method adopted was primarily the restriction of agricultural production. Farmers were paid substantial sums of money, so-called 'benefit payments', on condition that they agreed to restrict their production to an extent indicated to them by the Government. The money for these benefit payments which were to compensate farmers for crop restriction did not come out of the Federal Treasury as such but was raised by means of a 'processing tax', levied at the first domestic processing of the particular commodity, as for instance, at the milling of wheat, but paid ultimately in the main by the urban consumer of the agricultural products.[1] This method of crop restriction was applied to the most important 'basic' products of American agriculture, corn and hogs, wheat, rice, tobacco, and cotton. In addition the Act provided for marketing agreements and licences for the purpose of raising the prices of these and other agricultural products (especially dairy products). These too were essentially monopolistic in character and the benefits they conferred on the agricultural producers were paid for by the consumers in the price of the products.

The crop restriction scheme of the A.A.A. was carried on for three years until it was declared unconstitutional by the Supreme Court in January 1936. Administratively it worked considerably more smoothly than the N.R.A., and by the end of 1935 its immediate objective of raising agricultural prices and increasing the farmers' share in the national income had certainly been largely achieved. Whereas in March 1933 farm prices stood at 55 per cent of their pre-war level, the average figure for 1933 was 70, for 1934 90, and for December 1935 110.[2] These figures alone are not very significant, since other prices also rose. But the farm-industrial price ratio, too, increased from 55 per cent of the pre-war level in March 1933 to 64 for the average of 1933, 73 for 1934 and 90 for December 1935.[3] The initial rise can largely be ascribed to the restriction policy of the A.A.A. In 1934 nature came to the assistance of the Administration's policy. A devastating drought and the spread of soil erosion and dust storms are estimated to have rendered some 75 million acres permanently uncultivable and reduced the efficiency of a further 25 million by 90 per cent in 1934 alone; and they wrought further havoc in 1935.[4] The combined result of crop restriction and drought was an actual dearth of some agricultural products, and in 1934 and 1935 corn and some wheat had to be imported. Between 1932 and 1935 the cash income of farmers also increased from $4,328 million to about $6,800 million.[5] How much of this rise was directly due to the restriction policy and benefit payments of the A.A.A. it is impossible to say. It was certainly effective in raising the farmers' share of the national income. On the other hand, it is extremely doubtful whether the A.A.A. restriction policy did anything to increase total purchasing power. It can only have had that effect to the extent to which those who ultimately paid for the price increase and benefit payments (chiefly the urban consumers of foodstuffs) would have spent less on industrial products

---

[1] The question of the incidence of the processing tax involves a controversial and highly technical economic problem. But broadly speaking the statement above is probably generally accepted.

[2] Radice and Hugh-Jones, op. cit., p. 170.

[3] ibid.   [4] ibid., p. 169 f.   [5] ibid., p. 170 f.

than was spent by the farmers. The increased farm income between 1933 and 1935 was clearly effective in stimulating the consumption goods industries; but that effect was primarily due to those measures for the relief of the farmers which constituted a net contribution to the total national income out of the Federal deficit.

Against the gains of the crop restriction policy in terms of a better distribution of the national income and possibly some increase in effective demand of consumers must be set the waste of natural resources and manpower which this policy implied. There is no need to enlarge upon the absurdity of a policy of restricting the production of foodstuffs in a country where a substantial proportion of the people were gravely undernourished, to say nothing of the immense potential unsatisfied demand for foodstuffs the world over. In the conditions of 1933 no action of the U.S.A. Government could have tapped the potential world demand for American agricultural products. And even internally the main problem was the cyclical decline and maldistribution of the national income. Complete recovery and a better distribution of the national income would have gone a long way towards the solution of the agricultural surplus problem. To that extent, Government purchase of surpluses for storage or relief distribution in kind on a larger scale than was actually undertaken would have been a better policy than crop restriction. But the American problem of agricultural surpluses was not merely a cyclical problem. There was a real problem of surplus productive capacity of some products of American agriculture, especially wheat and cotton, for which there would have been no adequate demand even in conditions of full employment and prosperity, at any rate within the U.S.A. In the case of these two commodities there was a real need for a reduction of production. Even here, however, a reduction which left millions of acres and men idle instead of turning both over to the production of other agricultural commodities, such as meat, vegetables, or dairy products, the real demand for which was expanding with changes in nutritional tastes, or ultimately, if necessary, absorbing any surplus agricultural manpower in industry, meant waste of the nation's wealth. In the depth of the depression, the market even for dairy products, meat, and vegetables was probably inadequate to support increased production. The restriction policy of the A.A.A. however, hardly took into account the long-run problem. Its contribution to a solution was inadequately planned[1] and

---

[1] As a result of the fact that the crop restriction schemes of the A.A.A. were planned on a regional instead of a national basis, it happened that farmers in the South who were paid for restricting their production of cotton began to grow wheat instead, whilst farmers in the Middle West who were paid for restricting their output of wheat began to grow cotton.

incidental to the immediate object of saving the agricultural population from destitution. It was not until 1936, after the original A.A.A. had been declared unconstitutional, that a new scheme linked the old policy of crop restriction on a large scale to a real and vital social objective, that of soil conservation.

VII. GOVERNMENT LENDING AND SPENDING

WE have so far described those measures of the New Deal recovery policy which were designed, on the one hand, to stimulate private investment and, on the other hand to raise effective consumers' demand by means of a redistribution of the national income. During the first year these measures predominated in the New Deal recovery policy. As we have seen, they formed the basis of the two greatest legislative efforts of the Roosevelt Administration, the N.R.A. and the A.A.A.

But from the beginning the New Deal consisted largely of measures which involved net contributions out of Government deficits to the total purchasing power of American consumers and which were intended to stimulate the demand for consumption goods and, directly or indirectly, for capital goods. It was this policy of the 'net contribution' or 'compensatory fiscal policy' which, at first in response to urgent social problems rather than by conscious design, gradually became the centre of the New Deal and its most effective contribution to the economic recovery of the U.S.A.

In view of the importance of this type of recovery policy, not only in the U.S.A., but also in other countries, during the nineteen-thirties, the principle on which it worked must be briefly discussed.

The Government net contribution could assume two forms which differed in important respects in their purpose and effect. One form was simply the distribution of money by the Government directly to consumers, in the shape of relief or otherwise. The new net income would be spent by consumers and would thus stimulate production and employment in the consumption goods industries. Its effect would not stop at that. The new income created in the production of consumption goods would further stimulate production, new employment, new income, and so forth. This cumulative process, however, would not continue indefinitely; for part of the new income created would not be spent but saved; and in addition some of the consumption expenditure would be on imported goods and would, therefore, benefit income and employment abroad. For these reasons, the beneficial effect on the consumption goods industries of the injection of any one dose of money into the economic system would soon peter out.

On the other hand, the increased production of consumption goods could also be expected to stimulate investment and production in the capital goods industries which would create further employment and income, new expenditure and new investment. Since the capital goods industries had, as always in cyclical depressions, suffered most, this indirect effect of Government expenditure on investment was particularly important. The expectation that rising consumers' demand, by raising profit expectations, would provide the initial stimulus for a revival of private investment activity (which could then be expected to carry the economy forward to full recovery without further additional Government expenditure) was considered by the New Deal authorities as its chief merit as a recovery policy and gave rise to the conception of 'pump priming'. In fact, as events were to prove, the effectiveness of Government relief expenditure in stimulating the capital goods industries and new investment was for several reasons much less certain than was thought at the time. In the first place, the stimulus to the production of capital goods was largely dependent on the *growth* of consumption expenditure, since a *constant* level of production in the consumption goods industries merely required the upkeep and replacement of existing machines and factories some of which would have taken place in any case whether there was any new demand or not. Moreover, since during the depression large stocks of consumers' goods had accumulated, and all industries had suffered from considerable excess capacity, the increased demand could for some time be satisfied without new investment. Most important of all, the amount of investment undertaken depended, not on the actual demand for capital goods arising out of the increase in purchasing power, but on the profit expectations of entrepreneurs, which might bear no relation to real demand and real opportunities for profitable investment. Broadly speaking, low profit expectations during the early stages of the recovery were likely to retard the indirect effect of Government relief expenditure on new investment (though in the later stages of recovery excessive optimism might lead to that disproportionate investment and inflation which had characterized earlier booms).

Government relief expenditure, therefore, could in the most favourable circumstances be expected to induce a revival of private investment activity which, in a cumulative process, would lead the economy to full employment. In that case, as the recovery proceeded, the Government net contribution could be gradually reduced and, if necessary, replaced by deflationary measures (especially increased taxation), in order to avoid the development of inflation. If Government expenditure, for the reasons just mentioned, failed to induce this cumulative process, its effects on recovery would be confined to a revival of the consumption goods industries and that minimum of investment necessary to meet the rise in consumers' demand. This in itself might produce a substantial degree of recovery. But inadequate investment would leave the economy short of a state of full employment and the recovery would depend on the continuation of Government expenditure out of budget deficits.

The Government net contribution could, secondly, take the form of expenditure on public works. Instead of distributing money directly to consumers and relying on private entrepreneurs to undertake new investment in response to the increase in demand for consumption goods or as other profitable investment opportunities offered themselves, the Government could itself undertake new investment. This form of Government expenditure was in many respects preferable as a recovery policy. Whereas increased consumers' purchasing power could at best have only an indirect and uncertain effect on the capital goods industries which in the depression were most in need of revival, public works would create a direct demand for their products. From that point of view, public works, such as afforestation or road building which required relatively little materials per labourer employed, were obviously less valuable than housing or electrification schemes which required a relatively large expenditure on machinery and materials. Moreover, whereas the distribution of money would stimulate different constructional industries in proportion to the demand for their products, and regardless of their needs, public works could be selected so as to assist the most depressed sections of industry.[1] Lastly, Government expenditure on public works would result in the creation of material assets for the community, either in the tangible form of income-earning enterprises, such as houses or public utilities, or in the intangible form of valuable social utilities, such as roads, forests, public parks, or soil conservation.

On the other hand, Government expenditure on public works had two important disadvantages as compared with the direct distribution of money to consumers. In the first place, the time needed for the preparation and execution of public works programmes would mean a considerable delay before money spent on public works could provide financial relief to the unemployed and before it could stimulate the consumption goods industries.

[1] Whether this was also an advantage in the long run is more doubtful; for it meant that public works were liable to be used so as artificially to maintain in being industries which, in view of technological changes or changes in demand, ought to have been allowed to contract. See also below, p. 260 f.

Moreover, part of the money thus spent would increase profits of corporations and private entrepreneurs who would save a larger proportion of their increased income than recipients of Government relief. The effect on consumers' demand of the expenditure of any given sum would, therefore, not only be slower but possibly somewhat smaller. For this reason, relief expenditure was clearly preferable to public works expenditure as an emergency measure in 1933 when the primary need was the relief of destitution and the substantial increase of the real income of the masses of the American people.

Another, and in the long run more serious, objection to a policy of Government expenditure on public works was that, so long as the Government relied for the most part on private enterprise to undertake the amount of new investment necessary for full recovery, any public investment in spheres normally reserved to private enterprise was liable to have a discouraging effect on private investment activity and would at best only replace private investment. In some spheres, such as that of public utilities, the advantages of public ownership could be held to justify public investment even if it had that effect. In general, however, this consideration made it appear advisable to confine public works schemes in the main to spheres which would not ordinarily attract the private investor, such as road building or reafforestation, even though such schemes were generally less effective in stimulating the constructional industries. This objection, of course, would lose much of its force in case of a continued failure of private investment. In that case, public investment might have to take the place of private investment on a large scale in order to achieve complete economic recovery. But for a Government, which had neither the intention nor perhaps the political power to transcend in this way the limits of the free capitalist system, the possible effects of an extension of public investment on private investment activity constituted a serious obstacle to the effective use of that vital instrument of recovery.

One other aspect of the policy of Government spending must be briefly discussed. Both forms of Government expenditure, whether on relief or on public works, involved, and were indeed based on budget deficits. Government expenditure financed out of current revenue (that is to say, broadly speaking, out of taxation) could have increased effective consumers' demand to the extent to which it redistributed the national income so as to diminish saving and increase spending. But in the depression the discouraging effect on business activity of steeply progressive taxation would have far outweighed any favourable effects of this method of raising consumers' demand.[1] Government expendi-

---

[1] There was, in theory, an alternative method of financing large Government

ture could therefore only be effective in promoting recovery if it constituted a 'net contribution' of additional purchasing power, and that meant in practice[1] if it was financed by Government borrowing.[2] The fact that the policy of Government lending and spending involved budget deficits and a rising national debt was of considerable psychological and some economic importance.

In the first place, a policy of budgetary deficits offended the canons of orthodox fiscal policy. Orthodox public finance required that the State budget should be balanced year by year. The principle was based on a fundamental confusion between the private business-man and the State. It ignored the fact that whereas the private business-man must default unless he is able to meet his expenditure out of income, the State can directly or through the banking system create new money. It also ignored the fact that the state can and the business-man cannot perform the vital function—which someone or other *has* to perform in the modern economy—of controlling the volume of money circulating in the economic system, a function which incidentally involves the creation of new money (credit) when its quantity has been unduly reduced by a deflationary process. In the *laisser faire* economy this function had been performed almost unconsciously by private banks acting on a profit basis, subject only to central bank control and, indirectly, to the rules of the international gold standard system. The only innovation introduced in this respect by a compensatory fiscal policy was that the

expenditure without unbalancing the budget. If the Government had during the previous period of prosperity accumulated a reserve fund out of unspent revenue this fund might have been used during the depression to compensate for the decline in income and purchasing power of consumers. Until the recent development of the theory of the compensatory fiscal policy, however, no Government had thought it necessary to accumulate reserves. It is doubtful, moreover, whether the accumulation of sufficiently large reserves during a boom would be politically and economically practicable. Politically, a policy of steep increases in taxation might find little understanding or support at a time of growing prosperity. Economically, it would be difficult, though probably not impossible, to avoid severe deflationary effects. The proposal also gives rise to problems connected with the possible methods of holding the reserve fund. But if practicable it provides the soundest financial basis for Government trade cycle control by means of compensatory public expenditure.

[1] In theory, the Government, instead of inducing the banks to create money by offering them interest on Government securities, might itself have created money. This would have made possible Government expenditure without any rise in the internal debt. Some small part of the net contribution was, of course, financed by the printing of notes. But the issue of new currency on anything like the necessary scale would have led to a panic fear of inflation and would in fact have made further control of the banking system and credit structure impossible. The other alternative of a public bank which would lend money to the Government at interest rates just sufficient to cover costs has already been discussed (see above, p. 36 f.). As to whether it was politically possible in the U.S.A. in 1933 and whether it would not equally have led to a disastrous collapse of business confidence, it is impossible to dogmatize.

[2] To the extent to which the Government securities were taken up by the banks the money was, of course, newly created by the latter. But there was no reason

function of controlling the volume of money was taken over by the State and became an instrument of deliberate economic policy. The prevalent prejudice against an unbalanced budget was none the less important. For the appearance of 'unsound' public finance was liable to have a depressing effect on business confidence. What was gained on the swings of public expenditure was, therefore, liable to be lost in part on the roundabouts of private investment. In the second place, since the budget deficit had to be financed, not by the simple creation of money by the Government, but by borrowing at interest, it involved an increase in the national debt. Here again much of the popular fear of a rising national debt was due to false economic reasoning. Since the budget deficit was financed internally, the national debt was not in itself a 'burden on the nation'; for it was owed by the nation to itself and need never have been repaid as long as its constituent loans could be regularly replaced on maturity by new loans. Moreover, with the progress of economic recovery, a considerable proportion of deficit expenditure would be self-liquidating. Most of the money spent on public works would result in real assets, some of which would actually produce new Government revenue sufficient to meet interest and amortization charges. What is more important, all the income generated, directly or indirectly, by Government expenditure would help to increase the yield of taxation. Thus even without any increases in the rates of taxation much of the money spent by the Government would automatically come back to it in the form of increased revenue. Lastly, if 'pump-priming' was successful it would be possible, and even necessary in order to avoid an inflationary boom, to increase the rates of taxation and thus Government revenue. It was only in connection with the payment of interest out of taxation that a high national debt would prove awkward, since in practice it would involve an enforced redistribution of

to fear that, in the depression, the injection by the Government of large quantities of new money into the economic system would lead to inflation. The fact that the banks lent the newly created money to the Government instead of, as normally during the recovery, to private investors, did not alter the fact that, as long as a large proportion of the productive resources of the country were idle, private producers would react to rising demand based on additional consumers' purchasing power, by expanding production rather than by raising prices. With the gradual progress of recovery inflationary price and wage increases would, of course, result from additional 'net contributions'. The theoretical limit to reflation would be a state of full employment of all productive resources when increased money demand could not possibly lead to increased production. In practice the limit would be reached some time before unemployment of workers and of means of production had disappeared. Owing to the immobility of labour and means of production, 'bottlenecks' would arise in certain industries which would result in cost and price increases. Moreover, in an economy which, like that of the U.S.A., contained many strongly monopolistic sections, prices might be raised even before any real 'bottlenecks' appeared, before, in technical language, the marginal cost curves of individual industries began to rise.

the national income in favour of the relatively narrow section of bondholders at the expense of the wider community of taxpayers. It is true that even this disadvantage could be minimized by progressive rates of taxation which, in effect, would go a long way towards cancelling out this redistributive effect. But, if the service on the national debt was very large in proportion to the national income, this might necessitate taxation at rates which would have a discouraging effect on private investment activity. This problem, admittedly a serious one within the framework of a free capitalist economy, was the only real problem to which a growing national debt could give rise. It was a problem, however, which was raised in a far more acute form by the need to curb an inflationary boom in the later stages of recovery and will be discussed in that context.[1]

When the Roosevelt Administration in 1933 began its expansionist policy of Government lending and spending out of budgetary deficits it did not break altogether new ground. The first departure from orthodox budgetary policy had already been made by the Hoover Administration. As, with the development of the depression during 1931 and 1932, Government revenue diminished severely, the Hoover Administration had not—as the theory of orthodox public finance would have required—raised the rates of taxation sufficiently to keep the budget in balance, but had tolerated substantial budget deficits. In 1932 it had even gone beyond this passive 'expansionist' policy by the establishment of the R.F.C. and a programme of public works and relief. However, as we have seen, the pre-New Deal loan policy of the R.F.C. did next to nothing to increase consumers' purchasing power and the public works policy of President Hoover never got properly under way. Although the Federal deficits for the years 1931, 1932, and 1933 were all substantial, the positive benefits they conferred on the economy by counteracting the deflationary pressure of the depression was, therefore, entirely inadequate to maintain purchasing power and employment.

Nor can it be said that the Roosevelt Administration embarked on the policy of lending and spending with a very clear conception of its economic significance. The primary objects of its first large-scale measures of this kind were the relief of destitution and unemployment and the lightening of agricultural and urban indebtedness. It was only gradually, and with the frequent and unsolicited support of mass pressure for financial relief, that a conscious policy of compensatory Government expenditure crystallized out of disconnected emergency measures.

Among the first measures of the New Deal involving Government expenditure on a very large scale were two which combined

[1] See below, p. 70.

the object of increasing consumers' purchasing power with the more immediate task of liquidating the frozen assets of the country's banks and other credit institutions. The second part of the Agricultural Adjustment Act of May 1933 established the Farm Credit Administration, to which farmers could apply for loans with which to pay off their existing mortgages. About half the farmers of the U.S.A. were weighed down by mortgages at high interest on which most of them had defaulted during the depression, involving in their bankruptcy hundreds of rural banks, and which at any time constituted a crushing financial burden. The object of the Farm Credit Administration was to re-finance farm mortgages at lower rates of interest. The Act succeeded in reducing interest rates paid by farmers from over 5 per cent to $3\frac{1}{2}$ per cent and thus reduced their indebtedness by more than a quarter. By September 1937 Government credit agencies held 37 per cent of the farm mortgage debt of the country.[1] In June 1933 the Government took similar action to deal with the parallel problem of the mortgages on urban house property. A public corporation (Home Owners Loan Corporation) was set up which gradually bought up one-sixth of urban mortgages from the banks, trust companies, and building societies which held them, and arranged for new mortgages at substantially lower rates of interest and for longer terms with the house 'owners'. Up to June 1936, when its power to lend expired, Home Owners Loan Corporation lent just over $3,000 million.

Since the bulk of the money lent under these two Acts was used to repay mortgage debts and, therefore, for the most part flowed back to the banks and other private credit institutions, it can have had little direct effect in raising consumers' purchasing power. But by restoring liquidity to a large part of the banking system it put these banks in a position to grant new credits and thus removed an important potential obstacle to recovery. Moreover, the reduction of interest charges and of the debt burden on farmers and urban house owners increased the net income and therefore the effective demand of two large sections of American consumers. In this indirect way, the expenditure on loans to farmers and house-owners promoted recovery for the same reasons as relief expenditure.

Government lending for the purpose of debt reduction, however, formed only a small part of Government expenditure and, for the reasons just mentioned, an even smaller proportion of the 'net contribution' of the New Deal to effective consumers' demand. The bulk of it took the form of Government expenditure on relief and public works. Relief expenditure, as the quickest

[1] J. Strachey, op. cit., p. 189.

method of giving financial aid to the impoverished sections of the population, naturally predominated during the first year of the New Deal; but the first large public works programme was at any rate authorized as early as June 1933. In practice it is difficult to draw a clear line between the two types of Government expenditure of the New Deal. In order to avoid the appearance of the 'dole', most of the grants of Government relief were ostensibly linked to some additional social purpose, such as the purchase of agricultural surpluses or the performance of some sort of useful work. Though much of this work performed by unemployed on relief tended to be somewhat perfunctory and most of it was deliberately selected so as to require the employment of a maximum number of men with a minimum demand for materials and tools, a good deal of it created valuable social capital and hardly differed from some of the public works schemes. On the other hand, some of the money appropriated for the Public Works Administration was in the end allotted to Government relief agencies. No useful purpose would be served here by a detailed description of all the various methods of Government lending and spending of the New Deal. It will be sufficient to mention the most important measures that were adopted.

The main relief programme of the New Deal was inaugurated by the passage of the Federal Emergency Relief Act of May 1933, which for the first time authorized the Federal Government to make direct grants to the States and other local authorities, of money to be paid out to the unemployed. The Act appropriated $500 million, to which further sums were added at intervals by subsequent legislation, and set up the Federal Emergency Relief Administration which until August 1936 remained responsible for the administration of relief both to unemployed and to farmers, and which during this period distributed altogether over $4,000 million. Besides this main relief agency other bodies disbursed money for relief purposes. The Civil Works Administration which was set up in the autumn of 1933, though intended as an emergency substitute for the public works programme which was slow in getting under way, was in fact more concerned with providing immediate relief to the unemployed than with the execution of public works projects and must be considered primarily as a relief agency. During the four months of its existence it spent nearly $1,000 million. In addition, much of the money that continued to be lent by the Government through the R.F.C. and other agencies, especially to farmers, amounted in practice to direct financial relief and constituted a direct contribution to consumers' purchasing power.

Actually the largest single net contribution to consumers' purchasing power out of Federal deficit did not take the form of relief. Under the Veterans Bonus Act, passed in 1936, over the President's veto, nearly 2,000 million dollars' worth of bonds were distributed to war veterans and about half of these bonds were promptly cashed and spent. By any normal standards, the 'veterans' bonus' was a scandalous piece of political 'log-rolling'. But given the circumstances of the depression it is almost unfortunate that the President's veto postponed it by two years. In 1934 or 1935 a net contribution to consumers' purchasing power of these dimensions would have constituted a valuable stimulus to recovery. By 1936 'bottlenecks' had already begun to appear and the war veterans' distribution was largely responsible for a rapid rise in prices and thus indirectly for the disastrous reversal of the policy of Government spending of 1937, which resulted in the slump of the autumn of that year. The fact that the President vetoed the earlier passage of the Bill confirms the impression that until about 1936 at any rate, the net contributions to purchasing power of the New Deal were not really part of a thoroughly thought-out recovery policy.

Legislation authorizing large-scale public works expenditure also belongs to the first months of the New Deal. Part II of the N.R.A. set up the Public Works Administration with an appropriation of $3,300 million (increased in 1934 by a further $500 million) to be spent on public works by the Federal Government and other public authorities. Not all of the original appropriation was allocated to regular public works projects. Some $1,000 million were allotted to special agencies such as state highway systems which normally received Federal grants-in-aid, the Farm Credit Administration, the Civil Works Administration, the Emergency Housing Corporation and the Tennessee Valley Authority. Only the last two of these could really be considered as administering public works proper. Moreover, of the rest about one-third was diverted to Army and Navy purposes. The remainder, however, was spent on a regular construction programme, undertaken by Federal and non-Federal authorities, and, co-ordinated, not altogether adequately, by a National Planning Board (after June 1934 National Resources Board). Though planned on a large scale the public works programme had at first a subordinate position to other measures of 'pump-priming' in the recovery policy of the Roosevelt Administration and, owing to administrative difficulties, few of the projects got under way before 1934. During the following years the emphasis on the public works policy increased. In April 1935 a second public works programme was adopted with an additional appropriation of $4,000 million to be administered partly by the P.W.A., partly by a new agency, the Works Progress Administration. After the abandonment of Federal relief expenditure in

1936 these two agencies became the chief regular channels for Government spending out of budget deficits.

The budget deficits which resulted from all these measures were naturally considerable. They amounted to $3,600 million in 1934, $3,000 million in 1935, $4,200 million in 1936, and $2,700 million in 1937. For various reasons the formal budget figures do not indicate precisely the actual net contribution to purchasing power of the New Deal expenditure. According to Mr. Gayer's estimates, the net income-generating expenditure of the Federal Government during the first four years of the New Deal amounted to $1,800 million in 1933, $3,200 million in 1934, $3,200 million in 1935 and $4,025 million in 1936.[1]

We have now completed our survey of the main types of recovery policy which were embodied in the New Deal of the first Roosevelt Administration. It need hardly be repeated that this approach cannot do justice to the New Deal as a whole. In particular, the important social reforms which were undertaken and, in spite of great obstacles, on the whole successfully carried out, have had to be omitted from this analysis. We have been concerned only with those measures which were primarily intended to promote the recovery of the American economic system. It remains to examine the degree to which recovery was achieved.

VIII. THE AMERICAN RECOVERY 1933–7

THE four years from 1933 until the slump of the autumn of 1937 undoubtedly saw a substantial recovery of the American economy. The Federal Reserve Board index of production rose from 64 in 1932 (1923–5 = 100) to an average of 116 for the first nine months of 1937, which contrasts with the peak in 1929 at 121. Thus by 1937 industrial production had recovered from about half of the 1929 level to within 5 per cent of that level. The national income which, according to Department of Commerce estimates, had fallen from $81,100 million in 1929 to $40,000 million in 1932, rose to $69,800 million in 1937[2] which, if allowance is made for the fact that the price level was considerably lower in 1937 than in 1929, indicates a similar advance. But, substantial though the recovery was,[3] it could hardly be considered satisfactory. Even had it regained the level of 1929 it would have meant that in eight years during which the working population of the U.S.A. had grown from 48 millions to 53

[1] J. A. Schumpeter, *Business Cycles*, vol. ii, p. 1,002.
[2] Cf. League of Nations, *World Economic Survey*, 1937–8, p. 136.
[3] According to an eminent American authority, 'the speed of the recovery, up to this point (1937), was clearly one of the most rapid in our history. . . . The recovery was, moreover, one of the longest in American experience.' (A. H. Hansen, *Fiscal Policy and Business Cycles* [Allen & Unwin, 1941], p. 83.)

million[1] and industrial productivity had increased as a result of technical progress and inventions, the richest and most productive country in the world had made no economic progress whatever. This long-term stagnation was, of course, reflected in the unemployment figures. In 1929, with an index of production of 121, there were anything up to three million unemployed. In 1937, with an index of production at 116, there remained over eight million unemployed (of whom 1·7 million were employed on public works). Even considering a figure of 2·5 to 3 million as the irreducible minimum of unemployment, this meant that by 1937 the U.S.A. still fell short by some four to five million of a condition of full employment.[2]

Two questions arise: first, to what extent can the recovery that was achieved be ascribed to the expansionist measures of the New Deal? Secondly, what are the reasons for the inadequacy of the recovery?

The clue to the answers to both questions will be found in an analysis of the nature of the recovery. It differed in several striking respects from the normal type of cyclical upswing of which the prosperity of the U.S.A. in the nineteen-twenties may be considered a good example. The most outstanding difference was the relative failure in investment expenditure during the later period. During the seven years of prosperity from 1923 to 1929, average total investment expenditure amounted to $18,500 million compared with an average national income of $77,000 million.[3] During the recovery of the nineteen-thirties, consumption expenditure, industrial production, and national income nearly regained the level of 1929. But investment expenditure, which had fallen in 1933 to about $5,000 to $6,000 million, never rose higher than about $12,000 to $13,000 million in 1937.[4] Moreover, this relative decline in total investment expenditure was not evenly distributed over all types of investment. On the one hand, business capital expenditure, comprising replacement and maintenance as well as new investment in industrial plants and equipment, practically maintained the same ratio to consumers' expenditure; but non-business capital expenditure comprising residential and public construction,[5] as well as foreign

[1] J. Strachey, op. cit., p. 206.   [2] ibid.
[3] A. H. Hansen, *Full Recovery or Stagnation?* (Black, 1938), p. 290 f.
[4] ibid., p. 207.
[5] The decline of public construction, that is to say, of capital expenditure by public authorities other than the Federal Government, is of special significance. With regard to trade cycle control by means of a compensatory fiscal policy, local (which in the U.S.A. means State and municipal) authorities occupy an intermediate position between the central government and private enterprise. In theory there is no reason why local authorities, whose budgetary policy is as little dependent upon profit considerations as that of the central Government, should not assist in the task of evening out fluctuations in private investment by compensatory capital expenditure. Where, as in the U.S.A. or Great Britain,

investment, showed a considerable relative decline. In the second place, replacement and maintenance expenditure accounted for a far larger proportion of total business capital expenditure than new investment. Lastly, statistical investigations have shown that, whereas during the nineteen-thirties increases in investment expenditure constantly preceded increases in consumption expenditure, the order was reversed during the nineteen-thirties.[1]

These facts strongly suggest that the American recovery of the nineteen-thirties differed fundamentally from previous cyclical recoveries. Whereas in the past cyclical recoveries had generally been initiated by a rising demand for capital goods in response to renewed business confidence and new investment opportunities, and had only consequentially led to increased consumers' income and demand for consumption goods, the recovery of 1933–7 seems to have been based and fed on a rising demand for consumers' goods. This rising demand for consumption goods brought about a full recovery of the consumption goods industries. It also led to some derived demand for capital goods and some additional new investment. But, instead of leading the recovery, private investment activity seems to have been restricted more or less severely to what was necessary to meet this derived demand. The result was a substantial recovery of the American economy which yet fell short of the goal of full employment, and which, moreover, remained largely dependent on the continuation of large 'net contributions' out of budget deficits.

In the light of these facts there can be little doubt that the particular recovery which did take place was the direct result of

local authorities have normally been responsible for a far larger proportion of regular public investment than the central Government, it is particularly desirable that *all* normal public investment expenditure should be kept at a minimum during periods of prosperity and should be expanded as soon as there is danger of a slump. On the other hand, quite apart from constitutional and administrative difficulties, local authorities have to rely for funds with which to finance *additional* public works on normal credit facilities or on subsidies from the central Government. In that respect their position differs in principle little from that of private firms (although it is in practice somewhat easier to prevent local authorities from treating such subsidies as a welcome aid to investment which cannot in any case be postponed, rather than as an inducement to undertake additional investment).

In the U.S.A. the state and local Governments, which until the New Deal were responsible for all relief, found themselves in desperate financial straits by 1933 and, although the Federal Government freed them from this responsibility, they pursued an orthodox policy of reducing their capital expenditure so as to balance their budgets as far as possible. As a result, state and local public works expenditure declined steadily from $3 milliard in 1929 to $1·1 milliard in 1935. The public works expenditure of the Federal Government, though it increased considerably, was quite inadequate to compensate for this decline. If all public authorities are considered together, therefore, the surprising fact emerges that it was not until 1936 that public investment expenditure exceeded its normal predepression level (A. H. Hansen, *Fiscal Policy and Business Cycles*, p. 85 f.).

[1] A. H. Hansen, *Full Recovery or Stagnation?* ch. xviii.

the expansionist measures of the New Deal. For it was the Government's 'net contributions' to consumers' purchasing power which were directly responsible for the rise in consumers' demand. They also prove beyond any doubt that a policy of Government deficit expenditure, even if that expenditure takes the form of distribution of money directly to consumers rather than of public investment expenditure, can lift an economy out of a depression. It is still arguable—as has in fact been contended by the opponents of the New Deal—that a policy of *laisser faire* would have achieved better results. This hypothetical question cannot in the nature of the case be finally settled. But some more light can be thrown on it if we turn to our second question.

The facts cited above show that the inadequacy of the American recovery from the great depression was in the main an inadequacy of real investment. They show that the policy of 'pump-priming' on the whole failed in its major objective. When the Roosevelt Administration began to embark on compensatory Government expenditure as a conscious recovery policy it did so in the hope that 'pump-priming' would serve as an initial stimulus which was to taper off as private investment gradually took hold with increasing vigour, carrying the economy to full recovery. In fact private investment, though responsive to derived demand for capital goods, failed to take the lead throughout these years and public investment was not nearly adequate to fill the gap. The question why the recovery of 1933-7 remained incomplete, therefore, resolves itself into the question why private investment activity failed to take the lead; why 'pump-priming' failed.

No simple answer can be given to this important question. Part of the explanation is probably to be found in the deterrent character of certain measures of the New Deal. In this connection the Securities Act of 1933, which provided legal and administrative safeguards against the repetition of the Wall Street boom of 1929, is often mentioned; but what effect the Act had in restraining speculators had probably no permanent influence whatever on investment activity. Again, the attitude of the New Deal authorities towards public utilities in connection with the T.V.A. gave rise, it has been said, to 'a growing uncertainty as to the profitability of any investment undertaken by them in view of the possibility of extended Government competition with them.'[1]

More important than the direct influence of these and other, possibly ill-advised measures, was the general political hostility of the business world to the New Deal. During the first year of the Roosevelt Administration the political atmosphere was favourable, for private industry was crying for help and was attracted by the monopolistic nature of the N.R.A. As the de-

[1] League of Nations, *World Economic Survey 1937-8*, p. 21.

pression lifted, however, and the industrialists were beginning to feel stronger, the opposition began to grow. Opposition to State intervention in the economic system, hostility against the progressive social reforms of the New Deal, fear of the results of its 'unorthodox' policy, and ignorance of the benefits which this policy in fact conferred upon themselves, turned the business world into bitter enemies of the Roosevelt Administration. They succeeded in destroying, through the instrumentality of the Supreme Court, the regulatory measures of the New Deal (an action which, as we have seen, was probably a blessing in disguise), and their influence was primarily responsible for the disastrous reversal of the expansionist policy of the Roosevelt Administration in 1937. It is not suggested that, because of their hostility to the New Deal, the entrepreneurs engaged in any deliberate 'strike of capital'; but it is probable that their lack of confidence had a depressing influence on business activity and private investment.

The fact, however, that replacement and maintenance expenditure responded readily to the rise in consumers' demand and that the failure of private investment activity was to be found mainly in the spheres of new investment in industry, residential and public construction and foreign investment, suggests that the unfavourable political atmosphere may not provide the whole, or even the main explanation of the deficiency of private investment activity. It appears that one of the contributory causes of the inadequate recovery of the nineteen-thirties was a relative failure of factors which had been primarily responsible during the nineteen-twenties for stimulating private investment.

The prosperity of the post-war decade had been due largely to the opportunities for profitable investment presented by a pronounced building boom, by foreign demand for American capital, and by the rise of a number of new industries, such as the motorcar industry. During the nineteen-thirties all these three spheres failed to act in the same degree as independent stimuli to private investment. The residential building boom of the nineteen-twenties, which had been one of the most important foundations of prosperity, failed to revive after the great depression. After the exceptional depression of the building industry during the slump, residential construction showed a substantial increase after 1933. But by 1937 it was still 30 per cent below the 1929 level.[1] What little opportunity for the investment of American capital abroad presented itself in the depressed condition of world trade during

---

[1] S. Kuznets, *National Income and Capital Formation*; quoted T. Wilson, op. cit., p. 183. The reason for this decline was partly that, owing to the strong monopolistic position of the cement and brick cartels, and to a lesser extent of the building unions, building costs remained very high throughout the depression.

the nineteen-thirties was insufficient to attract the American private investor after the disastrous experience of 1930–1. As a result American foreign investment, which had amounted to some $500 million per year and which had financed a huge export trade during the nineteen-twenties, dropped to insignificant amounts during the depression and was finally replaced by a net repayment of loans. Next to expanding internal and external demand for capital goods the most important stimuli to capital formation and private investment in a capitalist economy are advances in technique and innovation which give rise to new industries. During the nineteen-twenties the remarkable growth of the automobile industry had provided a large sphere for new investment and had constituted one of the foundations of prosperity. It appears that in this sphere too, opportunities for profitable investment were smaller after the depression. During the years between 1920 and 1929 the index of average productivity in the manufacturing industries had increased by 41·6 points; between 1929 and 1937 the increase amounted to little more than half that figure (21·6):[1] the electrical industry was the only major group which showed a rising rate of growth of productivity, and although this technical advance was an important stimulus during the nineteen-thirties it was insufficient to offset the decline in other industries. The most important single factor was the fact that the automobile industry ceased to expand at its former rate. Productivity rose by only 6.3 points compared to an increase of 74.9 points between 1920 and 1929, and whereas the increase of output of the industry during the nineteen-twenties had been far ahead of all other major industries it was 4 points lower than the average in 1937.[2] Similar though smaller declines took place in some other new industries, such as petroleum and rubber, whose great expansion during the nineteen-twenties had shown the influence of technical progress as a stimulus to investment.

The absence, or relative decline, of profitable investment opportunities during the nineteen-thirties in the very spheres in which new investment had been greatest during the post-war decade must have been a major factor in retarding the rate of real investment and may have been largely responsible for the inadequacy of the recovery of the nineteen-thirties. If this is the case, the contention of the opponents of the New Deal policy loses much of its force. For in that case, it is clearly most unlikely that —even if the adverse effects of many of the New Deal reforms on business confidence are taken into account—private enterprise unaided by expansionist measures would have brought about a fuller recovery.

[1] T. Wilson, op. cit. p. 184. [2] ibid.,, p. 185.

C

The question whether 'low business confidence' or the relative failure of investment opportunities had the greater effect in retarding investment activity is not of purely academic interest. For on the answer to this question depends in part the remedy which would have been available to the American Government and the lesson to be drawn from the experience of the New Deal. If the relative lack of success of 'pump-priming' can be put down to the lack of confidence of private enterprise in the prospects of success of the expansionist policy of the Roosevelt Administration it is not impossible that that policy, even in the form of direct contribution to consumers' purchasing power, would have succeeded if it had been carried on longer and on a larger scale. Sooner or later, *entrepreneurs* would have realized that investment undertaken in the expectation of further increases in consumers' demand brought a profitable return. Even if it is granted that 'low business confidence' was at least as much due to political hostility against the radical tendencies of the Roosevelt Administration in general and the social reforms of the New Deal in particular as to the prevailing prejudices against 'unsound' fiscal policies, the solid attractions of a steady demand, coupled with (*ex hypothesi*) normal investment opportunities, would probably have been sufficient to ensure the success of 'pump-priming'. On this assumption also, there is a reasonable hope that 'pump-priming' of the New Deal type would by itself provide an adequate remedy against depressions, once the implications of a compensatory fiscal policy are generally understood.

If, on the other hand, as appears more likely, the relative failure of opportunities for profitable investment in specific fields was the more important reason for the deficiency of private investment, the distribution of money to consumers on an adequate scale would probably not have been feasible. For in order to replace the investment opportunities of the nineteen-twenties in the spheres of residential building, new industries, and foreign investment by investment opportunities in the shape of growing consumers' demand would probably have required an amount of Government expenditure which would have been politically quite impossible. In that case, the remedy would have been to supplement private investment with public investment on a larger scale than was done through the public works policy of the New Deal. In retrospect, one can almost say that the inadequacy of the American recovery was due to the complete failure of public investment expenditure under the New Deal to fill the gap left by the decline in private investment activity. From 1932 until 1937 private investment expenditure was on the average $8·6 milliard per year below the 1925-9 level of $14 milliard.[1] In order

[1] A. H. Hansen, *Fiscal Policies and Business Cycles*, p. 87.

to compensate for this decline, therefore, Federal public works expenditure should have reached this average figure of $8·6 milliard. In fact, Federal investment expenditure (including aid to local authorities) during these years averaged only $1·2 milliard per year; and, if the decline in state and municipal construction expenditure is taken into account, public investment as a whole made, as we have seen,[1] until 1936, no positive contribution whatever towards recovery.

Nor can there be any doubt that public investment on a much larger scale would have been possible. Obviously, there was no *absolute* lack of investment opportunities in the sense of opportunities of applying the idle productive resources of the country to the production of new capital equipment. At most, the difficulty was that what investment opportunities presented themselves did not appear sufficiently profitable to attract the private investor. Although constitutional difficulties stood in the way it should certainly have been possible, by concerted policy and larger Federal subsidies, to prevent the decline of, if not to expand, State and municipal construction expenditure. In all probability, moreover, slum clearance, road building, reafforestation, soil conservation, housing, electrification, and a hundred other fields would have provided ample scope for public investment which would have made valuable additions to the nation's capital equipment without being unduly competitive with private enterprise and, therefore, unduly discouraging to private investment activity.

Even should it have been impossible to extend productive public investment greatly without automatically reducing private investment to the same or a larger extent there would, in theory, have been two solutions. On the one hand, productive public investment could have been carried further regardless of the effects on private investment activity. If carried far enough, this would undoubtedly have been successful in achieving full recovery, though it would have meant considerable inroads on the system of private enterprise. Whether such a policy would have been politically feasible in the U.S.A. of the nineteen-thirties is, of course, quite a different matter. Alternatively, the same result in respect of full employment might have been achieved had the Government embarked on unproductive investment, of which the most obvious example is armaments. This, in essence, as we shall see later, was the secret of the German recovery under the Nazi régime.

[1] See above, p. 61, note 5.

THE recovery of the American economy came to a sudden end in the autumn of 1937, and was followed by a brief but disastrous slump which for a time threatened to wipe out completely the hard-won gains of the preceding years. It appears that even the limited recovery which had been achieved could not be maintained. We may conclude this analysis of the New Deal with a brief consideration of the events of 1937–8.

Until about October 1936 the course of the recovery had belied those who had foretold inflation as the inevitable consequence of the 'unsound' budgetary policy of the New Deal. After the initial sharp rise during 1933 prices had remained steady. Between July 1935 and December 1936, when the largest net contributions were made, production expanded rapidly, but the cost of living index rose by only two points. Towards the end of 1936 however, partly owing to outside factors, such as the sudden stimulus given to American raw material exports by the European rearmament programmes and the drought of 1936 which forced up agriculture commodity prices, partly owing to the sudden bulge in consumers' demand and expenditure which resulted from the veterans' bonus payments, prices began to rise more rapidly, and in the spring of 1937 the price increase gave rise to commodity speculation and a large increase in business inventories. There is evidence that, although the economy was still far from full employment, 'bottlenecks' had begun to appear in some sectors of industries as a result of a genuine, if temporary, scarcity of specialized factors of production; though it seems probable that these bottlenecks would mostly have widened again after a time under the pull of a steady demand. At any rate, the Roosevelt Administration grew alarmed by the inflationary symptoms. The opponents of the New Deal, especially among big business and finance, raised a hue and cry about the imminence of inflation. Influenced by this clamour, and at the same time confident that the economy had by now acquired sufficient momentum to enable it to go forward under the impetus of private investment, the Administration decided early in 1937 to take vigorous steps to check the 'inflation'.

In December 1936 the policy of 'gold sterilization' was adopted which prevented most of the imported gold from being added to the reserves of the banking system; during the spring of 1937 the reserve ratios of the Federal Reserve Banks were twice raised in order to check the expansion of credit by the banks. Since bank credit had not even reached the limits set by the new reserve ratios this measure can only have had a psychological effect. What was much more important, the Administration decided severely to curtail Government expenditure. Actually, it was not proposed to remove the budget deficit for 1937 entirely. But other factors, of which the most important was the inflow of funds to the Government from the insurance contributions that had been imposed on workers and employers alike by the Social Security Act of 1935, led to an even greater decline of the deficit than was intended. The Government net contribution which, swollen by the veterans' bonus, had amounted to about $4,100 million in 1936, is estimated to have dropped in 1937 to $985 million. In February 1937 it fell for the first time for several years to below $100 million per month and did not materially exceed this figure again until April 1938.[1]

These measures not only succeeded in checking the symptoms of inflation; they were followed by a slump almost as deep as and even more precipitate than that of 1929. The inventory boom collapsed in March 1937. In September the downward trend began. In the six months between October 1937 and March 1938, some four and a half million workers lost their jobs. The Federal Reserve Board index of production dropped from 116 for the first half of 1937 to 75 for July 1938, only eleven points above the bottom of the great depression. The national income, which had risen to $72,000 million in 1937, had fallen by the beginning of 1938 to a figure corresponding to no more than $50,000 million per year.[2]

What had at first been dismissed as a 'business recession' had developed into a slump of catastrophic dimensions. In March 1938 the Roosevelt Administration realized that only an immediate resumption of Government expenditure on a large scale could prevent a prolonged depression. The President therefore proposed in April, and Congress authorized in July, a new programme of expenditure on relief and public works (the latter this time having by far the major share), of $2,000 to $2,500 million and new R.F.C. loans up to $1,500 million. The mere announcement of this policy in April caused the stock market to turn upwards after six months of rapid decline. From July onwards, when the new Government expenditure became effective, recovery proceeded almost as quickly as the slump the year before. Before the end of 1938 the index of production had regained the 100 mark and employment had increased by 1·2 million.[3] The shortness of the depression was partly due to the fact that the slump had taken the form of an inventory crisis. But this alone would not account for the rapidity of the recovery. The events of 1937–8 clearly showed the extent to which the economic prosperity of the U.S.A. remained dependent on the intervention of Government expenditure.

[1] J. Strachey, op. cit., p. 216.   [2] ibid., p. 226.   [3] ibid., p. 233.

Nor can there be much doubt that the Administration allowed itself to be stampeded into the reversal of its expansionist policy by a cry of inflation which, at any rate in 1937, had little justification. In the spring of that year the U.S.A. was still so far from a state of full employment, the remaining reserve of unemployed labour was still so large, that existing bottlenecks—due largely to the unfortunate coincidence of the veterans' bonus, the drought, and European rearmament demand—would almost certainly have disappeared after a few months. The question, however, remains whether, even without these incidental factors, the American Government would not sooner or later have been faced with the same problem.

The events of 1937 suggest that owing to the immobility of factors of production and, it should be added, also owing to the monopolistic character of many American industries, additional Government deficit expenditure was bound to result in inflationary price increases in some sectors of the economy long before unemployment and unused capacity over the country as a whole were fully absorbed. It seems doubtful, therefore, whether monetary control alone which was not supplemented by direct forms of intervention to increase the mobility of labour (especially a system of state-controlled training of skilled workers) and by measures of price and wage control, could ever have achieved more than a 'three-quarters' recovery which left a substantial proportion of the working population unemployed.

The experience of the U.S.A. in 1937 also illustrates the difficulty of controlling the flow of new purchasing power into the economic system in the last stages of the recovery. The problem is partly to judge accurately the actual net contribution that will result from any given budget policy; partly to prevent the speculative boom which is liable to develop as soon as prices begin to rise with the emergence of bottlenecks and which may more than offset any planned reduction of Government expenditure. The latter danger points to the necessity of fairly stringent control of credit and investment if the economy is to be maintained in equilibrium at the peak of recovery.

Chapter Three

UNITED STATES: FOREIGN ECONOMIC POLICY

I. THE BACKGROUND

THE great depression, as we saw in the first chapter,[1] suddenly laid bare the international economic problem created by the transformation of the U.S.A. from a debtor to the leading creditor country in the world. For half a century before 1914 the U.S.A. had, with the assistance of foreign capital, built up her industry behind a tariff wall which had become a political institution while she had paid her creditors with agricultural and raw material surpluses. The war of 1914–18 had compressed into a span of five years a process which without it might have taken a decade or two. In 1919 the U.S.A. was owed some $2—4 milliard on private account, in addition to $10 milliard of political debts. But no attempt was made to adjust the American balance of trade to the new position by turning her export surpluses into import surpluses. Whether such adjustment would have been possible or not without severe internal dislocation, the needs of Europe, first for relief and then for American capital, made it easy to shelve the problem for a decade. The American tariff was raised further in 1922, and the disequilibrium was concealed by an orgy of foreign lending which more than covered interest and amortization payments due to the U.S.A. and enabled her to maintain throughout the post-war decade a large annual export surplus. The return flow of capital to the U.S.A. during the Wall Street boom revealed the first cracks in this precarious structure, and with the slump and depression it collapsed. As American lending ebbed and ceased and short-term capital hastened back from Europe, the incongruity between the protectionist policy and export surpluses of the U.S.A. and her creditor position became apparent.

But there was never a less propitious time for a too-long-postponed adjustment of American commercial policy than the beginning of the worst internal depression. Over the ineffectual protest of a thousand American economists and the claims of a few groups interested in American foreign trade (such as investment bankers, importers, and automobile manufacturers), traditional Republican protectionism, supported by vested interests firmly entrenched in Congress, produced in 1930 the Hawley-Smoot Act which raised the American tariff higher than ever.

[1] See above, ch. i, p. 12 f.

In the conditions of the world economy at the onset of the great depression, even the most liberal foreign trade policy of the U.S.A. could not have prevented violent disturbances. But the policy that was actually followed contributed, perhaps more than any other single factor, to the international economic chaos and collapse of international trade of the succeeding years.

The events that followed were reviewed above. The Hawley-Smoot tariff gave the signal for the first wave of tariff increases which by the end of 1931 already involved some twenty-five countries. In some cases American foreign trade policy served as the excuse rather than the direct cause of the resort to isolationist policies elsewhere. But the decline in American demand which, though mainly due to the internal slump, was aggravated by the further restrictions on imports, together with the withdrawal of American short-term capital, were largely responsible for the pressure on the balances of payments of the debtor countries of Europe and South America which forced them to curtail their imports and to choose between depreciating their currencies or adopting exchange control. Deprived of the support of American loans, with rapidly shrinking gold and foreign exchange reserves, and unable to increase or even maintain its exports to the U.S.A., one debtor country after another went into default on its external obligations to the U.S.A. During 1933 the problem of political debts was liquidated by the general default in payments on war debts to the U.S.A. by all Governments except Finland, and by 1934 there were total or partial defaults in connection with 32 per cent of American-held foreign bonds.[1]

The depression not only resulted in the loss of a substantial proportion of the foreign investments which the U.S.A. had bought during the preceding two decades by her export surpluses; American foreign trade suffered more severely from the depression and the rapidly growing obstacles to international trade than that of any other important country. Between 1929 and 1932 the physical volume of American exports dropped by nearly one half, compared with a drop of one-quarter in world exports,[2] and the decline in the value of American trade amounted to nearly 70 per cent for both exports and imports.[3] Unlike the other large industrial countries, the U.S.A., whose exports and imports were fairly evenly balanced between primary commodities and manufactures, did not derive any compensating benefit in the form of an improvement in her terms of trade from the disproportionate fall in the prices of the former. On the contrary, the chief sufferers

[1] A. D. Gayer and C. T. Schmidt, *American Economic Foreign Policy*, Report to Twelfth International Studies Conference, 1939, p. 127.
[2] Gayer and Schmidt, op. cit., p. 166.
[3] League of Nations, *World Economic Survey*, *1932–3*, p. 214.

from the slump in American exports were the American farmers and especially the producers of the agricultural staple commodities, cotton and wheat, who more than most American manufacturers depended on foreign markets.

During the nineteen-thirties the problem of the maladjustment of the American balance of trade and payments was brought little nearer solution. While the U.S.A. ceased to lend abroad on a large scale, she remained the world's largest creditor. In spite of the extensive defaults the U.S.A. continued to receive large sums year by year in interest on her foreign investments. To these receipts was added after 1934 a large and steady inflow of capital, in search of speculative gains and a haven of refuge from the political and economic uncertainties of Europe. American foreign economic policy, however, was determined exclusively by the needs of the American domestic economy. The very first act of the Roosevelt Administration in this sphere, the devaluation of the dollar, though it reduced the cost of debt payments to the U.S.A. in terms of foreign currencies, on balance seriously aggravated the problem. American commercial policy did indeed, under the guidance of Secretary of State Cordell Hull, undergo a notable transformation. During the thirties the traditionally protectionist U.S.A., in striking contrast to the trend towards State control of trade and bilateralism elsewhere, appeared as the champion of 'freer trade'. But this policy, though superficially sounder in its method, pursued the same object as the restrictionist policies of the countries of Europe; to relieve the internal depression by selling as much and buying as little as possible. Its relative failure was in no small part due to the profound international maladjustments for which American policy had itself been partly responsible.

II. THE DEVALUATION OF THE DOLLAR

IN our analysis of the New Deal we have already discussed the devaluation of the dollar in 1933 as a factor in the American internal recovery. It remains only to consider its effects on the external economic position of the U.S.A. and on the rest of the world.

With the partial exception of France, the U.S.A. was the only country which throughout the years of the depression remained free from the embarrassment of an adverse balance of payments and dangerous pressure on her gold and foreign exchange reserves. Owing partly to the fact that the depression, and with it the decline in demand, spread from the U.S.A. to the rest of the world, partly to the initial high American tariff, and partly to heavy withdrawals of short-term balances from the U.S.A.

C*

during the years 1930–3 by foreign countries in payments for American goods, the U.S.A. throughout these years maintained a large favourable balance of trade. Despite defaults her income from foreign investments remained large enough more than to cover her invisible imports in the form of tourist expenditure, immigrant remittances and the deficit on her balance of shipping services. On two occasions, first after the depreciation of the pound in the autumn of 1931, and again during the first half of 1932, large speculative short-term movements which by their erratic behaviour had helped to wreck the gold standard in country after country threatened even the U.S.A. But on both occasions the enormous gold reserves which the U.S.A. had accumulated during the post-war decade provided a more than adequate buffer, and the outflows were soon halted. Broadly speaking, the U.S.A. was the main beneficiary—if the term may be used in this context—of the international payments disequilibrium and adverse capital movements which forced the European debtor countries off the free gold standard. If any country could afford to maintain the gold parity of its currency and a free gold standard it was the U.S.A. Yet in 1933 the U.S.A., too, abandoned the gold standard and devalued the dollar.

To some extent the action of the U.S.A. was part of the game of competitive currency depreciation. The depreciation of the pound and the other currencies of the sterling group and of Japan had given these countries a considerable competitive price advantage over the U.S.A. in international markets. During 1932 Great Britain is stated to have increased her share of world trade by 16 per cent over the previous year and Japan by 29 per cent,[1] and, while it is doubtful in view of the disproportionate fall of the internal American price level whether even at the end of 1932 the dollar was seriously overvalued, Americans believed that the decline in the American share of world trade by 22 per cent between 1929 and 1932[2] was partly due to the price handicap resulting from the maintenance of the gold parity of the dollar. But though the desire to stimulate American exports may have acted as a subsidiary motive, the main reason which induced the Roosevelt Administration in April 1933 to abandon the gold standard and devalue the dollar was, as we have seen before, the belief that the fall in the external value of the dollar would by itself raise the internal price level and thus promote recovery.

The devaluation of the dollar by 41 per cent had some undoubtedly beneficial results for the U.S.A. It constituted a reinsurance against the danger of capital flight, and it ensured a more than adequate gold basis for the policy of credit expansion

[1] Gayer and Schmidt, op. cit., p. 166.
[2] P.E.P., *Report on International Trade*, p. 246.

of the New Deal. It also—and this was a more doubtful advantage —in effect raised the American tariff by 60 per cent, and gave a 40 per cent bounty to American exports which more than wiped out their previous competitive handicap. But these benefits were obtained at the cost of other countries and at the expense of increasing the already existing disequilibrium in the American balance of payments.[1] Whether the net result even for the U.S.A. herself was favourable is, as we have seen, by no means certain.

The announcement by President Roosevelt of the intention of the American Government to devalue the dollar in April 1933 came as a bombshell to the World Monetary and Economic Conference which had just met in London and destroyed what little hopes there were of agreement between the gold standard countries, on the one side, and the sterling bloc and the U.S.A. on the other, on the central question of currency stabilization. At a time when exchange rates were just settling down after the first shock of the British departure from gold and the wave of depreciations that followed it, the devaluation of the second most important currency brought new confusion. During the summer of 1933 rapidly rising prices in the U.S.A. eased the strain on other countries which might otherwise have been expected from the depreciation of the dollar. By the end of the year, however, the first flush of recovery in the U.S.A. was over, and after the stabilization of the dollar in January 1934 its undervaluation caused an acute strain on the balances of payments of most other countries. Those countries which had already depreciated their currencies merely suffered the loss of most of the competitive advantage which their export trades had obtained from depreciation, though some of the sterling countries, particularly Australia, were forced into further depreciation by the downward pressure on their export prices and the return of short-term capital to the U.S.A. The countries which, like Germany, had protected their currencies and balances of payments by exchange control were driven still further in the direction of bilateral controlled trade. The worst hit countries were those that were still clinging to the gold standard. They were forced to new and ever more stringent measures of internal deflation, or to new restrictions on imports, or both. Thus in France during 1934 the general level of prices was reduced by 16 per cent with further depressing effect on

---

[1] In one respect the devaluation of the dollar reduced the disequilibrium. Since most of the debts due to the U.S.A. were dollar debts, their value, and the cost of interest and amortization payments to the debtor countries, were automatically reduced by 40 per cent. This effect was not unimportant; it was largely responsible for the temporary resumption of debt payments by Germany and Hungary in 1934. But part of this reduction merely served to offset previous appreciations due to currency depreciations in the debtor countries and its effect on the American balance of payments was probably more than outweighed by the effect of the devaluation on the balance of trade.

economic activity, and fresh trade restrictions helped to cut the import surplus by approximately half. In the Netherlands the import balance was cut from 40 to 27 million florins; in Switzerland from 62 to 50 million Swiss francs. The two countries of the gold bloc where such measures were not effectively taken were forced, Italy into exchange control and Belgium into devaluation.[1]

The devaluation of the dollar resulted in an immediate rise by more than 100 per cent in the American export surplus.[2] It is practically certain, though difficult to prove statistically, that the dollar was undervalued, at least until about 1935 or 1936. But even a devaluation which had merely restored to the U.S.A. her international position prior to the currency depreciations elsewhere would have increased the existing maladjustment. For, that position was, as we know, itself untenable in the absence of continued capital exports. From 1931 until 1933 large outflows of short-term capital had taken the place of long-term loans in providing foreign countries with the dollars necessary to purchase more from the U.S.A. than she bought from them. One result of the devaluation and the restabilization of the dollar on a gold basis was that the movement of 'hot money' was reversed. From 1934 onwards short-term (and long-term) capital flowed into the U.S.A. in large volumes. The export surpluses and payments due to the U.S.A. being no longer offset—but, on the contrary, reinforced—by capital movements, the balance had to be paid for in gold.[3] The result was that from 1934 onwards immense quantities of gold flowed from all over the world to the U.S.A.[4]

Neither the export surpluses of the U.S.A. nor the capital movements to the U.S.A. during the years after 1934 were wholly or even mainly due to the devaluation of the dollar. But the

[1] League of Nations, *World Economic Survey, 1934-5*, p. 8 f.

[2] F. W. Fetter, *U.S. Balance of International Payments*, Foreign Policy Reports, 15 May 1936, p. 57.

[3] Defaults and the devaluation of the dollar considerably diminished the receipts of interest and amortization payments on American foreign investments during the nineteen-thirties. But during the five-year period between 1934 and 1938 these receipts still amounted to a total of over £1,250 million, or an average of £250 million per annum. (*Statistical Abstract of the United States*, 1939.)

[4] Concurrently with the gold purchase policy the U.S.A. embarked on a silver purchase policy. Though put forward under the guise of a policy of bimetallism the policy of buying silver at home and in the world market at anything from twice to three times the world price had no rational justification; it was in fact a racket engineered by the senators for the 'silver states'. The policy which was continued throughout the decade not only cost the U.S.A. some $900 million between 1934 and 1938, paid for in American exports—an inefficient subsidy to American silver producers but perhaps a minor burden on the American people —it also incidentally exerted a severe deflationary pressure on China and Mexico and forced the former to abandon the silver standard and the latter to demonetize silver. The silver purchase policy well illustrates the responsibility for international economic order which rests on the large countries merely because of the magnitude of their operations; what in the U.S.A. was merely a major scandal spread depression and chaos on the other side of the globe.

devaluation prevented such adjustments in the American balance of payments as might have resulted during these years from the depreciations of foreign currencies and the rise in American price levels and import demand. At the best, it assisted the American recovery by stimulating exports and giving further protection to the home market at the cost of selling American goods abroad for largely useless gold. At the worst, by its immediate disturbing effect on world economic conditions and its long-run effect in diminishing the purchasing power of other countries for American exports and preventing a 'spilling over' of the American recovery, it actually retarded the revival of American foreign trade.

III. THE CORDELL HULL TRADE PROGRAMME

IN 1934 the Roosevelt Administration launched its 'New Deal' for American foreign trade, which has rightly been identified with its sponsor and tireless proponent, Secretary of State Cordell Hull. In one sense the term 'New Deal' fits the Cordell Hull trade programme of reciprocal tariff bargaining; for its major object was to assist in the recovery of one sector of the American economy, the depressed American export industries. In another sense, the analogy is misleading; for while the New Deal meant a large, though perhaps reluctant, step towards Government intervention in economic life, the great aim of the Cordell Hull trade programme was, by a curious contrast, to reduce state intervention and restore the free play of market forces in international trade.

During the years of the depression, as we saw, American foreign trade had fallen to less than a third of its former value, with disastrous consequences to the American export industries. In similar circumstances, Great Britain in 1932 was able to attempt to compensate her industries for the loss of foreign markets by abandoning free trade and thus enlarging the home market. This course was not open to the U.S.A., traditionally protectionist and already surrounded by unconscionably high tariff walls. The American export industries could not hope to find in the home market an adequate substitute for their former export trade. This applied especially to American agriculture, by far the most important and most depressed of the export industries. A revival of American agricultural exports, at least to pre-depression levels, was the only alternative to immense structural changes in the American economy, involving the virtual abandonment of part of the traditional agricultural industries of the U.S.A.

In 1933 it was clear to everyone that the steep decline of international trade between 1929 and 1932 was largely due to the obstacles to international trade, in the form of tariffs, import quotas, and exchange control, to which country after country had resorted in its efforts to ward off the impact of the world depression. It was also increasingly realized in the U.S.A. that not the least of these obstacles to the revival of American exports was the high American tariff; that commerce is a 'two-way process'; and that foreign countries could not increase their purchases of American products or meet their financial obligations to the U.S.A., even if they wished, unless the U.S.A. provided them with the necessary dollar exchange either by renewed lending, for which there was little inclination, or by purchasing their goods. In 1934 Secretary of Agriculture Wallace insisted that 'America must choose' between the abandonment of high protectionism and the abandonment of her agriculture. In practice the farmers were by no means unanimous in their support of the Democratic 'free trade' platform. The most powerful vested interests behind the Cordell Hull 'freer trade' policy were the financial and banking interests, which saw that a substantial reduction of the American tariff was the only alternative to further defaults on their large foreign investments of the nineteen-twenties and the continued breakdown of foreign investment activity.

The most straightforward remedy would have been a unilateral reduction of tariffs by the U.S.A. Such unilateral action alone could have brought about the change-over in the American balance of trade which her creditor position required, and in view of the immense importance of the American import market it would have given a powerful stimulus to international trade and thus to American exports. But there were few if any voices in the U.S.A. in favour of this proposal which would undoubtedly have raised considerable problems of internal adjustment and which stood no chance of acceptance by a Congress still steeped in protectionist ideas and influenced, if no longer controlled, by the vested interests of protected industries. In the long run, it was American industry, grown to maturity behind the protective tariff, rather than American agriculture which stood to gain from a revival of world trade; and the fact that many American industries, such as the motor-car industry, were now capable of outbidding all competitors in the world markets was not unconnected with the decline of protectionism in the U.S.A. But in the depth of the depression most American industries preferred the safety of the tariff to the venture of competition, and high-cost producers, well organized into powerful pressure groups, strenuously and vociferously opposed any reduction in the tariff which appeared to threaten their internal markets.

In these circumstances Secretary Cordell Hull chose the compromise policy of bilateral bargaining with foreign countries for the reciprocal reduction of trade barriers, which had the advantage that it could be carried through with a minimum disturbance to American producers for the home market while at the same time making certain that foreign countries would reciprocate for American concessions by equivalent concessions to American exports.

The decision to abandon the traditional autonomous tariff policy of the U.S.A. in favour of a policy of bilateral bargaining raised the question whether the U.S.A. should also abandon the principle of 'equality of treatment' which, expressed in the unconditional most-favoured-nation clause, had since 1923 formed the explicit basis of American commercial policy; whether the U.S.A. should follow the general trend towards bilateralism. Under the impact of the depression most important European countries were resorting to bilateral bargaining either in order to overcome shortages of foreign exchange or for the exploitation of superior bargaining power; in either case, with the result that international trade was being canalized into bilateral channels. Owing to the maladjustment in the American balance of international payments which forced most debtor countries to circumvent their shortage of dollars by diverting their purchases to other countries, American exports were suffering more than those of any other country from adverse discrimination. The U.S.A. might have endeavoured to correct the maladjustment in her balance of payments which was largely responsible for this development. On the other hand, the U.S.A. might also have retaliated by discriminating in her turn against foreign countries. In fact, the U.S.A. adopted neither course. The principle of 'non-discrimination' became the keystone of the Cordell Hull trade programme, and bilateral tariff bargaining was reconciled with multilateralism by the inclusion of the unconditional most-favoured-nation clause in all trade agreements.

There is no doubt that, by contrast to the commercial policies of many other Powers during the nineteen-thirties, the Cordell Hull trade policy was inspired by a genuine spirit of idealism. It rested on the conviction that all countries, including the U.S.A., had to make an effort to revive international trade, that the chief obstacle to such a revival lay in the tariffs, import quotas and exchange controls which had grown up everywhere during the years of the depression, that the tendency towards bilateralism was contributing to the strangulation of international trade by confining it into bilateral channels, that the benefits to be derived from discrimination in any form were ultimately based on the exploitation of weaker countries, and that a revival of international trade, therefore, presupposed a reduction of those trade barriers and a renunciation of bilateral and discriminatory trading methods. Yet—ignoring for the moment the question as to the soundness of these convictions—it may be doubted whether they would have prevailed if the policy of non-discrimination and *laisser faire* had not accorded with the special interests and position of the U.S.A.

The same factor which rendered American commerce particularly liable to discrimination by foreign countries made it somewhat more difficult for her to retaliate. In conditions in which each country was eager to push its exports and curtail its imports, one of the chief elements of bargaining power lay in the possession of an adverse balance of trade. The country with an import surplus could threaten to cut down its purchases unless the other countries bought more of its goods. In this respect, the U.S.A. was badly placed. With the exception of some of the British colonies and Dominions (which were unassailable owing to the triangular character of British-American-Empire trade) there were few countries with which the U.S.A. did not have a favourable balance of trade. This 'handicap' was not insignificant. At the same time, there is no doubt that the economic power of the U.S.A. was quite sufficient to enable her to stand up against any country in a free fight. What is more important, the U.S.A. was not as pressed to take advantage of what opportunities for discrimination she possessed as were most European countries. In almost all European countries (including after 1934 even the countries of the gold bloc) adverse balances of payments necessitated, or at least provided arguments in favour of, import restrictions and bilateral balances of trade so as to obviate the use of foreign exchange. In the U.S.A. as we know, there was no balance of payments problem in this sense. Most important of all, however, was probably the fact that, partly owing to the sheer size of the U.S.A., partly owing to the long period of protectionism, the foreign trade of the U.S.A. was relatively less important to the American economy as a whole than in any other country except Russia. In 1933 the foreign trade (imports plus exports) of the U.S.A. was equivalent to only 7·3 per cent of the national income, compared with 25 per cent in the case of Great Britain, 23·5 per cent in the case of France, and 19·5 per cent in the case of Germany.[1] It is not suggested that for that reason foreign trade

---

[1] League of Nations, *Statistical Year Book 1937–8*. In 1933 the corresponding figure even for Russia (7·6 per cent) was still a little higher than for the U.S.A.; but during the following years the growth of the Russian national income brought the ratio, in the case of Russia, down to 3·2 per cent. The figure for France is almost certainly far too high, the reason being that the only available figures for the French national income probably underestimate it by anything up to 30 or 40 per cent.

did not matter to the U.S.A. or that the character of her commercial policy was a matter of indifference to American business men, farmers, bankers, workers, and consumers. But there can be no doubt that her relative independence of foreign trade placed the U.S.A. in a better position to forgo the advantages to be obtained from discrimination in favour of a policy which in the international sphere upheld the principles of *laisser faire* liberalism, still the dominant philosophy of capitalist America. In a sense, the U.S.A. during the nineteen-thirties could afford the luxury of relying in her commercial policy on free private enterprise and the free play of market forces. We shall see presently that where, as in the case of American agricultural surpluses, the free play of market forces failed to solve the problem and where opportunities for discrimination presented themselves, the U.S.A., too, resorted to measures which were difficult to reconcile with the principle of 'equality of treatment'.

IV. RECIPROCAL TRADE AGREEMENTS

IN 1934 the Roosevelt Administration secured the passage of the Trade Agreements Act which was to provide the legal basis for the execution of the Cordell Hull trade programme. It empowered the President to enter into trade agreements with foreign countries for the reciprocal reduction of tariffs and other trade restrictions. The Act authorised the President to reduce American tariffs, though he could not decrease any one duty by more than 50 per cent. It also provided that any reductions of duties should, on the unconditional most-favoured-nation principle, be extended automatically to all other countries, with the proviso, however, that the President could withhold such benefits from countries which discriminated against American commerce. The Act, which was originally passed for a period of three years, was renewed in 1937 and again in 1940.

The Trade Agreements Act itself constituted an important reform and a victory for the Hull policy. For fifty years and more tariff-making in the U.S.A. had been a game of sectional interests and political intrigue which by itself had tended to raise the American tariff walls. By virtually handing over the power of altering the tariff from Congress to the Administration the Act helped to eliminate one of the worst features of American political life and for the first time made possible a commercial policy which, whatever its merits, was at least determined by wider considerations of national interest.

Between 1934 and the outbreak of the present war the U.S.A. concluded trade agreements with twenty countries. Half of these were with the tropical or semi-tropical countries of Latin

America. Since their products were mostly non-competitive with American industries and since all of them depended largely on the American market for their surpluses, trade agreements with them met with little difficulty. In return for tariff concessions on specialized American products the U.S.A. agreed to keep most imports of their tropical products on the free list. The position was similar with regard to a second group of countries including Finland, Sweden and, with certain qualifications, Canada. American trade with the two former was mainly non-dutiable and the agreements for the most part stabilized the existing tariff status. The agreements with Canada, the first of which was concluded in 1935, and the second in conjunction with the Anglo-American pact of 1938, were of greater importance mainly because of the large volume of trade between the two countries. In 1935, Canada provided a market for one-seventh of American exports (constituting one-half of Canada's total imports), and depended on the American market for more than one-third of her own exports. Moreover, the importance of the American market to Canadian exports, together with the difference in size between the two countries, meant that the relatively limited tariff concessions made by the U.S.A. hardly disturbed her vast domestic economy but affected a large proportion of Canadian production. They consisted chiefly of promises to allow continued free entry to Canadian forest products and raw materials and some tariff concessions on dairy and other minor agricultural products in return for reductions of duties on many American manufactures and promises of most-favoured-nation treatment.

The real test of the Hull trade programme lay in the ability to reach agreements with the industrial countries of Europe. The products of these countries were more or less competitive with those of American industries and subject to high American duties. These countries still constituted the main potential markets for American agricultural surpluses, and they had gone furthest in imposing tariffs and other obstacles to foreign trade. Moreover, since with most of them the U.S.A. had a favourable balance of trade, she was in a weak bargaining position to press her demands. With some of them agreements were successfully concluded. In the cases of Holland and Switzerland their low tariffs and highly specialized products, and in the case of the former the fact that the U.S.A. was a large customer for the raw materials of the Dutch East Indies, facilitated the conclusion of agreements. Agreements involving minor concessions on both sides were also obtained with France, Belgium, Czechoslovakia, and Turkey. But the outstanding success of the Cordell Hull policy was the conclusion in 1938, after protracted negotiations, of an agreement with Great Britain. On any showing, an agree-

ment for the reduction of tariffs between the two leading commercial countries of the world, which together bought 28 per cent
of the world's imports and sold 24 per cent of the world's exports,
was a step forward in the promotion of freer world trade. The
achievement was particularly impressive because British industrial exports were very largely competitive with American manufactures and because Great Britain, which represented the largest
potential market for American agricultural and raw material
surpluses, had since 1932 pursued a policy of restricting imports
from the U.S.A. in favour of Dominion and Empire products.
Although the negotiations, which were beset with difficulties, did
not result in concessions as large as had been hoped, the pact
meant the first reversal of the British policy of imperial preference,
increasing protection, and bilateralism, and represented a substantial victory for the Cordell Hull policy of 'freer trade'.
However, it must not be forgotten that special circumstances here
favoured the success of the Cordell Hull policy. Great Britain
throughout the nineteen-thirties wavered between her traditional
policy of liberal multilateral trade and the new course of controlled bilateralism; and she was prepared to pay a price for the
political asset, in the year of Munich, of an agreement with the
U.S.A. Negotiations with Spain and Italy which were opened in
1934 and 1935 never achieved any results; and there was never
any hope of bringing Germany and Japan into the trade agreement network. On the other hand, outside the Hull programme
a trade agreement was reached in 1935 with the U.S.S.R. by
which the U.S.A. pledged most-favoured-nation treatment in
return for a Russian promise to increase her purchases of
American goods to an agreed total.

V. RESULTS OF TRADE AGREEMENTS

HOW far can the Cordell Hull trade policy be said to have been
successful?

The figures for the total reductions of trade barriers achieved
make impressive reading. By 1938 the efforts of Secretary Cordell
Hull had succeeded in bringing some 60 per cent of the total
foreign trade of the U.S.A. into the scope of trade agreements.[1]
The U.S.A. had obtained concessions, either in the form of
improved treatment or guarantees of existing treatment, on more
than half her exports to the countries with which agreements had
been concluded (equal to about 30 per cent of total American
exports on the basis of 1937 statistics).[2] In return the U.S.A. had
reduced duties on some 45 per cent of dutiable imports and

---

[1] D. H. Popper, 'Six Years of American Tariff Bargaining', *Foreign Policy
Reports*, 15 April 1940, p. 31.   [2] ibid.

guaranteed continued free entry for 65 per cent of imports previously on the free list.[1] There is no question that these reductions assisted in the revival of American foreign trade and indirectly of world trade. But the undeniable beneficial effects of the agreements are easily exaggerated.

The reduction of American duties in particular did little more than scratch the surface of the American tariff wall. A large number of peaks were filed down, but the average level of American tariffs remained very high.[2] It would be unfair to put the blame for this fact on the Administration. Already hampered by the 50 per cent clause of the Trade Agreements Act, it was only by the most skilful negotiations and constant struggle with powerful pressure groups at home that the State Department achieved the limited reductions that were made. Almost every reduction raised an outcry from some vested interest of high-cost producers who believed their interests to be threatened,[3] and there can be little doubt that any more forward policy would have jeopardized the precarious chances of renewal of the Trade Agreements Act in 1937 and 1940. In theory, the fact that all the concessions made by the U.S.A. in any one agreement were, on the most-favoured-nation principle, extended to all other countries should have greatly increased the total effect of each concession in terms of reduced trade barriers. In practice it made little difference. Unwillingness to grant benefits to third countries without reciprocal concessions and the fear that such benefits might reduce the incentive to conclude reciprocal agreements led to the practice of violating the spirit if not the letter of the most-favoured-nation principle by confining concessions to the products of which the partner to the agreement was the chief supplier and by meticulous specification of items; in some cases this attitude even prevented reductions of tariffs which might otherwise have been made.

The unwillingness or inability of the U.S.A. to set a strong pace in tariff reductions naturally restricted the scope of the concessions she obtained from foreign countries. As far as specific concessions to American exports are concerned, there is actually reason to believe that the U.S.A. made a good bargain in the

[1] D. H. Popper, op. cit.

[2] To give some examples: expressed in *ad valorem* equivalents on the basis of 1937 prices duties under trade agreements still amounted to 66 per cent for whisky, 75 per cent for wrapper tobacco, 54 per cent for manganese ore, 87—54 per cent for certain high-priced wool fabrics, and 60 per cent for certain cotton laces (ibid., p. 32). Many of the concessions, especially on agricultural imports, were, moreover, restricted by 'tariff quotas' under which lower duties were applicable only up to a fixed maximum volume of imports.

[3] The Trade Agreements Act provided for elaborate safeguards to domestic producers such as a complicated system of consultation and administrative hearings and the right to legal action, all of which greatly hampered the State Department in its efforts.

trade agreements as a whole. On the other hand, the Cordell Hull programme failed almost completely in its second major objective, the reversal of the trend towards discrimination and bilateralism in world trade in general and the removal of discriminations against American commerce in particular. In each of the treaties the U.S.A. obtained a promise of most-favoured-nation treatment. But in practice this meant little. Where tariffs were concerned other countries employed the same methods of evasion as the U.S.A. herself. But in most countries tariffs had assumed an entirely subordinate role as a method of trade control and discrimination. Much effort and ingenuity were expended by the State Department in devising formulae by means of which quotas, licensing arrangements, rationing of foreign exchange, barter agreements and so forth could be fitted into the scheme of the most-favoured-nation principle.[1] But combating these new devices with the most-favoured-nation clause was like fighting a mechanized army with bows and arrows. The most-favoured-nation principle was based on the conception of international trade between free competitive market economies. Exchange restrictions and quantitative limitation were the methods of a system of State-controlled trade from which market forces were largely eliminated. 'Discrimination' was of the essence of this system.

The net results of the efforts of the Cordell Hull policy to ensure equality of treatment for American commerce were virtually nil. The only real achievement in this direction was the (very partial) reversal of the policy of imperial preference by Great Britain in the Anglo-American Trade Agreement; and here the value of the U.S.A. as a potential ally in war had a good deal to do with the success. The Trade Agreements Act, as we saw, empowered the President to retaliate against countries discriminating against American commerce by withholding from them the benefits of most-favoured-nation treatment. In practice this weapon was deprived of much of its efficacy by the deliberate

[1] In the case of quantitative limitation of imports the object sought was to ensure for the U.S.A. a fair share of total imports. The formula applied was based on the calculation of the U.S. share during a 'representative' period. But experience showed that it could not provide non-discriminatory treatment. Apart from the technical difficulties in applying the formula, the definition of the 'representative' period was obviously a matter of opinion and the formula could not take into account shifts in the competitive position of producers in different countries. Under systems of State-controlled trade which prevented the operation of market forces the very concept of price equilibrium lost much of its meaning. The problem was even more hopeless in the case of exchange control: no conceivable formula could prevent evasion by any one of the innumerable methods of discrimination open to the exchange control authorities: accumulation of balances, delay in payment to exporters, variations in exchange rates, rationing of foreign exchange to importers, hidden export subsidies, etc. What results were here achieved depended entirely on the goodwill of the Governments concerned.

minimization of these benefits, and little use was made of it. With the exception of Australia which was on the 'black list' for only a few months, Germany was the only country which in this way was acknowledged to discriminate against American trade. The discrimination practised everywhere else was either ignored or explained away, as in the case of Great Britain by the fiction of considering the Empire as a political unit.

The partial successes obtained by the Cordell Hull programme are reflected in the development of American foreign trade during the decade. Between 1932 and 1937 the dollar value of American foreign trade rose steadily from $2,934 million to $6,433 million.[1] In 1938 the upward movement was reversed, principally because of the economic recession, and in 1939 only part of the lost ground was regained. Clearly, the broad trends of American foreign trade depended on the progress of domestic and world recovery and on other factors such as drought, rearmament and wars. But there can be no doubt that the reductions in trade barriers which were achieved were responsible for a certain proportion of the increase in trade since 1934. More detailed evidence should be obtainable from a comparison between the development of American trade with 'agreement' and 'non-agreement' countries. The results are interesting though not conclusive. American exports to 'agreement' countries expanded much more rapidly than to 'non-agreement' countries,[2] and the same is true of the American share in total imports of the former as compared with the latter.[3] On the other hand, the relative share of the 'agreement' countries in American imports not only failed to rise but in some cases actually declined.[4] These facts suggest that, judged by the prevailing criterion of assisting recovery by maximum exports and minimum imports, the trade agreements represented a good bargain for the U.S.A. Actually, though this conclusion is probably correct, there is reason to believe that the tariff reductions at most emphasized changes in the direction of American trade which would have taken place without them.[5] The degree of success and failure of the Cordell Hull programme in bringing about a revival of American foreign trade is perhaps best summed up by two figures: Between 1933 and 1937 the U.S.A. increased

[1] D. H. Popper, op. cit., p. 32.   [2] ibid.
[3] The share of the U.S.A. in the imports of 16 'agreement' countries rose from 12·2 per cent in 1933 to 19·7 per cent in 1938; for the 20 most important 'non-agreement' countries (including the United Kingdom, Turkey, and Venezuela) the corresponding figures are 12·1 per cent (1933) and 14·5 per cent (1938) (ibid.).
[4] Gayer and Schmidt, op. cit., p. 82.
[5] From unofficial investigations it is by no means clear that exports of American products, which received improved customs treatment in foreign countries by the trade pacts, as a general rule increased more rapidly than other exports. Nor does it appear that exports of manufactures have risen more rapidly to countries which granted concessions than to others (ibid.).

her share of world trade by nearly 20 per cent;[1] but in 1937 the total value of her foreign trade was still only two-thirds and its volume only three-quarters of what it had been in 1929.[2]

The failure of American export trade to revive to anywhere near the pre-depression level meant that the problems of the American export industries remained largely unsolved; and the outstanding problem was that of American agricultural surpluses. During the twenty years preceding the great depression several factors—the growth of powerful competitors in the British Dominions and South America during and after the World War, agricultural protection in Europe, and changes in nutritional tastes and population trends—had combined to reduce the world demand for the staple products of American agriculture. But no corresponding reduction had taken place in American agricultural production. During the nineteen-twenties American foreign lending had enabled American agriculture to hold on to its export markets in spite of its handicap of high costs (due largely, though not entirely, to the American tariff and to a large debt burden— itself the legacy of war-time expansion). The depression had brought matters to a head. Prices had collapsed, markets had shrunk, and trade restrictions had grown apace. By 1933 the problem of American agriculture had become well-nigh insoluble. The decline in exports represented a loss of markets equivalent to the production of from ten to fifteen million acres farm land.[3] The only alternative to a revival of exports to pre-depression levels was the abandonment of a large proportion of the production of the American agricultural staple commodities—a social and economic problem of colossal dimensions. On the other hand, there was little hope of any such revival as long as the American tariff prevented foreign countries from obtaining the dollars with which to buy American products and together with the mortgage debt burden, kept the cost of American production well above the level at which American farmers could compete with other overseas producers. The New Deal tackled the problem at both ends by restricting production and by attempting to revive exports by reducing costs and lowering the American tariff. But all its measures, and particularly the cautious tariff reductions, barely touched the problem; while the efforts of the Administration to save the farmers from destitution aggravated it: price subsidies to the farmers encouraged production in the U.S.A., and the efforts of the Government to maintain world prices by keeping American surpluses off the market encouraged production in

[1] From 9.9 per cent in 1933 to 11·8 per cent in 1937 (League of Nations, *Statistical Year Book 1937–8*).
[2] *Statistical Abstract of the United States*, 1939, p. 472.
[3] L. A. Wheeler, 'The American Farmer Looks Ahead' in *The Annals*, vol. 211, September 1940, p. 28.

other countries, while the constant threat of the release of vast Government-held stocks depressed world prices. In 1938 the position was as bad as ever. Total agricultural exports, which had fallen between 1929 and 1932 from $1,693 million to $662 million,[1] still amounted to only $827 million.[1] Cotton exports, which had fallen from $920 million in 1929 to $345 million in 1932, stood at $228 million in 1938,[3] and, although cotton acreage had been reduced to the 1900 level, prices were one-third below the 1935–7 average and there was a carry-over of thirteen million bales—more than the whole year's crop and domestic consumption.[4] Wheat exports, which had slumped even more steeply during the depression, also declined further during the recovery. In the late summer of 1938 wheat was selling at the lowest price in five years. There was a carry-over of 153 million bushels in July 1938; for the summer of 1939 the surplus was estimated at 257 million bushels, the largest since 1933.[5]

By 1938 it was obvious that the Cordell Hull trade policy could do nothing to solve this problem. American wheat and cotton could not be sold abroad at prices remunerative to the American farmers. The U.S. Government, therefore, in 1938 embarked on a policy of export subsidies. In August 1938, a wheat and flour subsidy programme was inaugurated; in the fiscal year ending June 1939, 94 million bushels of wheat (including the wheat equivalent of flour) were sold abroad at an average price of 29 cents a bushel (as compared with a farm price of 55·3 cents).[6] Similarly, a cotton export programme providing for a bounty of 1·5 cents per pound became effective in 1939 under which some six million bales were sold abroad during the first six months of operation.[7] In 1939 the U.S.A. even resorted to direct barter to get rid of unsaleable surpluses. Under an inter-governmental barter plan with Great Britain the U.S.A. exchanged 600,000 bales of cotton for 80,000 tons of rubber to be held for war reserves. These measures clearly ran counter to the fundamental aim and spirit of the Cordell Hull trade programme.[8] Supporters of the Hull policy saw in them temporary emergency measures rendered necessary by the refusal of the rest of the world to return to a liberal system of free international trade. Others saw in them proof of the failure of free market forces and the price mechanism to rectify fundamental economic maladjustments.

[1] L. A. Wheeler, loc. cit.   [2] U.S. Statistical Abstract 1939, p. 644.
[3] ibid., p. 645.   [4] Gayer and Schmidt, op. cit., p. 102.
[5] ibid., p. 101.   [6] D. H. Popper, op. cit., p. 40.
[7] D. H. Popper, loc. cit.
[8] This was not the first instance of discrimination in American commercial policy. Ever since 1902 the U.S.A. had given Cuba preferential treatment in the form of a 20 per cent reduction in American duties. This double-column tariff was maintained throughout the nineteen-thirties and was explained away by reference to the 'colonial' status of Cuba.

THERE is undoubtedly some truth in the view that the relative failure of the Cordell Hull policy of 'freer world trade' was due to the unwillingness of the rest of the world to co-operate in the American effort to revive international trade, or to put it positively, to the fact that all the major Powers in a pursuit of what they conceived to be their own national interests were carrying on policies which tended to reduce the volume of international trade. But this is hardly the whole truth.

In the first place, the commercial policy of the U.S.A. during the nineteen-thirties was hardly less determined by the national interests of the U.S.A. than the commercial policies of other countries. It is true that the Cordell Hull policy of 'freer world trade' was based on a definite conception of a liberal *world* economy, which the commercial policies of Germany, Great Britain, Italy, France, Japan, and most other countries were emphatically not. But with certain qualifications, it is clear that this difference was due to the peculiar circumstances of the U.S.A.—her creditor position, the competitive power of her industries, her freedom from pressure on her balance of international payments, the relative independence of the American economy of international trade, and the strength of *laisser faire* liberalism in the U.S.A.—rather than to any marked preparedness to forgo national advantage in favour of international peace and order.

Moreover, as we saw before, the trend towards economic isolationism in Europe during and after the great depression had, to say the least, received a considerable impetus from the maladjustment of the American balance of payments, and the incongruity between her creditor position and a strongly favourable balance of trade. The Cordell Hull policy did nothing to remedy this situation. It is true that it aimed at a reduction of the American tariff and that it was severely handicapped in its efforts by the enormous heights which the tariff had reached in 1930 and by the opposition of vested interests. But the reasons for this failure go deeper. The Hull trade programme was not really concerned to adjust the American balance of trade to her creditor position. On the contrary, its main object was to aid the domestic recovery of American industry and agriculture; and, however much it was realized that commerce is a 'two-way process', that object implied that, other things being equal, the State Department endeavoured to push American exports so as to increase employment at home and was chary of allowing increased imports which would compete with American industries. In the U.S.A., no less than in the other industrial countries, the economic depression and the needs of domestic recovery constituted an insuperable obstacle to a policy compatible with international equilibrium and a revival of international trade.

As a result, the U.S.A. throughout the nineteen-thirties maintained a large annual export surplus. Only in one year, 1936, did the American balance on current account (including goods, services, and interest and dividend payments) show a deficit; and this was largely accounted for by exceptional circumstances, especially the drought which reduced agricultural exports and increased agricultural imports.

During the nineteen twenties the American surplus on current account had been offset by American foreign lending. With the depression American private foreign investment ceased, not to revive again during the nineteen-thirties. After the bitter experience of wholesale defaults American capitalists showed no desire to place their money in foreign issues, a reluctance which was heightened by the uncertain political and economic conditions of the world.[1] With the exception of some investment in Canadian bonds, the only lending undertaken by the U.S.A. during the nineteen-thirties consisted of loans by the American Government. The total amount lent abroad in this way, however, was very small.[2] Moreover, the foreign loan policy of the American Government, like its commercial policy, was subordinated to the immediate needs of the American economy. With the exception of one or two loans to China in support of the Chinese currency, all Government loans were deliberately designed to stimulate, and in some cases actually made conditional upon the purchase of, American exports. They therefore contributed nothing to an adjustment of the U.S. balance of payments.

In the absence of American foreign lending the debt payments to the U.S.A. and the American export surplus could only be paid for in gold. From January 1934 onwards, when the stabilization of the dollar stopped the outflow of short-term capital, gold poured into the U.S.A. in immense quantities. During the period between January 1934 and June 1939 net imports of gold

[1] In addition, resentment at the default by the former Allies on war debts and the view that loans made by American bankers to the Allies had helped to draw the United States into the World War on the Allied side resulted in the passage of the Johnson and Neutrality Acts which placed embargoes on loans to foreign Governments which were in default on obligations to the U.S.A. and to belligerent Governments respectively. But it is unlikely that these enactments prevented any foreign lending which would otherwise have taken place.

[2] The Reconstruction Finance Corporation lent $17 million to China and $4 million to Russia; the Export-Import Bank, which in 1934 became the main Government foreign loan agency, had by January 1939 made commitments amounting to $200 millions, but only $61 million had actually been disbursed of which $35 million had been repaid (Gayer and Schmidt, op. cit., pp. 131 and 134).

amounted to nearly $10,000 million.[1] In 1929 the U.S.A. had already owned 38 per cent of the world's monetary gold. In 1939 the reserves of the U.S.A., valued at over $16,000 million amounted to 59 per cent of the world's stock of monetary gold.[2]

It is true that, except in 1938 when the steep decline in American imports (due to the fall in American demand during the 1937 slump) resulted in an abnormally large export surplus, this inflow of gold cannot be explained by the favourable American balance on current account. Most of it represented capital movements which bore no relation to current international payments. To some extent the inflow of capital into the U.S.A. was itself due to the high price of gold fixed by the U.S.A., which enormously increased production and stimulated the disgorging of gold hoardings in India. For the most part capital flowed to the U.S.A. for a variety of reasons beyond the control of the American Government, chiefly the desire of foreign capitalists to profit from the expected rise in security and real estate values after the unprecedented collapse during the slump and to safeguard their money against currency depreciation and other dangers in their own country. It would obviously have been unwise, even if it had been possible, to adjust the American balance of trade to the vagaries of these movements of 'hot money'. The fact remains that the maladjustment of the American balance on current account greatly aggravated the problem.

For the U.S.A. the inflow of gold constituted a minor embarrassment which was relatively easily dealt with by the 'gold sterilization' policy adopted in 1936. If it was tragically absurd for the U.S.A. to give away year by year the products of American industry and agriculture in return for practically useless gold, it was also unfortunately true that even the gold buried at Fort Knox was still worth more than idle machines and unemployed labour. The indirect results of the maladjustment were much more damaging. As long as the United States sold more to foreign countries than she bought from them, her debtors were not only unable to resume payments on their defaulted obligations, but were constantly under pressure to transfer their purchases from the U.S.A. to other countries which were prepared to buy from them. In addition, the drain of gold to the U.S.A., which was aggravated by the one-way movement of 'hot money' and in turn stimulated it, provided a constant inducement to the debtor countries to find new methods of international trade, by clearing and barter, which would obviate the use of gold and foreign exchange. The continued disequilibrium of the American balance

[1] H. J. Truebold, 'Gold: an American Dilemma', *Foreign Policy Reports*, 1 September 1939, p. 146.
[2] ibid., p. 151.

of payments thus contributed directly to the trend towards bilateralism and indirectly helped to defeat the Cordell Hull programme.

Clearly, it would be absurd to lay the blame for the international economic chaos of the nineteen-thirties on American policy. The disequilibrium of the American balance of payments was only one factor which contributed to the collapse of the international exchange system and to the break-up of the international economy into national units and economic blocs. On balance it was probably less important than the failure to co-ordinate the various national attempts to counteract the domestic depressions by different and contradictory policies, the breakdown of the international commodity market, the shortsightedness of many of the policies pursued independently by each country, and the deliberate subordination of commercial policies to considerations of military security and preparation for war. Moreover, that disequilibrium itself was not the deliberate creation of American policy: it was due to the inadequacy of American policy in the face of accumulated maladjustments in the American and world economies. This leads us to the final point.

Our considerations so far are not incompatible with the conclusion that the Cordell Hull policy, while sound in principle, failed largely because for various reasons—the opposition of vested interests at home, the requirements of domestic recovery policy, the folly of foreign countries—it did not go far enough. The question arises whether the policy of 'freer trade' was in itself sound. It was clearly right in aiming at the restoration of a system of multilateral international trade, in realizing that the trend towards bilateralism and autarky meant a loss of the advantages of international exchange in terms of comparative costs. But it is more than doubtful whether it was right in its implicit assumption that this aim could be achieved by the mere removal of tariffs and other obstacles to the free play of market forces in international trade. To a very large extent the growth of these artificial barriers to international trade and the development of State control were due to the fact that the world war and the depression had resulted in fundamental maladjustments which had outgrown the corrective power of the price mechanism and the free play of market forces. The problem of the American agricultural surpluses was merely one instance of this general malady. It is true that the attempts of national Governments during and after the depression to protect their domestic economies and national economic interests by unco-ordinated and too often shortsighted actions had often merely increased these maladjustments. But this by no means proves that, *in the absence of any international system for the co-ordination of national policies to take the place of the old gold standard mechanism,* any alternative policies would have achieved better results. Nor does it prove that the maladjustments which had, in part at least, been responsible for the breakdown of the old system could have been corrected by the mere reliance on market forces in international economic relations. The results of the Cordell Hull experiment themselves suggest that by 1931, and even more by 1939, a large measure of conscious control, or, if we like, planning, both national and international, had become the precondition of any return to a beneficial system of multilateral trade.

Chapter Four

GREAT BRITAIN

1. INTRODUCTION

BRITISH economic policy during the nineteen-thirties presents in many ways a remarkable contrast to that of the U.S.A. In the U.S.A. commercial policy played a relatively subordinate part as compared with the spectacular internal recovery policy of the New Deal. In the case of Great Britain, nearly all the most decisive changes of policy and contributions of Government intervention to the recovery belong to the sphere of foreign economic policy, in so far as it is legitimate to make a rigid distinction between two spheres. The internal and external policies of the two countries, moreover, present further contrasts. Whereas the U.S.A. witnessed in the New Deal an attempt on the largest scale to solve the problem of depression and unemployment by far-reaching State intervention in the economy, British internal economic policy during the nineteen-thirties hardly departed from orthodox practice: the State on the whole confined its intervention to measures intended to provide suitable conditions for a recovery of private enterprise. Again, on the face of it at least, the new course in British commercial policy after 1932 seems to stand at opposite poles from the commercial policy of Secretary Cordell Hull which we considered in the preceding chapter. Some of these differences between British and American policy may, on closer inspection, turn out to be less decisive than would appear at first sight. But the contrast is sufficiently striking to demand some preliminary explanation. Such an explanation may also provide some of the background to our analysis of British policy.

To some extent, the contrast is accounted for by the difference in the origin and character of the great depression in the two countries. For Great Britain, the initial causes of the depression were external: the collapse of the American import market, with its further repercussions the world over, led to a severe decline in British visible and invisible exports. Since the British economy was far more dependent on foreign trade, the cumulative internal effects of this decline were correspondingly greater than a similar decline would have been for a relatively self-sufficient country like the U.S.A. Great Britain, secondly, was faced in 1931 with an urgent balance of payments problem from which the U.S.A. was free. Finally, for various reasons, the British internal depression was relatively milder than that of the U.S.A. All these three factors, however, were in a sense merely reflections of a more fundamental difference between the economic positions of the two countries at the onset of the great depression.

For Great Britain, as we saw in the first chapter, the world depression did not mean, as for the U.S.A., a sudden collapse after a period of unprecedented prosperity, but rather the climax of economic difficulties under which she had laboured ever since the war of 1914–18. In the last resort, these difficulties, above all the relative stagnation of her staple export industries, were due to long-term changes in Britain's position in the world economy—the rise of powerful industrial competitors which even before the end of the nineteenth century had begun to challenge her predominant position in world markets, the gradual exhaustion of opportunities for development investment in new territories which had formed the basis of a large part of Britain's foreign trade, the growth of competing industries behind tariff walls which characterized the economic progress of the new countries of the Western and Southern Hemispheres, and technological changes which militated against her three most important exports—coal, cotton goods, and steel. All these changes which inevitably necessitated and in normal circumstances might have been accompanied by gradual adjustments in the structure of the British economy were enormously hastened by the war. During the post-war decade, what efforts were made to encourage the development of new exports, on the one hand, and the transfer of labour and capital to new home-market industries, on the other, were wholly inadequate to cope with the large-scale maladjustment that had thus arisen. On the contrary, the return to the gold standard at the pre-war parity in 1925—itself in a sense a reflection of the failure to appreciate fully the extent to which conditions had changed since 1914—imposed an additional handicap on British exports and aggravated the tendency towards a growing import surplus and pressure on the British balance of payments.

The changes in the economic position of the U.S.A. which the war had hastened or brought about, and the problem which resulted from the failure throughout the post-war decade to make adequate planned efforts towards adjustment, were no less great than in the case of Great Britain. But the changes and the nature of the adjustment required in the two countries, were in opposite directions. The U.S.A. had suddenly emerged from the war the second largest creditor country and the most powerful and richest industrial nation in the world. In her case, the adjustment that ought to have taken place was in the direction of a larger volume of imports, if only to enable her debtors to discharge their obligations. It was an adjustment which was easily obviated by a large volume of foreign investment during the post-war decade; but which became immeasurably more difficult when, with the great depression, the American home market collapsed. Great Britain, on the other hand, was confronted by the long-term changes in her international economic position with two alternatives. She could either try to regain her former position in world markets, which in the circumstances involved shifting some of her productive resources from her stagnant staple export industries towards new lines of production that stood a better chance of competing in world markets. In practice, it is very doubtful whether this course by itself could have provided a solution in the economic conditions of the post-war world, though more might have been achieved in that direction, at any rate before 1929. Alternatively, she could write off part of her former export trade as lost and endeavour to re-employ the productive resources thus set free in production for the home market to replace the imports which she was no longer in the position to import from abroad. These two policies were, of course, not mutually exclusive; nor should it be assumed that the second alternative in a generally expanding economy need have implied anything more than a relative increase in the importance to British industry of the home over the world market. In practice, the failure to pursue either course with sufficient determination left some one to one and a half million British workmen unemployed throughout the nineteen-twenties. But the important fact is that when, under the impact of the world depression, Great Britain, in common with most other countries, resorted to a restrictive commercial policy of *sauve qui peut*, the shift did not, as in the case of the Hawley-Smoot tariff in the U.S.A., aggravate the existing maladjustment, but in fact served to adapt the British economy in some measure to its changed international position.

II. THE ABANDONMENT OF THE GOLD STANDARD

THE turning point in the course of the world depression as far as Great Britain was concerned came with the abandonment of the gold standard and the depreciation of the pound in September 1931.

The events which led up to it have been reviewed before.[1] Ever since the return to the gold standard in 1925, Great Britain had experienced difficulties in maintaining the pound at the pre-war parity at which, largely for reasons of prestige, it had been re-aligned to gold. The high exchange rate had meant an additional handicap for the British export trade while the efforts of the

[1] See above, p. 20 ff.

authorities to protect the gold reserves had obliged them to pursue a deflationary monetary policy which further depressed economic activity at home. One of the effects of the world depression was greatly to aggravate the British balance of payments problem. Between 1929 and 1931, the value of British merchandise exports fell by nearly half and invisible exports—mainly shipping income and income from overseas investments—by nearly 40 per cent. At the same time, the volume of imports hardly fell, with the result that, in spite of a large improvement in Britain's terms of trade due to the disproportionate fall in the prices of her foodstuff and raw material imports, the British balance of payments on current account deteriorated from a surplus of over £100 million in 1929 to a deficit of over £100 million in 1931.[1]

The only method of correcting such a maladjustment of the balance of payments under the rules of the gold standard was deflation, a reduction of British prices and/or incomes sufficient to reduce imports and stimulate exports so as to restore the balance. Ruthlessly pursued, such a policy might have achieved the objective at the cost of sacrifices of income (which would have fallen almost entirely on the industrial workers), increased unemployment, and in all probability political and social conflict. In the conditions of contracting world income and demand of 1930–1, moreover, deflation would have been effective in removing the deficit in the balance of trade by reducing British import demand rather than by expanding British exports and would thus have exercised a further deflationary effect on the rest of the world.

In the circumstances, a reduction in the exchange rate of the pound was undoubtedly a preferable method of adjustment for the rest of the world as much as of Great Britain herself. The British Government, however, did not favour devaluation as a deliberate policy. The maintenance of the old parity of the pound was considered a matter of prestige. There was as yet in 1931 no precedent for a controlled devaluation of an important currency, and while there was in Great Britain little of that fear so widespread on the Continent that devaluation inevitably involved internal inflation, the view still prevailed that a fall in the value of a country's currency was a sign of financial weakness and 'not done'. Devaluation moreover was (erroneously, as we shall see) expected to raise internal prices, and was therefore thought to involve a further substantial loss of income from foreign investments by reducing the real value of some £100 million of interest payments on investments fixed in sterling. Another factor which undoubtedly weighed with the British authorities was the fact

[1] *Statistical Abstract for the United Kingdom.*

that devaluation would be considered abroad as a breach of faith with those who had deposited large sums of money in what was thought the safest place in the world.

These arguments might have prevailed, at least for a time, if the international financial crisis of the summer of 1931 had not taken the decision out of the hands of the British authorities. The panic flight of foreign capital from London during July, August, and September, which followed the Austrian and German financial crisis and the forecast in Great Britain of a substantial budget deficit, rapidly exhausted the gold and foreign exchange reserves of the Bank of England and utterly defeated the last minute efforts to maintain the gold standard. On 20 September, the Bank was forced to suspend gold payments and on the following day the gold standard was officially abandoned. The pound promptly depreciated by 20 per cent and before the end of the year by another 10 per cent of its former gold value.

For the remainder of the decade, the pound was operated as a managed currency. Unlike the dollar after 1934, it was not re-stabilized on a gold basis. Excessive exchange fluctuations, however, were prevented by the establishment in 1932 of an Exchange Equalization Account which was armed with £150 million (augmented by a further £200 million in April 1933 and by yet another £200 million in June 1937) in order to smooth out short-term fluctuations in the exchange rates with the dollar and franc without, on the other hand, preventing long-term trends from taking their effect. In practice, this latter limitation of its scope does not seem to have been strictly observed. The steady accumulation of gold by the Exchange Equalization Account for most of the decade[1] suggests that it was operated so as to prevent an appreciation of the pound which would otherwise have taken place.[2] As long as France remained on the gold standard, the

[1] The value of the Bank of England's gold reserve, including the holdings of the Exchange Equalization Account, increased from £121 million in 1932 to £840 million in March 1938 (F. W. Paish, 'Twenty Years of the Floating Debt' *Economica*, August 1939, p. 266). Part of this increase is accounted for by the rise in the sterling price of gold during this period (due mainly to the gold policy of the United States) which increased the sterling value of the original £121 million to £200 million. But the bulk of the increase was due to purchases of gold by the Exchange Equalization Account.

[2] During the years 1932 and 1933 this tendency of the exchange rate to rise might be accepted as evidence that the pound was undervalued. By 1934, however, that undervaluation had certainly disappeared, mainly owing to the devaluation of the dollar and most other important currencies (except those of the gold bloc). The continuation of the tendency after that date was mainly due to large inflows of 'refugee capital'. Since these funds were liable to be withdrawn at any time, it would have been dangerous to allow these inflows to raise the exchange value of the pound, quite apart from the fact that such an appreciation would have handicapped British exports. The cautious policy of the British authorities was justified in March 1938 when fears of war led to heavy withdrawals of capital from London. If the account had not accumulated gold, this would have resulted in a sharp fall of sterling. As it was the demands were easily met by the release of gold.

British and American Exchange Equalization Accounts were able to operate on the franc. When in 1936 the franc, too, at last succumbed, a Tripartite Monetary Agreement ensured an alternative method of stabilizing exchange rates by co-operation between the Exchange Equalization Accounts of the three States.

There can be little doubt that the abandonment of the gold standard and the depreciation of the pound, which were generally considered at the time as a disaster of the first magnitude constituted in fact the first important step towards helping Great Britain out of the depression.

In the first place, the 30 per cent reduction in the value of the pound gave an indiscriminate encouragement to British exports, while at the same time exercising a protective effect on the British home market. Whereas until 1931 the overvaluation of the pound had handicapped British exports, British exporters enjoyed for at least two years after 1931 a definite competitive advantage in world markets.[1] The abandonment of the gold standard thus, at a crucial moment during the depression, gave a valuable stimulus to economic activity in Great Britain. Great Britain, moreover, was in the unique position of being able to obtain this advantage without any worsening in her terms of trade which a devaluation normally involved. On the contrary, it is not unlikely that, partly owing to her preponderant role as a world importer and partly also to the immediate devaluation of the currencies of her most important sources of imports, the fall in the value of the pound actually accentuated the tendency of her terms of trade to improve which had begun in 1929 with the disproportionate fall in agricultural and raw material prices as compared with the prices of manufactures.

It is true that this direct favourable effect of the depreciation of the pound on economic activity in Great Britain was to some extent counteracted by its external repercussions. Great Britain was not the first country to be forced by the depression to devaluate its currency. A number of South American countries and Australia and New Zealand, the chief victims of the catastrophic slump in agricultural prices, had preceded her in 1929 and 1930. But the repercussions of the British action corresponded to the importance of Great Britain as an import market and international creditor, and to the importance of the pound in international commercial transactions. The whole of the British

[1] The relief given to British foreign trade by the fall of the pound is liable to be underestimated because it consisted mainly in warding off much of the additional shrinkage that would otherwise have accrued, at least in 1932. Total British exports continued to decline throughout most of 1932. But exports to some countries began to revive between 1931 and 1932 and the improvement in the competitive position of British exports in world markets showed itself in a substantial increase in Great Britain's share of world exports between these two dates.

Empire, with the exception of South Africa, Canada, British Honduras and Hong Kong, followed the British example at once and maintained the old relationship of their currencies to sterling. A number of other countries which relied largely on the United Kingdom as a market for their products, including the three Scandinavian countries, Portugal, and Egypt, also left the gold standard and 'pegged' their currencies to the pound. Nor were the repercussions confined to these countries. Once begun, the process of exchange depreciation spread both through the automatic mechanism of the balances of international payments and the desire of each country to protect its export trade. Between September 1931 and August 1932, twelve countries, in addition to those of the 'sterling bloc', left the gold standard. When the devaluation of the dollar in 1933 led to a second wave of exchange depreciations, the gold standard as an international exchange system, whose substance had already largely evaporated, virtually disappeared also in its outward form. In its place stepped openly managed national currencies and currency blocs, with or without exchange control. These exchange depreciations *pro tanto* diminished the competitive advantage which British exports had obtained. They also resulted in an unprecedented degree of instability of exchange rates which undoubtedly imposed a certain handicap on international trade during the nineteen-thirties, though the seriousness of that handicap has sometimes been exaggerated.[1] The fall in the value of the pound and of a large group of other currencies, finally, imposed a severe deflationary pressure on the countries that remained on gold. It accelerated the depression in France and the other 'gold bloc' countries whose exports were severely cut. The consequent decline in their demand for British goods must also be taken into account in reckoning up the gains of depreciation for Great Britain. The total adverse reactions on British exports of all these repercussions, while impossible to estimate, were undoubtedly considerable. But they hardly offset the stimulus which the depreciation of the pound had imparted to the British economy and which was probably the decisive factor in the early British recovery.

Nor was this the only advantage to Great Britain of the abandonment of the gold standard. The policy of allowing sterling to depreciate, by removing the immediate pressure on the British balance of payments, placed the British Government in a position to pursue a far more independent internal policy than

[1] The emergence of the 'sterling bloc' considerably reduced this handicap for Great Britain; the advantage of exchange stability within the Empire probably contributed to the concentration of the trade of the Empire countries into inter-Empire channels during the nineteen-thirties which was in the main the result of Imperial preference.

would have been possible under the gold standard rules. In practice, as we shall see later, no advantage was taken of this opportunity as far as budget policy was concerned. But the return flow of foreign capital which immediately followed the departure from gold as well as the subsequent accumulation of gold by the Exchange Equalization Account, part of which was added at intervals to the active gold reserves of the Bank of England, paved the way for the adoption of a vigorous policy of 'cheap money'. This also provided the chief motive for the refusal of the British Government to restabilize the pound on a gold basis. In view of the persistent tendency of the pound to appreciate after 1932, it is unlikely that the 'cheap money' policy would in fact have been impeded by balance of payments difficulties. But the cautious policy which was actually pursued freed the British Government from all risk on that score.

It might be maintained that the advantages which Great Britain derived from the abandonment of the gold standard and the depreciation of the pound were largely obtained, as in the case of the devaluation of the dollar, at the expense of aggravating the economic difficulties of other countries. The comparison, however, ignores the fact that the circumstances in which the two countries abandoned the gold standard differed profoundly. The devaluation of the dollar was an entirely voluntary decision which, owing to the immensely strong balance of payments position of the U.S.A. was, as we have seen, in all probability not essential to the American recovery. Great Britain, on the other hand, was placed by the depression in a position in which—quite apart from the events of the summer of 1931 which might conceivably have been avoided by a more cautious policy—something had to be done to correct the maladjustment in her balance of payments on current account. Great Britain was buying more from abroad than she could pay for by current visible or invisible exports. For a time, this deficit could have been met by the repatriation of British foreign assets. But borrowing could not in the long run provide a solution. In the circumstances, short of deflation, the only alternatives were an adjustment in the exchange rate of the pound or drastic import restrictions (which in the circumstances would probably have had to take the form of exchange control of the type later adopted in Germany). Either course was bound to increase the economic difficulties of other countries. Moreover, in assessing the effects of the British devaluation on other countries two points must be kept in mind. The first is that, to the extent to which it gave a direct stimulus to the British recovery, its adverse effects were later offset, if not outweighed, by the increase in British import demand which accompanied the recovery. The second is less obvious but hardly less important. The

British abandonment of the gold standard made devaluation 'respectable'; directly or indirectly, as we have seen, it led a large number of countries which might never have risked such a step if it had not been for the British example, to devaluate their currencies. The effect of this mass devaluation (i.e. revaluation of gold in terms of national currencies) was equivalent to a large increase in the world's stock of gold and, given the still generally prevailing convention of relating credit policies to gold reserves, was as salutary in its reflationary effects as an addition to the physical quantity of gold stocks would have been.

III. PROTECTION AND IMPERIAL PREFERENCE

THE abandonment of the gold standard was followed six months later by a second spectacular change in British policy, the final abandonment of free trade in favour of a general tariff and imperial preference.

a. The General Tariff. Ever since the beginning of the present century, the question of protection versus free trade had been an issue in British politics. Great Britain had adopted free trade at a time when her industrial and commercial supremacy assured her a virtual monopoly in world markets. When towards the end of the nineteenth century this monopoly began to be seriously challenged the merits of free trade immediately began to be questioned. During the pre-war boom, protectionist ideas had made little headway. Even after the war, the electorate still gave a decisive vote in favour of free trade in the general election of 1923. But during the following years, protection began more and more to be looked to as a remedy for Britain's ills. It is doubtful whether economic reasoning played the decisive part in this process. Great Britain was suffering from heavy unemployment which tended to be attributed to the fact that foreign countries were increasingly closing their markets to British exports while British industries were meeting with growing competition in the British home market. The great depression added new arguments to the protectionist case. In introducing the Import Duties Bill to Parliament in February 1932, Mr. Chamberlain managed to adduce seven reasons in its favour: its purpose was to correct the balance of payments, to obtain fresh revenue, to ensure against a rise in the cost of living, to decrease unemployment, to render production and distribution efficient, to facilitate negotiations with foreign countries over tariffs, and to consolidate Imperial preference.

While not all these arguments would bear equally close examination, it is clear that the protectionists in Great Britain had a far stronger case than their opponents in the free trade camp—

which included at the time the majority of economists—were prepared to admit. The free traders had two main arguments against protection, first, that it diminished the advantages in terms of comparative costs which Britain had obtained from international division of labour and trade, and secondly, that protection could do nothing to relieve unemployment since the favourable effect on the home market would be offset by its adverse reactions on the export industries. The first argument which had traditionally been the strongest in favour of free trade was the weakest in conditions of large-scale unemployment. To the extent to which the imposition of a tariff stimulated economic activity at home the gain due to the re-employment of idle resources far outweighed the loss due to the higher costs of home-produced over imported goods. So long (though it should be added, *only* so long) as a large proportion of the country's resources were unemployed, considerations of comparative costs lost much of the relevance which they possessed on the implicit assumption of full employment. In the immediate conditions of the depression, the second argument against protection was far more to the point. It was based on three considerations. Protection, it was said, by raising costs would impose an additional handicap on British exports in world markets; at the same time it would reduce foreign demand for British goods by reducing the purchasing power of foreign countries for British products; and, thirdly, it would invite retaliation. The first point was in practice largely taken care of by exempting raw materials, with few significant exceptions, from the tariff. The second ignored the fact that while a tariff inevitably reduced the proportion of domestic purchasing power spent on imports, it did not in conditions of large-scale unemployment necessarily reduce the total volume of imports, since by stimulating economic activity it would raise total money incomes and effective demand. The net effect, therefore, might even be a higher absolute volume of imports after than before the introduction of protection. This is what in fact happened in Great Britain, though in her case protection was only one of the causes of the recovery and of the growth in import demand. The danger of retaliation was a very real one. Great Britain, however, could claim with a good deal of justification that until 1932 she had been the chief victim of restrictive measures by other countries. The adoption of protection, moreover, provided her with a powerful bargaining weapon which, as we shall see presently, she used with considerable effect. On balance, the protectionists could hold out a reasonable hope that protection would stimulate recovery and diminish unemployment in Great Britain.

The free traders could still argue that this provided a valid case for protection before September 1931 but that after the abandonment of the gold standard, the same results could have been achieved by some additional depreciation of the pound. It is true that the effects of a general tariff were similar to those of a further depreciation of the currency. But there were several reasons why a tariff was preferable. The most important one was that, whereas depreciation affected all goods and industries equally, tariffs could give differential protection. This was in itself an advantage where for economic, military, or other reasons exceptional protection was considered desirable for specific industries. In addition, however, it meant that the incidence of protection could be adjusted so as to obtain the maximum advantage with regard to Britain's terms of trade. The tariff also, as has already been mentioned, provided Great Britain with a bargaining weapon in subsequent trade negotiations. It yielded revenue and at the same time avoided the loss of real income from foreign investments which additional depreciation would have implied. Finally, additional depreciation might have involved the risk of additional speculation against the pound and a renewed flight of capital.

Even before 1931 the swing towards protectionism had left some traces on the British statute book. Duties on a number of manufactures which had been imposed during the war primarily for the purpose of saving shipping space and a further set of import duties imposed immediately after the war on articles the home production of which was considered vital for strategic reasons had both come to stay. During the nineteen-twenties, a number of other protective duties had been introduced for a few commodities. But the scope of all these duties was small and in 1930 the essentially free-trade character of the British commercial system was still intact. In 1930, more than 80 per cent of imports from foreign countries into Britain were still admitted completely free of duty.

The abandonment of free trade in 1931–2 proceeded by several stages. The formation of a predominantly conservative National Government after the crisis elections of November 1931 led to a flood of import orders in anticipation of a general tariff. To prevent this, two emergency measures were rushed through Parliament which empowered the Government to impose duties up to 100 per cent *ad valorem* cn imports of manufactures and heavy duties on early fruit and vegetables. In February 1932, the Import Duties Act laid the basis of the new tariff structure. The emergency duties were replaced by a general 10 per cent *ad valorem* tariff on all imports except those on a free list containing most raw materials and foodstuffs. The Act, which left all other existing duties in being, further empowered the Government to impose higher duties on the recommendation of an Import Duties

Advisory Committee. In practice, most manufactured imports were subjected to 20 per cent duties, but higher rates than these were imposed on a number of commodities, notably iron and steel, home producers of which were considered to have a specially strong case for protection. The Act did not apply to Empire products. It thus laid the basis for the system of Imperial preference which was consolidated six months later by the agreements concluded at Ottawa between the United Kingdom and the British Dominions and for which the general tariff was partly designed to pave the way.

b. Imperial Preference. Protectionism in Great Britain had from the beginning been bound up with the idea of Imperial preference. The economic development of the British Empire during the nineteenth century had been founded on the exchange of the raw materials and foodstuffs of the Empire for the manufactures of British industry based on a constant flow of British capital to the Colonies. In its origins, the idea of Imperial preference was, political and emotional factors apart, an attempt to maintain the benefits of this system in the face of foreign competition and changing conditions. When the British Dominions began, before the war, to protect their nascent industries by tariffs they granted preferences to British products. As long as Great Britain herself, however, maintained free trade she was unable to reciprocate with preferences for Empire produce. Some preference on a small scale was given to Empire goods on the duties imposed from 1916 onwards. But during the post-war decade, the Dominion raw-material producers who found increasing difficulty in marketing their large surpluses and keeping up the prices of their products grew increasingly dissatisfied with the existing arrangement. As far as Great Britain was concerned, the main motive for the adoption of Imperial preference was probably political, the desire to strengthen the political unity of the Empire; but British exporters undoubtedly hoped to benefit by the exclusion of foreign competitors from the Dominion markets. By 1932, the economic relations of the Empire had diverged far from their former simple structure of bilateral specialization and exchange. In 1929, only 25·7 per cent of the total trade of the British Empire represented inter-Empire trade, while 74·3 per cent was with foreign countries. But that very fact appeared to provide ample scope for a diversion of Empire trade into inter-Empire channels. In addition, the British investor could in the absence of continued capital exports expect interest payment on his Empire investments only by means of an import surplus from the Dominions.

In the Ottawa agreements, the United Kingdom, in return for minor tariff concessions and increased preferences for British

D*

goods in Dominion markets (most of which were obtained by increases in Dominion tariffs on foreign, rather than by reductions of duties on British, imports), promised continued free entry into the British market to all Dominion products (except meat with regard to which Empire producers were to be given an expanding share of British imports under a quota system) and guaranteed margins of preference which were made effective by the imposition of new or additional 'Ottawa duties' on a number of foreign foodstuffs including, among others, wheat, maize, butter, cheese, and other dairy products.

The adoption of Imperial preference, while it may have strengthened the political and economic bonds between the countries of the British Empire had the effect of making many other countries which had formerly supplied the British market, especially the Balkan and South American countries, liable to economic and political penetration by Germany. Whether or not this disadvantage outweighed the advantages of Imperial preference is a question of political judgement which is beyond the scope of this report. From a strictly economic point of view, it is doubtful whether Imperial preference justified the hopes which had been set on it. In the Dominions, the owners of the growing secondary industries for whom Great Britain was necessarily the most formidable competitor were as suspicious of it as the depressed domestic agriculture of Great Britain which was threatened as much by cheap Empire as by cheap foreign competition. Moreover, it was insufficiently realized that in the case of commodities, such as wheat and some British manufactures of which the Empire as a whole had an export surplus, even the producers would gain little since the increased competition of foreign producers outside the Empire would depress world prices.

In 1933, the system of Imperial preference was extended to the Crown Colonies. The Import Duties Act of 1932 had granted preference to Colonial goods in the British market. The Colonial Governments were now 'invited' by the British Government to grant preference to British Empire goods. In nearly all the Colonies, the grant of preference took the form of increased tariffs on foreign goods accompanied by rebates on Empire products. The tariffs which amounted to nearly 100 per cent *ad valorem* on some goods such as rubber-soled boots and shoes and 75 per cent on cotton piece goods were followed in 1934 by a system of import quotas in all Colonies except where international conventions or the interests of the entrepôt trade stood in the way. The quota system as also many of the tariffs were primarily designed to keep out cheap Japanese textiles, which had begun to oust the more expensive Lancashire products from the Colonial markets.

The closing of the traditional Open Door in the British Colonies was a far reaching change of policy. By making it more difficult for foreign countries to export to the Colonies, it deprived them to that extent of access to their raw material resources and lent plausibility to the colonial claims of the 'have-not' powers. While it benefited the British export trade, it *pro tanto* depressed the standard of living of the native populations. This is not incompatible with the undoubted fact that without the preference which they enjoyed in the United Kingdom market the primary producers of some of the Colonies, such as the West Indian sugar producers, would have suffered even more from the world depression than they did.[1]

c. Agricultural Protection. The general tariff and the Ottawa treaties by themselves left virtually unprotected the industry which was suffering most from outside competition, agriculture. The Government was here faced with the dilemma that, in contrast to British industry, British agriculture had most to fear from competition by Dominion producers whose products, under Imperial preference, enjoyed free entry into the British market. A compromise was found in a system of protection based on fairly severe restrictions on foreign food imports, some quantitative limitation of Empire imports, and internal assistance to the British farmer.

British agriculture had suffered a long and continuous decline since the eighteen-seventies of the last century. It was the price paid by Great Britain for her industrial supremacy and policy of cheap food for her industrial population. During the post-war years, falling world prices and high comparative costs hastened the decline. In 1931, the acreage under wheat was the lowest on record. The depression gave a further blow to British agriculture. The slump in world prices fell most heavily on the high-cost producer in the one remaining free market.

While British agriculture was well fitted to produce on competitive or nearly competitive terms such high unit-value

[1] In defence of the system of Colonial preference, as of Imperial preference generally, it has been argued that the balance of payments position of the sterling area as a whole *vis-a-vis* the rest of the world made it desirable to direct Colonial imports into inter-Empire channels, so as to economize in dollars and other foreign exchange which could not easily be obtained by increasing exports from the sterling area. It is true that the protagonists of 'non-discrimination' have tended to neglect the significance which balance of payments considerations of this kind assumed with the breakdown of the system of multilateral settlement of international payments, and that such considerations may render preferential arrangements similar to Imperial preference unavoidable during the transitional period following this war. But as applied to the adoption of Imperial preference in 1932 the argument is at best an *ex post facto* rationalization. It was certainly not the motive behind the adoption of Imperial preference, and it is very doubtful whether the diversion of trade into inter-Empire channels due to Colonial preference was quantitatively significant for the balance of payments position of the whole sterling area.

products as milk, eggs, fruit, vegetables, high-quality meat, poultry and fish, it could not possibly hope to compete with foreign producers in the production of most staple foodstuffs, such as cereals, sugar and, with certain qualifications, cheap meat. Whereas, therefore, some protection for the former crops was well worth while, there was, from a purely economic point of view, little to be said in favour of general agricultural protection. The National Government, however, favoured the view that Great Britain could afford to pay a price for a prosperous domestic agriculture which it considered desirable both for social and strategic reasons and in 1933 launched a vigorous programme of protection and internal assistance.

The few new tariffs on agricultural products which had been introduced in 1932 and the Ottawa import quotas on foreign meat, had served the purpose of substituting Empire imports for foreign imports and were of little benefit to the British producer. In 1933, import quota schemes were introduced which were designed to provide the home producer with a practically guaranteed market for an expanding output though even here the quota normally favoured the Empire exporter. The effect of the quota schemes may be illustrated by that for bacon, which was almost the leading British import commodity. By voluntary agreement with the foreign producers and later by compulsory quota foreign, and especially Danish, imports were severely curtailed. The result was a fall in foreign imports from 12 million cwt. in 1932 to 7½ million cwt. in 1938. Nearly one quarter of these imports were replaced by imports from Canada, which rose from a mere 324,000 in 1932 to over 1·5 million cwt. in 1938. But the British farmer reaped the main benefit from the reduction in imports from Denmark. Within five years, the number of pigs in Great Britain rose by nearly 20 per cent, and there was a considerable increase in the amount of bacon cured at home. The bacon scheme was followed in 1933 and 1934 by similar schemes limiting, by voluntary agreement or compulsion, imports of dairy products, eggs, poultry, potatoes and sea fish.

Protection from foreign competition was coupled with internal measures of assistance to agriculture which may conveniently be mentioned here. The Agricultural Marketing Act of 1933 provided for the organization of marketing schemes designed to improve efficiency of production and maintain agricultural prices. The most important of these schemes, that for milk, was in essence a State organized discriminating monopoly based on the maintenance of a relatively high price for liquid milk part of the proceeds from the sale of which was used to subsidize the producers of milk for domestic processing who had to compete with cheap Empire imports of dairy products. A similar concealed subsidy, the cost of which in this case was shared by the domestic consumer of bread and the foreign exporter of wheat, underlay the Wheat Fund set up in 1932 to encourage wheat production. Some other branches of agriculture received direct government subsidies, such as the sugar industry which, between 1924 and 1935, was paid £30 million (to which should be added £10 million revenue loss on preferential excise duty).[1] Further subsidies were paid at various times to the livestock industry, to producers of oats and barley, and to herring fishing. Lastly, some producers such as those of potatoes and hops were assisted by legal restrictions on home production and others again by legal minimum prices.

This comprehensive system of assistance on the whole succeeded in restoring a fair degree of prosperity to most branches of British agriculture. Output rose by one-sixth[2] and the prices of nearly all products were considerably higher by 1937. The number of employed workers continued to fall, but the decline was certainly retarded. The cost of the system of agricultural protection and assistance was shared between the foreign exporters of foodstuffs and the British consumer. The latter, however, was enabled to bear it with relative ease because of the exceptionally low prices of imported foodstuffs during the first years after the slump.

d. Additional Protection to Industry. British industry, too, received some additional protection after 1932. The Import Duties Advisory Committee, upon whose recommendations changes in the tariff were made, occasionally during the nineteen-thirties recommended reductions of duties, especially on raw materials, where a reduced rate was expected to confer substantial benefit on export industries. A number of goods were at intervals added to the free list. But, partly because the changes were made piece-meal, usually on application from the vested producers' interests concerned, and because the interests of consumers had little chance of making themselves heard except where the consumers were themselves powerfully organized industries, the general tendency during these years of recovery was for tariffs to rise and for more onerous specific duties to replace the earlier *ad valorem* rates. By 1938, both the number of articles subject to import duty and the average rate of duty were substantially higher than at the end of 1932. Not all the additional duties served the purpose of protecting the home market. Some were temporarily imposed as retaliatory measures, such as the 20 per cent *ad valorem* duty imposed on certain imports from France in retaliation for French discrimination against British goods; others, in order to assist British export industries in negotiations

---

[1] F. Benham, op. cit., p. 54.   [2] ibid., p. 215.

with foreign competitors, such as the increase to 50 per cent of the duty on iron and steel products during the negotiations between the British steel industry and the International Steel Cartel in 1935. Most of the increases, however, were made on straightforward protectionist grounds. In addition, in the case of a few minor industries, where tariffs for one reason or another were considered inappropriate, subsidies, import licences and quota schemes were employed.

IV. THE BAN ON FOREIGN LENDING

THE third important change in British external economic policy was the virtual discontinuation of foreign investment after 1931. Before the war, Great Britain had been by far the leading international creditor country. Almost the whole of the annual surplus on her balance of payments on current account had been regularly lent and invested overseas. The value of her foreign assets was, in round figures, about £4,000 million, yielding some £200 million a year. The economic basis of her capital exports had been mainly the export of capital goods for the opening up of new areas of agricultural and raw material production, chiefly in the British Empire, but also in the Argentine and other foreign countries. The war had fundamentally changed her position. The need for development investment in the large overseas primary producing areas had greatly diminished; and the capital needs of these countries for the construction of secondary industries were increasingly met out of domestic capital resources. Great Britain herself had become a debtor on a large scale to the U.S.A. who, in turn, had assumed the function of the leading lender nation. After the war, Great Britain had continued to lend abroad. A growing proportion of her foreign lending, however, had taken the form of loans to foreign Governments. Whereas her pre-war development loans and direct investment had not given rise to balance of payments difficulties since they directly stimulated foreign demand for British goods, loans of the Dawes, Young and League of Nations Reconstruction type at best promoted British exports only indirectly. Partly for this reason, Great Britain was lending on a larger scale than her balance of trade and payments position warranted.

In 1931, British foreign lending virtually ceased. In view of the uncertainty as to the economic prospects in foreign countries and the future exchange value of their currencies, it is doubtful whether, even without Governmental intervention, private foreign investment in new issues would have regained its pre-depression level. In fact, the Government did intervene. After the crisis of September 1931, a complete, though unofficial, embargo on foreign new issues was imposed. In January 1933, this embargo was relaxed in favour of British Empire borrowers who were again given practically free access to the London market. But the embargo on new foreign issues remained in force throughout the nineteen-thirties and Treasury permission to foreign borrowers was granted only in exceptional circumstances.

The immediate purpose of the embargo on foreign investments was monetary. It was designed to facilitate the internal 'cheap money' policy of the British Government. In practice, the embargo on new issues did not prevent capital export altogether because sterling could still be freely transferred into foreign currencies and the ban did not apply to purchases by British residents of existing foreign securities. Such transfers and purchases which in some years assumed substantial proportions could only have been prevented by exchange control which the British Government was not prepared to impose. In addition, the embargo was intended to prevent pressure on the British balance of payments. If the British Government could have been certain that money lent abroad would directly or indirectly result in a corresponding increase in foreign demand for British goods, there would have been little force in this argument. As regards their effect on the volume of employment and economic activity in Great Britain, there would have been nothing to choose between internal and foreign investment. However, in the conditions of the nineteen-thirties, there was no longer any guarantee that this would be the case. In the circumstances, there was a strong case for restricting foreign lending to loans which were made conditional upon the purchase of British goods. The failure of the two leading lenders, Great Britain and the U.S.A., to resume foreign investment on the old scale after the depression was undoubtedly partly responsible for the inadequate revival of international trade during the nineteen-thirties. But the cause of this failure must be sought primarily in the unwillingness (or inability) of private investors to bear the risks of foreign investment in the insecure political economic and financial conditions of the nineteen-thirties and, in the case of Great Britain, in the changes in world economic conditions which made it impossible for a country with a none too strong balance of payments position to allow complete freedom to private foreign investment and leave the balance of international payments to look after itself.

V. EXPORT POLICY

ON a long view, the adoption of protection by Great Britain was itself an attempt to meet the problem presented by the loss of markets for the British staple exports. Its object was to compensate British industry for the loss of foreign markets by an artificially enlarged home market. But it was obvious that protection could not solve the immediate problem of the British export industries. At the best, the shift of labour and capital from the cotton, coal and shipbuilding industries to the new industries of the South which mainly benefited from the increased home demand was a slow and difficult process. In any event, Great Britain continued to depend for most of her foodstuffs and raw materials on foreign imports which in the main had to be paid for by exports. Both the problem of continued large-scale unemployment and the requirements of the British balance of payments made a revival of British exports essential. Having safeguarded the home market, therefore, the British Government turned in 1933 to the task of pushing British exports.

In one respect, the adoption of protection itself had facilitated this task. Great Britain had acquired an extraordinarily strong bargaining position. Having never bargained before she was now able to use the new tariff and import restrictions to obtain concessions for British exports in foreign markets. Between 1932 and 1935, the British Government took advantage of this favourable position by concluding a series of bilateral trade agreements with foreign countries. The most important of these agreements were those with the Argentine, the Scandinavian and Baltic States, Poland and Russia. All these countries were in a particularly weak position because their exports to the United Kingdom far exceeded their imports from the United Kingdom. Some of them, moreover, had specialized in the production of certain commodities for the British market (Danish bacon, Argentine beef) and depended on it while themselves taking only a relatively small proportion of British exports. As a result, Great Britain was able to obtain most of her concessions from them by mere promises *not to increase* duties and *not to reduce* quotas. Although many concessions were made to foreign producers, they were not comparable to the advantages gained by British exporters. This form of bargaining by its nature involved the diversion of British trade into bilateral channels. But in the circumstances the costs due to the loss of advantages from multilateral trade were mainly borne by the foreign countries.

In the agreements with the Scandinavian and Baltic States concluded in 1933 and 1934, the most important concessions obtained by Great Britain were minimum quotas on British coal at a considerably higher level than previous purchases by these countries. Great Britain also obtained tariff concessions on a number of goods especially cotton and other textiles, coal, and iron and steel products. The concessions made in return by Great Britain were in the main confined to promises of tariff stabilization, though some tariff reductions were granted on timber, fish, and paper, and most-favoured-nation treatment was promised with regard to agricultural as well as industrial imports. The agreements with Soviet Russia in 1937 and Poland in 1935 were similar in character. The agreement with the Argentine, though as regards the volume of trade involved the most important of all, really belongs to a different category since, from the British point of view, its main object was to secure the liquidation of outstanding debts. Minor agreements were also concluded with France, Germany, and some other countries. In relation to these countries, however, Great Britain enjoyed no markedly superior bargaining power and was unable to obtain one-sided concessions. The agreement with Germany of 1933 was actually the only instance before the Anglo-American trade agreement of 1938 of substantial reductions in duties made by Great Britain (in return for a minimum coal quota).

Judged by the end which it was designed to serve, the British policy of bilateral trade agreements was on the whole very successful. While the share in British imports of the group of countries with which trade agreements had been concluded (except France and Germany) fell even more heavily between 1932 and 1936 than the share of other foreign countries, British exports to these countries showed no decline and even increased slightly.[1] The countries that suffered most from this decline in British imports were Denmark and Argentina, both of which also showed the largest increase in British exports. Coal exports to the Scandinavian and Baltic states nearly doubled in four years.[2] To some extent these gains were offset by the increased competition from the former suppliers of coal to these countries, Germany and Poland, which British exports encountered in the Mediterranean countries. The gain to the coal industry of the North-East and Durham was in part the loss of South Wales. But, even if this factor is taken into account, the policy of bilateral trade agreement undoubtedly benefited British export trade as a whole.

The official trade agreements were supplemented by three other methods of stimulating exports. In the first place, the British Government assisted British exports by the careful control of British foreign investment activity and by a system of state insurance for private commercial credits to foreign importers. The object of British foreign loan policy during the nineteen-thirties, for the reasons mentioned above, was to direct what little foreign lending was permitted into channels where it would directly benefit British foreign trade. While British Empire borrowers were granted a fair degree of latitude in the London capital market, the only exceptions to the embargo on foreign

[1] P.E.P., *Report on International Trade*, p. 285 f.   [2] ibid., p. 286.

loans were (*a*) loans which would be spent by the borrowing country entirely on British exports (visible or invisible) and (*b*) loans for the purpose of strengthening the sterling reserves of countries within the sterling area (and thus ensuring the maintenance of this economic bloc with its attendant advantages to British trade).

Further compensation to the British export trade for the breakdown of long-term foreign investment was provided by extending the functions of the Export Credits Guarantee Department. By underwriting private commercial credits granted to foreign purchasers it relieved the British exporter of some of the risks attending export trade in a world of unstable exchanges and exchange control and encouraged the grant of medium-term credits for the financing of British exports. The work of the Department, which continued to be run on a commercial basis, expanded greatly after 1931. The total value of its policies guarantees and contracts increased sixfold between 1933 and 1937 and in the second half of the decade included a number of very large loans to foreign Governments. Even these, however, though in some cases motivated by political rather than purely economic considerations, fitted into the general principles of British foreign loan policy during the nineteen-thirties since they were under direct Government control and conditional upon the purchase of British goods.

In the second place, the British Government during the nineteen-thirties began to assist British industries in various ways in the conclusion of private international agreements, either by tariff manipulation or by granting them official sanction. These agreements which played an important part in British trade relations during the decade were of three kinds. There were, first, private purchase agreements between British exporters and foreign importers which were concluded in parallel negotiations with the official trade agreements with the Baltic and Scandinavian countries and in which the foreign importers committed themselves to purchase definite quantities of specific British products. Secondly, British industries concluded a number of bilateral barter agreements with other industries in foreign countries.[1] These two types of agreements did not differ except in scope and efficacy from the official bilateral trade agreements and, on a smaller scale, benefited British export trade in much the same way.

More important than either of these was the third type, international cartel and commodity control agreements, though most

---

[1] e.g., the barter agreement of 1934 for the exchange of Welsh coal for French pit-props and the agreement between the Lancashire and Indian cotton interests of the same year.

of them dealt with raw materials and, with the important exception of iron and steel, did not directly affect United Kingdom trade. Their purpose was to maximize producers' earnings either by restricting production or by the division of markets between the producers at a fixed and agreed price level. Some of the pre-1929 schemes, especially the Stevenson scheme of rubber restriction and Copper Exporters Incorporated, had broken down as a result of the expansion of outside production and reclamation provoked by the excessive rapacity of the monopoly producers. The later schemes which by 1936 covered most of the important raw materials and some finished goods embodied the lessons of these experiences, though the interests of consumers continued to receive scanty attention. British manufacturers were on the whole slow in joining hands with their foreign competitors; but by 1937 British industries were more or less closely involved in international cartel agreements covering among other commodities, steel and steel products, coal, aluminium, coke, nitrogen, railway rolling stock, wheat, zinc, heavy chemicals, and molybdenum. In addition, British financial interests had a large hand in commodity control agreements, concluded in most cases directly by the governments of the producing countries, for the control of Empire production of copper, rubber, lead, sugar, tea, and tin.

Whether these international cartels and commodity control schemes in practice benefited British exports is by no means certain. With the breakdown of the international commodity markets during the depression some international control designed to adjust the world supply of raw materials to demand and to smooth out excessive price fluctuations had undoubtedly become necessary. But in the hands of international monopolies and cartels this control tended to be exercised primarily in the interests of the producers and operated so as to restrict output below the optimum. A manufacturing country like Great Britain could benefit from increases in raw material prices at best only indirectly. One or two of the agreements, of which the agreement between the British Iron and Steel Federation and the International Steel Cartel was the most important example, certainly hampered the British export industry. It represented a victory of the heavy industry over the much larger engineering and constructional industries which suffered from the increase in the price of their most important raw material.[1]

Lastly, some of the depressed British export industries, in par-

---

[1] The Board of Trade index of iron and steel prices (1930 = 100) rose from 91·5 in 1932 to 100·5 in 1935, 129·6 in 1937, and 139·1 in 1938, as compared with the general wholesale price index which rose from 85·6 in 1932 to 89·0 in 1935, 108·7 in 1937 and 101·4 in 1938.

ticular coal, cotton and shipbuilding, received special Government assistance in the form of subsidies or otherwise. The purpose of these measures, however, was not so much to stimulate British exports as to assist these industries in the task of adjustment to the loss of foreign markets. While it was undoubtedly hoped that by internal reorganization and cost reduction these industries would be placed in a better position to compete with the often heavily subsidized industries of other countries, even the subsidies were not export subsidies in the ordinary sense of the word and are more properly dealt with in the context of internal economic policy.

VI. DEBT COLLECTION

A THIRD objective, in addition to protection and the stimulation of exports, which assumed a surprising importance in British commercial policy during this period was 'debt collection'. The need for this arose with the spread of exchange control over most of Europe and South America. Difficulties in obtaining free sterling resulted in long delays in payments to British exporters and the accumulation of substantial commercial debts to Great Britain in most of these countries. In addition, some of them, especially Germany and the Argentine, owed large sums to British creditors in interest on British loans and direct investments.

In order to secure the payment of these debts, Great Britain between 1933 and 1938 concluded payments and clearing agreements[1] with many of these countries.[2] While these agreements showed considerable differences in detail, the principle underlying all of them was that all or most of the sterling proceeds of British imports from the foreign country were earmarked in the first place for repayment of outstanding financial or commercial debts and in the second place for purchases of British exports. The proportion of the total sterling proceeds for which Great Britain was able to obtain an undertaking that they would be used for one or the other of these purposes varied mainly with her bargaining power. Thus, in the important agreement with the Argentine (1933), a country which depended largely on the British market, the latter, in return for a British promise not to restrict imports of Argentinian meat below the Ottawa level, obliged herself to allocate practically 100 per cent of the sterling exchange arising out of export to the United Kingdom to the payment of interest on her public debts and repayment of other

[1] For a definition of the difference between payments and clearing agreements, see below, ch. vii, p. 187 n. 3.
[2] Payments agreements were concluded with Argentina, Uruguay, Italy, Germany, Hungary, Rumania, and Yugoslavia; clearing agreements with Spain, Italy, Turkey, and Rumania.

debts to private British investors and traders. Similarly, having first by the threat of impounding German sterling credits by compulsory clearing secured a transfer agreement with Germany which provided for full payment of the British share of the Dawes and Young loans, Great Britain, in the various payments agreements concluded with Germany, secured the earmarking of more than half the sterling proceeds of German exports for payment to British exporters and a further proportion (fixed at 10 per cent in the 1934 agreement) to the repayment of outstanding commercial debts. These agreements, however, left Germany with a considerable amount of free exchange. In the agreement with Brazil, finally, with whom Great Britain did not have the bargaining weapon of a passive balance of trade, she had to content herself with a promise of the allocation of certain agreed sums to meet outstanding debts and of most-favoured-nation treatment in this respect.[1]

The object of debt liquidation necessarily came into conflict at times with the other objective of British commercial policy, the promotion of British exports. Wherever Great Britain had an import surplus with another country the accruing sterling exchange was available either for debt payment or for purchases of British exports. In practically all these cases, Great Britain in her payments and clearing agreements gave preference to the liquidation of old debts over the promotion of new trade. In two cases, Italy and Turkey, this principle was carried so far as to provide for a reduction of British exports to the countries concerned. In one sense, it was obviously sound policy to use outstanding debts rather than British goods to pay for imports from abroad. At the same time, this policy meant that in the interest of British investors opportunities of stimulating British export trade and thus speeding the recovery of the British export industries were missed.

VII. THE TREND TOWARDS BILATERALISM AND TRADE CONTROL

ONE significant aspect of British commercial policy during the nineteen-thirties which stands out from this brief summary and which requires a word of comment was its general trend away from *laisser-faire* towards increased state intervention and quantitative control. In this respect the adoption of protection was relatively unimportant. For the tariff, even if it reduced the volume of foreign trade below what it would otherwise have been (which, as we have seen, is by no means certain), left foreign trade to be determined in its volume and direction by the price mechanism. The real breach with the *laisser-faire* system lay in

[1] H. J. Tasca, *World Trading Systems* (International Institute of Intellectual Co-operation, 1939), p. 83.

the supersession of the free play of market forces by State control and diversion of foreign trade from its 'natural' channels which was apparent in much of British commercial policy. The system of Imperial preference, of course, already involved such diversion: preferential tariffs deliberately discriminated in favour of Empire as against foreign imports. The quota system constituted an even more direct interference with the price mechanism. But the most far-reaching extension of State direction of trade resulted from the bilateral trade, purchase, payments, and clearing agreements. The tendency towards the bilateral balancing of trade with each country in itself meant a diversion of trade from the channels which it would have taken if market forces had been allowed free play (in so far as that trade would have taken place at all under free conditions). In practice, State control was carried a good deal further by many of the detailed provisions of these agreements—provisions for the purchase or exchange of specified quantities of goods,[1] for the maintenance of the proportion of the various classes of goods supplied in previous specified years,[2] for the exchange of goods at arbitrarily determined prices and/or exchange rates,[3] and many others. The same trend towards State control, as we have seen, was noticeable in British foreign loan policy. And the commodity control schemes, though most of them were operated not by the State but by private enterprise, were indicative of the same tendency.

By 1939, the British foreign trade system was still very far from that of Nazi Germany. In the main, British trade was still conducted on open and competitive principles. Not only was her trade with the British Empire, which in 1938 amounted to nearly half her total foreign trade, carried on under relatively free trade conditions, but even in her trade with the rest of the world market forces still played the predominant part. With certain qualifications, private traders could buy and sell where they liked; with certain qualifications again, foreign exchange was freely available for all commercial purposes. How far, however, Great Britain had moved away from the old system of free multilateral trade, is illustrated by the fact that by 1938 nearly half her total trade with foreign (non-Empire) countries was conducted under bilateral trade, payments or clearing agreements, and by applying to British commercial policy the test of the principle of 'non-discrimination' which, as we saw, formed the ostensible basis of American commercial policy during the nineteen-thirties. Formally, Great Britain adhered throughout the nineteen-thirties to the principle of the most-favoured nation-clause which embodied

---

[1] e.g., in the purchase agreements with the Scandinavian and Baltic countries.
[2] e.g. in the payments agreement with Germany of August 1934.
[3] e.g. in the payments agreement with Rumania of August 1935.

the conception of 'non-discrimination'. The clause was incorporated in all her trade agreements, and, apart from Imperial preference which was officially defended on the ground that the British Empire countries stood in a special political and economic relation to the United Kingdom, Great Britain in fact on the whole meticulously refrained from discriminating in her own tariff and quota policy between different foreign countries. What Great Britain did do on the largest scale was to induce foreign countries, by skilful exercise of her bargaining power, to discriminate in her favour. It was to discrimination in this form that Great Britain owed much of the success of her policy of export stimulation and debt collection.[1]

It is important for an understanding of British policy to realize that this drift away from *laisser-faire* and multilateralism was not entirely deliberate or even voluntary. In part, of course, it was due to the determination of Great Britain to take advantage of her strong bargaining position to secure preferential treatment for her exports and in the payment of outstanding financial claims. But to a large extent it was due simply to the growth of State control of trade elsewhere. In its efforts to maintain British commercial and financial interests in its trade relations with the exchange control countries of Europe and South America the British Government was reluctantly forced to adopt the same methods. This fact is most obvious in the attempts to solve the problem of debt collection. But it also underlies much of the trend towards discrimination in British export policy. The classical argument that a country will benefit by free trade even if the rest of the world is protectionist may have been true as long as protection took the form of non-discriminatory tariffs. It had certainly ceased to be true with the growth of monopolies and cartels, on the one hand, and the use of quotas, discriminatory tariffs, preferential systems, export subsidies, and exchange regulations, on the other, and in a world in which a number of coun-

---

[1] In some cases, discrimination assumed forms which differed but little from those practised under the German system of trade control. Thus, the agreement with Denmark of 1933 stipulated that if Danish imports of textiles from any country other than the United Kingdom increased during any six months by more than 30 per cent the two Governments should discuss measures to 'preserve or restore an economic level of prices.' Designed as a safeguard against German or Japanese competition, this provision implied an unusual degree of control by one country over the foreign trade of another with third countries. Again, under the Anglo-Turkish Export Credit Guarantee Agreement of 1938 a joint Government organization was set up for the sale of Turkish products in the British Empire and against foreign exchange freely convertible into sterling, to foreign countries for the purpose of providing Turkey with sterling exchange with which to purchase British products. This arrangement, like similar methods used by Germany, was essentially parasitic in nature since it ultimately depended upon the existence of other free exchange countries which had no bilateral arrangements with Turkey. In effect it meant that free exchange made available by, say, American imports from Turkey was earmarked for purchases of British products (cf. Tasca, op. cit., pp. 128–30).

tries conducted their entire foreign trade on the basis of State control and the exercise of discriminatory monopoly. To give but one illustration: in criticism of the British method of making foreign credits conditional upon the purchase of British exports, it has been argued that 'unless it is assumed that competitive power is lacking, there does not seem to be any important reason why German trading methods cannot more efficiently be met by free credits'.[1] Now it is clear that one of the reasons for the widespread use of such methods by Great Britain was that many of her export industries had ceased to be able to compete with more efficient foreign rivals. Exploitation of bargaining power to that extent took the place of improvements of efficiency or of changes towards exports in which Great Britain possessed greater comparative advantage. But that is not the whole story. In competition with a country which, on the basis of complete State control of foreign trade, can conduct its foreign trade by means of discriminatory monopoly (e.g. carry on trade with whole countries at a loss so as to obtain a hold on these markets and compensate for this loss by gains in other directions) and which, moreover, as did Germany, uses political and military pressure in addition to economic bargaining power, a country which relies on free trading methods, that is, on the capacity to bear risks and losses of private exporters and the efficacy of the price mechanism, is bound to be at a disadvantage.

The fact that the trend of British commercial policy towards trade control and bilateralism was to a large extent imposed on a reluctant British Government by the general trend in this direction over a large part of the world accounts in part for the striking contrast between the professions of the British Government and the practice of its commercial policy during this period. While the practice tended steadily towards increased protection and trade control, the British Government frequently expressed its regret at the growth of 'artificial barriers' to international trade and disclaimed responsibility for this development. To critics this attitude appeared blandly hypocritical. And it is undoubtedly true that the British Government, like any other, was much more acutely aware of any damage that was done to the trade of its own country by the growth of trade barriers and 'discriminatory practices' elsewhere than of injuries inflicted upon other countries by its own policy. But up to a point, this contrast was also due to an inadequate awareness of the fact that the intensification of economic nationalism during the depression and post-depression years was at least as much the effect as the cause of the breakdown of the old world economic system. Whether or not an international *laisser-faire* system was capable of functioning

[1] Tasca, op. cit., p. 135.

smoothly in a world composed of national economies which to varying degrees had substituted planning, State control and monopolistic organization internally, that system had collapsed in 1931 as a result of large structural maladjustments and the world depression. The old automatic mechanism for the co-ordination of national policies having broken down and no effective system of planned international co-ordination having taken its place, each country, acting on an immediate view of its own interests, almost inevitably pursued a policy which gave rise to new difficulties and problems elsewhere.

The last two years before the outbreak of the present war did bring a number of modifications of British commercial policy which could be interpreted as the first steps towards a reversal of the course which it had followed since 1931. The Anglo-American trade agreement of 1938 led to the first appreciable reduction of the British tariff since 1932 and involved a partial reversal of the policy of Imperial preference. In return for considerable concessions for British products in the American market, Great Britain not only reduced her duties on some manufactures but also abolished or reduced several of the Ottawa duties on raw materials and foodstuffs. The British Government undoubtedly welcomed this important step towards the removal of some of the barriers to international trade. But the fact cannot be ignored that this departure from the course of the preceding years was, at any rate, assisted by political considerations. In the autumn of 1938 the agreement was of inestimable political value to Great Britain as evidence of an Anglo-American *rapprochement*. Although the American gains in terms of tariff concessions hardly exceeded those obtained by Great Britain, the agreement in a sense constituted an important victory for Cordell Hull's policy of 'freer trade' over the general trend of British commercial policy during the nineteen-thirties. Political and strategic factors also account for some other changes in British foreign economic policy during the last year before the outbreak of war. The British trade drives of 1938 in South America and South-Eastern Europe which meant that for the first time since 1932 British trade policy concentrated on regions outside the sterling area, and the large loans granted by the Export Credits Guarantee Department to Turkey, Poland, Greece and China in 1938 and 1939 which involved a considerable breach with earlier British foreign loan policy, were both preliminaries of economic warfare rather than evidence of a fundamental change in British commercial policy.

VIII. INTERNAL RECOVERY POLICY

IN contrast with British external economic policy, the internal recovery policy of the British Government during the nineteen-thirties was remarkable for its orthodoxy. The great depression did not lead to any marked increase in State interference in, or control of, the economic system. It was left to private enterprise, aided only by protection from foreign competition, 'cheap money' and minor internal measures of assistance to lift the British economy from the depression.

The most important positive contribution of internal Government policy to the British recovery was the adoption of a policy of 'cheap money'. The policy was tried first in 1930. The flow of funds to London after the collapse of the Wall Street boom induced the Bank of England to reduce the bank rate to 3 per cent and early in 1931 to $2\frac{1}{2}$ per cent. But the attempt failed completely to reverse the decline and came to a sudden end with the crisis of the summer. After the departure from gold in September a second attempt was made and this time cheap money came to stay. The policy of cheap money took three main forms, war loan conversion, expansion of the 'cash' of the joint stock banks, and government control of new capital issues.

The War Loan which formed one-third of the total internal public debt and was redeemable at par between 1929 and 1947 dominated the gilt-edged market. Its conversion from a 5 per cent to a $3\frac{1}{2}$ per cent basis in the summer of 1932, therefore, was an effective method of forcing down interest rates on long-term securities at a time when it was obviously impossible to reinvest on better terms elsewhere. The conversion operation successfully completed, the Government took strong and persistent action to expand the cash basis of the banks by increasing the issue of Bank of England notes on the basis of gold acquired by the Exchange Equalization Account, and by open market operations. The banks were thus enabled to increase loans and investments and to lower interest rates. The most important part of the control of new capital issues was the unofficial ban on foreign lending which has already been mentioned. It served to increase the volume of capital available to British borrowers and to keep down interest rates in Great Britain.

The cheap money policy was extremely successful in its immediate object of forcing down interest rates available to industry and increasing the amount of credit. Between 1925 and 1929 the average level of the Bank rate and the yield on War Loan was nearly 5 per cent and private borrowers with first-class security had to pay at least $\frac{1}{2}$ per cent more. Between 1932 and 1937 the government could borrow on long-term at $3\frac{1}{2}$ per cent and on short-term at little more than $\frac{1}{2}$ per cent and interest rates on loans to other borrowers and mortgage charges were correspondingly reduced to a level considerably below that to which they would have fallen during the depression in the absence of Government intervention. What was more important, credit was not only made cheaper but it was also far more readily available to potential borrowers.

Despite lower interest rates, bank advances to private borrowers did not increase greatly and remained below the level of the later nineteen-twenties. Over 80 per cent of all conversion and refunding loans issued in London between 1932 and 1938 were for the British Government and half the rest for Empire Governments.[1] Lower interest rates, however, once psychological conditions for a trade revival had become favourable, gave an additional stimulus by raising share prices. The reduction of national debt charges by £30 million was not without importance in view of the orthodox budget policy of the British Government since it meant lower taxation. Increased investment by the banks in bills and securities of money for which they could not find borrowers led to a large increase in bank deposits and thus helped many firms and industries to become sufficiently liquid to finance increased production without recourse to the banks. Above all, the fact that large mortgages were easily obtainable from building societies and other credit institutions, as well as the reduction of mortgage charges, played an important part in assisting the building boom which was the main feature of the British recovery. There is little evidence that 'cheap money' was any more effective in Great Britain than in the U.S.A. in *directly* stimulating new investment. On the other hand, in so far as the abundance of cheap credit after 1932 raised effective consumer demand for houses, it did give a direct stimulus to economic activity, over and above its general effect in removing any obstacles to recovery in the shape of credit stringency and high interest rates.

The British Government also took steps at intervals to assist some of the most depressed British industries by means of Government subsidies, loan guarantees, and measures intended to encourage internal reorganization by the industry concerned.

The beneficiaries were primarily the great British export industries, localized in the 'depressed areas', coal, cotton, and shipbuilding. The first of these to receive direct assistance had been the coal industry which had suffered intensely from the loss of export markets. Subsidies had been paid to the coal industry during the immediate post-war slump and again in the winter preceding the General Strike. In 1928, this policy was discontinued after some £23 million had been expended and was not renewed by the National Government, which instead continued rather ineffectually to encourage the owners of the industry to

[1] F. Benham, op. cit., p. 231 f.

set their house in order. The production quota scheme of the Coal Act of 1930 was found to hamper coal exports and had to be revised in 1934. The cotton industry suffered from serious over-capitalization as well as the loss of markets. The Government, through the agency of the Bank of England, supported the policy of purchasing and scrapping redundant spindles by means, not of a direct subsidy, but of a large loan guarantee which enabled the industry to borrow the necessary money at a low rate of inter-est. The shipping and shipbuilding industries had suffered severely during the depression and the British Shipping Act of 1935 provided for two subsidies: a tramp shipping subsidy primarily designed to raise freight rates by restricting competi-tion for freight among tramps, and a loan to shipbuilders for the building of new and the modernizing of old ships conditional upon the scrapping of old vessels. Under the first scheme £4 million were paid out and under the second £3,500,000 were advanced. By 1937, the position of both industries had consider-ably improved and the subsidies were discontinued only to be reintroduced on a larger scale in 1938.

In principle, this policy of assisting the depressed export industries, on the one hand, to improve their competitive ability in world markets and, on the other hand, to adjust their capacity to the loss of world markets in so far as that loss was due to permanent changes in technological and economic conditions, was perfectly sound and the logical corollary to the change-over in British commercial policy. In practice, these measures suffered from two grave defects. In the first place, the vested interests concerned either, as in the case of the coal industry, offered stubborn resistance to reorganization which the Government made no real attempt to overcome, or alternatively, as in the case of the shipping and shipbuilding industries, made reorganization the excuse for restricting capacity so as to maintain prices at levels which secured them monopoly profits. As in the case of the agricultural marketing schemes discussed before, Government assistance to British industry during the nineteen-thirties largely served to speed the process of monopolization and cartellization which by the end of the decade covered all the most important industries of the country. In the second place, and partly as a result of this, these measures were far more effective in restricting capacity in the contracting industries than in ensuring the transfer of labour, and where possible capital, to new employment in expanding lines of production. Some attempts were made to stimulate transfers of labour from the depressed areas to the prosperous South, to attract new industries to the depressed areas, and to retain unemployment. But these measures met with very limited success, and it was not until the outbreak of the war that the needs of war production led to a real revival of prosperity in the depressed areas.

The most striking fact about British internal economic policy during the decade, however, is that Great Britain was the only one of the five countries with which we are concerned which did not resort to a policy of budget deficits to promote internal recovery. The Labour Government which was in office at the beginning of the depression, did make some half-hearted attempts to devise a compensatory public works policy. But planned on a totally inadequate scale and hampered by the Government's weak political position, by Treasury opposition and by the immense practical difficulties of improvising a public works programme at the last minute (particularly in a country where, as in Great Britain, local authorities are responsible for the bulk of public capital expenditure), the efforts amounted to little. The revelation by the May Committee in 1931 of the prospect of a budget deficit was sufficient to put an end to these attempts; and the formation of the National Government signified a return to strict financial orthodoxy. Determined to balance the budget at all costs, the Government resorted to a policy of drastic deflation. An 'economy campaign' was launched throughout the country and an emergency budget in September 1931 combined heavy increases of direct and indirect taxation and unemployment insurance contributions with cuts in all items of Government expenditure, including expenditure on education, the road fund, salaries and wages, rates of unemployment benefit and grants to local authorities. Some of these measures fell hard on those who had been most hit by the depression, particularly the 'means test' for unemployment benefit, and they undoubtedly tended to reduce consumers' purchasing power and demand, but they succeeded in balancing Government expenditure and revenue and facilitated conversion. Business confidence was stimulated by the return of a 'sound' Government with 'sound' principles of public finance. The depreciation of the pound relieved the pressure on the balance of payments. At the end of 1932 business began to revive. The British default on war debt to the United States, war loan conversion, and the new protective duties helped to ease the financial position of the Government. With the progress of recovery the yield of taxes increased and expenditure on unemployment relief diminished. Thus from 1932 onwards it was relatively easy to maintain a balanced budget without recourse to further deflationary measures. The British national debt increased slightly from £7,413 million in 1931 to £7,800 million in 1935. But this increase—which was mainly due to the Exchange Equalization Fund and was largely offset by the gold acquired by the Fund—was negligible compared with the rate of increase of the national debts of the U.S.A. or Germany during the same period.

THE primary object of British economic policy, like that of nearly every other country during the nineteen-thirties, was recovery, and in discussing its effects we must begin with the question to what extent it achieved that object.

Now, the British recovery between 1932 and 1937 was certainly remarkable. During the nineteen-twenties, Great Britain had lagged behind the other large industrial countries. After the depression, the position was almost reversed. By 1937, Great Britain's indices of economic activity were considerably ahead of those of France and the U.S.A. and most other countries and had in most respects passed the peak pre-slump levels of 1929. The volume of industrial production had risen by 50 per cent since 1932 and was over 20 per cent larger than in 1929.[1] Unemployment, though it had been reduced to less than half of what it had been in 1932, was still higher than in 1929 and at the peak of the 1937 boom still affected nearly 10 per cent of the insured population.[2] But the number of persons employed (excluding agricultural workers) had increased from 10·2 millions in 1929 to 11·5 millions in 1937[3] and there had been a striking increase in industrial productivity.[4] Industrial profits were at least 10 per cent higher than before the depression and money wages, despite a 5 per cent fall in the cost of living, were some 7 per cent higher than in 1929.[5] The national income which had fallen during the depression to £3,850 million[6] is estimated to have reached in 1937 the figure of £5,200 million.[7]

What distinguished the British recovery of the nineteen-thirties from most earlier cyclical upswings in Great Britain was the fact that it was predominantly a home-market recovery. After the temporary improvement in economic conditions which followed the abandonment of the gold standard in 1931 and which must largely be ascribed to the competitive advantages which British exports had obtained, exports followed rather than led a recovery which was based on a rapidly expanding production for the home-market. The volume of British foreign trade which had been halved by the depression increased steadily from 1933

[1] Board of Trade index of industrial production.

[2] *Statistical Abstract for the United Kingdom*, 1938; the lowest percentage was 9·7 per cent in September 1937.

[3] ibid.

[4] According to the estimates of the London and Cambridge Economic Service, net physical output per worker increased during the short period from 1930 to 1935 by as much as 25 per cent (Special Memorandum, No. 47, G. L. Schwartz and E. C. Rhodes, *Output, Employment and Wages in the United Kingdom, 1924, 1930, 1935*, p. 3).

[5] F. Benham, op. cit., p. 218.

[6] Colin Clark, *National Income and Outlay* (Macmillan, 1937).

[7] *The Economist*, 15 April 1939.

onwards. Moreover, whereas during the nineteen-twenties Great Britain's share in world trade had steadily declined, it more than held its own during the nineteen-thirties.[1] But neither exports nor imports kept step with the increase in industrial production nor even regained their pre-depression level; and what was even more significant, imports throughout these years rose at a more rapid rate than exports.[2] Whereas in the past British imports had followed exports, they now rose in response to the increase in home-demand for raw materials and foodstuffs which accompanied the domestic recovery.

The character of the recovery showed itself in striking changes in the internal economic structure of Great Britain. Ever since 1914, the stagnation of the British staple exports had led to a relative decline in the proportion of total industrial output produced for export relative to production for the home-market. During the nineteen-thirties, the domestic recovery hastened this tendency despite the absolute rise in the volume of British foreign trade. Production for export which is estimated to have accounted in 1914 for nearly one-third of Britain's total industrial production and which had declined to 27 per cent in 1924 and 22 per cent in 1930 is estimated to have declined further to 17 per cent in 1935 and 15 per cent in 1938.[3] This tendency, in turn, was reflected in large occupational and migratory shifts. In the first place, the shift of labour out of the old British staple export industries of the North and Wales, to the South which had begun during the post-war decade continued at an increased rate. While the numbers engaged (whether employed or unemployed) in coalmining declined by 22 per cent, in the cotton industry by 32 per cent, and in the shipbuilding industry by 14 per cent, and the numbers engaged in 'manufacturing' as a whole rose by only 12·5 per cent as compared with an increase of 16·6 per cent in the total number of insured workers, a few new industries, especially the motor and aircraft, the electrical engineering and rayon industries and most occupations providing 'services', such as Government service, public utilities, road transport, and building showed increases well above the average. The numbers engaged in building and contracting, in particular, expanded by 42 per cent.[4] Owing to the localization of the old industries mainly in the North and the new ones mainly in the South, there occurred

[1] Britain's share of world trade amounted to 13·72 per cent in 1933, 13·61 per cent in 1937, and 13·90 per cent in 1938.

[2] The value of British exports increased from £416 million in 1932 to £596 million in 1937, the value of imports from £625 million in 1933 to £952 million in 1937. But at these figures exports were still 29 per cent and imports 14 per cent below their 1929 level (*Statistical Abstract for the United Kingdom*).

[3] H. Clay, 'The Place of Exports in British Industry after the War' *Economic Journal*, vol. 52, June–September 1942, p. 146.

[4] *The Economist*, 6 January 1940, p. 21.

a corresponding migration of workers from Wales and the North-West towards the London area, the South East and South West.[1]

These figures show that Great Britain not only experienced a quick recovery from the depression but also went a good way during these years towards solving the long-term problem of adjustment which we mentioned at the beginning of this chapter. The home-market expansion had absorbed a considerable proportion of the country's productive resources which the long-term decline in world demand for her old staple exports had deprived of employment. That this solution was still incomplete is shown by the continued high level of structural unemployment concentrated in the depressed areas which accounted, together with a relatively large amount of frictional unemployment, for most of the 1·3 million unemployed that still remained at the peak of the recovery in 1937.

The intractability of this problem was not unconnected with a second major change in the structure of the British economy which should be mentioned here, the rapidly increasing monopolization of British industry which was one of the outstanding features of British economic development during the nineteen-thirties. By 1939 there were few important industries (the coal industry was a notable exception) which were not dominated by one or two or three large firms or combines. In addition, trade associations—in their turn co-ordinated by the Federation of British Industries—had grown up in most industries which endeavoured, with varying degrees of success, to regulate sales, maintain prices, and ensure co-operation against recalcitrant firms. The organization of employers was paralleled by the further growth of trade union organization on an industrial basis. Government policy, as we have seen, did a good deal to further this development, in the belief that it would increase efficiency of production. In practice, it is very doubtful how much of the increase in industrial productivity that did take place can be ascribed to the effects of monopolization; while, on the other hand, there can be no doubt that the trend towards monopolization heightened still further the rigidity of the British economy and, owing to the natural tendency of monopoly towards restriction of output, operated as a powerful brake on economic expansion.

The fact that Great Britain, apart from the major problem of structural unemployment, achieved what was by all counts a highly successful recovery without having had to resort to State intervention on any large scale seems at first sight to contradict the conclusions which we reached in our analysis of the New Deal. The question arises why private enterprise succeeded in

[1] *The Economist*, 6 January 1940, p. 21.

Great Britain in lifting the economy out of the depression without the stimulus of public investment on the scale which became necessary in the U.S.A., and, as we shall see later on, also in Germany, France, and Sweden.

Part of the answer to this question must be found in the fact that the stimulus which in those four countries was supplied by public deficit expenditure was provided in Great Britain by the devaluation of the pound and protection, and to a lesser extent also by cheap money. There can be no doubt that all three measures stimulated and hastened the revival of private investment and economic activity in Great Britain. The devaluation of the pound, as was pointed out before, supplied the first check to the slump and placed Great Britain for two years in a relatively favourable international economic position. The fact, moreover, that Great Britain was the first country to abandon the gold standard meant that it was also the first country to be able to pursue, and next to Finland and Sweden, the first actually to initiate, an expansionist monetary policy. The contribution of protection to the recovery is harder to assess. It is not enough to acclaim its beneficent results on the basis of *post hoc ergo propter hoc*, simply because the beginning of the British recovery in fact almost coincided with the imposition of the tariff. The fact that, as we shall see presently, the chief feature of the recovery was a phenomenal boom in residential building, which was certainly not the direct result of protection, suggests that protection was at any rate not the decisive factor in the recovery. Nor, on the other hand, can it be maintained that the favourable effects of the tariff on the home market were offset by its indirect adverse reactions on the export industries. The fact is that British exports had declined severely during the slump and there is no prima facie reason to assume that British exports would have made a better recovery than they did had Great Britain maintained free trade. The tariff certainly stimulated production for the expanded home-market and encouraged investment in the protected industries, especially iron and steel. On balance, there can be no doubt that it was a significant factor in the home-market recovery. Again, cheap money, as was mentioned before, played an important part in the building boom and assured that the recovery was not impeded by credit stringency. Finally, in the peculiar conditions of Great Britain in 1931, even the orthodox budget policy may have been initially a favourable rather than an unfavourable factor. In view of the prevailing conceptions of 'sound' public finance among British public opinion and the business world in particular, the determined stand of the National Government by the principles of financial orthodoxy probably had a favourable psychological influence, while the Government's

E

'economy' measures were relieved of their deflationary character by the expansionist effect of the devaluation of the pound and the subsequent credit expansion.

Yet it may be doubted whether these various policies would have sufficed to bring about an otherwise unaided recovery of private enterprise if conditions in Great Britain had not, for two reasons been peculiarly favourable to a large cyclical upswing.

In the first place, the very fact that Great Britain never fully shared in the prosperity of the nineteen-twenties probably assisted her recovery from the great depression. It has been suggested that one of the basic reasons for the comparative failure of the New Deal was the exhaustion during the prosperity of the post-war decade of investment opportunities in two or three outstanding fields. In Great Britain the position was reversed. Much new investment which had been postponed during the years of semi-stagnation after 1925 was undertaken after 1932. The American prosperity of the post-war decade had rested mainly upon the opportunities for investment provided by the growth of new industries, such as the motor-car industry, and by a pronounced building boom. In Great Britain the same investment opportuni-ties 'carried' the recovery of the nineteen-thirties. There was con-tinuous and rapid progress in the motor-car, electrical, rayon and some other new industries; and in 1932 began the residential building boom which became the outstanding feature of the British recovery. The rate of house building increased from an average of about 140,000 houses per year between 1920 and 1930 inclusive (of which nearly two-thirds were built with State assistance), to 200,000 in 1932, 267,000 in 1934, 329,000 in 1935 and 346,000 in 1937 (of which more than three-quarters were built by private enterprise without State assistance).[1] The number of workers attached to 'building' rose from 857,000 in 1932 to 1,035,000 in 1937 and through its indirect effect on other indus-tries the housing boom is estimated to have been responsible for perhaps a third of the increased employment during the recovery.[2]

The basis of the building boom was the large underinvestment in building during the nineteen-twenties, and the urgent need for new and better housing in England ever since the war. But this need had to be converted into effective demand before it could lead to a spontaneous building boom. To some extent this was accomplished by the ample supply of cheap credit to purchasers of houses. The reduction in mortgage rates, as well as low build-ing costs, also played a part in encouraging investment in housing. Nor must it be ignored that, once the building boom (and the recovery in other industries) had got under way, the increase in

[1] *Statistical Abstract for the United Kingdom.*
[2] F. Benham, op. cit., p. 224.

investment and employment itself provided new flows of purchasing power and effective demand for new houses. But it is
doubtful whether cheap money could have stimulated a building
boom of such proportions if it had not been for the second
favourable circumstance which formed the background to the
British recovery.

As an importer of foodstuffs and raw materials and exporter
of manufactures, Great Britain benefited greatly from the disproportionate fall in the prices of the former which was one of
the chief features of the world depression. Between 1931 and
1935, a representative unit of her commodity exports purchased
a volume of imports 20 per cent greater than before the slump.
It was this improvement in her 'terms of trade' which was chiefly
responsible for the surprising fact that the real incomes of consumers in Great Britain who were not unemployed increased
substantially during the years of the great depression.[1] The reduction in the amount of money that had to be spent on imported
food and other necessaries is estimated to have released some
£250 million of consumers' purchasing power which became
available for expenditure on houses and other 'luxuries', such as
motor cars (the sale of which increased by 50 per cent between
1930 and 1936). The windfall of an almost unprecedented improvement in the terms of trade would not by itself have stopped
the slump or produced a recovery. But coupled with devaluation,
protection, and cheap money (the first two of which actually
accentuated the improvement) it may be said to have provided
that initial stimulus to recovery which in Germany and the U.S.A.
was artificially produced by heavy Government expenditure.

The British recovery continued undisturbed until the end of
1937 when the American slump of that year threatened to spread
to Great Britain. It is impossible to say whether the British
economy would once again have revived unaided had a depression been allowed to develop. It must be assumed that by 1937
the impetus of the residential building boom had largely spent
itself. And it is improbable that in the conditions of world trade
of 1937 Great Britain would have derived the same benefit from
an improvement in her terms of trade as during the great depres-

---

[1] Between 1929 and 1935 the cost of living fell by no less than 25 per cent as
compared with a fall in average wage rates of only 6 per cent. Part of this
increase in real incomes and consumers' purchasing power was, of course, due
to the striking increase in industrial productivity during these years which has
been mentioned before. But though important in its long-term effects on the
national income, this increase in productivity can hardly have been quantitatively important in its effects on consumers' purchasing power and on the course
of the trade cycle. The improvement in Britain's terms of trade, on the other
hand, is estimated to have been directly responsible for an increase in the British
national income by about 5 per cent (British Association, *Britain in Recovery*
[Pitman, 1938], p. 20).

sion. As it happened the slump was caught before it could assume dangerous proportions by the large rearmament programme which got under way in that year. For the remaining years of peace, Great Britain joined the group of countries whose economy was based on rearmament as the prime mover of economic activity.

This analysis, on the face of it, suggests that in so far as the British recovery was actively assisted by Government policy, that assistance largely took the form of measures which helped Great Britain at the expense of other countries. This is in fact the burden of the criticism which has frequently been levied against it. The criticism raises two questions: in the first place, it is worth inquiring how far it can in fact be said that British policy was detrimental to the rest of the world. In the second place, it may be asked what other policy was open to the British Government. We may conclude this chapter with a brief discussion of these two questions.

Now there can be no doubt that the initial impact of both the devaluation of the pound and of the adoption of protection and Imperial preference by Great Britain was gravely to increase the economic difficulties of most other countries. The repercussions of the fall of the pound have been outlined before. The British adoption of protection had the immediate effect of increasing the difficulties of the primary producers of South America, Denmark, and South Eastern Europe, and of Great Britain's leading industrial competitors. Against these effects, however, must be set the favourable reflationary effect which these measures had on Great Britain and which were transmitted to the rest of the world through the increase in her demand for the products of other countries. In the conditions of the world in 1931 and 1932, any expansionist factor which was capable of stemming or reversing the general decline of world income and demand was beneficial. The early British recovery in fact constituted such a factor. That does not mean that all countries which suffered from the British policy of import restriction were compensated by the spilling over of the British recovery.[1] But the fact that British

[1] The chief reason why this was not in fact the case to a much larger extent must be seen in the policy of Imperial preference which for that very reason stands in an entirely different category from the devaluation of the pound and the general tariff. At the best, it could benefit the United Kingdom and the Dominions only at the expense of their foreign competitors in Empire markets, without any compensatory expansionist influence on the world economy as a whole. It was primarily responsible for the striking changes in the direction of British foreign trade which occurred during the nineteen-thirties. The chief change was a diversion of British imports away from foreign sources and in favour of the Empire. Between 1931 and 1936, the share of the Dominions in British imports rose from 28·7 per cent to 39·2 per cent, while the share of European countries fell from 42·7 per cent to 34·2 per cent, and that of non-European foreign countries from 28·6 per cent to 26·6 per cent. The Empire producers benefited from the diversion of trade from the chiefly non-European producers of foodstuffs and raw materials, while the influence of the British

imports began to rise earlier than those of any other major country provides a powerful argument for the view that the net effect of British policy on the world as a whole was on balance favourable.

The question may still be asked whether the same degree of internal recovery and the same beneficial external effects could not have been achieved without the initial detrimental effects on the rest of the world, had Great Britain adopted a vigorous expansionist policy of the New Deal type. Now there are no economic reasons why this should not have been possible. There can be no doubt that a substantial increase in public investment expenditure, supplemented perhaps by some degree of control of private investment, could have provided as effective a stimulus to recovery as currency depreciation and protection. The reason why no such policy was attempted was that the National Government, supported by powerful sections of public opinion and the majority of economic experts, rejected any policy involving budget deficits as 'unsound' and public works as 'ineffective'.

At the same time, the fact must not be ignored that the British balance of payments problem placed Great Britain in a very different position from that of the U.S.A. In the first place, it is practically certain that the adoption of an expansionist policy, based on public deficit expenditure, would in the conditions of Great Britain of 1931 have led to renewed large-scale capital flight; the success of such a policy would, therefore, in all probability have presupposed the imposition of exchange control of capital transactions. In the second place, there is no reason to assume that the adoption of such a policy would have enabled Great Britain to maintain her traditional free import policy. The effect of an autonomous British recovery would have been to raise British import demand and to aggravate the existing balance of payments deficit. In all likelihood, balance of payments difficulties would sooner or later have forced Great Britain to resort to import restrictions, whether in the form of further currency depreciation[1]

tariff was chiefly responsible for the relative decline of imports from Europe. The direction of British exports was changed to a much smaller degree by Imperial preference. The Dominions' share in British exports rose by only 5·5 per cent between 1929 and 1936, and the actual decline of British exports to the Dominions was almost as severe as that of British exports to Europe during this period. As regards the British balance of trade with the Empire, too, the results of Imperial preference were decidedly disappointing. In 1929, Great Britain had possessed a slight export surplus in her trade with the Empire. By 1936, this export surplus had been turned into an import surplus of £126 million which was paid for by interest and amortization payments on British investments in the Empire.

[1] Since further depreciation of the pound would probably have severely worsened Britain's terms of trade and might have been quite ineffective in correcting the deficit on her balance of payments on current account, it is probable that the adjustment would have had to take the form of selective

or direct import control.[1] An expansionist policy would, therefore, have involved a far greater extension of State intervention in the economy in Great Britain than it did in the
U.S.A. In all probability it would have meant the transformation
of the British economy into a largely State-controlled, if not
planned, economic system.

It may be argued that this would in fact have been the best
policy for Great Britain, both from her own point of view and
from that of the rest of the world. A vigorous and well-directed
policy of public works and public investment expenditure might
not only have produced a speedier recovery and alleviated the
problem of large structural unemployment in the depressed areas
which kept unemployment in Great Britain at one and a third
millions at the peak of the recovery; it would also have meant that,
instead of exercising an initial deflationary effect on other countries by cutting down imports in order to stimulate employment
at home, Great Britain would at most have had to prevent her
imports from increasing, as a result of her domestic recovery,
beyond what she could pay for by exports. Such import restrictions would probably not have had to be as severe as those imposed in 1932 and would have followed rather than preceded the
beneficial reflationary effects of the British recovery on the rest of
the world.

But it is futile to criticize the British Government for its failure
to adopt an expansionist policy of the New Deal type unless the
implications of such a policy in the circumstances of Great
Britain in 1931 are taken into account. It need hardly be added
that in 1931 these implications made such a policy politically
impossible internally, and even in the rest of the world Governments and public opinion might have resented such a transformation in Great Britain even more than they resented the policy
which was actually pursued.

import restriction, either by tariffs or quotas, or by the extension of exchange
control from capital transactions to import control.

[1] Theoretically, it might have been possible to avoid import restrictions by
covering the deficit on the British balance of payments by means of repatriation
of British foreign investments. On a relatively small scale, such repatriation
actually served during the nineteen-thirties to cover part of the British merchandise import surplus; and, for a country with such vast foreign capital assets,
this method, while clearly not feasible in the long run, might have been unob-
jectionable for a period of years. In practice, the mobilization of these assets
might have presented considerable difficulties. It is doubtful how far the attractions of investment in a Great Britain enjoying a rapid recovery would have
offset the deterrent effects of exchange control, state control of investment and
the other methods by which this recovery would have been brought about:
while the compulsory mobilization of foreign assets in peace-time would have
constituted a formidable administrative and political problem.

Chapter Five

FRANCE

IN 1930 the economic prosperity and financial strength of
France seemed to place her in a better position than any other
leading capitalist country to weather the storm of the great depression. As it turned out, France was the only country which
enjoyed no appreciable economic recovery throughout the following decade. For five years, from 1931 to 1935, the obstinate efforts
of successive Governments to maintain the gold standard by a
policy of deflation merely resulted in increasing economic depression, financial crises, political instability, and social unrest. In
1936 the victory at the polls of the *Front Populaire* put an end
to deflation. There followed nine months of hectic efforts to
promote recovery by an expansionist programme modelled on the
American New Deal. But errors of policy, political difficulties,
and other factors combined to deprive the Blum experiment of
what success it might otherwise have had. A brief revival of
economic activity in the latter half of 1936 was followed by another spell of stagnation; and in December 1937 the French
economy suffered renewed decline under the impact of the 1937
slump.

I. THE VICIOUS CIRCLE OF DEFLATION

FRANCE was at first not seriously affected by the world depression. The stabilization of the franc in 1928 at one-fifth of its
pre-war value had given France a flying start. With a price-level
considerably below that of her leading competitors France enjoyed an exceptionally strong economic and financial position.
French visible and invisible exports began to fall after 1929 with
the decline in world demand and the slump in the tourist trade.
But until 1931 France was to all intents and purposes untouched
by the depression. Industrial production actually continued to
increase until May 1930 and remained above the average level
of 1925-9 until well into 1931.[1] It was the series of defensive
measures adopted by other countries in the face of depression
and financial crisis, and in particular the waves of exchange
depreciations of 1931 and 1933 which started the French economy
on the downward path.

The depreciation of the pound and a group of other important
currencies in 1931 more than wiped out the competitive advan-

[1] League of Nations, *Review of World Production 1925-1931*, p. 50.

tage enjoyed by French exports owing to an undervalued currency—an advantage that had already been diminished by the slump in world prices. After 1931 France had to contend not merely with the decline in world demand for her products, rising tariff walls abroad, and increased competition from other countries seeking to push their exports, but in addition with a high level of French costs and prices in terms of the depreciated currencies of her competitors. This disparity between French and world prices was at the root of France's economic difficulties after 1931. Its direct effects were a gradually increasing strain on her balance of payments, internal economic depression, and growing budget deficits.

a. The balance of payments problem which bulked largest in most other countries at the beginning of the depression presented at first little difficulty in France. The French balance of trade (including services) did in 1931 become adverse for the first time since 1926. But this constituted at first no danger to the franc. France possessed an immense reserve of gold and foreign exchange, and during the first three years of the depression she shared with the U.S.A. in the function of serving as a haven of refuge for capital seeking security from exchange depreciation in the debtor countries. Far from losing gold, therefore, France between 1929 and 1932 actually doubled her gold reserve.[1] In 1932 the inflow of refugee and speculative capital was large enough to account for an addition of 700 million francs to her gold reserves in spite of the now adverse balance of trade of nearly 200 million francs.[2] After 1933 the position changed. The devaluation of the dollar widened the disparity between French and world prices, and, as the economic position of France deteriorated while other countries were beginning to recover, the flow of capital was reversed. Although the technical monetary position of France remained strong, the strain of a regular deficit on current account in her balance of payments, aggravated by periodic flights of capital and speculative attacks on the franc in anticipation of a possible devaluation, became after 1934 a constant threat.

b. The fall in visible and invisible exports put an end to French internal prosperity. France did not experience a sudden slump. But towards the end of 1931 industrial production began to decline, unemployment figures rose in spite of the peculiar safety valve of the repatriation of alien workers, agriculture suffered from the competition of cheap imports, and there were all the signs of an incipient depression.

c. The decline of economic activity in turn made it increasingly difficult to balance Government revenue and expenditure. Falling

[1] League of Nations, *Statistical Yearbook 1937–8*, p. 245.
[2] ibid., p. 212.

tax receipts and heavier expenditure on social relief resulted in growing budget deficits which, in view of the prevailing conceptions of sound public finance, reacted unfavourably on the one hand on business confidence and economic activity and, on the other hand, on confidence in the stability of the franc and on the balance of payments.

France's first reaction to the decline in her export trade and internal prosperity was, like that of most other countries, recourse to protectionist measures. French agriculture and industry had traditionally enjoyed tariff protection. But in 1927–8 France had consolidated 72 per cent of her tariffs in commercial treaties which could not be altered without delay and the risk of controversy. The emergency protectionist measures adopted by France, therefore, took the form of import quotas which were imposed on a wide range of imports and were freely used as bargaining weapons in trade negotiations. In August 1933 it was decided to reduce existing quotas to one fourth of their previous amount and to use the remaining three-fourths as bargaining counters. This ruthless method was immediately successful in some cases. But here, as elsewhere, protection led to reprisals. Heavy reductions of imports helped to diminish France's large import surplus and to alleviate the strain on her balance of payments. But import quotas could not solve the fundamental problem of the disparity between the level of French and world prices.

The simplest remedy would have been to readjust the level of French costs of production and prices in terms of gold by following the example of other countries, abandoning the gold standard and devaluing the franc. France, however, was in the fortunate or unfortunate position that owing to her immense gold reserves she was in no danger, at any rate until about 1934, of being *forced* off the gold standard. And devaluation as a voluntary recovery measure was barred by the popular fear of inflation and in particular by the opposition of the large class of small savers and *rentiers* on whom the Radical Socialist Governments depended for political support. Nor was France prepared to follow the example of Germany and impose exchange control. The result was that French economic policy was dominated until 1936 by the efforts of successive Governments to maintain the existing parity of the franc in the face of ever increasing difficulties.

The only alternative to the abandonment of the free gold standard was deflation. Cost reductions, it was hoped, would restore the profitability of private enterprise, price reductions would stimulate exports and relieve the strain on the balance of payments, and drastic reductions in public expenditure would enable the Governments to balance the budget. From 1931 until

E*

1934 prices and wages were slowly but continuously reduced and the Radical Governments made regular attempts to balance the budget. But no sooner, after a great effort, had some approach to equilibrium been achieved than fresh exchange depreciation elsewhere called for another. By 1934, after three years of gradual deflation, economic and political conditions were worse, the strain on the balance of payments greater and the budget problem more intractable than ever. France and the four other 'gold bloc' countries were now the only ones that still adhered to a free gold standard and they were most exposed to the deflationary pressure exerted by events in the rest of the world. For another two years National Governments in France struggled to maintain the franc by a policy of *déflation à outrance*. But deflation acted as a vicious spiral, with each of the three major economic troubles reacting back unfavourably on the other two.

a. By means of import restrictions and deliberate reductions of the internal price level, assisted after 1933 by rising foreign demand for French goods, the French Governments were able somewhat to improve the French balance of trade and to that extent relieve the strain on the balance of payments (though in the process the total value of French foreign trade declined to one-third of its 1929 level).[1] But the adverse balance of trade was the least important problem. The gravest menace to the stability of the franc consisted in the movements of 'hot money', and these were increased rather than diminished by the indirect effects of deflation. The problem became acute in 1934 with the return flow of capital to the U.S.A. following the stabilization of the dollar. Thereafter as economic activity declined and further deflation encountered increasing resistance, distrust of the stability of the franc—strengthened at intervals by political campaigns in favour of devaluation—led to a steady flight of capital which usually diminished when a new Government inspired confidence by an uncompromising affirmation of the deflationary policy and rose when a new budget deficit was revealed. Speculative attacks on the franc accompanied and aggravated these panic outflows of capital. As a result of these capital flights and private hoarding of gold, the gold holding of the Bank of France fell from 83,000 million francs in 1931 to 57,000 million francs at the time of the accession of the *Front Populaire* Government in 1936.[2] In ordinary circumstances 57,000 million francs' worth of gold would have been a more than sufficient safeguard. But by 1935 the recurrent crises had assumed such proportions that gold losses within a few weeks amounted to a considerable proportion of this

[1] J. C. de Wilde, *Political Conflict in France*, Foreign Policy Reports, 1 April 1936, p. 21.
[2] G. Peel, *The Economic Policy of France* (Macmillan, 1937), p. 41.

reserve. Moreover, each financial crisis heightened political instability, and had a further depressing effect on business confidence and economic activity.

b. Deflation, it was hoped, would stimulate recovery either by restoring profitability to private enterprise or by leading to a fall in interest rates and thus encouraging private investment. In fact it did neither. Money wages were cut between 1930 and 1935 by 12 per cent.[1] But cost reductions could never catch up with the decline in demand and prices which resulted from these very reductions in money wages, salaries, and the decrease in employment. On the other hand, though the cost of living fell slightly more than money wages,[2] and real earnings of employed manual workers increased, further efforts to reduce wages and salaries met with ever increasing resistance and political opposition from workers and government employees who resented the imposition of greater and greater sacrifices. Entrepreneurs, in turn, anticipating further falls in prices, tended to postpone new orders. Interest rates remained high, chiefly owing to capital exports, hoarding and the heavy demands of the Government on the credit facilities of the capital market. But even had interest fallen, as had been hoped, that in itself would have improved matters little in the circumstances. For profit expectations, depressed by constantly falling prices, social unrest and the regular budget deficits which were generally regarded as the clearest symptoms of France's economic disorder, were so low that interest rates would probably have had to be negative to encourage new investment. Economic activity, therefore, declined steadily. By 1935, the volume of industrial production had fallen off by one-third, the number of workers employed had fallen by one-fourth, the number of unemployed on relief had risen to half a million, and there was a steady rate of bankruptcies of well over a thousand a year.[3]

c. Deflation failed most obviously to solve the budget problem. Repeated drastic cuts of Government expenditure, primarily at the cost of Government employees, war veterans, and retired functionaries, aroused growing dissatisfaction and political opposition but were quite incapable of reducing the budget deficit. Total Government expenditure actually increased after 1933 as the serious international situation and the growth of unemployment called for larger expenditures on armaments and relief of distress. At the same time, tax revenue fell with the decline in economic activity and the Government had to cover the growing operating deficit of the State railways. The annual budget deficits, which

[1] League of Nations, *Statistical Yearbook 1937–8*, p. 70. The corresponding figure for Great Britain was 4 per cent.
[2] By 18 per cent; ibid., p. 290.   [3] J. C. de Wilde, loc. cit.

totalled 35,000 million francs for the years 1932-5,[1] were met by borrowing and resulted in an increase of the French national debt from 264 milliard francs in 1932 to 333 milliard at the end of 1935.[2] In different circumstances this large excess of Government expenditure over revenue might actually have helped to maintain purchasing power and economic activity. But it was not viewed in this light either by the French Governments or the French public. Both regarded the budget deficits as a calamity, and the mere fact that this view was generally held tended to make it true. The revelation of each new budget deficit had a depressing effect on business confidence and swelled the flight of capital abroad. The export and hoarding of money completely offset the potential favourable effect of the budget deficit in maintaining consumer purchasing power. Besides, capital flight and hoarding, and the general distrust in the credit of the Government, kept interest rates high and made Government borrowing increasingly difficult. Unable to obtain sufficient credit from private lenders the Governments had to rely on the Bank of France which, imbued with the principles of financial orthodoxy, coupled reluctant grants with demands for further deflation and other political conditions.

The last and most desperate attempt to balance the budget and promote recovery by deflation was made by the Laval Government in the latter half of 1935. By July 1935 price reductions in France and rising prices in the U.S.A. and Great Britain had narrowed the gap between French and foreign prices to about 9 per cent,[3] and a moderate devaluation of around 15-20 per cent might have been enough to start a recovery similar to that which had followed the devaluation of the Belgian currency a few months earlier. The Laval Government, however, armed with sweeping powers, embarked instead on the most drastic and thorough-going deflation. Five hundred and nineteen emergency decrees imposed a 10 per cent reduction in the expenditure of all public authorities, involving, with minor exceptions, a further flat 10 per cent cut in all salaries and wages, and similar cuts in interest rates and retail prices of some commodities, in order to lower the cost of living. It was hoped by these means to reduce the budget deficit by 11,000 million francs; but the reduction actually realized was only 6,460 million[4] and in June 1936 the budget deficit, partly owing to increased armaments expenditure, was again 6,500—7,000 million francs.[5] The efforts of the Government to reduce prices were even less successful. In order

---

[1] G. Peel, op. cit., p. 174.

[2] J. C. de Wilde, loc. cit.

[3] R. Marjolin, 'Reflections on the Blum Experiment', *Economica*, May 1938, p. 178.

[4] League of Nations, *World Economic Survey 1935-6*, p. 294.   [5] ibid.

to placate the farming population, who would not stand for further deflation, the Government took steps to raise farm prices by increasing Government agricultural subsidies and reinforcing quota restrictions on agricultural imports. The net result was a renewed widening of the gap between French and foreign prices and a progressive rise in the cost of living which fell heavily upon the workers. In the spring of 1936 popular discontent with the *'décrets de misère'* led to the sweeping victory at the polls of the left wing coalition of the *Front Populaire*, followed by the first wave of 'stay-in' strikes; and in June the Blum Government assumed office, pledged to repeal the decrees and reverse the policy of deflation.

II. THE BLUM EXPERIMENT

THE Blum experiment lasted from June 1936 until March 1937. In its essentials it was a repetition, in very much less favourable circumstances, of the American experiment of the New Deal. Like the New Deal, it was an attempt to solve the economic problem of the capitalist economy by methods which, while not theoretically incompatible with the smooth functioning of that system, rightly or wrongly aroused resentment, fear, and opposition among those on whose confidence and initiative that system chiefly depended. Like the New Deal, it began with measures designed to combine the promotion of economic recovery with the improvement of the standards of life and work of the masses of the population. If it failed to an extent to which the New Deal can never be said to have failed, it was not because its errors of policy were any greater but because the French social system lacked the resilience of the U.S.A., its economic resources were smaller and the degree of social cleavage was greater.

The Blum experiment consisted in the main of four policies which may be examined roughly in the order in which they were applied: (*a*) a policy of raising money wages; (*b*) devaluation of the franc; (*c*) a reflationary policy based mainly on public works; (*d*) the forty-hour week.

a. Raising Money Wages. The policy of raising wages and improving labour standards dominated the first stage of the Blum experiment. The choice of this particular—and, as the experience of the N.R.A. had shown, mistaken—form of expansionist policy by the Blum Government was, at the time of its assumption of office, no longer entirely voluntary. The Government was confronted by a sympathetic strike movement which had swept through France—the result of years of wage deflation, growing unemployment, and in 1936 rising costs of living. In the circumstances no Government could have resisted the demands of the workers without danger of provoking civil war. The Blum Government immediately prevailed upon the employers' organization to end the strike by conceding to the workers, in the Matignon Agreement, average wage increases of 12 per cent and the right of collective bargaining, and passed legislation introducing a forty-hour week and holidays with pay. The forty-hour week was not enforced until after September, and then gradually. But rapidly rising wage-rates and holidays with pay are estimated to have increased money earnings by 18 per cent to 20 per cent between June and September 1936.[1] The increase in real earnings and purchasing power, however, was nil; for as costs of production increased, prices rose in proportion.[2] In a closed economy this parallel rise of wages and prices would have meant merely that the policy was futile; it would have done neither harm nor good except possibly for its psychological effect on business confidence. In France, however, until the depreciation of the franc in September, the rise in French prices widened the gap between French and world prices which, for wholesale prices, amounted to 20 per cent in June and 27 per cent in September.[3] The increased disparity of price levels largely accounts for the further deterioration of economic conditions which took place during these three months. The volume of exports dropped by 6 per cent, industrial production (partly owing to holidays with pay) by 9 per cent, and unemployment increased by 6 per cent.[4] After September wages continued to rise, and the enforcement of the forty-hour week further increased wage-costs. But while the effect of these wage increases on purchasing power remained negligible[5] and was certainly not favourable to economic recovery, they probably

[1] R. Marjolin, op. cit., p. 178.

[2] Actually, since, as was pointed out above (see page 44 n. 1), wages constitute only one part, though the most important part, of costs, prices would have risen by a smaller percentage if it had not been for the fact that the costs of imported raw materials also rose, partly owing to the general rise in world prices, but chiefly owing to depreciation of the franc after September. As it happened, the rise in raw material prices over the whole period of the Blum experiment was exactly the same as the rise in wage-costs—about 60 per cent, and the rise in the wholesale prices of 60 per cent exactly reflected this rise in the costs of production. (M. Kalecki, 'The Lesson of the Blum Experiment', *Economic Journal*, March 1938, p. 27 f.)

[3] R. Marjolin, op. cit., p. 178.

[4] ibid., p. 179.

[5] This is probably an overstatement; for as a result of various Government measures—especially subsidies to farmers, the establishment of the Wheat Office which reduced the margin between the price of wheat and flour, rent control and stable transport costs (the Government covering the railways deficit) —retail prices and the cost of living rose much more slowly than wholesale prices (by about 27 per cent)—and over the period of the Blum experiment as a whole there was probably some redistribution of the national income in favour of the industrial workers and the 'big capitalists' at the expense of salaried employees and the fixed income groups. But it is doubtful whether this redistribution had, on balance, any favourable effect on consumers' demand (Kalecki, op. cit., pp. 29–35).

ceased in September to have an unfavourable influence on the
level of economic activity.

b. Devaluation. The electoral victory of the *Front Populaire*
had been the signal for a new and unprecedented flight of capital.
Between April and June fear of, and speculation on, a possible
devaluation by a left-wing Government pledged to end deflation
had resulted in the loss of more than 11 milliards of gold and
foreign exchange by the Bank of France.[1]

Many realized at the time that in the circumstances any
expansionist recovery policy such as was planned by the Blum
Government could not possibly be carried out without a devaluation of the franc and the imposition of exchange control to stop
capital exports. The Government, however, took its stand on the
slogan of 'neither devaluation nor deflation' and for three months
confined itself to measures designed to encourage dishoarding,
to secure voluntary repatriation of capital, and to check currency
speculation. During July and August the Government was able
to arrest the flight of capital. But by September the rise in prices
and universal lack of confidence in the franc had made devaluation inevitable. Having secured itself against retaliatory depreciation by the Tripartite Monetary Agreement with Great Britain
and the U.S.A., the Blum Government, therefore, decided on
26 September to abandon the gold standard and devalued the
franc by 25 per cent.

The devaluation of the franc was followed by a considerable
improvement in economic activity. Exports rose from October
1936 until April 1937 by 12 per cent, industrial production from
August until April by 13 per cent, and unemployment fell between
October and April by 17 per cent.[2] This improvement cannot be
wholly ascribed to the devaluation of the franc. The revival of
production in August was probably partly due to the settlement
of the strikes and the subsidence of industrial friction. The fact
that unemployment fell faster than production increased is partly
accounted for by the work-spreading effect of the forty-hour
week and holidays with pay. French exports were assisted by the
rapid recovery in the U.S.A. and Great Britain. But the favourable change in French prices relative to foreign prices which
resulted from the depreciation of the franc was undoubtedly the
main cause of the temporary recovery. In October 1936, French
wholesale prices were only 3 per cent above English, and French
retail prices 6 per cent below English.[3] Although wages continued
to rise and raw material prices rose at about the same rate there
was now nothing to prevent entrepreneurs from passing on these
cost increases to consumers in the form of higher prices.

[1] League of Nations, *World Economic Survey 1935–6*, p. 295.
[2] R. Marjolin, op. cit., p. 179 f.   [3] ibid., p. 179.

On the other hand, the abandonment of the gold standard did not in France put an end to the flights of capital as had been hoped. A few milliard francs returned to France, but the expected large-scale repatriation of French capital failed to materialize. A law passed in October, requiring the surrender of hoarded and exported gold, was neither obeyed nor enforced. A Government of the Left which refused to put down industrial disorder, which carried out radical labour reforms and pursued an 'inflationary' budget policy, did not inspire confidence in business men and bankers, who preferred to keep their money abroad. The flight of capital continued, and the interventions of the British and French Exchange Equilization Accounts, while they absorbed the pressure on the franc, also prevented the franc from falling sufficiently to make it worth while for speculators to bet on its recovery. In spite of the depreciation, therefore, gold losses during the following six months amounted to 7,000 million francs.[1]

These capital exports, in turn, completely defeated the reflationary policy of the Blum Government. As long as entrepreneurs were in a position to invest their money in foreign securities[2], even measures which succeeded in increasing effective demand were useless because entrepreneurs could react by raising prices rather than expanding output. In the circumstances of France in 1936 exchange control to prevent capital flight was an essential precondition of an expansionist recovery policy. Exchange control, which was violently opposed by financiers and business men as an unwarranted interference with private enterprise, might have had a further initial depressing effect on business confidence; but by closing foreign investment outlets it would almost certainly have led to a revival of internal investment in response to a vigorous expansionist policy. This was realized by the left wing of the Front Populaire, which throughout pressed for the imposition of exchange control. But the Blum Government never sum-

[1] J. C. de Wilde, 'The New Deal in France' *Foreign Policy Reports*, 1 September 1937, p. 148.

[2] Obviously, French francs were not 'sent abroad' as the phrase goes. They were invested in foreign securities, but this meant merely that they changed hands within France. Both the failure of internal investment activity and capital exports were the result of low profit, or rather high risk, expectations in France. But capital exports not only provided an alternative investment outlet for liquid funds which had no favourable effect on the level of economic activity in France; they actually discouraged new investments in France both because they depressed the price of French securities sold in exchange for foreign securities (i.e. forced up the rate of interest) and because the desire for liquidity on the part of large numbers of persons may have tended to lower consumption expenditure. (All this applies, of course, only to sporadic capital flights; a continued flow of capital will, provided the country is off the gold standard, depress its rate of exchange in terms of other currencies: if capital exports continue long enough and the demand for the country's exports is sufficiently elastic to allow an expansion of exports as a result of the depreciation of the currency, the effect on home activity will also be favourable though the country's terms of trade are likely to deteriorate.)

moned up enough courage to take the step in the face of the opposition of its Radical Socialist supporters and the Bank of France and in the knowledge that London would view it with disapproval. The failure to impose exchange control at the very beginning of its term of office deprived the third policy of the Blum Government, its reflationary measures of Government deficit expenditure, of all efficacy.

c. *Government Deficit Expenditure*. The reflationary measures of the Blum Government were even less than the corresponding measures of the first year of the New Deal based on any conscious policy of compensatory budget deficits. The Blum Government hardly differed from its opponents among bankers and business men in considering budget deficits an evil. But it was determined to break the vicious circle of deflation—even at the cost of increased deficits. It therefore proceeded at once to restore in part the cuts in Government salaries, pensions, and veterans' allowances of the Laval decrees, and, in order to reduce unemployment, launched an extensive programme of public works which contemplated an expenditure of 20,000 million francs over a three-year period. Government expenditure was further increased by the application of the new social legislation to the railways and other state enterprises and by increased expenditure on armaments. The Government also had to cover the continued post office deficit. The result of these measures was a considerable excess of expenditure over receipts which was met by borrowing. In view of the misleading French system of budget accountancy, the actual deficits for the period of the Blum experiment are hard to gauge, but it has been estimated that, compared with the deficit of 21·2 milliard francs for 1936, the rate of Government expenditure during the first months of 1937 would have led to a total deficit for 1937 of 33·6 milliard francs.[1]

Budget deficits of this order might have been expected to provide a substantial stimulus to recovery by adding to consumers' purchasing power and demand. In fact, the real net contribution to purchasing power of the Blum Government was considerably smaller than the budget figures suggest, and it was cancelled out by the capital exports for which it was in part responsible. As prices rose the real effect of the increase in the budget deficit was *pro tanto* diminished. If the fall in the purchasing power of the franc is taken into account it appears that the real effect of the Government's net contribution was equivalent to an increase of only five milliard francs,[2] or 2½ per cent of the national income.[3] Contrary to the general view held at the

---

[1] M. Kalecki, op. cit., p. 38.   [2] ibid., p. 37.
[3] In the U.S.A. the Federal net contribution to purchasing power during the years 1933-6 was equivalent to about 5 per cent of the national income.

time, therefore, the reflationary measures of the Blum Government were in reality very moderate and probably in any case insufficient to stimulate business activity appreciably. In practice even the limited effect which these measures might have had was completely offset by the flight of capital. Up to a point this process was almost automatic. Apart from their general political opposition to the Blum regime it was their prejudice against 'inflation' and their view that budget deficits must lead to further currency depreciation which induced those who had capital to export to send their money abroad.[1]

As a result, to quote a forceful if somewhat misleading picture of the situation, 'a new franc put on the market was a franc which was promptly exchanged for sterling or for the money of some other country with a relatively stable political and monetary régime'.[2] Given the psychological and political circumstances of France, it is arguable that a cautious reflationary policy did more harm than good, since it did more to discourage private investment by depressing 'business confidence' than to encourage private investment by increasing effective consumers' demand—though the same would not be true of a really drastic expansionist policy based on public works and supplemented if necessary by some direct control of private investment. It is certain that without exchange control any reflationary measures were senseless.

d. The Forty-Hour Week. If the policy of raising money-wages was futile as a method of promoting economic recovery, the other half of the Blum programme of social reform, the work-spreading legislation, and particularly the forty-hour week, were probably a grave error. The flood of abuse which was heaped on the Blum Government after the event[3] by its reactionary opponents makes one more than ever reluctant to pass this judgement on what, on the face of it, appeared as an eminently desirable and progressive measure. But all the evidence goes to show that in the peculiar circumstances of France this particular method of improving the living conditions of the masses was incompatible with the economic recovery of France.

[1] The prejudice against budget deficits and the fear of 'inflation' were also largely responsible for another major obstacle to the expansionist policy of the Blum Government. The belief that the Government was heading for bankruptcy made private banks and other potential private lenders reluctant to lend it money. In striking contrast to the ease with which the Roosevelt Administration and the British National Government had been able to borrow, the Blum Government experienced constant difficulties in obtaining sufficient credit to cover the budget deficit and was forced to pay high interest. Moreover, the flight of capital, coupled with the increased demand for money resulting from the rise in wage-rates and prices, tended to keep interest rates high and prevented the application of a cheap-money policy.

[2] R. Marjolin, op. cit.

[3] At the time, in the summer of 1936, even the conservative Senate passed the forty-hour week law by large majorities (H. W. Ehrmann, 'The Blum Experiment and the Fall of France', *Foreign Affairs*, October 1941, p. 154 f.).

In so far as the forty-hour week and holidays with pay were not merely social reforms but parts of the recovery programme of the *Front Populaire*, their object was to 'spread work' and thus reduce the number of unemployed. In many other countries including the U.S.A. and Germany, 'work-spreading' measures had proved an effective short-term remedy to the most calamitous aspect of the economic depression, large-scale unemployment. In France the very object of 'work-spreading' was wrong except possibly as a short-term relief measure. For France never had an unemployment problem comparable to that of the other large industrial countries. For various reasons, chiefly the repatriation of foreign labour, the return to the land of many industrial unemployed and the decline in the natural increase of the French working population, French unemployment had never risen in proportion to the decline in economic activity. At its worst unemployment in France affected only 2·2 per cent of the total population as compared with 5·6 per cent in Great Britain, 11 per cent in the U.S.A. and 9·2 per cent in Germany. In 1936, short of a return to French industry of labour from abroad and from French agriculture, or a quite improbable increase in productivity, or a lengthening of working hours (which would probably have been ineffective because it would have lowered productivity), the total available labour supply was far below what was necessary in order to enable French industrial production to regain the pre-depression level. The situation was aggravated by the fact that French industry, grown apathetic through years of deflation and depression, had failed to maintain the reserve of skilled labour by taking on and training apprentices. As a result there was, on top of the shortage of total labour supply, a disproportionate shortage of skilled labour. In these circumstances, legislation which like the forty-hour week law and holidays with pay in effect reduced the available supply of labour[1] to little more than was necessary to sustain the volume of production at the lowest level of the depression, was bound to put an early end to recovery.

After a tardy beginning in September 1936, the forty-hour week law began to be enforced indiscriminately in the first months of 1937. By the beginning of February the law already applied to nearly two-thirds of all workers in establishments with more than 100 workers, and by June 1937 all but 40,873 (or 1·2 per cent) were subject to it.[2] The result was what should have been expected had the situation been correctly appreciated. In

---

[1] The forty-hour week in itself would have been relatively harmless if overtime had been permitted, in which case it would have been equivalent to a further increase in money wages. In fact, overtime, though not generally prohibited, was virtually excluded by prohibitive overtime rates.

[2] Marjolin, op. cit., p. 187.

March 1937, with a volume of production not much above the lowest level of the depression, France was rapidly approaching a state of 'full employment'. The forty-hour week law at one stroke eliminated partial employment. At the same time, unemployment, which had fallen from a maximum of 833,000 in March 1936 to about 400,000 to 500,000 at the beginning of 1937,[1] was no longer large enough to provide the labour market with the elasticity needed for a further expansion of production. The capital goods industries in particular were hampered by scarcity of skilled labour. In the first half of 1937 a large number of industries were unable to carry out all the orders they received and several were working at full capacity.

It was the artificially induced shortage of labour supply rather than the reversal of Government policy in February 1937 which put an end to the short-lived recovery of the previous six months. During the first months of the new year the recrudescence of distrust in the franc and of capital flight, continued industrial friction, a new strike wave, the rising budget deficit, and increased difficulty in finding credit to cover it, had made it obvious that something had to be done to meet the situation. At the end of February the Blum Government, pressed by the Left to take measures against the capitalists and impose exchange control, and by the Right to restore business confidence, capitulated to the latter and decided upon the virtual abandonment of its expansionist policy. Between January and June 1937 no further money was borrowed by the Government from the Bank of France. In practice, however, although the Government ceased to borrow, the scale of State armaments and investment expenditure does not seem to have been greatly reduced;[2] and, in any case, owing to the failure to impose exchange control a reduction of deficit expenditure was not likely to affect economic conditions any more than an increase, both being offset by capital movements.[3] On the other hand, the shortage of labour supply did prevent further recovery, and would have done so even if exchange control had made a continued reflationary policy effective. In spite of a further improvement in the ratio between French and foreign prices and in spite of the favourable influence of the boom conditions in Great Britain and the U.S.A., the French recovery which had followed the devaluation of the franc in September 1936 came to a stop in the spring of 1937. From April

[1] Marjolin, op. cit., p. 185.   [2] M. Kalecki, op. cit., p. 37.

[3] Actually it is very doubtful whether the unfavourable effect on economic activity of a substantial reduction in the Government net contribution would have been as completely offset by dishoarding and repatriation of capital as the favourable effect of increases in the net contribution was offset by capital flight and hoarding. In this case, however, the repatriation of funds that did take place (about five milliard in gold between March and June 1937) was probably sufficient to counteract the small actual reduction in Government expenditure.

onwards exports fell and the level of unemployment and industrial production remained stationary until October of that year,[1] when the contagion of the American slump resulted in a renewed decline.

The failure of the Blum experiment was not entirely or even mainly due to specific errors of policy, whether it be the forty-hour week legislation or the failure to impose exchange control. Any such interpretation is too narrow. The *Front Populaire* Government was brought to power by a popular revulsion against the hopeless and helpless policy of deflation. Its platform was above all to put an end to wage-cutting, unemployment and poverty, to raise the purchasing power and standard of living of the French workers. It incidentally included policies which, like the shortening of working hours, had for decades been among the legitimate aspirations of the industrial workers but which were disastrously inapplicable in the particular conditions of France in 1936, whatever the economic system. But this is almost unimportant as compared with the fact that the French capitalists were opposed to any such measures partly because they were in a better position to appreciate their effect, partly because these policies conflicted with their views of soundness and orthodoxy, partly because they saw in them an attack on their privileges. They therefore reacted by 'loss of confidence' and ca'canny. The Blum experiment failed because, in the circumstances of France, with an industrial working class exasperated by years of economic misery and Governmental bungling and a capitalist class prepared to use all methods at their disposal to sabotage a policy which they considered disastrous not only to themselves but to the country as a whole, only one of two policies could have succeeded. *Either* the Blum Government should have insisted on its radical policy, even if it meant forcing the capitalists into submission, by exchange control and more vigorous measures if necessary, *or* it should have provided the conditions in which the mainspring of the capitalist economy, the profit motive of the entrepreneurs, would effectively function. In practice it wavered between these two policies—partly no doubt because it feared, rightly or wrongly, that either policy ruthlessly pursued might lead to a degree of civil discord which would weaken France still further in a menacing international situation: on the one hand, it pushed forward its radical social reforms and deficit public works expenditure regardless of their effect on 'business confidence', it brandished the weapons of socialism and refused to suppress the strikes with the vigour recommended by the Right; on the other

---

[1] The index of industrial production actually fell from 105 in April to 100 in October; but this decline was probably accounted for by holidays with pay. (Marjolin, op. cit., p. 181.)

hand, it refused to impose exchange control and take whatever other measures were necessary to ensure the success of its policy.

The successors of the Blum Government in 1938 and 1939 firmly clasped the second horn of the dilemma: they sought to restore business confidence. The renunciation by the Blum Government in February 1937 of its reflationary policy and of any control of capital exports had been the first step in this direction, but it had failed either to solve the budget problem or to stop the flight of capital. In June 1937 its successor, after a renewed depreciation of the franc, went a step further by a policy of budgetary retrenchment which was greeted with satisfaction by business, but the autumn slump resulted in a new and severe setback, industrial production declining steadily from eighty-five in November to about sixty in August 1938.[1] In May 1938, however, the fact that French prices at last ceased to rise further, made possible the stabilization of the franc at the parity of 179 francs to the pound; and in November of that year the Daladier-Reynaud Government firmly set the new course by a series of financial reforms including heavy additional indirect taxation and civil budget economy; reduction of taxes that weighed on private investments; relaxation of price controls which hampered private enterprise; modification of the forty-hour week by the abolition of the five-day week, and reduction of overtime pay to non-prohibitive rates; extension of hours of work up to a sixty-hour week in the armaments industry; repayment of loans to the Bank of France out of windfall profits earned by the revaluation of gold reserves at the new parity; new borrowing from the bank (but no Government competition in the private capital market); and a cheap money policy (made possible by the steady return flow of capital from abroad in response to the stabilization of the franc and these reforms themselves). At the same time, economic activity was carried forward by an enormous increase in armament expenditure to an estimated amount of 46,032 million francs in 1939.[2]

Economically, the new policy was a success. Capital exports ceased and were replaced by a steady repatriation of capital from abroad. The Government was able to push down interest rates, the discount rate falling to 2 per cent in January 1939;[3] and from December 1938 industrial production increased rapidly. But not only was this success largely accounted for by that form of Government deficit expenditure which was alone without ill effect on business confidence, namely rearmament; it is impossible to judge the results of the break-up of the *Front Populaire* and

[1] League of Nations, *Statistical Yearbook 1937-8, 1938-9.*
[2] League of Nations, *World Economic Survey 1938-9*, p. 29.
[3] ibid., p. 28.

the new conservative course solely in economic terms. The destruction of the *Front Populaire* at the hands of the Conservatives left the industrial working class resentful and embittered and left the direction of French industry and finance in the hands of men who, while able for a time to run the economy successfully on their own terms, were prepared to deliver themselves up to Hitler rather than risk the danger of another attempt from below to oust them from their position of privilege.

Chapter Six

GERMANY: INTERNAL POLICY

THE general record of the Nazi régime in Germany tempts one to feel that there is but one economic lesson to be drawn from it: the necessity of removing the economic causes—economic insecurity, international economic disorder, and maldistribution of wealth—which were largely responsible for the rise of the Nazis to power. Even on a different level of argument, it seems that little can be learnt from an economic régime in which economic and commercial policy was completely subordinated to political objectives—preparation for war and the maintenance of the Nazi régime—in which the primary stimulus of economic activity was rearmament, and which achieved economic results within the framework of a repressive political system. Yet, positively and negatively, the economic development of Nazi Germany is at least as instructive as the economic experiences of the more orthodox capitalist countries during the nineteen-thirties. The Nazis alone achieved complete economic recovery, in the sense of the full use of all available productive resources, by means of an expansionist monetary policy. How far was this success due to the expenditure of economic effort on armaments rather than on an increasing standard of living? How far did it depend on the progressive imposition of controls on every phase of economic activity? Again, the Nazis developed a number of economic techniques—in the sphere of Government finance, planned State intervention, exchange control and the manipulation of foreign trade—which *mutatis mutandis* may well be applicable in a worthier cause.

I. THE GERMAN RECOVERY

WHEN Hitler was installed in power in January 1933 the German economy was still in a state of almost complete collapse. Since 1928 the national income had declined from 75·4 to 45·2 milliard RM.[1] The volume of industrial production was still nearly 40 per cent (in the investment goods industries 50 per cent) below the 1929 level[2] though it seemed to have passed the bottom of the depression in the autumn of 1932. Above all, some six to seven million German workers were unemployed. By 1938

---

[1] T. Balogh, 'The National Economy of Germany', *Economic Journal*, September 1938, p. 462.
[2] ibid., p. 463.

the Nazi régime could claim one outstanding achievement: unemployment had virtually disappeared and had in fact given way to an acute shortage of skilled labour; and industrial production was 25 per cent above the level of 1929. Measured by the yardstick of the employment of productive resources and the volume of production Germany had achieved full recovery. Our first task must be to explain this achievement.

The explanation is in essence very simple. The German recovery was brought about by a large and ever-increasing flow of Government investment expenditure. No official figures of public expenditure under the Nazi régime are available. But the best estimates show that total public expenditure rose from 6·7 milliard RM in 1932–3 to 9·7 milliard in 1933–4 and continued to rise at an increasing pace until 1938–9 it reached the immense figure of 31·5 milliard RM—equivalent to nearly half the total national income.[1] It was public investment expenditure on public works and armaments which, directly and through its effect on private investment, lifted the German economy out of the depression during the first two years of the Nazi régime; and it was Government expenditure on armaments, reinforced by State-controlled private investment, which after 1935 carried the economy to full recovery, maintained economic activity, and actually absorbed an increasing proportion of the nation's productive resources.

For a more detailed analysis of the process by which this flood of additional public expenditure stimulated economic activity it is necessary to distinguish between the first two years of 'work-creation' and the period of rearmament and war economy which began towards the end of 1934.

When the Nazis came to power they realized that their régime was bound up with their success or failure in dealing with the desperate economic position of the country and that the touchstone of success would be their ability to get rid of unemployment. During 1933 and 1934, therefore, Nazi economic policy concentrated on the task of stimulating economic activity of any kind and using every conceivable method of reducing the unemployment figures. In pursuit of this objective the Nazis characteristically did not rely on monetary measures alone. They resorted to innumerable devices of putting the unemployed directly to some work somehow. Considerable numbers were taken off the labour market by the introduction of compulsory labour service, a compulsory year on the land, and a vigorous campaign against the employment of women. Many also were absorbed by the rapidly growing (State and Party) bureaucracy and, probably even before the introduction of conscription in 1935, by the army.

[1] These are the figures given in J. Strachey, *Programme for Progress*, p. 266. They are based on other estimates.

Strong pressure was put on employers to increase or change their staff uneconomically. Short-time was enforced in some industries. Even wage-control may partly have been intended as a work-spreading measure.

All these measures were extremely important during the first two years in that they enabled Hitler to claim quick success in the reduction of unemployment. Even before the introduction of compulsory military service in 1935, the absorption of unemployed outside industrial production accounted for 1·5 million men—more than half the total reduction in unemployment during this period. But it would be wrong to infer from this that they constituted an essential part of the Nazi achievement of recovery. For these direct measures were coupled with an expansionist monetary policy which, based at first mainly on public works and later incidental to rearmament, was on a scale more than sufficient to abolish unemployment.

During the work-creation period additional public expenditure took three main forms:

a. In contrast to the New Deal, the Nazis did not resort to pure relief expenditure over and above the existing system of unemployment relief. Some of the additional public expenditure, such as that incurred by the measures just mentioned—especially the money spent on increased Government pay, the small sums paid to the labour service, and the system of marriage loans—did distribute purchasing power directly to consumers and, like relief expenditure, stimulate economic activity only by increasing effective demand. The indirect effect of this expenditure was probably not negligible. But the distribution of money was here incidental to the major objective of reducing unemployment directly (apart from the various other purposes which these measures served), and the public expenditure involved never formed a major proportion of total additional expenditure.

b. Some of the additional public expenditure went on financial assistance to private industry. Again in contrast to the U.S.A. (at any rate under Hoover) this financial assistance took the form, not of unconditional loans, but partly of state subsidies, partly of tax relief for certain specified forms of private investment (the former mainly for house repair and building, the latter mainly for replacement and extension of factories and machinery). This system of indirect incentives had formed the main part of the expansionist policy on which the last two pre-Nazi Governments had embarked in 1932. They had undoubtedly had some effect in stimulating private investment, though they had come too late to save the remnant of the Weimar Republic and though the Nazis reaped most of the benefit. The latter continued to use this method of stimulating recovery during 1933 and 1934. Since the

grants of financial assistance were conditional upon the undertaking of new investment their economic effects differed little
from direct public investment, though the latter was probably
the quicker and more certain method. The pre-Nazi Governments had preferred indirect incentives because they interfered
less with private enterprise. The Nazis were more concerned to
produce quick results than to preserve private initiative. From
the beginning they shifted the emphasis from indirect incentives
to direct public investment expenditure. In their policy towards
private investment activity regulatory, and later even restrictive,
State control gradually replaced indirect financial inducements.

c. From the start the bulk of the additional public expenditure
of the Nazis took the form of direct public investment expenditure. More than half of the five milliard RM expended under
the work creation programme of 1933-5 was spent on public
works schemes for the construction of strategic motor roads,
ordinary roads, public buildings, waterways, state railways, land
improvement, etc. In addition, it seems that already in 1933 and
1934 secret rearmament helped to supplement the official public
works programme, though it is unlikely that rearmament expenditure became an important factor before about November
1934.

By the end of 1934 the Nazi Government had spent at least five
milliard RM on top of normal budget expenditure. Of this total
about three milliard had taken the form of direct public investment expenditure (mainly on public works) which served directly
to bring into use idle factors of production. Moreover, the whole
of this additional expenditure had created new effective consumers' demand and had thus given a further indirect stimulus
to private investment.[1] By December 1934, before the indirect
effect of the work-creation programme had made itself fully felt,[2]
unemployment had fallen by more than three million, the
volume of industrial production had increased by 30 per cent,[3]

[1] The experience of the Blum experiment in France has shown that even a
large volume of additional Government expenditure may be completely ineffective
in stimulating economic activity if the increase in purchasing power is offset by
flight of capital. In Germany the expansionist recovery policy of the Nazi
Government was from the beginning safeguarded against this danger by
exchange control. The Nazis did not have to introduce exchange control, which
had existed in Germany since the financial crisis of 1931; and in the Nazi
economy prevention of capital flight was only one, and almost an incidental,
function of exchange control. But it is almost certain that in the inflation
psychosis of Germany capital flight would have developed when the Nazis
began to reflate on an unprecedented scale. There can, therefore, be little doubt
that for this purpose alone exchange control was an essential precondition of the
German recovery.
[2] This qualification is important, though, as will be seen presently, Government policy after 1934 was increasingly calculated to prevent this indirect effect
of public expenditure on private consumption and investment.
[3] T. Balogh, op. cit., p. 463.

and private gross investment had risen from 440 million RM in 1932 to 1,070 million.[1]

It is probable that from this point onwards no further *increase* in the rate of Government expenditure would have been required to carry the German economy forward to full employment. It is even conceivable that the Nazi Government could have abandoned any additional public expenditure once the work-creation programme was completed, in the hope that private activity, stimulated by this large dose of public expenditure and by a revival of German exports with the progress of world recovery, would absorb the remaining unemployed reserve of labour. We shall revert later to this important hypothetical question. The fact is that in 1935 economic recovery and 'work-creation' ceased to be the main objects of Nazi economic policy; they were replaced by preparation for war and economic self-sufficiency. As a result the rate of public expenditure of the first two years of the Nazi régime was not only maintained after 1934 but increased by leaps and bounds. During the three years between 1934–5 and 1937–8 annual public expenditure is estimated to have risen from 12·2 milliard RM to 22·0 milliard RM.[2] During approximately the same period public gross investment (almost entirely on rearmament) increased from 4·1 milliard RM to about 8–9 milliard RM.[3] To this should be added the increase in private gross investment (from 1·07 milliard RM in 1934 to 2·1 milliard in 1936)[4] which for the most part would undoubtedly have taken place in any case under the influence of derived demand though it was actually increasingly subject to, and directed by, State control.

It is not surprising that this enormous public expenditure and private investment activity quickly absorbed the remaining reserve of unemployment and carried economic activity in Germany to the limit of her resources. In fact, from 1934 onwards, the problem for the Nazi Government was no longer primarily how to absorb idle factors of production but how to ensure that what idle resources remained were absorbed into the industries producing armaments (and many goods, or substitutes for goods, previously imported from abroad)[5] rather than into industries

[1] T. Balogh, op. cit., p. 466.   [2] J. Strachey, *Programme for Progress*, p. 266.
[3] T. Balogh, op. cit., p. 466.   [4] ibid.
[5] The policy of 'autarky', of rendering Germany as far as possible independent of foreign imports, was from the beginning part of Nazi economic policy and it became a very important factor in the German economy with the Second Four Year Plan of self-sufficiency which was launched in 1936. Its significance will be discussed in greater detail in connection with German foreign trade policy. Here it is sufficient to point out that—except in so far as it was merely an attempt to overcome the actual shortage of foreign raw materials—its function in the process of recovery was similar to that of rearmament, though on a smaller scale. Like rearmament (or, on a closer analogy, like protectionism in other countries, including Great Britain) it promoted the German recovery by enlarging the

catering for civilian consumption demand. As time went on, it even became necessary to divert labour and capital already employed in producing 'unnecessary' consumption goods to the production of armaments and other 'vital' industries. The economic problem for the Nazi Government after 1934 became the problem familiar to people in this country in the shape of 'war economics'. It was solved by the Nazis by the gradual extension of central control to almost every form of economic activity and every corner of the economic system.

II. THE CONTROLLED ECONOMY

THE development of economic controls, like most other aspects of Nazi economic policy, followed no clear or preconceived plan. Regulations were issued, new offices of control and supervision were set up, as and when they became necessary. If it was found, as was usually the case, that the first set of regulations had been rendered ineffective by loopholes, new regulations were issued and new offices set up. What was lacking in forethought was made up by drive and ingenuity—and the Gestapo. Some of the most important systems of control completely changed their functions as the Nazi system developed. Wage control, imposed during the first months of the régime, partly at least, with the object of establishing a minimum wage level in the depressed industries, became (next to taxation) the chief method of keeping down consumption and preventing inflation. Control of the capital market, imposed in 1933 primarily to facilitate Government borrowing, became an instrument for the control of private investment. Most striking of all was the transformation of exchange control, imposed in 1931 by the Brüning Government as an emergency measure for the protection of the German currency and balance of payments, into one of the pivots of the whole system.

Behind this transformation was the acute shortage of foreign raw materials which from 1934 onwards lay like a millstone round the neck of the German economy. The causes of this shortage, which was only partly due to Germany's own policy, will be analysed in the following chapter. Its effects were extraordinarily far-reaching. On the one hand, it provided a motive, at least as urgent as strategic and ideological considerations, for the policy of self-sufficiency. On the other hand, it constituted the main driving force, as well as the most powerful weapon, for the extension of State control of the economic system. It was the need to

home market for German industry and agriculture; but like rearmament it was for political reasons (security from blockade) carried much further than economic motives warranted and necessitated the increasing curtailment of consumption in favour of investment.

ration scarce foreign raw materials which forced the Government to assume direct control of production even before the economy reached a state of full employment of productive resources in general. The dependence of most important industries on some foreign raw materials, in turn, put the entrepreneurs at the mercy of the exchange control authorities whose function it was to issue import permits. As a result, exchange and import control, as will appear presently, became the starting-point for most of the real, as opposed to the monetary, controls of the internal economy.

It is impossible to describe here in any detail the incredibly complicated institutional framework of the Nazi controlled economy. All that can be done is to outline the main types of control and the purposes they served. Leaving aside for the present the control of Germany's foreign trade and balance of international payments, the State controls that became necessary with the determination of the Nazis to rearm and render Germany self-sufficient at all costs, may be divided into two broad categories, control of consumption (by control of money incomes, on the one hand, and price control, on the other) and control of investment. In 1937 and 1938 the growing shortage of labour added to these two types of control yet a third, the control of the supply of labour.

a. Control of Consumption. Control of consumption was implicit in the decision to direct labour and capital from the production of consumers' goods to the production of investment goods. It meant that money incomes, increasingly earned in the production of capital goods, such as armaments, machines, factories, would grow much faster than the output of consumers' goods on which these incomes could be spent, a process which was sooner or later bound to lead to inflation. Now from a purely economic point of view, inflation, provided it was not allowed to get out of hand, might have served as effectively as rigid control of money incomes and prices to reduce real incomes and consumption demand. The Nazis might, therefore, have contented themselves, at least until a state of full employment was reached, with the modicum of control necessary to prevent a run-away inflation, and might have relied on the automatic working of inflationary price increases to keep down consumption expenditure.[1] For the Nazis, however, this course was ruled out by political considerations. Quite apart from the undesirable redistribution of income which it would have involved, the popular memory of the catastrophic German post-war inflation and the fear that rising prices would make it impossible to keep wages down without producing

[1] In the third year of the war the policy of allowing price increases, so as to reduce civilian consumption, was actually advocated in the German economic Journal, *Der Deutsche Volkswirt*; cf. H. W. Singer, 'The German War Economy in German Periodicals', *Economic Journal*, April 1941, p. 28.

severe social unrest, made it politically essential for the Nazi Government to prevent inflation at all costs. It was the fear of inflation which provided the most urgent motive for direct control of consumption and which, in particular, necessitated the extension of control from money incomes to prices and production.

i. Control of Money Incomes. The increase in money incomes which would otherwise have resulted from the continued growth of public and private investment expenditure was limited partly by taxation, partly by wage control.

During the great depression the last Republican Governments had, in pursuance of their deflationary policy, increased taxation to an extraordinarily high level. If the policy of the Nazis had been to raise the standard of living of the German people they would have lowered taxation as the tax yield increased with growing recovery. The Nazis, on the contrary and in violation of all promises, not only maintained taxation at depression level but even increased some taxes such as the tax on corporations, which was raised by 50 per cent. In 1932, at the end of several years of drastic deflation, taxation (including social insurance contributions) had already amounted to 25·4 per cent of the national income. By 1938, after five years of rapid recovery, this figure had been *raised* to 29·5 per cent.[1] While the increases in the rates of taxation that were made by the Nazis probably fell more heavily on higher incomes (which would largely have been saved) the bulk of this tax burden continued to be borne by the poorer classes who would otherwise have spent, or tried to spend, their increased earnings.[2] It is, therefore, clear that the Nazis maintained taxation at this level not only to absorb what would otherwise have been savings but also to limit any increase in consumption.

Taxation was from the beginning of the Nazi régime supplemented by rigid control of wage rates. As early as May 1933 the trade unions were suppressed and labour 'trustees' were appointed. During the first two years, as has been mentioned, wage stabilization was exercised largely with a view to establishing a minimum wage level in the depressed industries by ironing out wage anomalies and levelling up the wages of many classes of workers whom the trade union organization had left without adequate protection. This was in accordance with the general monetary policy of the Nazis in the expansionist phase, and with the 'socialistic' pose in their propaganda. But the wage earners constituted the largest class of potential consumers, and from 1934 onwards rigid measures to resist workers' pressure for

[1] T. Balogh, op. cit., p. 470 n. 4.

[2] Figures given by Mr. Balogh show that in 1928–9 51·3 per cent and in 1937–8 52·4 per cent of the total tax revenue was derived from taxes 'mainly on labour' (op. cit., p. 471).

wage increases (and after 1938, when full employment had been reached, even attempts of employers to attract workers by higher wages) became essential if inflation was to be avoided. Stabilization of wage rates alone did not, of course, prevent an increase in the money earnings of the working class as a whole, which rose by 8·7 milliard RM between 1933 and 1937.[1] But most of this increase was due to the increase in the number employed, the lengthening of working hours, and the promotion of workers into higher-paid categories. Only 13·4 per cent of the total increase was due to a rise in wage rates.[2]

ii. Price Control. The stabilization of wages, as we have seen, politically necessitated the extension of control to prices and production. The first extensive measures of price control had already been taken by the last Republican Governments as part of their deflationary policy. The Nazis at first attempted to confine themselves to restricting retail price increases. But it was obviously impossible to control prices without regulating costs. Step by step, therefore, the Government was forced to extend regulation to the whole cost structure. The most important element of cost was, of course, already taken care of by wage control. Control of raw material prices was first introduced in the case of imported raw materials, the exchange control authorities simply attaching price conditions to grants of import permits. By the end of 1934 price control had been extended to most home-produced raw materials, either on the basis of existing cartel agreements or in connection with agricultural price policy. The third element of costs, middlemen's profits, was regulated at first by fixing proportionate and later by imposing absolute profit margines. Exchange control was also deliberately used to reduce to a minimum fluctuations in the prices of imported commodities which could not be controlled. In 1936, under the pressure of rapidly rising world raw material prices and the intensification of investment under the Second Four Year Plan, the piecemeal system of price control which had grown up was replaced by a centralized system under a new Commissioner for the Formation of Prices, and in the 'Price Stop' Decree of November of that year price increases of any kind whatever (excepting wages and the capital and money markets which were separately controlled) were prohibited except by special Government permit.

In practice, prices of individual commodities were not kept rigidly stable. On the contrary, comprehensive price control

---

[1] T. Balogh, op. cit., p. 472.

[2] ibid., p. 472. Limitation of wage earnings was paralleled by limitation of dividends which was introduced in 1934. But it is most unlikely that a limitation of dividends to 8 per cent or even 6 per cent made any difference to the consumption expenditure of the owners of shares. The chief object and effect of the measure was to control investment.

made possible the use of planned price changes as an instrument for the direction of production and consumption. This method was used particularly in agricultural price policy. Agricultural prices had fallen disproportionately low during the depression; and during 1933 and 1934 the Nazis, in pursuance of their policy of assisting domestic agriculture both for social reasons and in order to promote self-sufficiency in the production of foodstuffs,[1] were primarily concerned to raise agricultural prices. By 1934, with the assistance of a poor harvest, that immediate object had been attained.[2] Henceforth, the general level of agricultural prices, too, was stabilized (at a level considerably above world prices). Price subsidies, paid for by levies on processing industries which were showing exceptional profits, and, in the case of one or two commodities, rationing kept down the prices to the consumers of the most vital foodstuffs. At the same time, deliberate price manipulation by the Government largely replaced the free price mechanism for the adjustment of supply to demand (or vice versa) and was used to induce such changes in agricultural production as long-run considerations of agricultural policy seemed to require.[3]

[1] Space forbids more than a reference to Nazi agricultural policy which in any comprehensive account of the Nazi economy requires a chapter to itself. The Nazis, from the moment of their accession to power, devoted immense efforts to the task of making Germany independent of foreign supplies of foodstuffs and agricultural raw materials, by raising agricultural prosperity, by stimulating the production of products of which Germany was short, by fairly large investments for the improvement of farming methods, land reclamation and drainage, by the supply of additional labour and by the compulsory improvement of distribution through State-controlled monopolistic marketing organizations. Compared with the dramatic success of Germany's industrial policy, the results of her efforts in the sphere of agriculture were meagre: output rose by a bare 7 per cent between 1933 and 1936 (C. W. Guillebaud, *The Economic Recovery of Germany* [Macmillan, 1939] p. 97); shortages of fodder imports led to an actual reduction in livestock; the continued flight from the land made shortage of agricultural labour a serious problem after 1936. By 1938 German agricultural self-sufficiency had made little progress, although substantial reserves of imported foodstuffs had been accumulated.

[2] The total returns to German agriculture were raised between 1932-3 and 1934-5 by 30 per cent, while at the same time reduction of taxation and interest rates on mortgages lowered farming costs (C. W. Guillebaud, op. cit., p. 59). From 1934 onwards the agricultural producers had the benefit of a guaranteed market and substantial economic security. But the peasant farmers obtained this security at the cost of the almost complete loss of freedom of movement through the Hereditary Farm Law of 1933; and agricultural wages remained far below the level of industrial wages. It was the great landowners, whose income rose from 300 million RM in 1933 to 2,100 million RM in 1938 (T. Balogh, op. cit., p. 479 n. 2), who derived the greatest benefit from the policy of self-sufficiency in bulk-foodstuffs.

[3] Thus, to give but one illustration, in 1937, when it was desired to increase the production of rye as against wheat (the yield per acre of rye on German soils being greater than that of wheat), the producer price of rye was raised by 20 RM per ton. In spite of this the consumer price of rye-meal and bread was kept unaltered, and the loss to the rye millers was made good by a special levy upon two other food industries, brewing and sugar, where relatively large profits were being made. (C. W. Guillebaud, op. cit., p. 162.)

F

This all-embracing system of control, while it required a large administrative organization and strict police supervision to enforce it, never became absolutely watertight; and as long as some commodities had to be imported from abroad it could not prevent German prices from rising to some extent with world prices. But price movements in Germany were very much smaller than abroad[1] (apart from the initial rise in agricultural prices), and by 1937 or so price control of all important goods had become sufficiently effective to eliminate all danger of inflation. Any surplus of money incomes over the available supply of consumption goods at the controlled prices simply could not be spent and had to be saved.

b. *Control of Investment.* But it was not enough to limit consumers' demand, so as to prevent inflation and ensure an adequate supply of savings (or in real terms, of factors of production) for public and private investment. The Nazi Government was determined that most investment should take the form of rearmament and the production of substitute materials. It therefore became necessary to canalize savings into the desired directions, or in other words to ensure that private investment was limited to projects determined by the state.

During the first, the 'work-creation', phase of the Nazi régime, State control of private investment was confined—apart from the vitally important prevention of capital exports by exchange control—to control of the capital market. In order to monopolize the resources of the capital market for its own purposes the Government as early as 1933 virtually prohibited private capital issues. The result of this control, which was later tightened rather than relaxed, was that much the larger part of all long-term lending in the capital market during the following years consisted of loans to the Reich.[2]

As long as there remained an ample supply of unused factors of production there was no need to impose further restrictions on the form which private investment assumed, since industry responded only too willingly to public investment demand in the shape of armaments contracts. Private investment could be stimulated indiscriminately by tax relief and other measures without danger that it would interfere with the rearmament

[1] Between March 1933 and January 1938 wholesale prices in Germany rose by only 16 per cent, as compared with 30 per cent in Great Britain, 34 per cent in the U.S.A., and 43 per cent in France. In Germany, moreover, the rise in prices was almost entirely confined to consumption goods; the price index of capital goods actually fell slightly. The fact that the volume of production nevertheless increased much faster in the capital goods industries shows the degree to which production was controlled.

[2] In 1928 public corporate borrowing had amounted to only 663 million RM in contrast to over 1,600 million RM private issues; in 1937 the relation was inverse, 3,150 million RM to less than 600 million. (T. Balogh, op. cit., p. 474.)

programme.[1] After 1934 it became necessary to restrict private investment for 'unessential' purposes and to induce or force private investment activity into the desired channels.

On the monetary side, control of profits (corporate savings) was added to control of the capital market. By the *Anleihestockgesetz* of 1934 dividends were limited to 6 per cent (in certain cases to 8 per cent); the surplus had to be handed over to the Government against its long-term obligations. Though it helped to prevent share speculation and conceivably had some effect in limiting the consumption expenditure of the recipients of dividends, the effect of the measure in diverting funds from private to State investment hardly corresponded to its social propaganda value. In 1934 the amount received by (i.e. lent to) the Government was only 30 million RM, less than 0·3 per cent of total profits for the year. On the other hand, the law stimulated enterprises to plough back their profits and to finance their capital expansion from their own resources, thus leaving the capital market free for Government issues. Gradually State control also restricted the freedom of industry to dispose of its undistributed profits. Through the 'corporate organization of industry' profits were utilized for a variety of purposes. Some of the burden of export bounties which were granted to individual exporters to offset losses due to the maintenance of the gold parity of the mark was imposed on industries collectively. In the same way, industries were forced to pay for subsidies to keep down the prices of certain goods to the consumer in spite of increased prices paid to the producers. Most drastic of all, private industry was 'encouraged' to finance a part, estimated at 30 per cent, of the investment in factories for the production of substitute materials under the Second Four Year Plan.[2]

Control of corporate savings was supplemented by meticulous supervision of actual real investment. The subsidies to indiscriminate investment of the work-creation period, such as tax relief for the renewal of plant, were gradually withdrawn after 1934. The establishment of new companies, and the extension of plant and building in nearly all important industries was prohibited. The authorities granted general and special exemptions which were in turn planned and varied according to state policy. Above all, exchange and import control, as already men-

---

[1] The virtual prohibition of private capital issues obliged industry to finance its investment largely out of its own resources. But public expenditure made this much easier by its effect on bank liquidity which in turn liquidated assets of industry which had been frozen during the depression, and by increasing profits.

[2] Even these measures left over a certain proportion of the greatly increased profits of industry which could be freely utilized by the entrepreneurs. It was mostly used to increase working and fixed capital.

tioned, was used to control output in all industries which depended directly or indirectly on imported raw materials.

The control of private investment enabled the Nazis to harness the energies and resources of private German industry to the purposes of rearmament and self-sufficiency over and above what was achieved by the normal methods of Government contracts and expenditure. Although in practice it was used increasingly to restrict investment in unessential industries it is worth pointing out that it also provided a reinsurance against any falling-off of private investment activity below what was necessary to achieve and maintain full employment.

c. Control of Labour Supply. Towards the end of 1937 the German economy approached a state of full employment. With the growing shortage of skilled labour, State control was extended to yet another sphere of the economic system, the supply and employment of labour. By the summer of 1937 unemployment was down to half a million men, most of whom were either temporarily out of work or unemployable. Moreover, the demand for labour had increased very unevenly. While some consumption industries still had a surplus of labour, the metal, building and other industries engaged in rearmament were beginning to feel an acute shortage of skilled labour. From 1936 onwards, therefore, the Nazi Government took steps to increase the supply of labour to industry in general and to the 'essential' industries in particular.

During the work-creation period the supply of labour had been artificially diminished by various devices. This policy was now reversed. Earlier work-spreading measures, such as compulsory short-time, were rescinded and hours of work, all restrictions on which in the armaments industries had already been removed, were lengthened. Great efforts were made to raise output by increasing the intensity of work—with the result that by 1938 even Government publications began to draw attention to the serious effects of the speed-up on the workers' health.[1] The ban on the employment of married women was lifted, and between August 1936 and 1937 alone some 200,000 women were newly employed. During the same period some 170,000 men were recruited to industry from other occupations.[2]

---

[1] J. Kuczynski, *The Conditions of the Workers in Great Britain, Germany, and the Soviet Union 1932–8* (Gollancz, 1939), p. 32 f. In spite of this intensification of work productivity under the Nazi regime increased much less than, for instance, in Great Britain [11 per cent as compared with 20 per cent between 1932 and 1937] (ibid., p. 33).

[2] Other measures designed to increase the supply of labour over and above the natural addition to the working population were subsidies for the employment of clerical workers and men above normal working age, measures to prevent loss of working hours due to frequent changes of employment, and a compulsory year of service for women.

Even more far-reaching were the measures taken to remedy the shortage of skilled labour in the essential industries. During 1937 and 1938 orders empowering the authorities to conscript labour, to transfer workers compulsorily to essential industries, and prohibiting the employment or dismissal of any worker without permission of employment exchanges almost completely abolished freedom of domicile and work and freedom of employment. These forceful methods were supplemented by energetic educational and other efforts to heighten the mobility of labour, such as vocational guidance and training of skilled workers which was partly undertaken by the State but was mainly enforced upon industry by orders requiring the employment of a high proportion of apprentices.

III. NAZI FINANCE

IT is not hard to see that Government expenditure on the scale on which the Nazis indulged in it could re-employ the productive resources of Germany. What many observers have found incomprehensible is how the Nazis were able to pay for this huge expenditure. As the Nazi rearmament bill mounted up, most people in this country, many in Germany, and probably at times even some members of the Nazi Government hoped for or feared—as the case may be—a 'financial collapse'. The impression was enhanced by the hand-to-mouth methods and complicated improvisations of Nazi finance and by the ruthless way in which the Nazis at intervals robbed Jews, foreigners and occupied countries, suggesting by implication the imminent danger of bankruptcy. Actually Nazi finance was neither miraculous (though ingenious) nor even unsound.

The fundamental point, which Hitler can claim to have grasped some time before the struggle against unemployment and the problems of war economics won for it wider recognition in the western capitalist democracies, was the relative unimportance of the monetary as compared with the real aspects of the economic process, the fact that what matters is not the cost in money terms of a given policy but its efficacy in making the most of the real resources, the labour, land, machines and factories, of a country. When Hitler proclaimed the 'primacy of work', he was expressing in a crude but effective slogan this principle which, partly no doubt by force of circumstance and sheer opportunism, became the basis of Nazi financial policy. Broadly speaking, the Nazis in their expansionist recovery policy concentrated on the job of putting the unemployed to work and left finance to look after itself.[1] In the same way, when it became necessary to limit con-

[1] One instance of this was the almost complete elimination of the stock exchange as an important factor in the economic structure of Germany.

sumption and control investment they relied in the first place on direct controls. The various forms of monetary control which we have described were extremely important. But their function was not so much to determine the allocation of productive resources, but rather to prevent monetary forces from putting undue pressure on the direct controls of production.

In the first period—the work-creation period—the increase in public expenditure was mainly financed by the creation of additional cash. The method used was that of bills of exchange rediscountable at the Reichsbank. Of the total cost of the work-creation programme, amounting to 5·1 milliard RM, 3·1 milliard RM came from this source.[1] This method of financing was continued after 1935 and was used both for rearmament purposes and for the execution of the Four Year Plan. The total amount of new money borrowed by the Government from the banks by the issue of these special short-term bills between 1933 and 1938 (an amount which was kept secret) is estimated at between 13 and 15 milliard RM.[2] Just as in the U.S.A. under the New Deal, the creation of additional cash was a perfectly sound method of financing as long as there was an ample supply of unused productive resources. It was this additional cash which in the hands of consumers turned potential into effective demand and brought idle factors of production into use to meet this demand. In a free economy the creation of additional cash by Government borrowing would have had to slow down with the approach to full employment if inflation was to be avoided, since under full employment additional money demand could not be met by increasing output but only by raising prices. The Nazis continued and even increased borrowing by cash creation (special short-term bills) after 1937. But by that time the rigid system of price and investment control which had been built up since 1934 was amply sufficient to prevent inflation. The additional cash could not be spent and was saved[3]—and reborrowed by the Government. In the Nazi controlled economy, therefore, any inflationary addition to the volume of money was cancelled out by forced saving, and the choice between financing public expenditure out of taxation, borrowing (out of savings), and cash creation (by special bills or even banknotes) became a matter of practical and political convenience.

In addition to cash creation, the German Government was able to raise large and increasing amounts by borrowing out of (more or less) voluntary savings. Having monopolized the resources

[1] T. Balogh, op. cit., p. 468.
[2] ibid., p. 469.
[3] This forced saving due to the restriction of consumption expenditure, largely accounts for the extraordinary liquidity of the German banks during recent years.

of the capital market for its own purposes the Nazi Government experienced no serious difficulty in placing long-term loans. As production expanded under stable wage conditions, profits available for voluntary and enforced investment in Government loans increased. Even small savings increased with the progress of recovery in spite of the heavy burden of taxation, as is shown by the fact that in 1937 savings deposits alone increased by 1,800 million RM.[1] During the later years control of consumption expenditure, profits and dividends somewhat blurred the distinction between voluntary savings and forced savings amounting practically to taxation, both of private individuals and industrial concerns. From this source the Nazi Government obtained a net total of well over 10½ milliard RM between 1933 and 1937.[2] Almost the whole of this borrowing took the form of long-term bonds which were mostly subscribed by the banking and savings banks system.

Both these forms of Government 'borrowing' together increased the German national debt from 11·7 milliard RM in 1933 to about 40–45 milliard RM in 1938.[3] It need hardly be pointed out again that the size, or even the rate of increase, of a country's national debt is of far less economic significance than has generally been assumed.[4] For those who are not yet convinced it can be mentioned that even the 1937–8 level of the German national debt worked out at only 40 per cent of the national income, while the British national debt, for example, stood in 1936, before the beginning of rearmament, at 220 per cent of the national income.[5] What increases the contrast—and this point *is* significant—the increase in the German national debt was almost entirely internal. By repudiation, default and repayment the Nazis actually diminished Germany's foreign indebtedness. Even the minor problem of redistribution of income involved in interest payments was of little importance to the Nazis. The German post-war inflation had completely wiped out the internal national debt, and the Nazis were able to start almost from scratch. Even in 1938 interest payments on the German national debt (assuming an average rate of 4 per cent) cannot have amounted to much more than about 1,500 million RM or 5 per cent of a total budget of 30,000 million.[6] Besides, strict control of investment obviated the danger that any increase in taxation necessary to meet the service on the national debt might discourage private investment activity.

[1] T. Balogh, op. cit., p. 474. [2] ibid., p. 475.
[3] G. Stolper, *The German Economy 1870–1940* (Allen & Unwin, 1940), p. 264.
[4] The question has been discussed *above*, ch. ii, p. 55 f.
[5] J. Strachey, op. cit., p. 267.
[6] E. F. Schumacher, 'The Economics of National Socialism' (unpublished Memorandum), p. 32.

For the rest the Nazis relied on taxation in one form or another to meet their growing expenditure.[1] Government revenue from ordinary taxation and customs receipts rose from 6·9 milliard RM in 1933–4 to 17·7 milliard RM in 1938–9.[2] To this must be added income from 'voluntary' contributions to party and other purposes (*Winterhilfe*) which are estimated to have yielded about 2·5 milliard during this period,[3] and the forced savings imposed through compulsory social insurance, which yielded considerable surpluses as unemployment diminished. Altogether about two-thirds of the total Government expenditure during the first five years of the Nazi regime was met out of taxation.

At first glance, it seems difficult to reconcile the two-and-a-half-fold increase in tax yields with the fact mentioned above, that, heavy as the burden of taxation on the German people was, the increase in that burden during these five years amounted to only 16 per cent. The explanation of the discrepancy lies, of course, in the rise of the national income.[4] Most of the increased tax revenue of the Nazi Government was due, not to higher rates or new forms of taxation, but to the greater yield of existing rates of taxation with growing money incomes. This fact is of great significance. For, since the rise in money incomes was for the most part the result of Government loan expenditure, it means that even without any further increase in the burden of taxation, a large proportion of the money borrowed or created by the Government to finance the public works and rearmament programme would have returned automatically to the Government in the form of increased tax yield. It means that a large proportion of the enormous public expenditure of the Nazis paid for itself; that, in a monetary sense, a large part of the German public works and rearmament programme cost nothing at all. In a real sense, of course, this part of the bill, too, was 'paid for' by the labour of German workers who had been thrown out of work, and the use of Ger-

---

[1] Of the three 'financial windfalls' referred to before, two, the repudiation of the foreign debt and Austrian and Czech gold, were entirely insignificant for internal finance, though both were very important as means of easing Germany's foreign exchange position. The confiscation of Jewish property did provide another significant source of revenue. But its importance has usually been over-estimated. Most of it took the form of forced realizations of assets to other private individuals or firms (usually much below market value). From these transfers of property the Nazi Government benefited only politically—by the heightened devotion of the beneficiaries. The Nazi Government did probably net a total of some 1—1·5 milliard RM from fines and confiscations of property which was mostly resold at a profit to private investors (the latter procedure functioning as a kind of open market operations). But this sum represented no more than 3—5 per cent of the total budget in 1938. There can be little doubt that the Nazis could relatively easily have raised the same amount by taxation and borrowing.

[2] J. Strachey, op. cit., p. 266.

[3] ibid.

[4] Increasingly severe measures against tax evasion also helped to raise the yield of existing taxes.

man factories and machines which had been allowed to stand idle during the great depression and were brought back into use by the flow of public expenditure.

This is, of course, not the whole story. The Nazis did increase the burden of taxation, and as the pace of rearmament increased a growing proportion of the real cost was borne by the German people in the form of a lower standard of living and by the depletion of some of the nation's capital equipment. To what extent this was the case will emerge from an analysis of the results of Nazi economic policy.

IV. THE RESULTS OF NAZI ECONOMIC POLICY

IN the nature of the case the achievements of Nazi economic policy between 1933 and 1938 cannot be measured in purely economic or social terms. The outstanding characteristic of that policy, at any rate after 1934, was that it was subordinated to a political objective, military power and preparedness for war. Judged by the end it was designed to achieve, Nazi economic policy was eminently successful. By 1938 it had made possible the creation of a war machine which in 1939 and 1940 enabled Germany to overrun the European Continent. It had in peacetime fully adapted the German economy to war purposes. And, to a much lesser extent, as will be seen later, it had succeeded in making Germany immune to blockade.

With this consideration in mind we can turn to the economic results of the first five years of the Nazi régime.

The outstanding economic achievement of the Nazis lay undoubtedly in the abolition of unemployment. There is no more striking evidence of the importance of this success than the fact that in return for the right to work and security of employment the masses of the German workers were prepared not only to forgo their claim for higher wages, but to acquiesce in the deprivation of their rights and liberties and even to accept if necessary a reduction in their standard of living. It is hardly an exaggeration to say that the fact that the Nazis from the beginning realized the overwhelming importance of the right to work and security of employment to the individual worker was *the* secret of their success. Together with the nationalist appeal and supplemented by the Gestapo and the concentration camp it provided the basis for the political stability of the régime.

On the face of it, the increase in the volume of German industrial production by 100 per cent between 1933 and 1938 was as remarkable an achievement as the abolition of unemployment. In 1938 the level of economic activity in Germany was 25 per cent above the pre-depression level of 1929, as compared with

F*

20 per cent above in Great Britain (where the depression had been much less severe), and 35 per cent and 40 per cent *below* in the U.S.A. and France respectively. But on closer analysis this achievement loses much of its impressiveness. The index of total industrial production conceals an unexampled divergence between the rate of growth of investment and production for consumption. Output in the investment goods industries rose by 162 per cent, in the consumption goods industries by a mere 36 per cent.[1] The result was that while capacity in most investment goods industries was enormously expanded, capacity in some of the most important consumption goods industries remained only partially employed. According to official figures only 65·1 per cent of the existing productive capacity of the textile and 54·5 per cent of that of the garment industry was in use.[2] Moreover the rate of increase in total output of German industry bore little relation to the needs of German consumers. The ratio of gross investment to national income increased from 18·2 per cent in 1928 to 23 per cent in 1937.[3] In other words, a quarter of the national income in 1937 and most of the total increase in the output of German industry under the Nazi régime did not benefit the needs of consumers at all, but took the form of capital goods. These figures in themselves might merely suggest that the German people forwent immediate consumption in favour of improving the nation's capital equipment. But a large proportion of this total 'investment' represented armaments which could in no sense be considered as an addition to the capital equipment of the nation: and while the industries producing armaments and factories and machines for the armaments industries were enormously expanded, investment in other spheres lagged behind. In most industries producing for civilian consumption (except those producing substitute materials under the Four Year Plan) gross investment was almost certainly insufficient even to maintain existing capacity. It has been estimated that already in 1935 there occurred a disinvestment of some 100—200 millions in the consumption goods industries.[4] The same is true of the German railways. Not only did the authorities fail to augment locomotives and rolling stock to meet the increased transport requirements, they even neglected necessary repairs and failed to replace outworn material. Again, residential building was wholly inadequate to meet the demands of a rapidly increasing number of house-

---

[1] Schumacher, op. cit., p. 15.

[2] T. Balogh, op. cit., p. 488. The stagnation in the textile industries was partly due to the fact that they suffered most from the shortage of foreign raw materials. But this shortage, as will appear in the following chapter, was itself largely, though not entirely, due to the preference given to war materials in German import policy and to the refusal to devaluate the mark.

[3] T. Balogh, op. cit., p. 466.

[4] ibid., p. 488.

holders, with the result that by 1938 the accumulated shortage amounted to between 1½ and 2 million dwellings.[1]

No doubt this unevenness in the growth of industrial output between production for consumption and investment, on the one hand, and between different forms of investment, on the other, was merely the price paid for military power. But it involved a far-reaching change in Germany's productive structure. Not only was the capacity of the German heavy industries doubled and their output tripled while the capacity of the consumption goods industries was not even maintained, with a corresponding shift in the geographical distribution and skill of labour; but the German economy was in every respect organized for the production of all the semi-capital goods which war requires. There was no conceivable other use for a great part of Nazi industry. Any attempt, if such had ever been contemplated, to switch the Nazi war economy to the needs of peace, would have faced the Nazis with so gigantic a social and economic problem that war would in any case have appeared as the line of least resistance.

What was the effect of Nazi economic policy on the size and distribution of the German national income? The total national income increased from 45·2 milliard RM in 1932 to 68·5 milliard RM in 1937.[2] But during the same period the income used for consumption increased by only 11 milliard RM to about 58·5 milliard as compared with 66 milliard RM in 1928.[3]

Only rough estimates can be made of the development of the real income of the working class. The money income of labour, after deduction of taxation and the fall in relief expenditure, is estimated to have increased by 3 to 5 milliard RM, i.e. by between 25 and 40 per cent.[4] But since employment during the same period increased by 47 per cent it is probable that this increase benefited mainly those previously unemployed and that many of those who had retained their jobs during the depression were actually worse off in 1937 even in terms of money earnings. At the same time, the official cost of living index rose by 8·9 per cent.[5] The real income of all workers (employed and unemployed), therefore, rose by only 7—17 per cent. Even this figure does not take into account the very considerable deterioration in the quality of certain goods and the fact that many others were not to be had at all or only in limited quantities. On the other hand, the worker benefited by a paid holiday and cheap facilities for 'approved' enjoyment of leisure. For the masses of the German people the Nazi régime brought little if any improvement in their real income and standard of living in spite of all the increase in employment, hours of work, economic activity, and output. From

[1] C. W. Guillebaud, op. cit., p. 146.   [2] T. Balogh, op. cit., p. 466.
[3] ibid., p. 467.   [4] ibid., p. 469.   [5] ibid., p. 482.

another point of view, however, it is equally significant that the Nazis were able, by putting to use all available resources of production, to carry through an immense rearmament programme without any appreciable deterioration of the standard of living.

There is every reason to believe that, at least during the first years of the Nazi régime, the capitalist class fared very much better. Increased production coupled with stable wages led to a rapid rise in profits from 6·6 milliard RM in 1933 to 10·4 milliard in 1936.[1] It is true that the corporation tax and other direct taxation took away a growing proportion of this increased income and that the limitation of dividends and, much more effectively, consumption control tended to reduce the inequality in purchasing power between different income levels. But it is very doubtful whether even by the outbreak of the war the relative share of the national income of the capitalist class as a whole had been reduced to any appreciable extent. Within the capitalist class, however, the distribution of income undoubtedly changed greatly in favour of the owners of the heavy industries and all those concerned directly or indirectly in the production of armaments (including the banks) and at the expense of the owners of consumption goods industries and small entrepreneurs in general. Moreover, as the Nazi controlled economy developed, the owners of private property in the means of production were increasingly deprived of their freedom to dispose of the income from that property and of the property itself. The Nazi system of State control of private investment and production meant that the individual business man *qua* entrepreneur lost most of the economic power that goes with the ownership of the means of production in the capitalist economy, while at the same time some of the biggest capitalists, especially the owners and directors of the armaments and allied monopolies, added to their power by becoming associated with the leaders of the party bureaucracy in the exercise of that very State control. It also meant that over a wide field within the German economy State control and planning replaced the profit motive as the determining factor in the allocation of productive resources. The profit motive continued to be relied upon in almost every sector of the economic system (in common with other elements in what is called the 'free play of market forces') but only where the State authorities believed that it would serve as a cheaper method ('cheaper' in terms of the amount of coercion and the size of the bureaucratic machine necessary to replace it) of achieving the desired result. The Nazis, however, did not substitute public for private ownership of the means of production—though the establishment of the State-owned Hermann Göring Werke under the Four Year Plan in

[1] T. Balogh, op. cit., p. 471.

1936 seemed for a time to point in this direction—and during the first years of the régime at any rate the capitalists were only too willing to surrender some of their power of control and some of their share in the national income as the price for the salvation from social revolution. Whether any except perhaps the biggest capitalists still shared this view in 1938 or 1939 is a question to which no categorical answer is possible.

V. THE SIGNIFICANCE OF REARMAMENT

WE may conclude this analysis of the internal development of the Nazi economy by considering briefly the question, raised earlier on, how far the success of the expansionist policy of the Nazis was due to the fact that public expenditure, to some extent from the beginning and overwhelmingly after 1934, took the form of expenditure on rearmament. Could full recovery have been achieved equally well by a policy devoted to raising the standard of living of the German people. The question is of course purely speculative and in its abstractness perhaps non-sensical. But some tentative remarks may throw some light on the merits of expansionist recovery policies.

Now there can be no doubt that rearmament represented by far the most effective and easiest method of promoting recovery by additional public expenditure. Rearmament was an ideal 'public works' policy. It stimulated directly the most depressed sectors of the German economy, the heavy industries and the constructional and building trades. Since the demand of the State for armaments represented completely additional demand, it did not in any way diminish existing investment opportunities and thus discourage private investment activity. Again, rearmament was the one method of large-scale public expenditure which was not only immune against the charge, however misguided, of 'extravagance' but which was certain of general approval on patriotic grounds. Rearmament, lastly, was but one aspect of the general Nazi policy of aggressive nationalism. The Nazis were able to enlist in support of their 'recovery' policy moral and psychological forces for which it would have been hard to find equally effective substitutes in connection with any economic policy aimed at a rising standard of living.

On the other side of the question it may be argued that the work-creation programme of the first two years of the Nazi régime in which armaments certainly played a relatively insignicant part, had by 1935 already provided so adequate a stimulus to private industry that the rearmament expenditure of the following years was entirely unnecessary from the economic point of view, and that from 1935 onwards the Nazis could have relied on private investment activity to carry the economy to recovery. There is every reason to believe that the expansionist measures of the last pre-Nazi Governments had been initiated with this end in view, and that at any rate the conservative majority of the first Nazi Government had looked on the work-creation programme in this light, as a policy of 'pump-priming'.

Three points can be urged in favour of this view. First, as we have shown, the Nazi work-creation programme was in many respects superior as a method of 'pump-priming' to the only comparable experiment, the American New Deal. A much larger proportion of the additional public expenditure took the form of public works which were, on the whole, carefully chosen so as to be 'non-competitive' and at the same time effective in stimulating some of the depressed investment industries. What financial assistance was given to industry was made conditional upon the undertaking of new private investment. And direct distribution of money to consumers was coupled with the absorption of unemployment. Secondly, exchange control ensured that the effect of public expenditure on effective demand was not offset by capital exports. Thirdly and most important of all, the Nazi Government—in striking contrast to the progressive Roosevelt Administration—was not hampered in its expansionist policy by 'low business confidence'. Any adverse effect which its unorthodox methods might have had on private investment activity was more than outweighed by the general character of its social policy, at least during these earlier years. German business which, rightly or wrongly, had thought itself threatened by imminent social revolution, breathed again under a Government which consisted largely of its own representatives and which by its rabid reactionary policy—the immediate dissolution of all left-wing parties, the destruction of the trade unions and the stabilization of wages at depression levels—appeared as the saviour and benefactor of private property.[1] It is arguable that these three factors together might have achieved without rearmament that full recovery which the New Deal failed to procure.

Yet is it difficult to accept this view without considerable qualifications. In the first place, it is most unlikely that the stimulus provided by the work-creation expenditure of five milliard

[1] The favourable attitude of the capitalists towards the Nazi régime helps to explain the rapid revival of private investment during 1933 and 1934. As a factor in the German recovery as a whole it is probably of little importance. Public investment expenditure was more than sufficient to offset any deficiency of private investment activity due to psychological causes. During the later years of the Nazi régime when profit expectations of a good many business men must have been low, State control of investment ensured that private investment absorbed what factors of production and savings were not required by the demands of the State.

RM would in fact have been sufficient;[1] any further public expenditure, however, would have faced the Government with the problem of finding effective and at the same time 'non-competitive' projects. This is not a very important point. But, secondly, it is impossible to divorce the favourable attitude of German business towards the Nazi Government from the nationalist character and programme of the new régime. One of the main reasons for the revival of business confidence in 1933 was that German business men had no doubt whatever that, as soon as internal and international conditions permitted, the Nazis would embark on a vast rearmament programme. In the eyes of the German capitalists who helped Hitler to power, his rearmament programme, together with his anti-socialist policy, provided the *raison d'être* of his régime. Lastly, the view assumes that Germany during the nineteen-thirties provided sufficient opportunities for profitable investment to ensure full recovery on the basis of private investment activity. The assumption may be correct. But the course of world trade during the nineteen-thirties, the contemporary experience of the U.S.A. and other considerations suggest that it is, to say the least, optimistic.

[1] Also, a large proportion of the public works schemes of the first two years—such as the system of national motor roads and many of the building projects (barracks)—already served military purposes.

Chapter Seven

GERMANY: FOREIGN ECONOMIC POLICY

I. THE OBJECTIVES

THE commercial policies of most countries during the nineteen-thirties can be summed up by saying that they tried to export as much and import as little as possible. There were two main reasons for this *prima facie* absurd policy. One was the pressure on the balances of payments and currencies of almost all countries except the U.S.A. which was due, in Europe chiefly to the international disequilibrium created by the creditor position of the U.S.A. and the volume of international capital movements, in the overseas primary producing countries chiefly to the disproportionate fall in the volume or prices of their exports relative to their imports. One method of diminishing this pressure was to 'improve' the balance of trade by curtailing imports and, if possible, increasing exports. The other reason for this policy which was quite as important and which persisted even where, as in the case of Great Britain after 1931, depreciation had largely solved the immediate balance of payments problem, was the internal depression. Other things being equal, exports maintained and imports diminished economic activity at home. It was the paramount need to maintain economic activity at home—first to counteract the slump and later to assist in the recovery—which was largely responsible for the absurd situation in which each country endeavoured to sell as much and buy as little as possible, and incidentally tried to sell more to others than it was willing to buy from them.[1]

The main difference between German commercial policy under the Nazi régime and the commercial policies of Great Britain, the U.S.A., France, and most other countries during the nineteen-thirties was that the second factor, the recovery motive, gradually ceased to operate in German policy. Until 1933 German commercial policy had been no less subordinated to the maintenance of economic activity at home than that of other countries. Her traditional policy of protecting her high-cost agriculture was intensified during the depression years by increased tariffs and import quotas; and the object of the frantic attempts by the German Government to maintain German exports during the

[1] It is probable that the 'maximum exports-minimum imports' policy has been reinforced by the fact that in most capitalist countries producer interests have as a rule been better organized and therefore been in a better position to influence policy than consumer interests.

years 1929–32 was at least as much to stem the internal depression as to secure an export surplus sufficient to cover debt payments. Even after 1933 the recovery motive did not disappear immediately or entirely. The protection afforded to German agriculture by exchange control, import quotas and tariffs which under the Nazi régime maintained German agricultural prices far above world prices, although its main objects were strategic and social, continued to have an economic element. There is also reason to believe that until about 1934 the efforts of the Nazi Government to stimulate German exports were in part motivated by the desire to increase employment within Germany.[1] But, as we saw before, with the decision of the Nazis to rearm at all costs the unemployment problem of Germany was potentially, and very soon actually, solved. After 1934, there was no longer any need to curtail imports and push exports in aid of domestic recovery. On the contrary, very soon the dependence of the armaments industry on foreign war materials and the growth of consumers' demand with a rising national income made an extension of imports urgently necessary; and with the approach to full employment the German export trade was actually hampered by scarcity of labour and other factors of production.

The solution of the recovery problem in Germany made possible, and even necessary, a commercial policy directed towards obtaining a maximum of imports from abroad for a minimum payment in the form of exports, in other words, towards maximizing the 'total gains from foreign trade' judged by the volume of goods available for home consumption rather than by the effect of foreign trade on domestic employment. In this connection, a technical point must be made which is essential for an understanding of Nazi commercial policy. Of the two component elements which enter into the 'total gains from foreign trade' in this sense, the *volume* and the *terms* of trade, the first is by far the more important. Normally a country will be able to increase its total gain by increasing the volume of its trade, even at the cost of the deterioration in its terms of trade (by selling at lower and buying at higher prices) which this is likely to involve; a deliberate improvement in her terms of trade, however, is liable to lead to so large a fall in the volume that the net result is a loss. For Nazi Germany, moreover, the absolute necessity of satisfying the growing import needs of the German war economy was the overriding consideration. Nazi commercial policy, therefore, deliberately subordinated considerations of cost to its major objective, the satisfaction of current German import require-

[1] The New Plan, adopted in September 1934, still mentioned the reduction of unemployment as one of its objectives. (H. S. Ellis, *Exchange Control in Central Europe* [Harvard University Press, Cambridge, Mass., 1941], p. 212).

ments, though by means of the exercise of discriminating monopoly it endeavoured to reduce the price that had to be paid for
these imports to the minimum. This fact, as will be seen, is of
considerable importance in assessing the achievements of Nazi
commercial policy.

In practice, the fundamental change of objective in German
commercial policy passed almost unnoticed. For, broadly speaking, Germany had to pay for her imports by selling exports just
as much as other countries (and Germany until 1934) had to
accept imports (or gold) if they wanted foreign countries to buy
their products. In the long run, Germany, like any other country,
had to balance the debit and credit sides of her foreign trade and
payments account. For Germany, moreover, the balance of payments problem was aggravated by her large foreign debt, the
exhaustion of her gold and foreign exchange reserves, and the protectionist policies of most other countries which stood in the
way of an expansion of her exports. As a result, most of the
efforts of Dr. Schacht and his successor were devoted to stimulating exports by every conceivable device and, where necessary,
reducing imports. But this superficial resemblance to the 'maximum exports-minimum imports' policy of other countries must
not be allowed to conceal the fundamental shift in emphasis of
German commercial policy under the Nazi régime. Nazi Germany, Hitler proclaimed, must 'export or die'. But for Nazi
Germany exports were solely a means for imports, the imports
required for rearmament and the accumulation of war reserves.

To secure the imports needed for rearmament and the essential
needs of German consumers was not the only objective of Nazi
commercial policy. In addition to ensuring the satisfaction of
current import requirements, it was also designed to assist in the
attainment of the second major objective of Nazi economic
policy, autarky. The influence of the Nazi policy of economic
self-sufficiency on German commercial policy under the Nazi
régime was considerably smaller than would appear at first
glance. The primary object of that policy was to safeguard Germany against the danger of blockade by rendering her independent of foreign supplies of foodstuffs and essential raw materials
which might be cut off in case of war. Of the three methods which
the Nazis used to attain this object, the first and most important
was to increase Germany's productive capacity of goods, or substitutes for goods, formerly imported from abroad.[1] While this
objective, as we have seen,[2] played a very important part in Nazi
internal economic policy (both in determining Nazi agricultural

---

[1] It need not be repeated that a subsidiary motive for Nazi agricultural policy
was the desire to maintain the German agricultural population for social and
political reasons.

[2] See above, ch. vi, p. 156, n. 5.

policy and in necessitating a large amount of additional investment in the substitute industries under the Four Years Plan) its
effect on German commercial policy was negligible. For what
little it achieved, in the years preceding the outbreak of war, in
reducing German import requirements was far outweighed by
the second method of attaining self-sufficiency, the accumulation
of war reserves of essential war materials. For the most part,
therefore, the effect of the drive for self-sufficiency on German
commercial policy during the pre-war years was to increase
rather than diminish Germany's need for imports.

In addition to the production in Germany of commodities
formerly imported from abroad, and the accumulation of war
reserves, however, the Nazis endeavoured to ensure security
against blockade by a third method which did have a decisive
effect on their commercial policy. By subjecting parts of Europe,
in particular the small countries of Central and South-Eastern
Europe, to German political and economic domination, they
hoped to enlarge Germany's *Lebensraum*, to increase the area and
sources of supply on which Germany could depend in times of
war, and thus reduce still further the danger of being starved into
submission by her enemies. It was this semi-political objective[1]
which led the Nazis to depart in their commercial policy from the
main objective of increasing the gains from international trade.
In her policy towards the Balkan countries, as we shall see,
Germany, at least until 1939, did not press her bargaining advantages to the fullest possible extent, being prepared to forgo for
a time the immediate economic benefits which her position as
sole buyer offered her, in favour of the longer-term objective of
political and economic domination and autarky.

The ruthlessness and efficiency with which the Nazis pursued
these objectives in their commercial policy was made possible by
rigid State control and planning of the whole of Germany's foreign trade, which in turn was based on the development and
exploitation by the Nazis of two instruments which they inherited
in rudimentary form from their predecessors, exchange control
and the clearing system. Both were originally forced on Germany

[1] Strictly speaking, there is little point in making rigid distinctions between
political and economic intentions, as for instance in the statement that 'on
economic grounds' Germany should have exploited her bargaining position in
relation to the Balkan countries and that her failure to do so was due to 'political'
considerations. For at bottom the ultimate object of both policies was, if we like,
political: preparation for war. The choice was between an *economic* policy of
immediate exploitation so as to assist German rearmament, or an *economic*
policy of 'generosity' so as to ensure political domination and security against
blockade. It might almost be said that the essence of the Nazi system was the
abolition of any clear distinction between political and economic ends and
means. Nazi political foreign policy was used at times for the attainment of
short-term economic objectives as much as economic policy was made to serve
political ends.

by the pressure of outside events during the great depression. Both were taken over by the Nazis and, at first almost reluctantly, transformed into powerful weapons of foreign trade control. Although the clearing system presupposed, and was in a sense merely a part of, exchange control, the two institutions served distinct purposes. Broadly speaking, exchange control became the instrument by means of which the Nazis established and maintained State control of German importers and exporters (and indirectly even of parts of the internal economy); while the clearing system became the chief weapon of the Nazis in furthering their politico-economic aims abroad.

II. EXCHANGE CONTROL

THE first measures of exchange control had been forced upon Germany by the financial crisis of 1931. Confronted with a flight of capital which had assumed catastrophic proportions, the German Government had had no choice but to suspend the free gold standard and impose control of capital exports. Even a devaluation of the currency would probably have been ineffective in stemming the outflow of capital; on the contrary, in the pathological state of German public opinion it might itself have precipitated new attempts at capital flight. During the following years, and especially after 1933, the increasing shortage of German gold and foreign exchange reserves and the necessity of safeguarding the work-creation and rearmament programmes against the danger of capital flight led to a constant tightening of the regulations against capital exports.

But capital exchange control alone could not solve the German balance of payments problem. The immediate cause of that problem was the cessation in 1930 of the inflow of foreign capital on which Germany had relied to cover her debt payments on reparations and private account. Germany was suddenly faced with the task of having to create an export surplus sufficient to enable her to meet her huge foreign obligations. During the first year of the depression a remarkable improvement in Germany's terms of trade, due to the disproportionate fall in the prices of her raw material imports as compared with her industrial exports, helped Germany to achieve a large favourable balance of trade. But this improvement was essentially a transient phenomenon, and as foreign markets for German exports shrank with the deepening world depression and growing trade restrictions, the pressure on her balance of payments increased.

One method of removing this pressure would have been to devaluate the German currency. But this was a step which the German Government felt unable to take in view of the nervous

state of public opinion which since 1923 erroneously but firmly
associated depreciation of the currency with run-away inflation.
Nor is it by any means certain that devaluation would in 1931
have been sound policy for Germany. A fall in the value of
the mark would have increased the money and possibly even the
real burden of the large German foreign debts, most of which
ran in foreign currencies. The fact that in Germany, in contrast
for instance to Great Britain, devaluation was unlikely to reverse
the outflow of capital considerably diminished its usefulness as
a remedy. It was uncertain whether at the onset of the depression
the demand for German exports would respond greatly to a
lowering of German export prices. Lastly, there was the danger
that devaluation of the mark would merely lead to reprisals in
the form of competitive depreciation of other currencies and a
further heightening of foreign tariff walls against German trade.
In the absence of any effective machinery for the co-ordination
of national policies, a devaluation designed to rectify an internationally dangerous maladjustment was just as liable to provoke
retaliation which would render it nugatory as one motivated solely
by the desire for national advantage.

Unwilling to devaluate the mark, the German Government
hoped to achieve the same result, a downward adjustment of
German prices, by the orthodox remedy of deflation. The heroic
efforts of the Brüning Government in this direction were not
entirely unsuccessful. But what little result was achieved—at the
cost of growing internal depression, unemployment and political
disintegration—was more than outweighed by the fact that in the
meantime the depreciation of the pound and other currencies
reduced the export prices of Germany's competitors, while the
British policy of protection and Ottawa further impaired German
competitive ability on international markets. As a result, German
exports began to decline faster than her imports; her export surplus in 1932 was barely one-third of the 1930 surplus;[1] and the
gold and foreign exchange reserves of the Reichsbank, which had
been cut in half by the flight of capital during 1931, continued to
decline.[2]

The failure of deflation to close the gap between German and
foreign prices, coupled with the continued though reduced drain
of capital abroad, meant that the demand for foreign exchange
exceeded the supply at the official rate and made it impossible to
confine exchange control to capital exports. In November 1931
a system of exchange rationing was introduced which allocated
to accredited importers a percentage of the foreign exchange used
by each firm during a base period, a quota which was gradually

[1] H. S. Ellis, *Exchange Control in Central Europe*, p. 380.
[2] ibid., p. 373 f.

reduced from 75 per cent to 50 per cent.[1] In 1932 also the first attempts were made to evade the foreign exchange difficulty by organizing foreign trade on a clearing basis, and to compensate German exports for the overvaluation of the mark by export subsidies based on concealed devaluation. The quota rationing of foreign exchange, however, involved as yet no direct control of foreign trade since it left importers free to use their ration as they wished;[2] and in spite of these measures the German system of exchange control could be and was until 1932 still considered as an emergency device to be abolished once deflation had succeeded in readjusting the German economy to the world price structure.

The decisive factor which changed both the character and the functions of exchange control in Germany was the abandonment of the hopeless policy of orthodox deflation by the Papen Government in 1932 and the initiation by the Nazis in 1933 of their vigorous expansionist recovery programme. Even the decision to embark on a reflationary recovery policy did not in itself necessarily commit Germany to the maintenance of exchange control of foreign trade. While capital exchange control undoubtedly remained a *sine qua non* of recovery by reflationary methods in view of the danger of capital flight and the depletion of Germany's foreign exchange reserves, the Nazis could probably, after an initial devaluation of the mark sufficient to re-establish equilibrium between German and foreign prices, have followed the example of Austria in gradually relaxing exchange control, other than control of capital exports, without fear that pressure on the German balance of payments would impede the internal recovery. This policy would have greatly eased the German balance of payments problem and avoided the drag on the revival of German foreign trade of the cumbrous mechanism of exchange control. Moreover, the arguments which had deterred the Republican Government in 1931 from devaluation had lost much of their validity. Whereas in 1931 devaluation would have been an unorthodox step justified only by Germany's need as a debtor to create an export surplus at the expense of her competitors and almost certain to be nullified by reprisals, in 1934 the German mark was

---

[1] Since during the same period import prices declined by some 30 per cent, the German Government could justifiably claim that this reduction did not involve a curtailment of imports.

[2] On the other hand, it is significant that not two months elapsed after the introduction of exchange control before the first use was made of it as an instrument of commercial policy. In August 1931 an order was issued under which foreign exchange was to be freely allocated for certain 'vital' imports, rationed for imports of semi-finished goods and not supplied at all for imports of coal and finished goods including food; the order was soon abandoned, but it provided a foretaste of things to come (H. S. Ellis, *Exchange Control in Central Europe*, p. 168).

seriously overvalued at the official rate in consequence of the
currency depreciations of most foreign countries and Germany
need merely have followed their example. Besides, the virtual
cancellation of reparations by the Lausanne Agreement of 1932
and the reduction of the interest burden on part of Germany's
short-term debt by the Standstill Agreements, together with the
windfall profits which Germany had reaped from the foreign
currency depreciations, had considerably diminished the force
of the argument against devaluation based on the fear of raising
the burden of the foreign debt.

The Nazi Government none the less rejected this course. The
chief reason for their persistent refusal to devalue the mark was
probably still the popular fear of inflation. The Nazi Government was even more anxious than its predecessors to maintain
the nominal gold parity of the mark for reasons of internal prestige. But there were other factors which rendered this policy less
attractive to the Nazis. In the first place, while the removal of
exchange control would not have prevented Germany from pursuing a reflationary policy, it would have forced Germany to
gear the pace of her recovery to the *tempo* of world recovery.
Rigid exchange control assured the Government of the maximum
freedom in their internal economic policy, even should they fail
in preventing reflation from raising German prices and regardless of the internal policies and economic conditions of other
countries. Far from preferring devaluation because it would permit a reintegration of the German economy into the world
economy, the Nazis preferred exchange control as an instrument
of economic isolation. Secondly, exchange control had, by 1934,
begun to reveal its potentialities as an instrument for State control
of the internal economy. The mere fact that the power of rationing foreign exchange gave the Government the whip hand not
only over importers but over all industries dependent on imported raw materials was in itself a sufficient argument against
its abolition. Lastly, devaluation would have meant a deliberate
worsening of Germany's terms of trade. This was a price which
some other countries had been willing to pay because for them the
stimulation of exports and curtailment of imports was a necessary
aid to internal recovery. For Nazi Germany, as we have seen, the
recovery problem ceased to matter after 1934. In these circumstances, the overvaluation of the mark was a positive asset since
it meant that Germany paid less for her imports in terms of her
exports, an asset to be abandoned (by export subsidies and selective depreciation) only where and when it was necessary in order
to sell the exports with which to purchase the imports required.
While it is doubtful whether the Nazi Government already viewed
the position in this light in 1934, their reluctance to increase the

prices of much-needed raw materials by devaluation probably played a part in determining their policy.

It was the refusal of the Nazis to devaluate the mark in spite of the abandonment of deflation which turned exchange control from an emergency device for the protection of the currency into a permanent instrument of foreign trade policy. The result of the revival of economic activity in Germany was a rapid increase in German import demand both for the raw materials needed for the expansion of internal production[1] and for foreign consumers' goods. On the other hand, German exports continued to decline, partly because the rise in German prices, which was not entirely avoided, increased the divergence between German and foreign prices, partly because of outside factors, especially the devaluation of the dollar in 1933–4. Moreover, as raw material prices rose rapidly with the beginning of world recovery, Germany's terms of trade began to move sharply against her. Under this manifold strain the German foreign exchange position rapidly deteriorated during 1933 and 1934.[2] It is safe to assume that the Nazi Government watched the depletion of German foreign exchange reserves with equanimity because it enabled them to declare truthfully that Germany was no longer in the position to maintain payment on her foreign debts.[3] In 1933 the German Government declared a partial moratorium on the transfer on

[1] It can be, and has been, argued that it was the Nazi policy of rearmament rather than the needs of recovery as such which necessitated larger German imports of raw materials. This view is hardly plausible. Short of a far-reaching change in the German economic structure, *any* recovery would have led to an increase of German import demand; and for the rest of the world (except possibly for Germany's creditors) such an increase was, after all, highly desirable.

[2] Between January 1933 and June 1934 the gold and foreign exchange reserves of the Reichsbank dwindled from about 1,000 to less than 100 million RM.

[3] This statement is, of course, not incompatible with the fact that once Germany's creditors ceased to lend money to her *and were at the same time not prepared to accept payment of their claims in the form of German imports,* full payment of her debt payments by Germany really was impossible. The only alternative to default would have been the creation of an export surplus by reduction of imports. But, assuming the size of the German debt as it was before the Lausanne and Standstill Agreements, and the 1933 volume of exports, that would have involved a further cut in German imports (after years of depression and deliberate inflation) by 50 per cent. Such a reduction would not only have meant, as some of Germany's creditors believed at the time, a lower standard of living; it would have resulted in acute food shortage and/or would have deprived German industry of the raw materials necessary to maintain production even at depression level, *a fortiori* making recovery impossible. It is true that by 1933 the cancellation of reparations had considerably reduced the magnitude of the problem; it is also true that the Nazi Government was no longer troubled by scruples on this score (as the Brüning Government undoubtedly had been). Schacht and the Nazis were determined to rid Germany of the burden of her foreign debt, for the contraction of which they did not hold themselves responsible. But in condemning the German default it is important not to ignore the extent to which the problem had become intrinsically insoluble, or the degree to which Germany's creditors themselves shared the responsibility.

long-term foreign debts, ingeniously coupled, as we shall see presently, with the promotion of German exports by concealed depreciation; in November 1934 the transfer moratorium was made complete. In the meantime, the German system of exchange control was breaking down. Between February and March 1934 the quota of foreign exchange allocated to importers was reduced from 50 per cent to 5 per cent and finally to a day-to-day allotment based on the Reichsbank's intake of foreign exchange. Orders could not be cancelled as quickly as facilities for payment were restricted, the volume of outstanding commercial debts increased, and foreign Governments began to apply pressure to safeguard the interests of their exporters.

In these circumstances the Reichsbank in September 1934 adopted a so-called New Plan which replaced the old system of percentage allocation of foreign exchange by a system under which a foreign exchange certificate had to be obtained for each individual transaction from one of twenty-seven Import Control Boards set up under the Plan before a definite order could be placed and the goods imported. The primary object of the New Plan was to solve the international payments problem by holding imports strictly to the available amount of foreign exchange, and by diverting purchases as far as possible to countries with which Germany had clearing agreements. In addition, import control was to ensure that preference was given to imports of raw materials, particularly those needed for rearmament, over imports of manufactures and foodstuffs to satisfy consumers' demand. It was this second objective, the qualitative selection of imports, which necessitated the substitution of direct import control for foreign exchange rationing. It soon appeared that control of imports, involving the rationing of importers, had of necessity to be extended to all subsequent users of the imported raw materials. At the same time, the new power of granting or withholding import permits enabled the Government, through the agency of the Import Control Boards, to extend its control of real investment, production and prices, in pursuit of its internal economic policy.

With the adoption of the New Plan, State control of German foreign trade became complete. On the import side, the volume, quality, price and source of every article was controlled directly. On the side of exports the New Plan did not contemplate direct control, except for prohibitions on the export of certain raw materials. But indirectly State control of imports obviously made the German exporter completely dependent on Government foreign trade policy.

THE system of clearing trade, like exchange control, was not a premeditated invention of the Nazis but grew out of the attempts, first of private traders, later of the Government itself, to escape the foreign exchange dilemma. The first impulse arose from the efforts of German import firms, unable to obtain foreign exchange, to enlist the assistance of German exporters for the arrangement of direct barter deals with their counterparts in a foreign country. Private compensation deals of this type which enjoyed a brief vogue during 1932 and 1933 made possible a certain amount of international exchange of goods which would otherwise have been prevented by lack of payment facilities. But since such deals were confined to exchanges of a definite quantity of goods and rarely involved fewer than four parties, this method of trading was limited in scope and excessively clumsy.

A more generalized form of barter developed during 1933 through the so-called Aski accounts, opened with German banks in favour of foreign exporters. The Aski accounts worked in effect like constantly renewed private compensation deals, the foreigner adjusting his sales to Germany (for which he received Aski marks) exactly to the volume of German goods (which he or another importer in his country purchased with Aski marks) for which he had use abroad. This system greatly extended the scope of barter trading but it soon raised in an acute form a problem which had already been encountered in the case of private barter deals. Owing to the overvaluation of the mark German exports suffered from a severe price handicap in foreign markets, with the result that the supply of Aski marks (the proceeds of German imports) constantly tended to outrun the demand. Foreign exporters could dispose of their holdings of Aski marks to potential importers only at a discount sufficient to compensate the potential importer of German goods for the price difference (the exporters in turn adding the premium to the price of the goods sold to Germany). The result was that the Aski system automatically tended to offset the overvaluation of the mark by the varying discounts at which Aski marks were sold abroad, at the cost of the German consumers of imports. At first the German Government attempted to limit the scope of this devaluation of the mark by allowing compensation dealings only for so-called 'additional' exports, that is, exports which could not have been sold at all at the official rate of exchange. But as the premium developed, German exporters were increasingly tempted to divert exports from channels bringing in free exchange to compensation channels. The difficulty of defining 'additional' exports and suppressing evasion led to increasing restrictions and the gradual abolition of Aski compensation trade after 1935.[1]

The technically most perfect form of barter trade which gradually ousted the earlier methods and became the framework of nearly 65 per cent of Germany's foreign trade was the system of clearing. Instead of leaving it to private dealers to search out possibilities of barter deals, the Government concluded general compensation or clearing agreements with whole countries. The essence of a clearing agreement consisted in the establishment in both countries of an account into which importers (and other debtors) paid, in their own currency, the sums they owed to their creditors in the other country and from which exporters to (and other creditors of) the other country were paid, again in their own currency. It had the advantage over both direct barter and Aski compensation, that it could be extended so as to include not only commercial but all other types of international transactions, such as debt payments, etc.[2] Clearing, on the other hand, initiated a new problem which did not arise in the case of direct barter or compensation trade, the problem of the 'uncleared balance'. Whereas private traders would embark on a barter deal only after they had made certain that the complementary orders had been placed and payments arranged, there was no certainty that the total trade between two countries would automatically balance. One method of achieving the necessary balance was to allow the exchange rate for each particular clearing account to fluctuate freely. In practice such violent exchange fluctuations so greatly increased the risk element in foreign trade that this method was rarely used. In the absence of freely fluctuating exchange rates, however, the balance could only be achieved by direct control of trade. In practice, therefore, the clearing system presupposed a considerable measure of State control of foreign trade in both countries.[3] On the other hand, the clearing system itself strength-

[1] The term Aski was retained for the German clearing agreements with the South American republics. These, however, were really clearing agreements proper under which the rates of exchange were fixed by agreement and substantial balances did not infrequently accumulate.

[2] Germany's first clearing agreements in fact originated on the one hand, in the efforts of Germany herself during 1932 to enforce payment of accumulated commercial debts to her exporters by the exchange control countries of South-Eastern Europe and, on the other hand, in the efforts of the creditor countries of Western Europe during 1934 to safeguard the interests of their nationals against the threat of default on Germany's foreign debt by establishing clearing accounts and setting aside a proportion of the proceeds of German exports for debt payment. Both types, therefore, had their *raison d'être* originally in financial rather than commercial considerations.

[3] It was this dilemma between violent exchange fluctuations and direct trade control which led a number of free trading countries, such as Great Britain, to insist on a modified form of clearing agreement, termed 'payments agreement', which necessitated State control of trade in only one of the two countries. Under the Anglo-German payments agreement Germany undertook to adjust her imports from Great Britain from month to month to British imports from

ened the powers of control of the Governments concerned. The fact that each clearing constituted, as it were, a closed system resulted in the establishment of a multiplicity of different rates of exchange between the respective currencies, rates which were often fixed afresh for each major transaction. Though the exchange rates were in theory fixed by agreement, this possibility provided the Government with the superior bargaining power with a supple instrument for controlling the volume and terms of its foreign trade.

The outstanding advantage of trade by barter methods, including clearing, was that it obviated the need for international means of payment, gold or foreign exchange. It was this which drove Germany and other countries whose gold and foreign exchange reserves had been exhausted by capital flight and adverse balances of payments, into adopting this method of trade. It is important to see clearly what this advantage really implied. Obviously it did not mean that Germany, for instance, no longer had to pay for her imports;[1] she still had to purchase her imports with exports, though the latter, instead of placing her in the possession of free foreign exchange, increased her clearing balance in the importing country. The only real difference between clearing and free exchange trade in this respect was that, whereas under the free exchange system a country whose foreign exchange reserves were exhausted could not import until it had acquired the necessary foreign exchange by means of increased exports—often rendered impossible by foreign tariff walls and the difficulty of finding foreign markets—the clearing system enabled a country to take the initiative by increasing its imports.[2] For a country which, like Germany in 1933, urgently required foreign imports, but whose export trade was hampered both by an overvalued currency and foreign trade restriction, this was in itself an important advantage. But this difference between the free exchange and the clearing system had a further important consequence. It meant that under the clearing system the onus of establishing the necessary balance in the clearing account gener-

Germany. This system made it possible for British imports to be conducted on a free exchange basis, though it meant that the volume of Anglo-German trade was determined exclusively by British initiative, Germany merely following suit. Incidentally, as we noted before, the Anglo-German payments agreement did not provide for a 1:1 ratio between British and German imports, but for a substantial German export surplus, the proceeds of which were in part set aside for debt payments, partly conceded to Germany in the form of free exchange.

[1] Nor, on the other hand, as is sometimes asserted, did it mean that clearing trade ruled out the possibility of export (or import) surpluses and thus made debt payments impossible; as we have seen, many clearing agreements provided for debt payments to be financed by export surpluses.

[2] In effect, a clearing agreement amounted to the reciprocal grant by the two parties, of loans, or rather overdrafts, conditional upon repayment in the form of exports.

lly rested with the country with a (temporary) export surplus.
For since a country which bought more than it sold in effect received goods without payment and merely increased its clearing
debt to the other country, it was the latter which had to assure
payment to its exporters either by increasing in turn its purchases
from the foreigner or, if need be, curtailing its exports. In so far
as this characteristic of clearing trade in itself placed a premium
on an expansion of international trade—and in certain circumstances this was undoubtedly the result—it was a decided merit
of the system. But it also constituted a powerful weapon in the
hands of a country which, like Nazi Germany, was alone eager to
buy in a world anxious to sell, particularly if that country was the
first to use the weapon of accumulating clearing debts on its
unsuspecting clearing partners. The possibilities of exchange
rates manipulation and the accumulation of clearing debts together turned the clearing system into a powerful weapon of
which the Nazi Government made full use in its foreign trade
policy.

All these advantages, some but not all of them highly dubious
advantages from the point of view of an international economic
order, of the system of barter and clearing trade were balanced
by an outstanding disadvantage. The whole point of the clearing
system consisted in the balancing of the credit and debit sides of
the balance of trade (or if other than merchandise transactions
were included, the balance of payments) of the country concerned
so as to dispense with international payments to settle (long-run)
surpluses. This, however, meant in practice that clearing confined
international trade to the bilateral exchange of goods between
pairs of countries. Though in principle there is no reason why
three or more countries should not arrange their foreign trade
in such a way that, while there is no balance between any two of
them, their collective obligations to each other cancel out, the difficulties in the way even of triangular clearing proved at the time
insuperable.[1] In practice, therefore, the reorganization of German
trade on a clearing basis involved the abandonment of some of the
advantages of international trade and in particular the loss of most
of the benefit, in terms of comparative costs, which Germany had
traditionally derived from her multilateral trade, based on her
sales of manufactures to the industrial countries of Europe and
her purchases of raw materials and foodstuffs overseas. We shall
later inquire how far the Nazis succeeded in reducing this loss by
exploiting the opportunities for discriminating monopoly afforded
by the system of foreign trade control.

[1] Some attempts at triangular clearing arrangements were made, e.g. between
Germany, Rumania, and Yugoslavia in 1939 and, in a more restricted form,
between Germany, Japan, and Greece. But they were isolated instances which
assumed no great importance during the nineteen-thirties.

Exchange control and the clearing system provided the Nazi with the instruments for a planned foreign trade policy. How were these instruments used?

IV. NAZI FOREIGN TRADE POLICY

THE New Plan, in laying down the policy of restricting import to the available amount of foreign exchange, merely underlined the obvious fact that the growing German import requirement would be satisfied only by an expansion of German exports. German exports, however, were hampered by the overvaluation of the mark which maintained German export prices considerably above the competitive level on international markets. On the face of it, therefore, Nazi foreign trade policy after 1934 was dominated by the efforts of the Nazi Government to overcome this artificial and largely self-inflicted handicap.

The methods which were used to stimulate exports varied considerably. Broadly speaking, it is possible to distinguish between four types of policies which Germany adopted respectively towards four groups of countries: (a) The countries with which Germany conducted trade on a free exchange (or payment agreement) basis; (b) creditor countries with which clearing agreements had been concluded; (c) the exchange control countries of South-Eastern Europe; (d) South America.

a. Free Exchange Countries. With a number of important countries, including especially Great Britain, the British Dominions and the U.S.A., Germany did not conclude clearing agreements. Imports from these countries, therefore, continued to require foreign exchange, to be obtained either by increased exports to the country concerned or to countries which were prepared to make available to Germany free foreign exchange or gold. It was with these countries that the overvaluation of the mark proved the greatest obstacle. As far as possible Germany under the New Plan tried to escape the difficulty by directing her purchases away from these countries to those with which she had clearing agreements. But a limit was set to this diversion by the fact that Germany depended on most of them either as sources of essential raw materials which she could not obtain elsewhere or as sources of free exchange.

In her trade with those countries Germany had resort to export subsidies. During 1933 and 1934 the funds for this purpose came almost entirely from windfall profits earned through repatriation of German bonds and scrip issued in lieu of debt payments. The imposition of exchange control had naturally led to a fall in the prices of German bonds abroad. As early as 1932 the Reichsbank had taken advantage of this by permitting exporters to purchase these bonds at their low prices and to use the profit from the resale in Germany to lower the prices of their exports, provided these exports were 'additional'. In 1933 this ingenious device was extended to debt payments, Germany permitting transfer of interest and amortization payments only at a discount (which her creditors were prepared to accept rather than have their accounts blocked in Germany). Both methods amounted in effect to a concealed devaluation of the mark; but whereas an all-round devaluation would have raised the prices of German imports, the cost was here, in effect, borne not by the German consumer but by Germany's foreign creditors.[1] When lack of foreign exchange compelled the German Government in 1934 to stop these capital exports by a complete transfer moratorium, this source of funds dried up. From 1935 onwards export subsidies were financed primarily by a levy imposed on German industry, each branch of industry being compelled to contribute part of its profits on sales in the home market.[2] Yet another form of subsidizing exports was to discount export bills at lower rates of interest than others.

Financial subsidies, however, proved inadequate to ensure the requisite volume of exports, partly because German firms found a slightly higher profit margin on export trade inadequate compensation for the trouble involved in export dealings under exchange control and preferred to sell in the booming home market. The German Government endeavoured to counteract this tendency by offering special inducements to exporters, such as giving absolute priority in the allotment of raw materials to the manufacture of goods for export and distributing Government orders among industrial concerns in proportion to the effort made by each in the promotion of foreign sales. In 1938 the Government even resorted to direct control in the form of export quotas assigned to each industry with penalties for failure to fulfil them.

Export stimulation by subsidies and direct control was not confined to German trade with free exchange countries. But in trade with the other three groups of countries these methods played a relatively subordinate part.

b. *Creditor Clearing Countries.* A number of Western Euro-

---

[1] Strictly speaking, of course, the windfall profits which Germany made at the cost of her foreign creditors might have been used to subsidize prices at home (or for any other purposes) while the funds for export subsidies might have been taken from any other internal sources. There was no necessary connection between the export subsidies and the losses of Germany's creditors.

[2] In 1935 this tax is estimated to have produced 750 million RM (J. C. de Wilde, 'The German Economic Dilemma', *Foreign Policy Reports*, 15 March 1937, p. 7). Internally, as we have seen, the tax formed one of several instruments for directing the profits of private industry into forms of investments considered necessary by the Government (in this case foreign trade).

pean creditor countries, including France, Switzerland, and Holland, had concluded clearing agreements with Germany in 1932 in order to earmark the proceeds of German export surpluses for debt payments to their nationals. But the clearing system, as we have seen, made it possible to increase imports freely without immediate payment. From 1933 onwards, therefore, Germany increased her purchases from these countries to such an extent (their exporters being only too pleased to sell) that not only did the German export surpluses disappear but Germany accumulated substantial debts in her clearing accounts with these countries. When the latter began to realize that they were in fact selling goods to Germany without immediate prospect of any repayment in the form of German exports they reacted by curtailing exports to Germany and, in the case of France, by substituting a payments agreement for the clearing agreement, thus making a repetition of the experience impossible. By rationing exports these countries were able to force Germany gradually to reduce her clearing debts. For Germany, on the other hand, trade under these conditions was just as disadvantageous as with free exchange countries, and during the following years German trade with these countries stagnated or declined.

c. *South-Eastern Europe*. The core of the explanation of Nazi trade expansion in South-Eastern Europe must be found in the fact that Germany alone was prepared to buy the primary products of these countries at remunerative prices. All these countries were producers of agricultural commodities, especially wheat and other cereals, pigs and tobacco, and depended for their necessary imports of manufactures on the sale of their agricultural surpluses. For various reasons, however—unsuitability of the soil, overpopulation, malorganization, and lack of capital resources—these countries had failed to keep step with the improvements in agricultural technique which had been applied during the first three decades of the century in the large primary producing countries of the Western Hemisphere and the British Dominions. With the collapse of agricultural prices during the great depression they altogether ceased to be able to compete with the overseas producers in international markets At the same time, most of their former European markets were closing the doors to their products. In this desperate situation Germany appeared as their saviour.

Germany, as we have seen, was prepared to buy Rumanian wheat, Hungarian maize, Yugoslav pigs, and Greek tobacco at higher than world market prices not only because purchases from these countries (all of which had been forced by the state of their balances of payments to adopt exchange control and had concluded clearing agreements with Germany) did not require payments in free exchange but because the Nazis were out to obtain political and economic control over this area in the event of war. It is important to realize that with the inability of the Balkan producers to charge competitive prices in international markets and the refusal of countries like Great Britain to assist them in their plight the German game was already half won. In practice Germany resorted to innumerable devices to increase her stranglehold on the Balkan economies.

The simplest and most effective was the accumulation of clearing debts. During 1935 and 1936 Germany increased her purchases from these countries through her clearing accounts. As her clearing debts accumulated, the Balkan exporters were unable to obtain payment, and in order to reduce the frozen balances the Governments of the Balkan States had to induce their importers to purchase commodities in Germany rather than elsewhere. Given equal bargaining power this form of blackmail worked only once with each victim.[1] France, Holland, and Switzerland, as we saw, had easily put a stop to it by cutting down exports to Germany. The Balkan countries, however, were not in a position to do so. Most of them made some attempts to expand their trade with other countries when they began to realize the dangers of excessive dependence on Germany, either by curtailing exports to Germany (a method which Turkey used with some success) or by insisting on payment in free exchange for part of their exports. But both methods presupposed the availability of alternative markets, and this remained the decisive factor.[2] Unable to sell their surpluses at remunerative prices elsewhere, they had no choice but to continue selling to, and therefore also buying from, Germany.[3]

Other methods by which the Nazis heightened the economic dependence of the Balkan countries on Germany included the dumping of Balkan products below cost price in other countries

[1] The German clearing debts with the Balkan countries were actually never very large. The combined clearing balances of the five countries (excluding Turkey) seldom exceeded 150 million RM, i.e. about 10 per cent of the total value of their exports (Royal Institute of International Affairs, *South-Eastern Europe*, second edition, June 1939, p. 198); they none the less helped Germany in getting a foothold.

[2] How important the availability of even one substantial alternative market was is illustrated by the direct effect of the imposition and removal of sanctions against Italy on Yugoslavia's bargaining power in her trade relations with Germany. The closing of Yugoslavia's most important alternative market by the imposition of sanctions in 1935 forced her to open her doors to the first German trade drive. When in 1936 sanctions were lifted Yugoslavia was promptly able to insist on a more favourable exchange rate in her clearing agreement with Germany. (H. S. Ellis, *Exchange Control in Central Europe*, p. 262 f.)

[3] A factor of some importance in assisting German trade expansion was the fact that, owing to the distribution of political power in most of the Balkan States, the interests of the agricultural producers who were chiefly concerned with finding markets for their surpluses generally prevailed over the weaker industrial interests which had to foot the bill.

(which had the twofold advantage of spoiling these foreign markets for Balkan exporters and bringing in free exchange for Germany); and, especially during the last two years before the war, the lavish grant of long-term credits (which actually cost Germany nothing, for the postponement of payment by the Balkan importers caused a lack of funds in the clearings with the result that the central banks of the Balkan countries had to advance money to their exporters, the credits being in fact financed not by Germany but by the Balkan Governments); direct barter agreements for the exchange of specific commodities on the basis of similar large-scale credits;[1] German willingness to sell (second-quality) armaments, often on 'credit', which in turn required further imports from Germany of ammunition, spare parts, and replacements; and, last but not least, direct political and military pressure.

Already by 1935 or 1936 Germany had succeeded in strengthening her economic hold on the Balkan countries to such an extent that she was able to exploit her position by turning the terms of her trade with the Balkan countries in her favour, that is, by insisting upon a higher exchange value of the mark in clearing agreements, by charging high prices for her exports, delivering goods of inferior quality or even goods which these countries did not want, refusing to deliver goods which could be sold in other countries for free exchange, and so forth. The extent to which Germany actually exploited her strong bargaining position is a matter of dispute. There can be no doubt that she used all these methods at one time or another with each of the Balkan countries. But substantial evidence has been adduced to show that, until 1939, Germany did not take full advantage of the opportunities of exploitation which her economic dominance over the Balkan countries presented.[2] The reason is not far to seek. Germany's main object in her trade expansion in South Eastern Europe was not to obtain cheap imports for her current require-

[1] Thus, in October 1938, Turkey was granted a credit of 150 million RM which was to be repaid in Turkish primary products; similar large credits were granted in 1938 and 1939 to Poland, Bolivia, and Argentina (H. C. Hillmann, 'Analysis of Germany's Foreign Trade and the War', *Economica*, February 1940, p. 79).

[2] An independent observer came in 1939 to the following conclusions which can be substantially accepted: 'It is true that (Germany) has been reluctant to assist the industrialization of these countries by supplying them with machines which they could not get elsewhere. But this has not been, in fact, of major importance. It is also true that there have occasionally been long delays by Germany in fulfilling orders (e.g. for aluminium or electrical plant), and that the quality of German textiles, machinery and other goods has fallen off during recent years—a tendency equivalent to a rise in price. But, taking a broad view, Germany has on the whole so far charged competitive prices for her goods, quality for quality—in certain cases to an extent suggesting subsidized dumping —and has not much restricted the types of goods which she will sell.' (R. I. I. A. *South-Eastern Europe*, p. 196 f.)

ments but to secure an area of economic dependence in the event
of war. With that object in view it was sound policy to forgo
some immediate economic gain in favour of the economic as well
as strategic advantages to be derived later from complete political
and economic domination. The policy itself, and the extent to
which it was successful, received striking illustration even before
the outbreak of war in the German trade agreement with Rumania
of March 1939, which went far beyond the scope of a normal trade
agreement in laying down a comprehensive plan for the reorganization of the whole Rumanian economy to fit in with Germany's
import needs.[1] The really significant point is that Germany did
not use her obvious predominance for purposes which could be
simply dismissed as 'exploitation', but for an adaptation of the
Rumanian economy to German requirements which was by no
means necessarily *economically* disadvantageous to Rumania. Her
treatment of the Balkan countries after the outbreak of war is,
of course, a different story.

d. *South America.* Next to South-Eastern Europe, South
America provided the main sphere of Nazi trade expansion. Like
the Balkan countries, most of the South American republics had
been forced during the depression to impose exchange control
and were prepared to trade with Germany on a barter or clearing
basis. Like the Balkan countries also, the South American countries were saddled with large agricultural surpluses. On the other
hand, owing to the fact that the South American countries were
able to sell at competitive prices, had strong financial and trade
connections with the U.S.A. and Great Britain, and were not so
amenable to political pressure, Germany's position towards them
was not nearly as strong as in South-Eastern Europe. The methods which Germany pursued in South America, therefore,
stood half-way between her Balkan policy and her policy towards
free exchange countries, relying partly on superior bargaining
power, partly on export subsidies.

During 1934 and 1935, the South American trade drive was
based on the system of Aski-compensation described before.
Since the value of Aski-marks was allowed to fluctuate (at varying
discounts) in accordance with supply and demand, this method
amounted to concealed export subsidies borne mainly by the
German consumers of South American goods. During 1935,
however, Germany replaced Aski-compensation by what

---

[1] The agreement laid down detailed plans for the reorganization of the Rumanian economy, the intensification of production of fodder, oil seeds and textile
plants, the cultivation of new crops, the scientific exploitation of Rumanian
forests, the technical improvement of Rumanian mines, communications and
public utilities, all to be carried out and largely financed by joint German-
Rumanian companies under the guidance of German experts—a scheme of
scientific and far-sighted colonial development. (ibid., p. 136 f.)

amounted to clearing agreements (though the name Aski was retained) with fixed exchange rates under which clearing debts soon accumulated. Germany was not strong enough in the South American market to insist on the official high exchange rate of the mark. In all her Aski clearing agreements with the South American republics the rates of exchange were fixed at varying discounts below the official rate in order to offset the German export price handicap. But from 1935 onwards accumulated clearing balances and the dependence of the South American countries on the German market placed Germany in a strong position. In the case of South America, the Nazis could entertain no hopes of obtaining complete economic control. It is therefore not surprising that, in contrast to German policy in South Eastern Europe, Germany, after 1935, appears to have taken full advantage of her position to turn the terms of trade in her favour.

Since it is obvious that Germany had to resort to these various and ingenious devices of export stimulation because the over-valuation of the mark raised her export prices above competitive levels in world markets it has been suggested that Germany in practice attempted to achieve by complicated and costly methods what she could have achieved, without State control of foreign trade, by devaluation; in other words that the advantage of over-valuation in allowing Germany highly favourable terms of trade had in fact to be sacrificed by concealed devaluation and export subsidies in order to enable Germany to export and import at all. It is true that the result of trade by Aski-compensation which lowered German export prices at the expense of increasing import prices, of export subsidies which were paid by German industry, and of the payment of higher than world prices to Balkan producers was in effect much the same as that of devaluation. But there was one profound difference. Whereas a devaluation of the mark by say 40 per cent would, *ceteris paribus*, have meant a flat increase of 66⅔ per cent in the prices of all German imports and a decrease of 40 per cent in the prices (in terms of other currencies) of all exports—regardless of the question whether in any particular market such a decrease was necessary in order to enable Germany to sell (and buy)—the policy actually pursued was one of 'selective depreciation', that is to say, a policy of lowering exports and increasing import prices (in other words, worsening her terms of trade) only where and when it appeared necessary in order to obtain the desired imports. The whole Nazi system of foreign trade policy was thus based on the exercise of what is technically called 'discriminatory monopoly'. Where her position as the only export outlet for a country's surpluses, or her successful employment of the blackmail of accumulated clearing balances, or direct political pressure placed Germany in a strong position she was able to obtain the raw materials or other imports she needed at relatively better prices than where these opportunities did not exist and she had to compete for markets and goods with other countries.

V. THE RESULTS

AS in the case of the internal economic policy of the Nazi régime, it is not possible to assess the achievement of Nazi foreign trade policy by the normal economic criteria. Nazi commercial policy pursued two politico-economic objectives, first, to supply Germany with the imports required for rearmament, for the essential needs of German consumers, and for war reserves, and secondly, to obtain for Germany an area of economic and political dependency in South-Eastern Europe primarily as an additional safeguard against the danger of blockade in war. It can hardly be denied that both these objectives were accomplished.

Though the shortage of foreign raw materials constituted throughout the years from 1934 until the outbreak of war one of the greatest, if not the greatest, economic problem of the Nazis, the policy of purchasing the requisite imports where they were to be had almost regardless of cost and of ruthlessly cutting down 'unessential' imports of consumers' goods in favour of essential raw materials[1] enabled them not only to meet the current needs of German industry but to accumulate in addition an unknown though undoubtedly substantial volume of war reserves.

Events have shown that the success achieved in the pursuit of the second objective was hardly less complete though, short of a political and economic history of these events, it is difficult to define this success with precision. Germany's willingness to buy the products of the Balkan countries at remunerative prices and under long-term contracts enabled her to increase her share in the foreign trade (both imports and exports) of the six Balkan countries from an average of less than one-fifth in 1933 to one-third in 1937 and, after the annexation of Austria and the

---

[1] The length to which this policy was carried is reflected by the shift in the share of the volume of German imports from finished goods to raw materials and semi-finished goods. Between 1932 and 1938 the share of the former declined from 8·3 per cent to 5·6 per cent while the share of the latter rose from 47·2 per cent to 52 per cent. It is an interesting reflection on Nazi agricultural policy (partly accounted for, however, by imports of war reserves) that the share of food imports actually increased between 1933 and 1938 from 38·7 per cent to 41·2 per cent. (H. S. Ellis, *Exchange Control in Central Europe*, p. 381.)

Sudetenland, to more than half in 1938.[1] As the buyer of half their surplus products and supplier of half their imports Germany was assured of a measure of economic predominance over these countries from which they were the less able to rid themselves owing to the failure, at any rate until 1938, of Germany's competitors to provide them with concrete assistance in the form of markets, credits and armaments. The British economic counter-offensive, when it did come in 1938, achieved a limited measure of success only in the case of Turkey. In Rumania, Hungary, and Bulgaria and, to a lesser extent, in Yugoslavia and Greece, economic penetration coupled with political and military pressure, had by the outbreak of war placed Germany in a position to adapt their economies to her own needs, both economic and political.

Strictly speaking, it is in such, rather than in precise, purely economic terms that the success of Nazi commercial policy has to be assessed. For its objectives were political as well as economic. Provided this fact is kept in mind, however, it is legitimate to consider the results of Nazi commercial policy in economic terms which may offer a basis for comparison with other countries and for an evaluation of the methods which the Nazis employed.

Even the purely economic achievement of Nazi commercial policy was far less meagre than has generally been assumed by those who condemned its methods. When Hitler came to power in January 1933 the value of German foreign trade had declined to 9,075 million RM (from 26,930 million RM in 1929), exports amounting to 4,871 million RM and imports to 4,204 million RM;[2] the gold and foreign exchange reserves of the Reichsbank had fallen from nearly 3,000 million RM in 1929 to 920 million RM;[3] and Germany was still saddled with a foreign debt of a nominal value of 19 milliard RM.[4] By 1938 the value of German foreign trade had recovered to 10,929 million RM, an increase

[1] GERMAN TRADE WITH SOUTH-EASTERN EUROPE
Percentage of each country's trade conducted with Germany.

	Imports			Exports		
	1933	1937	1938*	1933	1937	1938*
Hungary	19.7	26.2	48.1	11.2	25.6	50.1
Yugoslavia	13.2	32.6	50.0	13.9	21.5	49.9
Rumania	18.0	30.8	48.5	10.6	20.6	35.9
Bulgaria	38.2	54.8	57.9	36.0	43.1	63.6
Greece	10.3	26.1	31.1	19.7	27.3	43.2
Turkey	25.5	42.0	51.3	18.9	36.0	47.3

* 1938 figures including Austria and the Sudetenland. Figures from an unpublished memorandum of the R. I. I. A. on German Trade Policy.

[2] H. S. Ellis, *Exchange Control in Central Europe*, p. 380.
[3] ibid., p. 373 f.
[4] ibid., p. 231.

of more than 20 per cent;[1] Germany's foreign debt had been reduced to 10 milliard RM;[2] and the state of Germany's balance of payments and gold and foreign exchange was at least not much worse than in 1933.[3] It is true that the revival of Germany's export trade was greatly assisted by the world recovery and the consequent increase in demand;[4] it is also true that something like a third of the reduction in the German foreign debt was due to paper profits from foreign devaluations and real profits exacted by exchange control,[5] to say nothing of the fact that after 1934 Germany rid herself of the real burden of most of her long-term debt by default;[6] and it is true, lastly, that Germany found some relief from her foreign exchange difficulties in the sale of practically all her direct foreign investments,[7] and in such *coups* as the spoliation of Austria and Czechoslovakia.[8] But even taking

[1] H. S. Ellis, op. cit., p. 380; even taking into account the fall in prices, this meant that in 1938 the volume of German trade was still 30 per cent below the 1929 level; but it must be remembered that in 1929 German foreign trade was abnormally large owing to the inflow of foreign capital and German debt and reparation payments.

[2] ibid., p. 287; to these 10 milliard should perhaps be added Germany's accumulated clearing debts which, however, had by 1938 already been reduced to 250 million RM (ibid., p. 289 n. 1).

[3] By June 1934 Germany's gold and foreign exchange reserves had shrunk to 94 million RM and thereafter they never rose again above the 100 million mark for any length of time (ibid., p. 374 ff.); but after 1934 the question became largely irrelevant.

[4] On the other hand, it should be remembered that between 1933 and 1935 German import demand increased faster than that of any other country.

[5] It has been estimated that the paper profits which Germany made in consequence of the effect of foreign devaluations in reducing the value of German foreign debts amounted to 6 milliard RM between 1931 and 1937; of this, probably half was due to devaluations prior to 1933; the real profits made by Germany by depreciation of blocked marks and repatriation of German bonds at bargain prices have been estimated at 1—1·5 milliard RM (ibid., p. 288).

[6] Germany, however, continued to meet part of her debt service even after 1934. The transfer moratorium did not cover German short-term debts, which were regulated by the annually renewed Standstill Agreements. Under this arrangement Germany continued to pay interest and amortization charges, though at frequently reduced rates and substantial discounts, thus reducing her foreign short-term debt to only 1·1 milliard RM in 1937 (as compared with 6·3 milliard in 1931). Germany also continued to pay interest on part of her long-term debts through payment and clearing accounts, mainly because most of her creditors (with the notable exception of the U.S.A.) were in a position to enforce payment by impounding the proceeds of their import surpluses with Germany. Thus, according to German figures, 250 million RM in interest were transferred in 1935 and an equivalent amount was probably paid in 1936 (J. C. de Wilde, 'The German Economic Dilemma', *Foreign Policy Reports*, 15 March 1937, p. 12 f.).

[7] Germany's remaining holdings which, it is believed, were almost entirely liquidated during 1936-7, are conservatively estimated at 800 million RM (J. C. de Wilde, 'Germany's Controlled Economy', *Foreign Policy Reports*, 1 March 1939, p. 300). The sale of these foreign assets represented, of course, a net loss of capital.

[8] The rape of Austria secured Germany 248 million RM worth of gold and foreign exchange, apart from certain hidden reserves and 88·6 million RM worth of favourable Austrian clearing balances. But, though large, this spoil was barely enough to finance German imports in 1938 for a fortnight. (League

these factors into account, it must be conceded that, primarily owing to the successful operation of the New Plan[1] and a vigorous and thoroughly planned foreign trade policy Germany, despite her staggering initial handicaps, on the whole managed to hold her own in international trade throughout the nineteen-thirties. Contrary to what might be expected on a superficial interpretation of the Nazi policy of self-sufficiency and also contrary to assertions frequently made by foreign observers, Germany's share in world trade under the Nazi régime did not decline, but actually increased slightly from 9·05 per cent in 1933 to 9·2 per cent in 1938.[2] In view of the demand made on Germany's productive resources by the enormous expansion of internal production,[3] the maintenance even of her 1933 position in international trade represented a not inconsiderable achievement.

This result was undoubtedly obtained at considerable cost, even for Germany herself. Apart from intangibles, such as the subjection of German exporters and importers to the irritation of rigid exchange and trade control and the relatively minor economic burden of the large bureaucratic machine which was required to administer this system of control, this cost is represented mainly by the deterioration in Germany's terms of trade due to the conversion of 80 per cent of her trade on a bilateral basis.[4] By diverting her purchases from her former sources of supply to countries which were prepared to trade with her on a barter or clearing basis Germany was able to obtain imports which, no doubt partly owing to her refusal to devaluate, she could not have obtained elsewhere.[5] But, as the theory of compara-

of Nations, *World Economic Survey*, 1937–8, p. 182 f.) Moreover, Germany acquired Austria's strongly adverse balance of trade.

[1] There can be no doubt about the general successful operation of the New Plan. During 1935 and 1936 Germany actually secured substantial export surpluses (111 million RM in 1935 and 550 million RM in 1936) the proceeds from which were used to repay clearing debts, grant credits, and, in all probability, for secret imports of raw material reserves. (J. C. de Wilde, 'Germany's Controlled Economy', loc. cit., p. 300.)

[2] League of Nations, *Statistical Yearbook 1937–8, 1939–40*. These figures are based on the *value* of German and world trade; but since Germany's higher import prices were probably largely offset by her lower export prices it is unlikely that a calculation of the changes in her share in the *volume* of world trade would lead to very different results.

[3] By contrast, the increase in the U.S. share of world trade during the nineteen-thirties was accompanied by relative internal stagnation, while the enormous increase in internal production in the U.S.S.R. was accompanied by a still further withdrawal from international trade. The British recovery during the nineteen-thirties was also based largely on a diversion of productive resources from production for the export market to production for the home market.

[4] It is often suggested that in Germany's case the trend towards bilateralism in itself reduced the volume of Germany's foreign trade since the loss of Germany's export surpluses to the industrial countries of Europe was, it is alleged, greater than her gains in the Balkans and Latin America. The figures, however, do not bear out this assertion.

[5] Or only on even worse terms.

tive costs would lead us to expect, this diversion of trade from its 'natural' channels meant that Germany had to pay more for her imports, that her terms of trade were *pro tanto* worse. The actual total loss involved in the diversion of trade into bilateral channels cannot be precisely measured since the diversion itself affected both the import prices which Germany actually paid and those which she would have paid. But there is no doubt that Germany's import prices from the Balkan countries and South America were considerably above world prices for the same commodities.[1] Nor is this all. The diversion of purchases of particular commodities to new sources of supply frequently meant that Germany had to accept products of worse or better quality than she really wanted and materials to which German machinery had to be adapted at considerable expense. Both these factors have to be taken into account in assessing the cost of bilateralism.[2]

The Nazis, as we have seen, endeavoured to reduce this cost to a minimum by conducting the whole of Germany's foreign trade on the basis of discriminatory monopoly. By exploiting every opportunity which superior bargaining power assisted by political pressure presented to obtain the best possible terms of trade on any one transaction or in trade with any one country, and by offsetting losses in one direction by gains in another, Germany was undoubtedly able to reduce the cost of bilateralism and to improve her terms of trade considerably. Any quantitative estimate, however, of the magnitudes involved is impossible, not only because of the incredible intricacy of a system based on a multiplicity of different exchange rates, differential prices, subsidies, and a hundred other devices, but because it is impossible to know and practically impossible to estimate what the terms would have been if Germany had not made use of discrimination. It is conceivable that the gains from discrimination actually outweighed the costs of bilateralism. A more plausible assumption is that discrimination merely reduced these costs by a considerable margin.

[1] The price difference was only partially due to the fact that Germany diverted her purchases to less efficient producers. Most of it was due to the fact that most countries, if they could afford to do so, charged higher prices for the same commodity under clearing than for free exchange. Cotton may serve as an example. Germany diverted her purchases of cotton mainly from the U.S.A. to Brazil, Egypt, and British India, with the result that the average German cotton import prices in 1935 were 26·9 per cent above the world market price (New York). The difference between free exchange and clearing prices is illustrated by the fact that Egyptian cotton was quoted in 1936 at 105·6 RM per 100 kg in free exchange and 125·0 RM in barter (H. S. Ellis, *Exchange Control in Central Europe*, p. 250 f).

[2] To quote again the example of cotton, the fact that Egyptian and Brazilian cotton were of different quality from American cotton increased the costs of production of German textiles. Egyptian high-quality cotton was more expensive and thus increased costs directly; the coarse Brazilian cotton raised costs because it necessitated changes in German textile machinery and by lowering the quality of the finished products.

G*

On balance, therefore, it appears that the Nazi system of controlled bilateral trade enabled Germany to retain, and even slightly increase, her share of world trade at the cost of some deterioration in her terms of trade, which in real terms meant a greater expenditure of labour and other productive resources on the production of exports. The question remains whether Germany could have achieved the same or even better results if she had retained the system of free multilateral trade. A clear answer to this question is obviously impossible. But it is possible to isolate the factors which must be taken into account in evaluating the merits and demerits of the Nazi system of foreign trade.

Now we have already seen that the diversion of most of German trade into bilateral barter and clearing channels meant a loss to Germany, expressible as a deterioration in her terms of trade, which was probably considerable (though a large part of this loss was due to the costs of transition from one source of supply to another and to the preference of other countries for free exchange over clearing customers rather than to shifts to less efficient producers) and which would have been greater still but for the exploitation by the Nazis of methods of discriminatory monopoly. It is also clear that the substitution of State control for private enterprise in Germany's foreign trade, which meant the substitution of administrative decisions by exchange control authorities and economic experts for the profit incentive and experience of private business men, often led to the unnecessary loss of former German markets (though the figures given above for the volume of German trade leave it very doubtful whether on balance German foreign trade suffered by this change). But there is also a good deal to be said on the other side.

In the first place, without State control of foreign trade and the exploitation of all the devices of discriminatory monopoly Germany could never have achieved the second of her objectives, political and economic control of South-Eastern Europe. From any but the Nazi point of view this can hardly be regarded as a merit of the system. Secondly, and this is a much weightier consideration, it is by no means certain whether, given the state of the German balance of payments and of German and the world trade in 1933, Germany could have obtained the imports she needed for her rearmament recovery—or indeed for any full recovery—under a free multilateral system of foreign trade. Germany could in 1933 have devalued the mark so as to adjust German to foreign prices. But not only would any devaluation equally have involved a worsening of Germany's terms of trade; it is doubtful, in view of foreign trade restrictions and the relatively low elasticity of demand for German manufactures during the depression, whether a moderate devaluation which would have brought German into line with world prices would have increased German exports sufficiently to enable her to buy the imports she needed.[1] To assess these various factors is impossible. But it can plausibly be argued that in the circumstances bilateralism was, if not the only, at least the cheapest way of satisfying the rapidly growing import needs of the German economy, and that this would be true, though to a lesser extent, even if the German recovery had not taken the form of rearmament. Thirdly, the Nazi system of exchange and foreign trade control provided an invaluable, if not essential, instrument of control of the internal economy. This applies not only to capital exchange control without which, as has been argued before, the German rearmament programme and indeed any expansionist recovery policy would have been impossible; but also to the system of direct import control which was a vital part of the mechanism by which the Nazi Government directed investment into the desired channels and controlled prices and production. Whether this was an objective merit of the system or a merit only within the context of the Nazi policy of rearmament depends on one's views as to the possibilities of achieving and maintaining full employment in a free economy. Lastly, State control of foreign trade made it possible to maintain full employment at home irrespective of the state of trade abroad. By the appropriate adjustment of export subsidies and other methods the Nazis were able to smooth out fluctuations in the volume of German exports so that a decline in foreign demand was reflected, not in unemployment in the industries affected (with the possible cumulative effects on the rest of the economy) but in a worsening of the terms of trade the cost of which was borne, again not by the industries concerned alone, but by the economy as a whole (or that part of it which financed the export subsidies). State control of foreign trade therefore rendered Germany comparatively immune to the danger, ever present under the free system, of the contagion of economic depression.

In the light of this analysis it is at least arguable that, in the chaotic international economic condition which resulted from the breakdown of the former world economic system and from the great depression, Germany did better on the system of controlled bilateral trade than she would have done had she tried to maintain the old system of free multilateral trade. The last, and for our purposes almost decisive question which requires discussion

[1] Nor would there have been any point in an even larger devaluation. The elasticity of demand for a country's exports normally sets a narrow limit to the possibility of increasing import capacity by devaluation. Beyond a certain point any further devaluation will actually reduce import capacity since the deterioration in the terms of trade will outweigh the increase in the volume of exports.

is, how far the benefits Germany derived from this system were obtained at the expense of other countries.

Now it need not be emphasized that the methods of Nazi commercial policy, no less than its aims and objectives, were incompatible with an ordered world economy. But it is not enough to leave it at that. In the first place, it is important to realize that it was not the system of State control of foreign trade as such but the use the Nazis made of it which was harmful to other countries. Since 'power tempts abuse', this may seem a tenuous distinction; but it is one that should be made. The same applies to the Nazi system of clearing trade which, moreover, provided a new remedy to a genuine problem: the breakdown, under the strain of fundamental economic maladjustments and unregulated capital movements, of the old system of international payments. It is possible that, adapted to multilateral trade, an international clearing system may be found a more flexible substitute for the traditional gold standard system.

The internationally most objectionable aspect of Nazi commercial policy was, apart from the use of direct political chicanery and the open threat of force, its exploitation of discriminatory monopoly, which on the face of it would appear to have benefited Germany precisely to the extent to which it harmed the rest of the world. Even here three provisos must be made. First, Germany's opportunities for exploitation would have been very much smaller than they actually were if it had not been for the fact that Germany, having solved her own recovery problem, was able to concentrate in her commercial policy on maximizing her gains from foreign trade while most other countries were forced by their internal economic problems to try to sell their exports at almost any price. To a large extent the profits which Germany made by the use of her unscrupulous methods were due to the inability of most other countries to resist an offer to purchase their otherwise unsaleable surpluses. This consideration is directly relevant to the second point: it is by no means certain that even the countries which Germany exploited most did not on balance benefit, economically and in the short run, from their trade with Germany. This is almost certainly true of the Balkans if, as it appears, Germany did not, until the war, take full advantage of her strong bargaining position. But even had Germany exploited her position to the full the Balkan countries would still have been better off than they would have been if Germany had refused to buy their products. True, they would have obtained a smaller volume of imports for any given volume of exports; but since the volume of their trade would still have been much larger than it would have been without German purchases, their total gains would also have been greater; their losses 'on price account' would have been more than outweighed by their gains 'on income account'; their real income would have been improved. The Balkan countries purchased these material short-term gains by delivering themselves over to the tender mercies of Germany. But it is vitally important to realize that they could only have avoided this fate if *either* their economies had been sufficiently well organized to enable them to stand economically on their own feet *or* if during the nineteen-thirties some of the other great Powers, especially Great Britain and the U.S.A. had come to their assistance by opening their markets to Balkan products and by granting the Balkan countries long-term credits on generous terms for the reorganization of their economies. In her trade drive in South America, Germany was not deterred by long-term semi-political considerations from exploiting the strong bargaining position she had obtained by the accumulation of clearing debts. No precise data are available to show the net effect of the German trade drive on the real income of these countries. But it is not improbable that they, too, on the whole benefited during these years from German willingness to buy their surpluses, even though at a relatively poor price taking the period as a whole. The countries which in the circumstances really suffered directly and economically from the German policy of discrimination were, first, Germany's competitors in the South American and to a lesser extent in the South-Eastern European markets whose exporters were unable to compete individually with a powerful State monopoly, and secondly, the free exchange countries, especially the U.S.A., against whom Germany discriminated—and, it must be conceded, was forced by her foreign exchange difficulties to discriminate—in her purchases.

Third and last, it should be pointed out that the advantages which Germany obtained from the use of discriminatory monopoly would have been far less but for the fact that she alone made full use of these methods against a world which was either too weak to resist her or, if strong enough, unwilling to depart to that extent from the traditional *laisser-faire* system. If the U.S.A., Great Britain, Russia, France and Japan had played the German game and retaliated by discriminating in their turn against her and each other Germany would have gained little if anything and the result in the absence of any international co-ordination would probably have been even greater economic chaos.

Even this, however, does not mean that discrimination in international trade must at all cost be ruled out. Up to a point, the Nazis were not unjustified in claiming that their use of discriminatory methods was forced upon them by the conditions in which Germany found herself in the post-depression years. Moreover, discrimination, as we have seen, could in certain cir-

cumstances be advantageous not only to the country which prac-
ticed it but could actually, by making possible trade which would
not otherwise have taken place, benefit all concerned. Lastly, it
is impossible to ignore the fact that, with the growth of internal
planning and control of national economies, the chances are that
the trend towards greater control of foreign trade of the inter-war
period, with its greater opportunities for discriminatory practices,
will continue after the present war. In the chaotic condition of the
world economy during the nineteen-thirties discrimination undoubtedly represented a more dangerous weapon of economic
nationalism and exploitation than any that was available under
the *laisser-faire* system. But no international economic system is
immune against exploitation, which can ultimately be prevented
only by sanctions of one kind or another. The real lesson which
emerges once again is that the old world economic system which,
by the operation of the automatic gold standard mechanism, had
after a fashion co-ordinated national economic policies, had
broken down and that no effective system of control had taken its
place. In these conditions, ruthlessness in international economic
affairs was at a premium. In a world economic system, however,
which provides a framework within which national economic
policies must move—whatever the form of compulsion—a place
may well be found for the use of multiple prices (and discrimination essentially is no more than that) in international trade.

Chapter Eight

NOTE ON SWEDISH RECOVERY POLICY

IN the preceding chapters we have found reasons to believe that government intervention by means of a compensatory budget policy has on the whole proved the most promising approach to the problem of trade cycle control within a free capitalist economy. The country in which this type of policy was used most carefully and successfully during the nineteen-thirties was Sweden. A brief analysis of Swedish experience may, therefore, throw some additional light on the possibilities of overcoming, or even preventing, depressions by this method.

Sweden was not seriously affected by the world depression until late in 1930. Though falling world prices had begun to depress Swedish prices, industrial production and employment during most of 1930 actually exceeded the record figures of 1929.[1] When the depression did spread to Sweden it did so in much the same way as in the case of Great Britain. Exports—even more important for the Swedish than for the British economy[2] —declined first.[3] In the autumn of 1930 output and employment in the export industries, timber, wood pulp, iron and steel, and iron ore, began to fall, and during 1931 the slump spread to the industries producing for the home market.[4] For various reasons, to which we shall revert later on, internal purchasing power was relatively well maintained, and the depression in Sweden was not nearly as severe as, for instance, in the U.S.A. or Germany. But between 1929 and 1932 industrial output declined by 21 per cent[5] (by 34 per cent in the export and by 13 per cent in the home market industries),[6] and unemployment increased from a monthly average of only 14,000 in 1929 to a figure of 186,000 in March 1933—nearly one-third of the industrial working population.[7]

[1] Brinley Thomas, *Monetary Policy and Crises: A Study of Swedish Experience* (Routledge, 1936), p. 180.
[2] In 1929 the value of Swedish exports was equivalent to approximately 22 per cent of the Swedish national income, as compared with about 18·5 per cent for Great Britain.
[3] The value of Swedish exports fell from 1,812 million kronas in 1929 to 1,550 million in 1930, 1,122 million in 1931 and 947 million in 1932 (A. Montgomery, *How Sweden Overcame the Depression* [A. Bonniers, Stockholm, 1938], p. 35).
[4] ibid., p. 32 f.
[5] B. Thomas, op. cit., p. 24.
[6] A. Montgomery, op. cit., p. 33.
[7] G. Möller, *Swedish Unemployment Policy* (reprint from *The Annals*, May 1938), New York 1939, p. 17. Mr. Möller points out that these must be regarded as minimum figures and gives as a conservative estimate of the actual unemployment at the bottom of the depression the figure of 250,000.

In the autumn of 1931, Sweden, like Great Britain, was involved in the international financial crisis, and for much the same reasons—a rapidly growing import surplus temporarily concealed by inflows of foreign balances which were then suddenly withdrawn in the rush for liquidity during June—August 1931. It is not improbable that Sweden would in any case have followed Great Britain in abandoning the gold standard and devaluing the currency since, owing to the importance of the British market for Swedish exports, Sweden could hardly have afforded a high price level in terms of sterling. As it was, the Swedish authorities were left little choice. With its foreign exchange and gold reserves depleted, Sweden, after a brief final struggle, abandoned the gold standard a week after Great Britain in September 1931. During the next three months the krona, like the pound, depreciated by approximately 30 per cent.

The abandonment of the gold standard placed Sweden in a position to pursue an independent expansionist recovery policy. For the first year after the departure from gold little use was made of this opportunity. The continued import surplus and the depletion of the gold and foreign exchange reserves of the *Riksbank* allowed little margin for a vigorous expansionist policy, and fears of inflation led the authorities to pursue at first a monetary policy directed towards preventing internal prices from rising rather than towards stemming the continued decline in the price level. A series of fortunate accidents prevented a serious deflationary attack on wages,[1] and the Government was able to cover most of the budget deficit out of accumulated surpluses of the preceding boom years, without having to resort to serious deflationary increases in taxation or reductions of expenditure.[2] This cautious policy had some beneficial results. The maintenance of the krona at a low parity assisted Swedish exports and, reinforced by a large-scale, though unofficial, mobilization of Swedish foreign assets,[3] succeeded remarkably quickly in replenishing the foreign exchange reserves of the *Riksbank*.[4] The concealed and involuntary underbalancing of the budget helped to maintain internal pur-

[1] New wage agreements in Sweden are generally made in the autumn, and in the autumn of 1930 the depression had not yet set in. In 1931 fears of inflation following the departure from the gold standard made it difficult to press for wage reductions. In the autumn of 1932 the Labour Government came into power, again with the result that wage rates were maintained (cf. G. Wilson, 'Budgetary Policy' in *Democratic Sweden*, edited by M. Cole and Ch. Smith [Routledge, 1938], p. 74).

[2] Some increases in tax rates on income and property and on tobacco and alcohol were imposed in the spring of 1932.

[3] In 1932 exports of foreign securities exceeded imports by 115 million kronas (B. Thomas, op. cit., p. 198). During the first half of 1932 the shortage of foreign exchange also led to the use of a mild form of credit discrimination against imports (ibid., p. 195).

[4] Between December 1931 and December 1932 the net holding of foreign exchange of the *Riksbank* rose from 49 to 213 million kronas (ibid., p. 198).

chasing power. Towards the middle of 1932, also, the decline in prices was brought to a halt.[1] But on the whole the Conservative Government maintained a relatively passive role, and economic activity and employment continued on their downward path throughout 1932.

In September 1932 new elections brought into office a Labour Government ready to pursue a far more active and planned reflationary policy. Its first step was to strengthen still further the foreign exchange position of the *Riksbank* (and incidentally stimulate Swedish exports) by deliberately undervaluing the krona slightly in terms of sterling throughout the winter of 1932–3,[2] so as to increase the international safety margin for its expansionist recovery policy. When this object was largely obtained in the spring of 1933, the krona was pegged to sterling at the 1932 sterling rate, thus ensuring a stable exchange rate for Sweden's foreign trade with her most important market. The improvement of the foreign exchange position, in turn, made it possible to embark upon a policy of 'cheap money'. Interest rates were gradually reduced between 1932 and 1935,[3] though here as elsewhere 'cheap money' made little impression on the volume of borrowing at the bottom of the depression.[4] The chief innovation of the Labour Government, however, was its adoption of a policy of using the State budget deliberately as an instrument of recovery.

Sweden already had more experience than most other countries with public works as a method of counteracting or alleviating unemployment. Ever since the last war it had been the practice to create work for the unemployed rather than to provide cash relief; and in 1924 a State Unemployment Commission had been set up to co-ordinate State and municipal public relief works.

[1] B. Thomas, op. cit., p. 200.

[2] The sterling rate was kept about 7 per cent below the level to which it had fallen in 1932 and to which it was restored in 1933 (A. Montgomery, op. cit., p. 42 f.).

[3] The Kreuger crash in 1932 held up the reduction of interest rates, and the character of the Swedish banking system in any case made it difficult to pursue as vigorous a 'cheap money' policy as was possible in Great Britain. But in the course of 1933 the *Riksbank* was able to reduce the discount rate to the unprecedentedly low level of $2\frac{1}{2}$ per cent. The long-term rate moved downward more slowly but reached 3 per cent early in 1935. (H. Gaitskell, 'Banking System and Monetary Policy' in *Democratic Sweden*, p. 104.)

[4] B. Thomas, op. cit., p. 202 f. The enormous increase in the foreign exchange reserves of the *Riksbank* which reached a figure of 1,500 millions in 1938 was reflected in a big increase in the note circulation and the cash reserves of the commercial banks. The credit structure, however, was barely affected until about 1936. In Sweden, as to varying degrees in the U.S.A., Germany, and Great Britain, the money market throughout the period of recovery remained extraordinarily liquid, and despite low interest rates the banks were unable to find borrowers. The Swedish boom, therefore, must have been financed largely by industry itself (H. Gaitskell, op. cit., p. 104). The existence of such liquidity and large reserves, however, by itself had a favourable psychological effect on private investment, and easy money was probably a by no means negligible factor in the recovery.

The scope of these public works, however, was narrowly restricted by various rules,[1] the cost of the works which rested largely with the local authorities imposed an excessive burden on those with heavy unemployment, and in general public works served as a substitute for relief rather than as an instrument of a conscious anti-depression policy. With the severe all-round increase in unemployment after 1929 the system of relief works largely broke down, but it had paved the ground for a deliberate public works policy. Another favourable factor was the fact that the Swedish fiscal system already made a clear distinction between current and investment expenditure of the State. The budget was divided into current and capital account, and the principle was that, while current expenditure had to be met out of current revenue (taxation), capital expenditure which was not covered by income from past investments could be financed by borrowing provided it took the form of 'productive' investment yielding income out of which loans could later be repaid. This useful fiscal device, which acknowledged that State debts that had their counterpart in income-yielding assets were no more of a financial burden than the issued capital of private companies, considerably facilitated the adoption and acceptance by public opinion of a clear-cut policy of compensatory public investment expenditure.

The aim of the budgetary policy adopted by the Labour Government in 1933 was to counteract the fall in private investment, and at the same time provide work for the unemployed, by as large an increase as possible in Government investment—regardless of whether it was 'productive' (self-liquidating) or not—to be financed by loans which were to be repaid out of increased revenue during the recovery. Significantly, the Government made no attempt to gloss over the departure from strict financial orthodoxy which this policy involved. In presenting his budget in 1933, the Minister of Finance declared that 'the budget is based on the assumption that the international situation will undergo no appreciable change and that in Sweden there will be no spontaneous recovery, except to the extent that the policy of the State will help to bring it about. . . . In seeking to achieve this object, the State's financial policy must obviously play an important part.'[2]

The public works programme took three main forms: (1) The old relief works system (which it was hoped to abolish in time)

---

[1] The works had to be 'useful' but 'non-competitive'; the amount paid in wages had to constitute a large proportion of total costs; no works could be selected which could not be carried on through the winter and could not be undertaken, abandoned, extended or contracted according to the extent of unemployment; and the wages paid, to skilled and unskilled alike, were fixed at 15 per cent below the minimum wage for unskilled labour.

[2] Quoted B. Thomas, op. cit., p. 208.

was provisionally extended with some of its objectionable features removed. (2) A new form of 'emergency' public works (*beredskaps-arbeten*) was introduced which was free from most of the special restrictions imposed on relief works and, though financed by Government borrowing, were carried out under normal market conditions; that is, they were performed by contractors, not by direct labour, and normal trade union wages were paid for skilled and unskilled labour. The principle, however, that only works that would ordinarily have been executed by or through public (State and municipal) authorities were allowed to be undertaken as 'emergency' works was retained. (3) The system of 'emergency' works further included subsidies and (largely non-interest bearing) loans which were granted for State works and buildings of all kinds, road, railway and harbour construction, house building, improvements in forestry and agriculture, and the provision of smallholdings. Whereas the first two types were most important in providing immediate work for the unemployed, the third involved the largest expenditures[1] and was most significant from the point of view of stimulating the general economic life of the country. In addition, outside the exceptional public works programme, regular investment in State enterprises was increased as far as possible.

This comprehensive programme resulted, according to one estimate, in an expansion of public investment (including investment by local authorities and private persons directly due to Government loans and subsidies) from 380·5 million kronas during the two fiscal years 1931–3 to 832 million during 1933–5, an increase of 451·5 million.[2] Another estimate places the increase in public investment *per annum* between 1929–30 and 1933–4 at 267 million kronas.[3] During the same period private investment is estimated to have declined by 550 million.[4] Additional public investment, therefore, directly made up for about half the deficiency in private investment activity,[5] not counting its indirect effects.

[1] In the fiscal year 1933–4 expenditure on relief works amounted to 60, on 'emergency' works proper to 11·5, and on loans and subsidies to 96·6 million kronas; the corresponding figures for 1934–5 were 55, 10, and 76·9 million (G. Wilson, 'Public Works Policy' in *Democratic Sweden*, pp. 86, 88).

[2] G. Möller, op. cit., p. 20 f.; even the figure for 1931–3 exceeded that for 1929–31 by more than 100 million kronas—a measure of the involuntary expansion of State activity even under the predecessors of the Labour Government.

[3] Estimate by Dr. Alf Johannsen, quoted G. Wilson, 'Public Works Policy', op. cit., p. 89.

[4] G. Möller, op. cit., p. 22.

[5] This stands in striking contrast to the New Deal in the U.S.A., where, as we saw, total public investment expenditure did not even regain the 1929 level until 1936 and where even additional *federal* investment expenditure during the critical years 1933–5 amounted to less than 10 per cent of the deficiency in private investment activity.

The Swedish Government hoped to use the budget as an instrument of recovery without, on the other hand, bringing about a permanent increase in the national debt. Its departure from past practice went no further than the abandonment of the rule that the whole budget must be balanced year by year. It was determined to balance even the capital account of the budget over the period of the trade cycle as a whole. Thus, while it decided to borrow 168 and 196 million kronas in 1933-4 and 1934-5 respectively to finance 'unproductive' investment,[1] it at the same time—partly in order to lessen the objections to its unorthodox policy—actually reduced current expenditure slightly, so as to balance the current account, and imposed additional taxation to enable loans to be repaid within a period of seven years.[2] During 1933 and 1934, however, loan expenditure accounted for 27 per cent and 29 per cent respectively of the total budgets.[3]

The public works programme of the Labour Government had come two years too late to avert the slump. Its beneficial effects were further delayed by a strike in the building industry from April 1933 until February 1934 which almost paralysed building activity in the towns, though it was less severe in the country districts—a particularly unfortunate event because the public works programme relied heavily on stimulating the building industry. In the meantime, recovery had set in with a revival in Swedish exports. Unemployment reached its peak in March 1933. Improvement was slow until the late spring of 1934 when the public works programme began to be put into effect on a large scale. But from that date unemployment declined rapidly and steadily (with considerable seasonal fluctuations which are normal in Sweden owing to climatic conditions) to a mere 9,577 in August 1937 and 8,346 in August 1938.[4] Production began to revive in the second half of 1933 and rose steadily for the remainder of the decade. By the summer of 1937 the index showed a rise of approximately 60 per cent over the lowest point touched in 1932[5] and by the time of the outbreak of the war Swedish manufacturing output was nearly 50 per cent larger than in 1929.[6] The national income of Sweden regained its 1929 level as early as

---

[1] E. Wigforss, *That Swedish Budget* (reprint from *The Annals*, May 1938, New York 1939, p. 24). The amount actually borrowed in 1934-5 was somewhat larger than the budget provided for (226·3 million; G. Wilson, 'Budgetary Policy', loc. cit., p. 72); in addition, loans for productive investment also increased, but in this respect the new policy differed only in degree from earlier practice.

[2] These taxes, however, were specially selected so as to minimize their deflationary effects on the economy.

[3] G. Wilson, 'Budgetary Policy', loc. cit., p. 69.

[4] G. Möller, op. cit., p. 24 f.

[5] H. Gaitskell, op. cit., p. 105.

[6] B. Ohlin, *Economic Progress in Sweden* (reprint from *The Annals*, May 1938), New York 1939, p. 46.

1935[1] and by the end of the decade was estimated at nearly 40 per cent higher than before the depression.[2]

The trade revival enabled the Government easily to carry through its declared budget policy. Rapidly growing revenue[3] made it possible, without any further increases in taxation apart from those imposed in 1933,[4] to repay the whole of the money borrowed for 'unproductive investment' by 1938—in four instead of the scheduled seven years. The aggregate budget surpluses of the four boom years 1935 and 1936—1938 and 1939 actually exceeded by more than seventy million kronas the budget deficits of the preceding four depression years.[5] The national debt continued to grow, but this increase was entirely accounted for by 'productive' state investments the income from which was more than sufficient to cover debt services.[6]

On the financial side, therefore, the Swedish experiment with a compensatory fiscal policy was completely successful. In real terms the policy did not work out quite according to theory. The theory provided that public investment should be increased during the slump to compensate for the deficiency in private investment and contracted parallel with the revival of private investment during the recovery. The fact that the Labour Government did not come to office until the bottom of the depression and the delay caused by the building strike made any such timing in Sweden impossible. Additional public investment did not properly get under way until 1934 and actual expenditure of the public works appropriations continued well into the boom years of 1935-7. Moreover, it was found easier to initiate public works during the depression than to contract them during the boom. Productive public investment in State businesses and on social services, such as the provision of smallholdings and housing, increased steadily during the years of recovery. Some doubt has been expressed whether this continued increase might not have rendered difficult any expansion to meet further emergencies.[7] In practice, the Swedish Government was not called upon during the nineteen-thirties to face this problem.

[1] E. Wigforss, op. cit., p. 6.

[2] League of Nations, *World Economic Survey*, 1939-41, p. 80.

[3] Government income rose from 741 million kronas in 1932-3 to 1,227 millions in 1938-9 (E. Wigforss, op. cit., p. 25).

[4] In 1936 increased defence appropriations necessitated an increase in the surtax.

[5] Figures up to 1936-7 in E. Wigforss, op. cit., p. 25; 1937-8 and 1938-9 figures from League of Nations, *Statistical Yearbook, 1939-40*.

[6] The national debt increased from 1,805 million in 1930 to 2,237 millions in 1937; but while interest payable on the debt increased by only 5 millions from 86 to 91 millions income from productive investments rose by 42 millions from 148 to 190 millions (E. Wigforss, op. cit., p. 8 f.). The reduction in interest rates on Government bonds was, of course, partly responsible for this favourable development.

[7] G. Wilson, 'Public Works Policy', loc. cit., p. 92 f.

During the recovery, preparations were made to continue the compensatory public works policy in any future slump. At the end of 1937, a report was issued which analysed the capital expenditure plans of central and local authorities for future periods of five and ten years, so that schemes of development might be held in readiness. When the American slump of that year threatened a new world depression the Swedish Government actually took the precaution of introducing a special supplementary budget of 257 million kronas for 1938–9 which empowered it to spend this sum on additional construction if a new depression developed. In fact, Sweden was little affected by the recession. The American slump was reflected in a 20 per cent fall in Swedish pulp and paper exports; timber exports also declined; but rising prices for iron ore and increased exports of engineering products largely made up for this decline, with the result that Swedish exports as a whole fell by only 150 million below the record level of 1937,[1] and, partly owing to the continued building boom, economic activity and employment suffered no appreciable decline.[2] In the circumstances, the additional expenditure on public works became unnecessary.

How far can the spectacular Swedish recovery of the nineteen-thirties be attributed to the compensatory budget and public works policy of the Swedish Government? The question has been debated a good deal and in the nature of the case no conclusive answer is possible. But there is little doubt on the main points.

It is generally agreed that the initial upturn of the trade cycle in 1933 was due to a revival of Swedish exports rather than to the public works policy which did not really get under way until early in 1934. Between 1932 and 1933 the volume of the Swedish staple exports increased by anything from 20 per cent (timber and steel) to 80 per cent (iron ore).[3] Owing to the accumulation of stocks during the depression the increase was not immediately reflected in a corresponding fall in unemployment. But output in the export industries increased by 9 per cent before output in the home-market industries began to revive appreciably.[4] Some of the credit for this early recovery of Swedish exports is due to Swedish monetary policy which benefited the Swedish recovery in much the same way as the similar British policy did in Great Britain. But the main reason was that with regard to both the character and the destination of her exports Sweden was in a

[1] *The Economist*, 'Commercial History of 1938', 18 February 1939, p. 26.
[2] Between 1937 and 1939 the index of building activity rose from 104 to 133, output in the engineering industry from 131 to 139, and the general index of industrial production from 120 in 1937, after a decline to 117 in 1938, to 124 in 1939 (League of Nations, *Statistical Yearbook 1939–40*, p. 178).
[3] A. Montgomery, op. cit., p. 59.
[4] ibid., p. 58.

peculiarly favourable position. Four-fifths of the total of Swedish exports consisted of forest products (wood pulp 20 per cent, timber 16·5 per cent, paper and cardboard 10 per cent) and iron ore and iron and steel (18 per cent).[1] All these products were vital raw materials which the rest of the world could not well do without and which were therefore relatively little affected by the growth of protectionism during the depression. Moreover, world conditions particularly favoured at least two of them. It is true that the depression had reduced Swedish iron ore exports to one-fifth of the extremely high level they had reached in 1929,[2] and timber exports had also declined considerably. But world demand for wood pulp, which was needed in the rapidly expanding world production of paper and artificial silk, hardly fell off even during the worst years of the depression, and exports of Swedish iron ore also recovered quickly and after 1934 were lifted by the world rearmament boom to a level limited only by the productive capacity of the Swedish mines.[3] Another, less important, factor which favoured the revival of Swedish exports was the fact that Sweden's most important customer, Great Britain, was the first of the large import markets to recover from the depression. Though British imports from Sweden never regained their predepression level, their substantial increase in 1933[4] was probably partly responsible for the early recovery of the Swedish export trade. Swedish exports were not only in all probability responsible for the initial revival of the Swedish economy; they also continued to play a very important part in the Swedish recovery. How favourably Sweden was placed internationally is apparent from the fact that, with the one exception of Japan, Sweden was the only country whose exports increased by a larger percentage between 1932 and 1936 than its volume of industrial production.[5]

At the same time, it is quite clear that exports alone cannot explain the remarkable Swedish recovery. The policy of the Swedish Government was primarily directed towards stimulating recovery in the home market, on the pessimistic and as it happened not entirely justified assumption that Sweden could expect little aid in her domestic recovery from a revival of world economic conditions. Both the monetary policy (which by the devaluation of the krona in effect provided some protection for the

[1] League of Nations, *International Trade Statistics 1936*, p. 264.
[2] G. D. H. Cole, 'Sweden in World Trade' in *Democratic Sweden*, p. 227.
[3] Exports of iron ore rose from a monthly average of 160,000 tons in the spring of 1932 to a monthly average of 971,000 tons in the summer of 1937—a measure of the extent to which Sweden benefited from world, and especially German, rearmament (H. Gaitskell, op. cit., p. 105).
[4] From £13·4 million in 1932 to £15·9 million in 1933 (*Statistical Abstract for the United Kingdom*).
[5] G. Möller, op. cit., p. 30.

home market) and the reflationary policy were designed to promote recovery in Sweden relatively independently of what happened in the rest of the world. And there is a good deal of evidence that, from 1934 onwards, even the Swedish recovery—like that of most other countries during the nineteen-thirties—was predominantly a home-market recovery. The extraordinarily rapid expansion of exports was, at least in part, due to the fact that the volume of exports had fallen more than the volume of home-market production during the slump; and favourable as Sweden's international position was as compared with that of other countries, her exports in 1936 were actually still 2 per cent below the 1929 level while industrial production was 35 per cent above the level of that year.[1] No figures showing the increase in employment in the export as compared with the home-market industries are available. But Swedish authorities claim that, on the basis of the general development of Swedish industries during these years, it can safely be assumed that the absolute increase in employment was considerably greater in the latter.[2] Outstanding in the development of the home-market industries, in Sweden as in Great Britain, was the building industry which in Sweden gives employment directly or indirectly to nearly one-third of the industrial working population[3] and which, after the initial delay due to the building strike, experienced a boom that continued unabated for the remainder of the decade. The comparison with Great Britain where the building boom of the nineteen-thirties was almost entirely unsubsidized might suggest that the Swedish boom would equally have taken place even without the enormous increase in State investment—entirely in home-market industries and very largely in building and construction. The argument cannot be disproved without a detailed investigation of the types of building undertaken. But there is evidence of the important contribution made in Sweden by public investment expenditure. It is known that nearly half the total reduction in registered unemployment between October 1933 and October 1934 was accounted for by persons who found direct employment through 'emergency' public works,[4] and these figures do not take into account the indirect effects of the 300 million increase in State investment on economic activity and employment. There can be no doubt that the public works policy, though it came too late to set the recovery going, played a considerable part in assisting and accelerating the trade revival.[5]

[1] *Konjunkturinstitutet*, quoted G. Möller, op. cit., p. 31.
[2] ibid., p. 31 f.; cf. also B. Thomas, op. cit., p. 226 f.
[3] *The Economist*, Commercial History of 1938, 18 February 1939, p. 26.
[4] G. Wilson, 'Public Works Policy', loc. cit., p. 91.
[5] Moreover, it must be remembered that the Swedish public works and budget policy formed only part of a general expansionist policy. Space forbids a description of the other measures that were taken. But mention must be made of the

What then are the general conclusions which can be drawn from the Swedish experience?

It is not surprising that the Swedish experiment has been acclaimed as a model for future efforts towards trade cycle control. In several important respects it was greatly superior to the expansionist policies that were pursued simultaneously in other countries. The whole policy of the Labour Government was carefully worked out and, as far as that was possible for an opposition party, planned in advance. In contrast to the New Deal, the Swedish deficit policy placed most of the emphasis on investment which directly stimulated industry rather than on relief—though here especially it should be remembered that the Swedish depression was far less severe than that in the U.S.A. and the problem of poverty and destitution infinitely less acute than that which faced the Roosevelt Administration in March 1933. Moreover, most even of that part of the increased State investment which was not profitable in the business sense made useful additions to the nation's capital equipment; and in contrast to Nazi Germany the Swedish recovery did not rely on rearmament as the prime mover of economic activity.[1] Again, cautious handling of the budget made all this possible without any increase in the interest burden of the national debt. While, as we have seen, such an increase—even of the proportions it assumed in the U.S.A. and Germany—is no disaster, a compensatory policy on the Swedish model which leaves no aftermath of redistribution and taxation problems to meet the debt service is, of course, decidedly preferable. Lastly, the Swedish recovery progressed steadily from 1934 until the war without any catastrophic relapse such as occurred in the U.S.A. in 1937 and without any need to impose direct State controls on economic activity, beyond the monetary controls implicit in the compensatory fiscal policy itself.

Yet, none of these merits of Swedish policy in themselves prove that it provides a definitive solution to the problem of trade cycle control. Owing to the fact that even in Sweden a planned compensatory policy was not applied until the bottom of the depression had been reached, Swedish experience throws no light on the vital problem whether it is possible to prevent slumps and

agricultural policy of the Swedish Government which, by price regulation and Government purchase of stocks, succeeded in maintaining and increasing the purchasing power of the farmers. Like the policy of the American A.A.A. in that respect it assisted the industrial recovery by redistributing income in favour of a large and relatively depressed section of the community. The same object was pursued by large increases in State expenditure on social services, especially during the later years of the recovery.

[1] Defence expenditure was increased in 1936 but it remained a negligible factor. Even in 1937-8 the amount spent on defence was considerably less than that spent for instance on education (G. Wilson, 'Budgetary Policy', loc. cit., p. 73).

depressions altogether by this method. All that can be, and has been, claimed is that Swedish policy was remarkably successful in the task of recovery. Even this success, however, was achieved in what are generally admitted to have been very favourable circumstances.

In the first place, partly because Sweden had during the post-war decade enjoyed a period of smooth as well as rapid economic progress which left behind no major economic dislocations, partly because internal consumers' purchasing power was relatively well maintained, the Swedish depression was far less severe than that of the larger industrial countries. Secondly, as a small country, Sweden was able to safeguard her internal expansionist policy by monetary measures without having to consider the negligible repercussions of her policy on other countries. Whereas the devaluation of the pound and the dollar wrought havoc among the gold standard countries which in turn partially nullified the beneficial effects of devaluation on the British and American economies, Sweden could safely ignore the effects of her policy on the rest of the world, both from an international and from her own point of view. Thirdly, as we have seen, Swedish exports enjoyed, throughout the nineteen-thirties and particularly from 1934 onwards exceptionally favourable conditions. For a country which relies for so large a part of its national income and employment on foreign trade as Sweden the opportunities of pursuing an independent national policy of trade cycle control are inevitably smaller than for a relatively self-sufficient country. It is normally faced with the choice of either attempting to shift its economic structure to an appreciable extent away from production for export in favour of production for the home market, with the attendant friction and loss of income that this involves in the long run, or of waiting until a recovery of world prosperity is transmitted to its own economy by a revival of world demand for its exports. Though Sweden took some steps in the first direction, she was in fact rid of the dilemma by the exceptionally rapid revival in foreign demand for at least two of her three most important staple exports. Last not least, the Labour Government in Sweden was able to pursue its expansionist policy in almost complete freedom from the handicap which, as we saw, partly accounted for the relative failure of the New Deal—the antagonism of the business world to its policy which found expression in 'loss of business confidence'. There is some evidence that the dislike of the banks against the new Government slightly impeded the cheap money policy early in 1933.[1] But on the whole such unfavourable 'confidence reactions' were very slight and had no appreciable effect on the recovery. It is difficult to account for

[1] H. Gaitskell, op. cit., p. 104.

this difference between Swedish and American experience. The openness and clarity with which the Swedish Government from the beginning explained its policy may have had something to do with it. A more important factor probably was the fact that in the U.S.A. the ambitious social reforms of the New Deal and the sudden large-scale increase in State intervention in economic life were interpreted as an attack on the system of *laisser-faire* and private enterprise, whereas in Sweden both State intervention and social reform were already before 1932 an accepted tradition. Fundamentally the explanation probably lies in differences in the social structure of the two countries, the more even distribution of wealth, the more confined economic power of big business, the absence of sharp class cleavages in Sweden as compared with the U.S.A. Whatever the reasons, the fact that private enterprise responded readily to the stimulus imparted by the State undoubtedly contributed to the success of the Swedish expansionist policy.

None of these factors, except the second, can be put down entirely to 'luck'. The relative stability of internal purchasing power during the depression is partly explained by the accidental avoidance of wage deflation and by a substantial improvement in Sweden's terms of trade;[1] but the existing system of social insurance and relief and the considerable underbalancing of the State budget even before 1932 were probably at least as important causes. Swedish external monetary policy undoubtedly helped the Swedish export trade to take advantage of the favourable turn of world demand. Even Sweden's rapid and smooth economic progress during the nineteen-twenties, though partly due to Sweden's neutrality during the great war of 1914–18 and technological trends, such as the development of electric power and the expansion of world demand for paper, which favoured a country with Sweden's natural resources, can be fully explained only with reference to Swedish social, political, and economic policy during the preceding fifty years. Similar factors, as we have seen, are probably at the bottom of the difference between Swedish and American experience as regards 'business confidence'. All this, however, merely means that the relatively progressive social and economic policies pursued in Sweden during the preceding decades made it easier for the Swedish Government to deal with the problem of the depression of 1930–3. This is an important conclusion. But it does not alter the fact that the compensatory fiscal policy was put to far less severe a test in Sweden than in any of the other countries in which it was attempted.

The conclusion we reach seems to be that the compensatory budget policy was extremely successful in Sweden; that, if such

[1] B. Thomas, op. cit., p. 220.

a policy is to be adopted, the nineteen-thirties provide no better model; but that, owing to the peculiarly favourable circumstances in which Sweden found herself, Swedish experience supplies no answer to the question whether monetary measures of this type constitute by themselves an adequate remedy to the problem of the trade cycle.

Chapter Nine

INTERNATIONAL ACTION IN THE ECONOMIC FIELD

I. INTRODUCTION

IN the foregoing chapters of this report the economic events and policies of the nineteen-thirties have been reviewed principally in terms of the problems and interests of the countries that were selected for special study. Even this approach has shown that one of the basic reasons for the failure of the world to make the best use of its economic resources for the general welfare was the absence of any effective system of international co-ordination of national economic policies. Time and again, particular countries were, in the absence of such co-ordination, virtually forced by the pressure of events into actions which injured others and aggravated the general economic situation. Before summing up the major economic lessons of the inter-war period, it may therefore be worth while to review the attempts that were made during those twenty years to solve the world's economic problems by international action and to inquire into the causes of their failure. In doing so it will be necessary to go back beyond the nineteen-thirties to the nineteen-twenties; for one fact which has already emerged from our earlier analysis and which will be confirmed in this chapter is that the opportunities for creating a sounder world economic order were missed in the first post-war decade; by the beginning of the second decade, when the world depression was already under way, these opportunities had largely passed.

The history of international action in the economic field between the two wars falls into four periods. First, the immediate post-war years from 1919 to 1924, during which the world was faced with the immense tasks of reconstruction and adjustment arising out of the transition from war to peace, and which, to a far greater extent than has generally been realized, were the crucial period, both nationally and internationally, for the subsequent course of economic events. Secondly, the years from 1925 to 1929 when most of the problems of the previous period seemed to be solved and international action seemed to have lost its urgency in the prevailing atmosphere of prosperity. Thirdly, the years from 1930 to 1933 which witnessed the breakdown of the world economic system which the world had tried to resurrect during the previous decade and a series of desperate and entirely abortive attempts to cope with the catastrophe of the world depression by international action. And finally, the years from 1933 until the outbreak of war in 1939 when political conflict and preparation for, or fear of, war increasingly rendered nugatory what attempts were made to re-establish international co-ordination of national policies.

II. THE TRANSITION FROM WAR TO PEACE 1919–24

THE economic problems which faced the world at the cessation of hostilities in 1919 were immense. Internally, each of the belligerent countries was confronted with the difficult task of transforming its economy from war to peace production. In many parts of the European continent economic activity had altogether come to a standstill, calling for the immediate provision of foodstuffs to relieve famine, and of raw materials and equipment to restart production. Quite apart from the pressing problems of relief and physical reconstruction in the war-ravaged areas of Europe, there was the far more difficult because less obvious need to adjust national economies to the changes in the world economic structure that had come about during the war years (changes which in many cases did not reveal themselves for some time), as well as to the changed political structure of Europe that had emerged from the peace treaties—for the most part without reference to economic desiderata—and, last not least, to the profound changes in the balances of international payments that arose from both. All these problems had to be dealt with in conditions of political and social upheaval, continued international hostility and actual war which continued in some parts of Europe for several years after 1918.

In retrospect it is clear that only the most determined concerted international action could have coped with these enormous economic problems. The fact that no such action was taken on anything like the scale and with anything like the vigour required was at the root of many of the economic calamities of the next two decades.

The reasons for this failure were partly institutional and political; to an equal if not greater degree they were intellectual or social.

On the one hand, any effective international action in the situation following the Armistice would have required detailed preparation and the existence of an efficient international machinery. No such preparation had been made beyond the primarily political issues of the peace settlement and the enunciation of the general principles of political and economic liberalism which were to govern the new world order. Most of the rudimentary machinery for inter-Allied co-operation which had grown up during the war was disbanded, and the new international institutions which were set up in the course of 1919, the League of Nations and the International Labour Organization, were endowed with powers wholly inadequate to deal with any major economic problems during these first years. The only international authority which during the immediate post-Armistice years was in control of adequate power and resources for concerted international action in the economic field, the Allied Supreme Council, was for the most part too preoccupied with the immediate objectives of the peace settlement and too divided on major political issues to devote to economic problems the attention they required.

On the other hand, universal insistence in all countries on unfettered sovereignty in economic matters rendered any international action dependent on the willingness of governments to co-operate, which was in turn from the beginning marred by continued international hostility between the former enemies and, what was even more disastrous, by the political disputes which arose at once between the victor powers, France, Great Britain, and Italy, and by the withdrawal into isolation of the United States. There can be no doubt that this political factor, the absence of a secure political basis for international co-operation was then, and remained throughout, of absolutely fundamental importance. But it is not underestimating its significance to suggest that, in a sense, it was merely one aspect of what now appears as the basic failure at the end of the last war—the failure on all sides and in particular on the part of the victorious Allied Governments to appreciate the magnitude of the problems confronting them and, closely connected with this, the fact that at the basis of all national and international economic policy during these years lay the belief that the solution of the world's economic problems could be left to the recuperative power of private enterprise and to automatic economic forces.

In all the major capitalist countries the watchword of internal economic policy during the immediate post-Armistice months was 'de-control'. The same conception underlay the general approach to the international economic problems during the whole of the immediate post-war period. In so far as any general principle guided the actions that were taken for world economic reconstruction, it was the speediest possible restoration of the liberal world economic system which had existed during the nineteenth century. The failure to realize[1] that the problems con-

---

[1] To point out this intellectual failure is not to deny that the adoption of this policy was, historically, due to the fact that political power in most of the important countries was in the hands of those who, rightly or wrongly, believed that their interests demanded the minimum of State interference in economic affairs.

fronting the world required more positive action than the speediest possible removal of all impediments to and controls of private enterprise was relatively innocuous in relation to the immediate problems of relief and physical reconstruction which were sufficiently apparent (and sufficiently temporary) to call forth direct intervention; it was fatal in its consequences with regard to the major maladjustments in the world economy. For it meant that what international action in the economic field was undertaken was to a large extent misdirected and left the most fundamental economic problems untouched.

The only reference to economic matters in the Covenant of the League of Nations was Article 23 which obliged members of the League to 'make provision to secure and maintain equitable treatment for the commerce of all Members of the League'. Equitable treatment and the speediest possible removal of all barriers to international trade was also the keynote of every one of the international conferences on economic problems held during the post-war years.[1]

The generally prevalent view that the resumption of international trade, particularly between the newly created countries of Central and South-Eastern Europe, was an essential condition of the economic recovery of Europe, was undoubtedly correct. Something had to be done to alleviate the chaos which resulted from each of the thirty-odd States of Europe trying to hold on to what scarce raw materials, foodstuffs, and equipment it possessed, and to prevent the import of goods which would compete with whatever industries Governments thought it desirable to protect or build up. The mistake lay in the belief that, in the prevailing conditions of political insecurity, currency instability and acute scarcity of goods, this objective could be accomplished by the mere removal of Government controls, and in the failure to recognize that trade and exchange controls, prohibitions and

---

[1] In 1920 the Supreme Economic Council recommended the 'unrestricted interchange of commodities' and condemned the 'creation of artificial economic barriers' between the States newly created or enlarged as a result of the war. The Brussels International Financial Conference of 1920 again recommended that 'each country should aim at the progressive restoration of that freedom of commerce which prevailed before the war' and condemned 'attempts to limit fluctuations in exchange by imposing artificial control on exchange operations' as 'futile and mischievous'. In 1921 at a Conference at Ponteroso the Succession States of the Austro-Hungarian monarchy actually signed a Protocol pledging themselves to remove all import restrictions within a year and to agree on a date for the abolition of export restrictions; the protocol was never ratified and no substantial progress was made. Further resolutions of the same character represented virtually the only outcome of the economic conference of Genoa in 1922. During 1922–5 the League continued its efforts to promote agreements on the reduction of trade barriers, particularly in Central Europe and did a good deal of useful work on minor technical and legal problems connected with international trade. For a review of all these activities see League of Nations, *Commercial Policy in the Inter-war Period: International Proposals and National Policies*, Geneva 1942, ch. i and ii.

tariffs served to protect national economies against shocks to which they would have been exposed had economic forces been allowed free rein in the prevailing conditions of disequilibrium. In the circumstances, recommendations in favour of freer trade were useless without positive international action to correct existing maladjustments and, in particular, to provide material assistance by the Western Powers in the planned reconstruction of the economies of Central and South-Eastern Europe which throughout the first post-war decade constituted the economic storm centre of the Continent.

Some such steps in the latter direction were attempted in the immediate post-war years. At the International Financial Conference at Brussels in 1920 a scheme was proposed by which the Western Powers were to guarantee private loans to be granted under the auspices of an international commission to the impoverished nations of Europe for the financing of essential imports. The *ter Meulen* scheme, as it was called after its author, though it did not go to the root of the problem of the Central and South-Eastern European countries, which lay in the need for planned industrialization of this area as a whole with the help of Western capital, was a step in the right direction. In practice, even that scheme was abandoned as too ambitious. A second proposal for the economic reconstruction of Europe by concerted international action, including a suggestion to establish an 'international corporation for European reconstruction', brought forward by the British Government at the Genoa Conference of 1922, was little more than a political counter-move to the French policy of extracting reparations from Germany at all cost, and was in practice entirely overshadowed at the Conference by the political problem of Europe's relations with Soviet Russia and the Anglo-French dispute over the reparations problem. In 1921 an equally abortive attempt was made by the Economic Committee of the League of Nations to deal with the world problem presented by the acute scarcity of raw materials. There again the refusal of most countries to agree to any limitation of their freedom of action in economic matters and the prevalent opposition to State control led to the rejection of an Italian proposal for the international control of raw materials. The only outcome was yet another condemnation of 'artificial restrictions and duties on the export of raw materials'. By the time the report of the Committee was published, moreover, the post-war depression had substituted a glut for scarcity and the vital problem of controlling the production and prices of primary commodities had consequently lost its public interest.[1]

[1] The Raw Materials Enquiry incidentally became the test case for the definition of the scope of the League's economic activity and power. Most of the raw

Apart from the provision of relief both by private organizations and by the Allied Governments during the first two years after the war, the only instance of positive international action during this period consisted in the League of Nations schemes for the financial reconstruction of Austria and Hungary. In spite of financial assistance from the Allied Powers, Austria was by 1922 on the verge of financial collapse. At the request of the Supreme Council of the Allied Powers, the League of Nations prepared a scheme, based in part on the *ter Meulen* plan, for the financial reconstruction of Austria. A series of financial reforms designed to balance the Austrian budget and stabilize the currency were to be financed by a short-term loan guaranteed by foreign Governments, and carried out under the supervision of a Commissioner General appointed by the League of Nations. The plan was adopted after some delay, and on the whole successfully carried out. The success of the Austrian scheme led, during the following years, to a series of similar League loans which were granted successively to Hungary, Bulgaria, Greece, Estonia, and Danzig.

All these schemes were in the nature of relief rather than reconstruction, in the sense that they were designed to alleviate immediate financial or social problems rather than provide the basis for the construction of sound and viable national economies, and it is noteworthy that in the case of Austria in particular, international action in the economic field was greatly speeded and facilitated by political considerations, in this case the political interest of the Allied Powers in the maintenance of Austria's political independence. The fact, moreover, that the loans were used to cover budget deficits and to provide the basis for currency stabilization meant that they were not self-liquidating, either from the point of view of the countries which provided the credit, since the funds were not necessarily spent on imports, or from the point of view of borrowing countries, since the loans did not in themselves provide an economic foundation for subsequent payments of interest and amortization. These defects were in part responsible for the subsequent default of the debtor coun-

material exporting countries, and especially those of the British Empire, were anxious to restrict as far as possible the activity of the League in the economic field. Their representatives strongly opposed the proposed Raw Materials Enquiry, holding, in the words of the Canadian delegates, that the proposal might 'cause apprehension in the countries which disposed of raw materials such as Canada and the United States', and that the U.S.A. 'could never be expected to become party to this League so long as there is any suggestion or contention that you are going to interfere with the domestic affairs of that country'. Italy, on the other hand, supported by Switzerland, Sweden and Colombia, favoured the widest interpretation of the economic duties of the League. In the event, those opposing concerted action necessarily carried the day. While the division of opinion among the Powers on the scope of the League's activity in later years tended to vary with the subject under discussion, there was a natural tendency for 'haves' to be more suspicious about international control than 'have-nots'.

tries on nearly every one of the League reconstruction loans. On the other hand, it is doubtful whether anything short of a comprehensive scheme of international investment for the industrialization and economic reconstruction of the area of Central and South-East Europe as a whole would have sufficed, a scheme which would have presupposed a willingness to co-operate among the countries concerned which did not, in fact, exist. Nevertheless, the value of financial and currency stabilization at that time should not be underestimated. With all their defects, the 'reconstruction' loans proved one of the few successful examples of international action during the inter-war period.

The efforts that were made at nearly every one of the post-war international conferences and by the League of Nations to encourage the removal and reduction of restrictions on international trade were not altogether unsuccessful. Outside Europe and in several European countries including Britain, the Netherlands, Belgium and the Scandinavian countries, special war-time controls, exchange controls, and prohibitions on imports and exports had been very largely removed by the end of 1919. Most other European countries also followed, though more slowly, in removing quantitative controls. In most cases, however, quantitative restrictions tended to be replaced by higher tariffs as a second line of defence, and at no time were even the Western European and non-European countries prepared to put into effect the liberal recommendations which their experts, and even government representatives, at the international conferences were prepared to endorse.

III. PROSPERITY 1925-9

BY 1925 the world seemed to have overcome the problems of transition from a war to a peace economy. Fighting had died down and the political structure of the new Europe seemed at last settled. Most of the countries of continental Europe had succeeded in stabilizing their currencies after the devastating inflations of the post-war years. The German reparations problem which ever since the Peace Conference had overshadowed and poisoned all concerted international economic action seemed established on a tolerable basis by the Dawes settlement. The successful funding of the reparations obligations in fact seemed to have initiated an unprecedented revival of international lending. Except for the countries of Central and South-Eastern Europe, most of the world had abandoned quantitative restrictions on international trade, though tariffs everywhere remained at a markedly higher level than in 1913 and were continuing to rise. Economic activity everywhere was on the upswing after the severe world slump which had followed the hasty removal of Government controls. What was more important, by 1925 most of the world had returned to the gold standard, which seemed to have resumed its function as an automatic mechanism for the multilateral settlement of international payments, and the co-ordination of national monetary and economic policies.

In a word, events seemed to have vindicated the confidence in the power of the free capitalist economy to accomplish the tasks of adjustment.

As we know,[1] the appearance of equilibrium was largely illusory. In the first place, the gold standard was not in fact fulfilling its function as an automatic mechanism of co-ordination and adjustment. There were several reasons for this. One was that the rates of exchange at which the various currencies were stabilized were incorrectly chosen. Again, the new problem of erratic international movements of capital largely deprived the instrument of discount policy of its efficacy. With the failure of most countries to conform in their internal monetary policies rigidly to the 'rules of the game', the gold standard could no longer lead to an adjustment of national price levels. But the first of these new defects merely aggravated, and the second and third merely reflected, the basic cause of the defective operation of the resurrected gold standard during the nineteen-twenties, the fact that the structural maladjustments and disequilibria in the balances of international payments which had appeared after the war still persisted. The two most important of these, the German reparations obligations and the failure of the U.S.A. to adjust her balance of trade to her new creditor position, were not solved, but merely postponed and even aggravated, by the stream of American capital to Europe. Other structural maladjustments, such as the problem of the British export industries, continued as depressing factors, which the growing rigidity of the advanced industrial economies did not allow to be corrected by the operation of market forces alone.

In the second place, within a year or two of the world boom in industry, one of the most far-reaching of these maladjustments in the world economy, the tendency towards overproduction in agriculture relative to effective world demand (in particular for cereals), began to assume critical proportions. Though aggravated by the growth of agricultural protectionism in Western Europe for military and social reasons, and by the growing restrictions on outlets for surplus agricultural populations to the U.S.A. and other relatively sparsely populated countries, it was essentially a structural problem which could only have been solved by concerted and planned international action.

[1] See above, ch. i, p. 9 ff.

Thirdly, the world was still nearly as far off as during the previous period from that freedom of commerce which was the ideal aimed at by all international conferences. The persistence of quantitative restrictions on international trade in parts of Europe, the prevailing tariff instability, and rising tariff levels were for the most part merely symptoms of the absence of world equilibrium and of the attempts of individual countries to adjust their economies to the conditions of the post-war world. But they undoubtedly further impeded the working of the gold standard and, in many ways, increased the difficulties of adjustment for other countries.

Lastly, in addition to these three factors, all of which were in a sense aspects of the same problem, there was the inherent instability of the advanced capitalist economies which, as a major factor in the world depression, was to wreck all hopes of establishing an integrated world economy.

Looking back now we realize that it is to these four main problems, the failure of the gold standard in conditions of maladjustment in the productive structure of the world and the balances of payments of most countries, the problem of world agriculture, the obstructions to international trade, and the problem of trade cycle control, that international action during this period should have addressed itself. In practice—quite apart from the fact that in the prevailing atmosphere of prosperity international action seemed to have lost much of the urgency that it had possessed in the immediate post-war years—the very existence of the most important of these problems was barely recognized. The only one which was the subject of serious efforts by international action was the third, on balance the least fundamental of the four. The failure to attempt a solution of the more important problems by international action during the years from 1925 to 1929 was doubly unfortunate, because never at any time during the interwar period was there a better opportunity for their solution than during these years when rapidly expanding economic activity reduced the costs of adjustment to a minimum and when the political atmosphere for international co-operation was relatively more favourable than either before or after.

In the light of this analysis little need be said about what international action in the economic field was actually undertaken or accomplished during these years.

The main problem which throughout occupied the attention of international conferences and institutions was again, as during the first period, the reduction of barriers to international trade. Two major attempts were made to reach international agreement on this problem, the first directed towards the final suppression of prohibitions and restrictions, the second towards stability and reduction of tariffs.

The first, which constituted a direct continuation of the efforts in the same direction of the immediate post-war years and which lasted almost without interruption from 1924 until 1929, came, on the face of it, as near success as any major international action of the two decades. A diplomatic conference, summoned by the League of Nations to Geneva in 1927, after three years of preparations and attended by representatives of twenty-nine States, including all the great Powers, adopted an international Convention by which the parties undertook, subject to certain exceptions, to abolish all import and export restrictions within a period of six months and not to impose any such restrictions thereafter. After prolonged negotiations, in the course of which a great many exceptions and reservations claimed by nearly every country were allowed, a second conference decided in 1928 that the Convention thus amended would come into force if ratified by eighteen States before 30 September 1929. By that date seventeen ratifications were in fact deposited. But Poland finally refused to ratify owing to reservations made by Germany regarding trade in certain commodities which Poland considered essential for her economic life, and the majority of ratifications consequently lapsed. The Convention was formally brought into force by those States in which virtually no prohibitions existed, and by 1934 it had been denounced even by these. On the face of it, these facts suggest that an important step forward in the cause of international economic 'disarmament' suffered shipwreck at the last moment over a minor dispute which might have been overcome with a little more international goodwill. Yet, it is doubtful whether this is a sound diagnosis. The real question is whether the Convention, which deprived Governments of a powerful economic emergency weapon, could possibly have lasted, even had it come into force. It is impossible to believe that it could have survived for a month the whirlwind of the world slump and financial crisis.[1]

The tariff problem was the main item on the agenda of the World Economic Conference which the League Assembly had, in September 1925, decided to convene and which met at Geneva in May 1927. Declaring that 'substantial improvement in the economic conditions can be obtained by increased facilities for

---

[1] One minor success was achieved. Reservations regarding the export of hides, skins, and bones, put forward by several countries during these negotiations, led to a series of conferences in 1928 and 1929 the outcome of which was a convention for the renunciation of all prohibitions and the limitation of export duties on these commodities, a convention which was actually ratified and brought into force by eighteen states in October 1929. Since it was a convention to prevent restrictions on *exports*, it even survived the slump and depression.

international trade and commerce', that 'some of the causes which have resulted in the increase of tariffs and other trade barriers since the war have largely disappeared and others are diminishing', and that 'the time has come to put an end to the increase in tariffs and to move in the opposite direction',[1] the Conference recommended the reduction of tariffs by individual State action, by bilateral action through commercial treaties, or by collective action through the League. These recommendations of the Conference were universally acclaimed and endorsed, and were in fact followed during the next two years by a certain stabilization of tariff levels, based primarily on a system of bilateral commercial treaties, the most important of which was the Franco-German treaty of 1927. Some tariff reductions also followed, though they were too insignificant to have much bearing on the course of world trade. Attempts at collective action failed completely,[2] and within two years of the World Economic Conference the preparations for a new upward revision of the American tariff threatened to put an end to the lull in the tariff war. On balance, the net results achieved by all these efforts towards 'freer trade' were negligible, particularly if it is realized that a certain stability of tariffs would in any case have accompanied the years of prosperity.

The world agricultural problem was the only other of the four problems which appeared on the agenda of the World Economic

[1] League of Nations Document C.E.I. 44 (i), 1927, *Recommendations of the World Economic Conference 1927*.

[2] The two alternative methods proposed for the collective reduction of tariffs were that of 'maximum limits', i.e. the fixing of maximum limits to the duties imposable by any country on each category of merchandise, and that of 'percentage reduction', i.e. maintaining existing duties in each country as a basis and arranging for simultaneous and gradual percentage reductions in those duties. Both these methods raised insuperable difficulties. Abandoning this approach, the League of Nations Economic Committee then attempted, equally unsuccessfully, to bring about collective agreement for tariff reductions on particular groups of commodities.

Apart from the general unwillingness of Governments to abandon measures of protection which they considered essential instruments of economic or social policy (such as agricultural protection based on strategic or social considerations, or the tariffs of the primary producing countries designed to assist their policies of industrialization), and apart from technical difficulties in the way of changes which would upset the often carefully adjusted and balanced national tariff structures, there was one general obstacle to tariff reduction which was of fundamental importance, namely, the fact that any major changes in the tariff structure of a country were bound to involve social costs, in the absence of planned internal adjustment, and to injure 'vested interests', both of capital and labour. Where such changes in commercial policy were considered beneficial for the country as a whole, the obvious remedy would have been to provide facilities (in the form of direct financial assistance or of social services) to heighten the mobility of labour and, if necessary, compensation to capital. Such measures to transfer the burden of adjustment from special groups to the nation as a whole would not have silenced the opposition of vested interests entirely. But they would have helped to reduce one major obstacle to the reduction of trade barriers which did not involve the issue of 'economic nationalism'.

Conference of 1927.[1] But the character of the discussions and resolutions showed little awareness of the importance which that problem was soon to assume in world economic affairs. The Conference resolutions, apart from a recommendation to reduce agricultural protection to a minimum and to abolish export and import restrictions, confined themselves to vague generalities on such matters as the development of co-operative institutions and the advantages of international agreements between co-operative agricultural organizations. A more important proposal for the establishment of an international agricultural mortgage credit bank was referred back to the League for further inquiry.[2] None of the major issues involved in this immense problem, the creation of new outlets for the large surplus agricultural populations by industrialization and by a revival of international migration facilities, the international regulation of agricultural production, or the development of sound nutrition policies, were raised at the Conference. Nor were any further general attempts made to tackle the problem of world agriculture until 1931 when the disastrous slump in agricultural prices had brought agricultural producers all over the world to the verge of ruin.

The defective functioning of the revived gold standard did receive a good deal of attention by Governments and international bodies during these years. But apart from some direct co-operation between the major central banks, it was not until 1929 that attempts were made to approach the problem by international action. In that year, the League of Nations, through its Financial Committee, appointed a Gold Delegation to inquire into the working of the gold standard, and the Young Reparations Committee proposed the establishment of a Bank for International Settlements. The former step is significant primarily as evidence of the failure, even at that late date, to recognize the dimensions of the problem of the world monetary system.[3] The second was

---

[1] The third subject, in addition to trade barriers and agriculture, on the agenda of the World Economic Conference, was rationalization—that symbol of the years of 'normalcy'—and international industrial agreements. The rapid growth of international monopolies and cartels frequently throughout the inter-war period engaged the attention of international economic conferences. Occasionally the danger of their assuming a restrictive and predatory character was pointed out, but on the whole international conferences and authorities tended to view their development with favour—partly no doubt because the participants of these conferences were for the most part not predisposed, by either political persuasion or social background, towards opposition to business interests, but partly also because these cartels and agreements did constitute an element of stability and control in an increasingly unstable world.

[2] The proposal was subsequently taken up and actually became the subject of a draft convention; but the convention was never ratified, and the proposal lapsed.

[3] The terms of reference of the Gold Delegation instructed it to 'examine into and report upon the causes of fluctuations in the purchasing power of gold and their effect upon the economic life of nations'. (*Report of the Gold Delegation*, League of Nations Document C.502.M.243. 1932 IIA, p. 5.) This, four months

potentially of far greater importance. The original proposal of the Young Committee, though designed in the first place to facilitate the transfer of the German reparations payments, aimed at the creation of an institution which,. it was hoped, would gradually assume the functions in relation to national central banks that these central banks performed in relation to national banking systems. Such an institution, making vigorous use of its powers, might have been an invaluable instrument for the co-ordination of national monetary policies in the depression. In practice, the powers of the proposed bank were severely curtailed before it was established in 1930.[1] Moreover, since the Bank was deliberately put under the control of the governors of the national central banks, it is unlikely that it would have pursued a more enlightened policy than its mentors in fighting the depression, even had it possessed the powers to do so. This is not to deny that the B.I.S. fulfilled a number of useful minor functions in the sphere of international finance during the following decade and constituted a definite though limited achievement in the cause of international economic co-operation. The fact remains, however, that the world plunged into the great depression and financial crisis without any decisive international attempts to tackle the outstanding monetary problems.

Finally, and perhaps most important of all, no attempt was made at any time during the years of prosperity to prepare for international co-ordination of national policies in the event of a slump and depression—for the simple reason that the need for such action was not realized. There were few in any country who foresaw the catastrophe ahead; and in the absence of any national preparation to develop methods of trade cycle control, no international efforts in that direction could be expected.

before the Wall Street crash, appeared as the only problem in relation to the gold standard that required expert investigation! The Delegation, which deliberated for nearly three years, soon found itself forced by the course of events to bring under its purview a far wider and more urgent range of problems. Its report which appeared in 1932 is discussed below, p. 238 ff.

[1] The Young Committee had envisaged the B.I.S. not only as a means of facilitating the transfer of reparations and co-operation between national central banks, but as an instrument for promoting international financial relations and investment and 'for opening up new fields of commerce, of supply and demand'. To anticipate opposition from banking interests the Young Committee had already stipulated that the B.I.S. should not compete with existing banking institutions. During the discussions preceding the establishment of the B.I.S., it was shorn of the powers of making advances to Governments or opening accounts in their names, of issuing its own notes or accepting bills of exchange, and of undertaking operations in the money markets of any country without permission of that country's central bank. The abandonment of .the gold standard by most countries within the first years of the B.I.S.'s existence still further reduced its powers, since its banking functions 'on its own account' had been limited to currencies on gold.

IF the period of prosperity from 1925 to 1929, during which conditions for international economic co-operation had been relatively favourable, had been one of delay and inertia in that field, the next four years witnessed a succession of hectic attempts by international institutions and conferences to cope with the catastrophic events of the world depression, the financial crises, and the breakdown of the world monetary and trading system which it had been the aim of all the earlier efforts to re-establish. It is just possible that even in 1930 or 1931, given adequate knowledge of economics, preparedness in each of the major countries to sanction radical changes in the economic system, and all-round determination towards international co-operation, the disaster and chaos of the following years might have been prevented. But merely to state these conditions is to suggest that in practice, by the time the American slump and the world agricultural depression had got under way, the collapse of the existing structure of international economic relations had become unavoidable, although determined international action could un-doubtedly have done far more to alleviate the impact of the depression and the international economic chaos that accom-panied it.

What in fact happened was that, in addition to the two major obstacles which had prevented sound economic action during the previous decade—economic nationalism and the failure to appre-ciate the nature of the problems—all the attempts at international action during the years of the depression were vitiated by the pace of economic events. The urgency of domestic social and economic problems not only blinded Governments and public opinions to the need for international co-operation but in many cases did not allow Governments to postpone action until inter-national agreement could be reached. The fact that the depres-sion did not hit all countries at the same time, so that some were still enjoying prosperity when others were struggling with des-perate economic problems, further increased the difficulties of concerted international action. Again, the existing machinery for international action moved far too slowly to keep pace with the rate at which economic conditions were deteriorating and new problems arising; on several occasions the terms of reference of international bodies and commissions were out of date by the time their reports were published.

In the circumstances, it is not surprising that the record of all these attempts at international action is one of almost unrelieved failure. For the most part they were confined to attempts to tackle piecemeal the most urgent problems as they arose and, even where they did not constitute a mere acceptance of *faits accomplis* presented by unilateral actions of individual countries, they did not for the most part penetrate below the symptoms of the problems. Not until 1933 was any attempt made to deal comprehensively with the world's economic condition, and by that time even a sounder approach to the economic problems than was actually apparent could hardly have made headway against the increasing political disintegration of the world.

During the first year of the world depression the hope of stabilizing or reducing tariffs continued to monopolize attention in the field of international economic action. The renewed rise in tariffs after 1929, largely the reflection of the gathering slump in agricultural prices, led the League of Nations, at the instance of the British Government, to make a last attempt to deal with the tariff problem by concerted international action. In February 1930 an almost exclusively European conference met with the aim of reaching agreement on a 'tariff truce' and a possible reduction of tariffs. The idea of a tariff truce had to be abandoned in face of the opposition both from the Central and Eastern agricultural States and from the Western countries, like France, which had just embarked on a policy of intense agricultural protectionism. A Commercial Convention was signed by which the eighteen signatories, including Germany, France, and the United Kingdom undertook to prolong all existing commercial agreements for a year, and not to raise duties without prior consultation with the other parties. But by the time a second conference met in March 1931 to put the Convention into force, the further deterioration of economic conditions had removed any chance of agreement on these lines, and the Convention lapsed. The abortive Tariff Truce Conferences constituted the last general attempt towards tariff reduction. During the following years the League of Nations, through the Commission of Enquiry for European Union, continued its endeavours to achieve international agreement on reduction of trade barriers. But they were for the most part designed as contributions to the special problem of Central and South-Eastern Europe and are more suitably mentioned in that connection.

It was the international financial crisis of the summer of 1931 which first made it apparent that international action in the depression could not confine itself to the problem of 'trade barriers'. The financial blizzard which swept across Europe from Austria and the Balkans to Great Britain led to a series of emergency measures, none of which had any appreciable effect in relieving the chaos. The Hoover Moratorium on all inter-Governmental debts, proposed by the American President in June 1931, was a last-minute attempt to suspend one of the factors which had for years prevented international monetary equilibrium. At best, it could only have served to give a temporary support to international 'confidence'; in practice, the delay caused by French apprehensions over the possible loss of reparations deprived it even of that limited value. The international financial negotiations of the following two years for the liquidation and settlement of the foreign debts of the Central European countries, with their climax in the virtual extinction of the German reparations obligations at the Lausanne Conference of June 1932, constituted little more than grudging acknowledgements by the creditor Powers of the obvious fact that the depression had finally deprived the debtor countries of their ability to meet the enormous money obligations which their creditors had never allowed them to discharge in the form of goods and services.

Both the international debt problem and the rapid growth of obstacles to international trade, as well as political considerations, made the economic plight of the countries of Central and South-Eastern Europe the chief subject of international economic action during 1931 and 1932 and virtually the only one with regard to which international conferences before 1933 devoted their attention to economic as opposed to purely commercial or financial considerations. The catastrophic world agricultural depression, aggravated as it was by the growth of agricultural protectionism in Western Europe and the sudden cessation of the inflow of foreign capital, had wrought havoc with the agrarian economies and finances of these countries. Already in 1930 an international agricultural conference held at Warsaw, at which the Governments of most of the Balkan, Baltic and Danubian countries were represented, put forward on behalf of these countries a demand for financial assistance and preferential customs treatment for their cereals. The latter demand was taken up in 1931 by the Commission of Enquiry for European Union, and during 1931-2 various preferential tariff agreements on these lines were negotiated between France and Yugoslavia, Hungary and Rumania, and between Germany and the latter two countries. In the circumstances preferential customs agreements could have done little more than alleviate the problem of these countries. In the event, the proposals had to be abandoned owing to the opposition of the overseas primary producing countries, especially the British Dominions, who refused to concede the exception to their most-favoured-nation rights, which such preferential arrangements would have involved.[1]

[1] During the early post-war years the re-establishment of the Most-Favoured-Nation clause, as the cornerstone of a world system of non-discriminatory if not free trade, had been one of the chief objectives of the League of Nations in the

A more far-reaching attempt by the Western Powers to come to the assistance of the Danubian countries was provoked by the German-Austrian proposal for a customs union in March 1931. Both the Beneš and the Tardieu plans for the Danubian countries which were brought forward at a London conference of the four Great Powers concerned and again at the Stresa Conference, convened in September 1932 by the Lausanne Reparations Conference, were primarily intended as counter-moves to the German proposal, designed to keep Austria out of the political orbit of Germany. Both were based on the conception of a preferential customs régime within the Danubian group and still aimed, as the terms of reference of the Stresa Conference showed, at 'the removal of the present transfer difficulties, the suppression of exchange control', and the revival of the foreign trade of these countries, rather than at any more fundamental economic reconstruction. But in the immediate conditions of the depression, relief of their financial difficulties and export outlets for their agricultural produce were the two forms of assistance which these countries most urgently required. The scheme proposed by the Stresa Conference, which included (a) the establishment of a Currency Normalization Fund to be constituted by the larger Powers, as the basis of currency stabilization, leading to the gradual removal of exchange restrictions, and (b) a scheme for the revalorization of cereals, involving the grant of limited preferential tariff rebates by cereal-importing countries and/or financial contributions towards a cereal revalorization fund, would have gone some way towards meeting these immediate needs. In practice this scheme, too, came to nothing, the British Government refusing to participate in financial guarantees, while opposition to the preferential and revalorization proposals also came

sphere of commercial policy, and the acceptance of the clause by almost all countries by 1928 was widely considered as one of the League's outstanding economic achievements. It soon became apparent, however, that MFN treatment was difficult to enforce in the face of systematic efforts at evasion by many countries and, what was more important, that the obligation of MFN treatment actually tended to discourage, and insistence on MFN rights to prevent, reductions of trade barriers which might otherwise have been made. During 1927–31 the League Economic Committee worked hard by complex codification to make the MFN clause watertight against evasion. The second problem obtained considerable practical importance after the efforts towards general tariff reduction had been abandoned and had given way to attempts to achieve reductions of tariffs by regional preferential agreements. Apart from the instance mentioned in the text where insistence on MFN rights prevented a step towards the long-overdue economic unification of the Danubian area, the best-known illustration of the obstructive character which the MFN clause had assumed was the failure of the Ouchy Convention of July 1932 between the Oslo Powers owing to the refusal of the British Government to waive its MFN rights. What made the British attitude particularly open to criticism was, of course, the fact that Great Britain was at that very moment negotiating at Ottawa a preferential agreement of far greater dimensions, the immediate effect of which, moreover, was to raise not to reduce tariffs.

from other countries. With the failure of the Stresa proposals the Central and South-Eastern European countries were finally left to look for a solution of their economic difficulties in closer economic relations with Germany and the gradual submission to Nazi economic penetration.

So far nothing has been said about international attempts to deal with the world depression itself and the collapse of the world monetary system. The reason is that no such attempts were in fact made at any time between the beginning of the slump and the World Economic Conference in 1933. There is no need to enlarge upon the reasons for this failure. The gold standard system which had functioned precariously during the brief interval of prosperity could not possibly be maintained when the slump put an end to the flow of American capital to Europe and the depression further dislocated the balances of trade and payments of most countries. The failure to take action to halt and reverse the slump was almost equally inevitable. In the first place, whereas by 1930 the principle that the commercial policies of different countries were not matters of domestic interest only had come to be accepted, at least in theory, all the key points for anti-depression policies were unquestioningly considered within the preserve of economic sovereignty. Actually, since international action to halt the deflationary forces and bring about a revival of world demand, income, and employment could in the first place have been confined to the three or four large import markets whose level of economic activity and demand overwhelmingly determined that of the world as a whole, economic sovereignty need not have been an insuperable obstacle to effective action. The speed of events and the irregularity of the incidence of the depression were more important obstacles. But by far the most important reason for the failure to develop an effective international anti-depression policy was the obvious one that those who determined the economic policies of individual countries either did not know or felt unable to accept the policies which, as we now recognize, would have offered the best chance of providing effective remedies. So long as the Governments and vocal public opinion in most countries clung to principles of economic policy which were plainly inadequate if not positively harmful, effective international action was *a fortiori* impossible.

The degree to which faulty diagnosis and rigid adherence to orthodox policies (which in turn was largely based on conscious or unconscious opposition to any radical change in the existing economic system) dominated those who were responsible for the determination of national and international economic policies is shown by the report of the Gold Delegation whose appointment in 1929 was mentioned above. No action was ever taken on the report, which appeared in 1932, but it formed the basis of the deliberations on monetary policy of the World Economic Conference of 1933. The majority report which was signed by most of the Continental experts and bankers on the Delegation gave an astute analysis of the various factors—such as the great increase in international indebtedness, the rapid movements of international funds, the irregular character of long-term investment, the faulty choice of exchange rates, and the profound structural maladjustments of the world economy—which had prevented the smooth functioning of the gold standard during the post-war decade. But, in striking contrast to this analysis, its recommendations did not depart on a single point from the aim of restoring the very system which that analysis had shown to be incapable of functioning. 'The gold standard remains the best available monetary system.'[1] 'An internationally accepted standard' is desirable 'in order to facilitate the free flow of world trade'.[2] Among the measures which would make possible 'the return, within the shortest possible time, to the international gold standard system', the report demanded (a) 'the restoration of a reasonable degree of freedom in the movement of goods and services'; (b) 'a satisfactory solution for the problem of reparation payments and war debts'; (c) the acceptance by central banks of the fundamental principle that 'gold movements should not be prevented from making their influence felt both in the country losing gold and the country receiving gold. Not only should these movements not be prevented from exercising their influence but their working should be reinforced by other means—especially by changes in discount rates and by open market operation'; (d) national economic policies must be conducted 'on sound principles', involving above all balanced State budgets and the 'adjustment of costs of production and costs of living to the international economic and financial position'.[3] As conditions for the restoration of the free gold standard, these recommendations were no doubt appropriate; but in demanding *laisser-faire*, deflation, the adjustment of national monetary and economic policies to the vagaries of international capital movements, and the restoration of free trade, they not only sidetracked but went directly counter to the measures needed to overcome the depression. The two British members of the Delegation (and the Belgian Chairman) joined issue with the majority in a minority report, which, while its diagnosis of the causes of the collapse of the gold standard was far inferior to that of the majority report,[4] showed a much greater

---

[1] *Report of the Gold Delegation*, loc. cit., p. 23.
[2] ibid., p. 24.
[3] ibid., p. 24.
[4] The *Note of Dissent*, having stated that its authors were 'quite unable to associate [themselves] with the view that the . . . breakdown of the international

awareness of the impossibility of working the free gold standard in the prevailing conditions and did at least go so far as to urge the desirability of an expansionist monetary policy.[1] Neither of the two reports, however, showed the slightest awareness of the desperate urgency, for economic as well as social reasons, of using active Government intervention to raise effective demand and employment as a basis for a revival of economic activity.

The only international body which throughout these years consistently advocated the adoption of an active anti-depression policy, of the type to which in 1932 and 1933 a growing number of Governments began to turn independently, was the International Labour Organization. Already in 1919 the International Labour Conference had passed a resolution urging State members 'to co-ordinate the execution of all work undertaken under public authority with a view to reserving such work as far as practicable to periods of unemployment'. As the world depression deepened, the I.L.O again took up its advocacy of concerted international public works policies. A detailed scheme for the execution of extensive public works of an international character was submitted in April 1931 to the Commission of Enquiry for European Union of the League of Nations. The proposals were examined by various League Committees for two years, but the very fact that the ultimate decision was considered to rest with financial experts ruled out any chance of acceptance. In 1932, a five-year plan for public works for the Central and Eastern European area, worked out by the French economist Delaisi, was circulated by the I.L.O. to the Central and Eastern European Governments but was rejected by them and finally shelved by the Stresa Confer-

gold standard [was] primarily due to the various economic maladjustments enumerated by [their] colleagues', brought forward the argument that the 'appreciation in the value of gold . . . which began in 1929 . . . is the fundamental cause of the present depression' (ibid., p. 64), that 'the payment of reparations and war debts has been the basic cause of this one-sided distribution of gold' (ibid., p. 66), and that 'the breakdown of the gold standard must therefore be regarded as the combined result of the obligation to pay reparations and war debts on the one hand, and the unwillingness of the receiving countries to receive payment in the form of goods and services on the other'. 'To put the matter very briefly, we hold that the fall in the general level of prices has been the fundamental cause [sic] of the present depression, and that that fall was the result of the obligation to pay reparations and war debts combined with the unwillingness of the receiving countries to accept payment in goods and services, so that payment had to be made in gold' (ibid., p. 67). While the minority were right in emphasizing the enormous dislocating effect which reparations and war debts had exercised on the international balances of payments and the gold standard (a factor which was studiously minimized by the Continental experts who confined their references to it to the passing remark that 'the apparent impossibility of making such payments without increased economic productivity led to fresh capital borrowing' [ibid., p. 21]), their 'explanation' of the causes of the world depression was truly astonishing.

[1] The clash on policy between the majority and the minority reflected, of course, the policies of the 'gold bloc' countries, on the one side, and of the 'sterling bloc' on the other.

ence, again on financial grounds. In 1933 the representatives of the I.L.O. once more advocated a public works policy based on (a) the immediate initiation of 'large-scale public works, giving an assured economic yield, particularly in those countries where funds are at present remaining unused'; (b) co-operation 'between creditor countries and countries lacking capital, many of whom are debtors, in order to undertake for these latter countries large works likely to augment the national income and thereby to increase their capacity to meet external debts'; and (c) the co-ordination of these measures 'on an international basis so as to avoid the possibility, which might arise if individual action were taken, of a disequilibrium in the balance of payments of the various countries, detrimental to international monetary stability.' The World Economic Conference received their proposals 'with a marked spirit of respect',[1] but the refusal in some of the most important countries, especially the United Kingdom, to accept the principle of a public works policy *a fortiori* rendered international co-ordination impossible, and the proposal lapsed.[2]

The World Economic Conference of 1933 represented the final abortive attempt that was made to achieve an international co-ordination of economic policies. The Conference broke down over the impasse between the gold standard countries, which insisted that violent fluctuations in exchange rates were at least one reason why the removal of 'barriers to international trade', in the form of exchange controls, quotas, and tariffs, was impossible, and the U.S.A. and the countries of the sterling bloc, which refused to curtail their freedom to pursue an expansionist recovery policy by the return to the gold standard. In retrospect it is clear that the U.S.A. would have lost nothing by refraining from the devaluation of the dollar, the United Kingdom little by agreeing to restabilize the pound, and the gold

[1] International Labour Office, *Report of the Director*, 1934, p. 87.

[2] The I.L.O continued its study and advocacy of public works policies after 1935. In 1934 it published a comprehensive report on *Public Works Policy* (I.L.O., Studies & Reports, Series C. No. 19, Geneva 1935) which, largely on the basis of information obtained by a League inquiry (published in League of Nations, *National Public Works*, Geneva 1935), described the works undertaken in various countries in the preceding years and analysed the financial, economic, social, and administrative problems involved. The subject was again raised at the International Labour Conferences of 1934, 1936, and 1937. On the basis of a further report (*National Planning of Public Works in Relation to Employment*, Geneva 1937), the 1937 Conference passed a series of resolutions which led to the establishment in 1938 of an International Public Works Committee of the I.L.O. which was to facilitate the international co-ordination of national public works policies. The war broke out before the Committee came into effective operation; but the New York Conference of the I.L.O. in November 1941 made the existence of that Committee the starting-point of its plans for a post-war international public works policy. If these efforts of the I.L.O. had little, if any, direct effect on national policies during the nineteen-thirties, they did much to stimulate the growth of international public opinion on the subject, especially by emphasizing the need for international co-ordination.

bloc countries would have gained greatly by a downward adjustment of their exchange rates, which in turn would have enabled
them to abandon deflation and embark on a policy of internal
monetary expansion. But it is more than doubtful whether even
such a measure of agreement would have sufficed to re-establish
an integrated world economy. Quite apart from the fact that, by
the time the World Economic Conference met, German policy
was already in the hands of a Government which was fundamentally opposed to international co-operation, the World
Economic Conference showed no evidence of any principles
which could have provided the foundation for a new world
economic system. What spirit of international co-operation was
evident found expression in the economic principles of free trade
and *laisser-faire* which were patently inadequate to the practical
needs of social and economic policy. On the other hand, such
methods and policies as were beginning to emerge from the
attempts of Governments to meet these needs by a greater degree
of State intervention and control inevitably assumed the form of
independent and unco-ordinated national action.

V. DISINTEGRATION 1933-9

THE breakdown of the World Economic Conference of 1933
signalized the end of any general attempts at international action
in the economic field during the inter-war period. The chief
reason why during the remaining years of the decade international economic co-operation became increasingly hopeless was
undoubtedly the steady deterioration of the international political
situation. In 1931, Japan had launched her policy of aggression
in the Far East. In 1933, the depression brought Germany under
the sway of a régime which from then onwards systematically
prepared for war and set its face against any forms of international co-operation which did not assist that purpose. In 1935,
Italy made war on Abyssinia, and from the following year onwards preparation for war or defence largely determined the
domestic economic policies, and diplomatic considerations—
whether designed to improve their strategic position or as last-
minute efforts towards appeasement—the foreign economic
policies, of the Powers. The deterioration in international
political relations had the incidental effects that it increasingly
deprived the economic efforts of the League of Nations of what
weight they had formerly carried, that it hastened the general
tendency towards autarky and protectionism for strategic reasons,
and that, during the last years at any rate, efforts towards international economic co-operation could no longer be judged by
the same criteria as before; what during the previous decade

would have been welcomed as a step towards the improvement of international economic relations, now represented 'appeasement' on the larger political plane.

But the political factor was not the only one which stood in the way of concerted international economic action during these years. In the first place, the depression had finally swept away the world monetary system which throughout the nineteenth century, and after a fashion even during the first post-war decade, had served to co-ordinate national economic policies. Although the gold standard had in fact failed during the nineteen-twenties to function effectively as a co-ordinating mechanism, it had at least provided a standard of reference for national monetary and even, up to a point, commercial policies. During the nineteen-thirties, no such standard took its place. Each country pursued the prime objective of economic recovery (and, some of them, preparation for war) by the methods and principles of economic policy which its Government saw fit to adopt. To ensure for itself the maximum freedom of action and to safeguard its economy against outside disturbances became a predominant motive in the commercial and external monetary policies of nearly every country. In so far as any pattern of the world economy could be detected, it consisted in the emergence from the great depression of four or five great currency and trading areas, each grouped around one of the major Powers. Divided more or less sharply by differences in commercial, currency, and domestic economic policy, the members of each of these groups increasingly tended to concentrate their economic and trade relations within these areas. In the face of increasing divergences between national price levels and the disruption of international markets, the chances of a return to a world-wide system of free multilateral trade rapidly disappeared.

What was at least as significant as this 'disintegration' of the world economy, however, was the fact that after the depression a number of countries no longer accepted the fundamental premise of all the earlier attempts towards international economic action, the premise that the ideal to be aimed at was the restoration of the liberal world economic system of the nineteenth century.[1] For Germany, and to a lesser extent for Italy, Japan

[1] One Power, Soviet Russia, never throughout the inter-war period accepted this objective. But the difficulties between the Soviet Union and the capitalist world during these two decades were political rather than economic. During the years 1928-31, the outcries about Russian 'dumping' for a short time illustrated the difficulties of fitting the commercial policy of a planned economy into a liberal world trading system. But, with that exception, the small and diminishing importance of foreign trade for the Russian economy prevented that problem from becoming acute in the case of the Soviet Union. The transformation into a controlled economy of Germany, with her traditionally far greater share in world trade and her greater dependence on foreign resources, was bound to raise the problem far more acutely, though its difficulties were,

and the smaller countries within the German orbit, exchange controls (and, in so far as they were still used, quotas and tariffs) ceased to be temporary emergency devices or even (to a degree which was quite inadequately understood in the Western countries) 'trade barriers', and became the instruments and integral parts of a planned, or at least managed, national economy. It is largely the failure to recognize this fact which gives to all the reports, protestations and efforts towards 'freer world trade' of these years, both of the League of Nations and of the Governments of the Western democracies, their appearance of futility.

All the facts of this chapter point to the conclusion that a far greater degree of conscious planning and direction of economic affairs, both nationally and internationally, than the democratic countries were ever prepared to undertake, was an essential condition of a solution of the world's economic problems in the post-war world. But even if one accepts as a political fact the continued adherence of the Western democracies to a predominantly unregulated economic system, the existence side by side of planned (or managed) and market economies need not by itself have precluded international economic co-operation. What could not be expected was agreement between them entirely on the terms of one side. This is what all the international proposals of these years, from the Cordell Hull trade programme to the van Zeeland report, in effect amounted to. The reason why the initiative for international action during these years rested wholly with the liberal side was, of course, the obvious one that the totalitarian economies were being built up, in a spirit of aggressive nationalism, by countries preparing for war and as instruments of war. In the circumstances, the failure to work out any *modus vivendi* between liberal and planned economies was almost irrelevant. But it is not inconceivable that the need for such a *modus vivendi* may once again become a problem of fundamental importance.

What international economic action was attempted during the years between the World Economic Conference and the outbreak of the second world war falls mainly into three categories: (*a*) The efforts towards freer trade built around the American trade agreements programme, (*b*) a series of inquiries and reports by the League of Nations directed partly towards the same end of freer trade, partly towards finding a new approach to economic problems in the subordination of economic policy to social objectives, and (*c*) the last-minute attempts, initiated by the British Government, to find a way towards political appeasement

of course, aggravated out of all proportion by the inherent impetus towards economic expansion of the Fascist economic system and by the aggressive nationalism of the Nazi régime.

by means of economic agreement. Outside these three categories was (d) the Tripartite Monetary Agreement of 1936 which, directed towards a more limited immediate objective, proved the only relatively successful instance of international economic co-operation during this period.

a. We have described in an earlier chapter the strenuous efforts made by the United States, under the leadership of Secretary Cordell Hull, to promote freer world trade by means of a programme of bilateral trade agreements. The series of inter-American Economic Conferences, held at Montevideo in 1933, at Buenos Aires in 1937, and at Lima in 1938, at each of which the American States denounced unreasonably high tariffs, quotas, exchange controls and discrimination of all kinds and pledged themselves to co-operate in efforts to reduce trade barriers between them, were directly inspired by the new policy of the United States. They led to no appreciable results and did not, in any case, extend beyond the American hemisphere.

b. The League's economic activities after 1933 were entirely confined to inquiries and reports. The majority of these, which included the Inquiry into Clearing Agreements (1935), the report on Agricultural Protectionism (1935), the Raw Materials Inquiry (1936-7), two reports on the Present Phase of International Economic Relations (1935, 1936), the scheme of the Economic Committee prepared on the basis of the programme of the Tripartite Declaration (1937), and the Report on Exchange Control (1938) were inspired by the same aim, a return to the former system of free multilateral trade. For the three reasons suggested above, they all remained without practical results and little purpose would be served by analysing them in detail.

The *Report on Clearing Agreements* set out from the assumption that the system could only be regarded as a makeshift, tending 'constantly to reduce the volume and value of international trade and to subject it to forms of restraint that necessarily hamper its development',[1] and that it should be abolished as soon as possible. The solution proposed was the complete abolition of exchange control, to be facilitated by debt settlement and 'a less restrictive commercial policy which would afford minimum guarantees for export'; failing complete abolition of control over all international financial transactions, commercial transactions at least should be liberated from exchange control. Similar recommendations, supplemented by proposals to grant financial support to countries wishing to abolish exchange controls, were the only outcome of the *Raw Materials Inquiry*[2] which was set on foot in 1936 primarily to counter the colonial claims brought

---

[1] League of Nations Document, C.153.M.83, 1935, IIB, p. 15.
[2] League of Nations Document, A.27, 1937, IIB.

forward by Italy on the eve of her Abyssinian adventure. The same approach again underlay the *Scheme of the Economic Committee* of the League of 1937[1] under which the countries of Western Europe were to relax those restrictions which bore most heavily on the Central and Eastern European States, while the latter, helped also by the provision of financial assistance, were to reciprocate by the removal or relaxation of exchange control. The final contribution of the League to this subject, the *Report on Exchange Control*,[2] no longer assumed that all countries wished to return to a free-currency system, and it declared that the time was not propitious for collective action; but all its recommendations were again directed towards 'decontrol' as the chief objective. The two reports on the *Present Phase of International Economic Relations* are of interest primarily for their orthodoxy on all matters of internal economic policy, of which a wholly disproportionate emphasis on the importance of foreign trade was but one aspect.[3]

Side by side with these continued efforts towards 'freer trade', the League economic organization was led after the breakdown of the World Economic Conference of 1933 to seek a new approach to the world's economic problems in an emphasis on social objectives. The general principle that social objectives should form the end and criterion of economic policy had for many years been insistently advocated by the I.L.O.[4] which had

---

[1] League of Nations Document, C.358.M.242, 1937, IIB.

[2] League of Nations Document, C.232.M.131, 1938, IIA.

[3] 'Sound economy is inconceivable without the balancing of the finances of the State. The majority of Governments have made, and are making, great efforts to effect economies in their budgets.' 'The effect . . . of regulations which prevent those concerned from getting their money out of certain countries . . . is that those who have capital have lost confidence and refuse to consider either long-term or medium-term investments.' 'Public authorities . . . endeavour, not without success, to create directly all sorts of additional opportunities for work. . . . The State, dipping into the nation's reserves, endeavours . . . to effect an emergency allocation of the national wealth. . . . On the other hand, a nation's resources, especially in time of crisis, are not unlimited.' 'It is often supposed that Governments have at their disposal a number of powerful levers by which they can exercise a beneficial influence upon the national economic position. . . . Of course, as long as a Government is able to dip into the taxpayers pockets for relief . . . of certain classes of the population, there is some justification for this faith in its powers. A Government can also exercise considerable influence by a wise fiscal policy and a reasonable discount and credit policy. These instruments are effective in normal times but they must not be expected to produce the same results in times of depression. . . . Foreign trade, therefore, is the only really effective lever which the Government possesses for directing the course of internal economy at a given moment into a given channel. . . .' 'The economic system is not something dead or static, but an organism that is always growing. All we need is not to oppose its growth and then we can confidently rely upon its dynamic action.' (*Remarks on the Present Phase of International Economic Relations*, League of Nations Document C.344.M.174, 1935, IIB, pp. 11, 21, 22, 25, 26.)

[4] In particular, by its first Director, Albert Thomas. See, for instance, his *Report* to the Sixteenth Session of the International Labour Conference, Geneva, 1932, pp. 51–72.

done and continued to do valuable work in stimulating the improvement of labour standards and social policy in different countries by means of international conventions[1] and the study of social problems.[2] The first impetus towards a new emphasis in the League's economic activities on what came to be called 'consumer economics' came from the representatives of Australia who pointed to the need of millions of the world's population for more and better food as the obvious starting point for a solution of the economic difficulties of the world's agricultural producers. At their instance, the League in 1935 instituted an inquiry into 'nutrition in relation to health, agriculture, and economic policy', which resulted in the publication of a series of reports.[3] The same approach inspired the initiation in 1937 of an inquiry into the wider problems of raising general standards of living[4] which was undertaken by the League Economic Committee in co-operation with the I.L.O. and of a number of inquiries into related subjects, such as housing, public health, rural hygiene, population trends, and migration.[5]

[1] Without any powers to compel the adoption of its standards of social and labour policy by national Governments, the I.L.O.'s influence in this direction could never extend beyond assistance and encouragement. But there can be no doubt that a good many advances in national social legislation during the inter-war period can be attributed, directly or indirectly, to this influence. In this light, the record of 839 ratifications of some 60 conventions on conditions and hours of work, social insurance, and maritime and colonial labour regulations, presents a notable achievement.

[2] In this connection mention should be made of the work done not only by the I.L.O. but also by the economic organization of the League and, on a smaller scale, by the International Institute of Agriculture, in the sphere of research and the collection of statistics. The absence of reliable and comparable factual information was bound to constitute in itself a serious obstacle to any international economic planning. In spite of the limitations imposed by initially very inadequate research organizations, by lack of powers to compel national Governments (and industries) to furnish statistical data, and to some extent also by deficient insight into the policies which must direct and illumine factual research, the work of these international institutions in this sphere, which was relatively unhampered by political conflict, was alone sufficient to justify their existence.

[3] The most important of these were the report of the Technical Commission of the League Health Committee on *The Physiological Bases of Nutrition* (League Document C.H.1197, 1935), the *Report* of the Mixed Commission on Nutrition, published in four instalments during 1936–8 (League Documents A.12, 12 (a), 12 (b), 1936, IIB, and A.13, 1937. IIA) and a *Survey of National Nutrition Policies*, 1937–8 (League Document, C.478.M.321, 1938. IIA).

[4] The first, and owing to the outbreak of war the only, result of this inquiry was a memorandum written at the request of the Economic Committee by Mr. N. F. Hall, entitled *Preliminary Investigation into Measures of a National or International Character for Raising the Standard of Living* (League Document A.18, 1938. IIB).

[5] The consideration of consumption standards inevitably brought the League up against the very economic problems which were at the root of 'deficiencies of consumption' and poverty. Ever since 1930 the League had sponsored theoretical investigations into the problem of the trade cycle. One of the results of the 'social' approach was the belated appointment in June 1938 of a special delegation of the League Economic and Financial Committees to inquire into the 'practical measures for preventing or mitigating trade depressions'.

Judged by their direct effects on national economic policies during the nineteen-thirties, these League activities were as barren as the efforts of the League towards freer international trade. The emphasis on social objectives could not by itself solve the economic problems or overcome the political obstacles which prevented their realization. But, quite apart from the useful research to which it gave rise, it provided a valuable corrective to the confusion of thought which tended to turn shibboleths of 'finance', 'economic laws', and 'free trade', balanced budgets or gold standards, into ultimate criteria of economic policy, and pointed to a saner approach to economic problems.

c. Of the last-minute attempts to find a basis for international economic collaboration, the most ambitious was the van Zeeland Report. In April 1937, the British and French Governments requested the Belgian Premier, M. van Zeeland, to inquire into 'the possibilities of obtaining a general reduction of quotas and other obstacles to international trade'. The report, which was published in January 1938, was a conscientious attempt to adjust most of the earlier liberal proposals, that had been made by League committees and elsewhere, to the practical conditions as they appeared to its author, as the basis for a comprehensive scheme of international economic collaboration. It recommended a general agreement between Governments not to raise existing tariffs and to reduce exceptionally heavy duties; reciprocal trade agreements to be based on MFN, but exceptions to MFN to be allowed for the formation of regional agreements aimed at lowering tariff barriers; the suppression of industrial and the enlargement of agricultural quotas; the gradual relaxation and final abolition of exchange control, coupled with the necessary currency adjustments, to be facilitated by the removal of restrictions on capital exports in the creditor countries and the provision of credits by the latter to the exchange control countries to ease the transition; and the convening of a conference of the principal Powers with a view to the conclusion of a 'Pact of International Economic Collaboration', subject to political guarantees against the diversion of credits and financial facilities to 'warlike ends'. The political proviso alone was sufficient to rule out any attempts to follow up the report.

The same fate befell the last two British moves, the Düsseldorf negotiations for a comprehensive agreement between British and German industrialists of March 1939; and the alleged tentative British proposal of a £1,000 million loan to Germany, subject to a fundamental modification of Germany's foreign policy and other political conditions, of the summer of the same year, reports of which were never officially confirmed.

d. In July 1936, the Popular Front Government in France

decided at last to devaluate the franc, and opened negotiations with the British and American Governments to ensure by international co-operation that the adjustment should be carried out with the minimum disturbance. The outcome was the Tripartite Monetary Agreement of September 1936, which represents one of the few examples of successful international co-operation in the economic field during the nineteen-thirties. A declaration issued by the three Governments, in addition to declaring their intention to 'continue to use the appropriate available resources so as to avoid as far as possible any disturbance of the basis of international exchanges resulting from the proposed readjustment', also announced their agreement on the wider aim of the 'restoration of order in international economic relations and to pursue a policy which will tend to promote prosperity in the world and to improve the standard of living', to be approached by the development of international trade and in particular the progressive relaxation of the present system of quotas and exchange controls. But more important than this declaration, which was useful as a prop to 'confidence' rather than as a decisive move towards more far-reaching economic action, were the practical steps that were taken by the monetary authorities of the three countries to facilitate the adjustment, and their subsequent co-operation for the maintenance of exchange stability. Neither of these practical objectives was completely achieved. But the fact that the French Government would almost certainly not have risked undertaking this long overdue step without assurance of international co-operation shows that, in a limited field and given a minimum measure of agreement on wider political and economic objectives, successful international action was still possible.

Chapter Ten

THE LESSONS

IN the foregoing chapters of this report we have tried to assemble and analyse some of the historical raw material for a study of the economic lessons of the inter-war period. It remains in this final chapter to summarize the main lessons that have emerged.

We set out with the intention of concentrating on international economic problems. The discussions of domestic economic policies were intended as incidental to that analysis. One fact, however, which has emerged clearly is that the two spheres cannot be divorced. Domestic and international economic policies were throughout closely related and reacted constantly on each other. If it was true that few if any countries could hope to maintain prosperity and progress at home regardless of what happened in the rest of the world, it was equally true that there was little hope of an ordered world economy so long as the major countries were unable to cope with their domestic economic problems. Before we turn to the lessons in the international field, we shall, therefore, summarize briefly the main lessons in the sphere of internal economic policy.

I. INTERNAL ECONOMIC PROBLEMS

I. THE SCOURGE OF UNEMPLOYMENT

THE outstanding internal economic problem of the inter-war period in all the countries studied was undoubtedly unemployment. 'Next to war, unemployment has been the most widespread, most insidious, and most corroding malady of our generation: it is the specific social disease of western civilization in our time'.[1] It varied in intensity and incidence in the different countries, but in nearly every industrial country it held the centre of the social and economic stage in the inter-war years. It was a social even more than an economic evil. Its effects in terms of personal insecurity, maldistribution of income, and the deterioration of health, technical skill and morale were probably graver than the waste of resources and potential wealth it involved. At the same time, the pressure of the problem on national Governments was perhaps the decisive disrupting factor in international economic relations.

The mass unemployment experienced during the inter-war

[1] *The Times*, 23 January 1943.

period was of two main types.[1] On the one hand, there was special, localized (or 'structural') unemployment in industries which had been expanded during the war beyond the size required for peace-time conditions, or for which the demand had permanently shrunk as a result of technological, political or other developments. Typical of this class of unemployment was the problem of the 'special areas' in Great Britain, and some of the industries in Austria which had been geared to supply the much larger pre-war market of the Habsburg monarchy. On the other hand, there was the general unemployment, connected with the trade cycle, which was not confined to particular industries but was spread throughout the economy and reflected a general deficiency of effective demand or deflation. For some purposes it is important to distinguish between these two types of unemployment; in particular, it is important to remember that, while structural unemployment would have been less of a problem if aggregate effective demand could have been maintained, fiscal measures of trade cycle control directed towards maintaining the level of aggregate effective demand could not by themselves abolish structural unemployment. On the other hand, the two forms of unemployment cannot be treated in watertight compartments. Not only did large depressed areas, such as those of Great Britain, tend to spread depression over wider sectors of the economy, but some of the cyclical depressions of the inter-war period were themselves in part the consequence of structural maladjustments. The immediate post-war depressions of 1921–3 were largely the result of the failure to ensure an ordered adjustment of the capital goods industries to the smaller peace-time demand, after the abnormal expansion of the war and the reconstruction boom; and even the American slump of 1929 can in its origins be interpreted as the result of an over-expansion of some of the investment goods industries relative to the longer-term needs of the American economy for capital equipment.

The social consequences of unemployment during the inter-war period were such that Governments seemed justified in the eyes of their public opinions in giving the abolition of unemployment precedence over all other economic objectives and in attempting to set people to work almost regardless of the economic advantage and social benefit of the work they performed. Yet it would be wrong to think of full employment as an end in itself. Socially, what is wanted is not constant employment without

[1] Besides these two main types, there were other forms of unemployment which should not be ignored, such as the temporary unemployment of casual or seasonal labour, and brief periods out of work in between two jobs. The former may be reducible by appropriate measures; the latter is unavoidable and of course by no means undesirable. Yet both together may add up to substantial total levels of 'unemployed' in national unemployment statistics.

breaks, still less the over-employment of war-time, but a reasonable security of work and a reasonable minimum income for those who for no fault of their own are temporarily out of work. Economically, the intimate connection between the proper structural organization of national economies and the problem of the trade cycle suggests that the best solution to the unemployment problem may lie in a policy aimed at the most efficient use of resources for the satisfaction of changing needs, a policy of which the prevention of unemployment would be but one aspect.

2. SPECIAL UNEMPLOYMENT

The problem of special unemployment as exemplified in the British 'depressed areas' was largely due to international causes. Owing both to the lack of co-ordination of national economic policies and to the impediments to movements of goods and factors of production across national frontiers, such maladjustments generally affected industries that depended on foreign markets. Some aspects of the problem, therefore, are bound up with the creation of an efficient international economic system and will have to be discussed below. But the dimensions of special unemployment could have been greatly reduced if national Governments in the various countries had dealt with it more effectively. A word or two must therefore be said on it here.

At the end of the last war the view was still widely held that the problem of special unemployment would solve itself in time as a result of the play of market forces. If certain industries were unprofitable, labour and capital would gradually be withdrawn from them and transferred to new and expanding industries where their productivity would be greater. In fact, as we have seen, this did not happen on anything like an adequate scale; the British 'special areas', for instance, were hardly less of a problem at the end than at the beginning of the inter-war period.

Several factors combined to prevent the *laisser-faire* mechanism from working effectively. Psychological and other obstacles to the movement of labour out of the contracting industries, and the fear of losses of invested capital, were reinforced during much of the inter-war period by the depressed condition of the economy as a whole and by the brakes on expansion in some industries due to monopolistic restrictions on new entry, both by entrepreneurs and workers. Both these factors tended to limit the absorptive capacity of expanding industries for the labour released in those faced with contraction. Nor was such intervention as was attempted to deal with the problem always of the right kind. In some cases, the need for contraction was at first inadequately realized, and it was thought possible to evade it by short-time working and sometimes by the institution of production quotas which tended to keep up prices at the cost of maintaining excess capacity and inefficient units. In other cases, contraction was pursued vigorously—perhaps, at least from the point of view of subsequent war-time needs, too vigorously—but too little was done to ensure a smooth and speedy absorption in other employment of the resources thus set free. In Great Britain, the peculiar localization of the contracting industries presented a particularly difficult problem; for it turned whole regions into 'depressed areas' which, as such, deterred new industries from being established there and virtually forced any movement from contracting to expanding industries to assume the form of difficult migrations of workers to other parts of the country.

This problem of structural maladjustments and special unemployment of the inter-war period was essentially the same as the problem which has since then faced all belligerent countries at the outbreak of war, the problem of shifting a large proportion of their productive resources from civilian to war production. This is obvious in so far as the maladjustments of the inter-war period were merely the aftermath of over-expansion of certain industries during the last war; but it is equally true of maladjustments which were the result of technological or other changes. The experience of the last four years is, therefore, not irrelevant to the solution of the problem of structural unemployment. None of the belligerent countries relied on market forces alone to effect the contraction of consumption and other civilian industries and the expansion of the heavy industries and agriculture which the change over from peace to war involved. There is no reason to suppose that the methods which were obviously found necessary to meet the needs of economic mobilization—planned transfers of resources, including measures to heighten the mobility of labour, control of real investment, and reasonable compensation for losses of invested capital, all of them co-ordinated within the framework of an overall investment policy—can be completely dispensed with in meeting the, if anything more difficult, problem of economic demobilization at the end of the war, and the very similar problem of special unemployment due to other causes, although, in making such comparisons between war and peace, the difference in psychological and political conditions must always be borne in mind. Methods of control which have proved acceptable in war-time may prove politically impracticable, if not undesirable, however useful and indeed essential they may seem on technical grounds.

3. GENERAL UNEMPLOYMENT AND TRADE CYCLE CONTROL

The characteristic pattern of the cyclical unemployment of the inter-war period was a relatively simple one. The internal economy suffered some shock in the shape of a sudden fall in demand. In the U.S.A. it resulted in every case from internal factors. In most of the European countries the great depression of 1929–33 was the result of external factors, the cessation of capital import, withdrawal of short-term credits, or a sudden fall in the demand for exports. Whatever the initial shock, it reacted on the internal credit system in the form of a deflationary spiral, spreading unemployment throughout the economy in its course. The deflationary spiral was, in most countries, accentuated by orthodox Government financial policy as then conceived. The automatic effect of a depression was to reduce tax revenue and increase expenditure for the relief of the unemployed, and hence to produce a budgetary deficit. Orthodox finance demanded that the budget should be balanced annually, by rigid economies in expenditure and the imposition of additional taxes, a policy which, *ceteris paribus*, inevitably served to accelerate the deflation and produce further unemployment and shrinkage of income—although, given the prevalence of orthodox ideas on 'sound' and 'unsound' finance, any alternative policy was liable to have detrimental psychological effects.

The problem of cyclical unemployment and depression thus had two distinct aspects: first, how to safeguard economies against internal and, as far as possible, against external shocks; and secondly, how to prevent or counteract the cumulative deflationary spiral which those shocks set in motion.

(a.) Recovery

During the nineteen-thirties, the attention of Governments was perforce concentrated on the second aspect of the problem. Such attempts as had been made in the U.S.A. and other countries in 1928–9 to forestall a slump had been entirely unsuccessful. In the circumstances, Governments could at best hope to curtail the downswing; in most cases, large-scale intervention did not begin until the depression had lasted for several years and was directed towards 'recovery'. The experience of these years has taught us a good deal about this aspect of the problem of trade cycle control.

Neither internal nor external shocks would have resulted in such disastrous declines in income, economic activity and employment as the world witnessed in the industrial countries in 1921–3, 1929–33 and again in the U.S.A. in 1937–8, if they had not set in motion cumulative deflationary processes. The unregulated capitalist economy possessed no automatic mechanism of adjustment to such disturbances. On the contrary, the inherent working of the system tended to make every decline cumulative: a fall in effective demand led to unemployment, reduction of incomes, and a further fall in effective demand. The instability inherent in a system in which the level of employment depended on the profit expectations of individual investors was further aggravated by psychological factors, 'trade cycle consciousness' and other matters affecting 'business confidence'. Although, even in the conditions of the inter-war period, the cumulative deflationary spirals did not continue indefinitely, they tended, in the absence of State intervention, to last longer and assume more disastrous proportions than they had done during the nineteenth century when new investment opportunities in the shape of new inventions or in the sphere of foreign investment generally came to the aid at an early stage by raising profit expectations. During the inter-war period Governments were in all countries sooner or later forced to intervene. The various attempts to counteract the deflationary process and to promote recovery fell into four main groups:

1. Most countries endeavoured to improve their balances of trade by curtailing imports and pushing exports. Protection undoubtedly stimulated domestic employment, and in certain circumstances it did so without reducing the volume of international trade or injuring the interests of other countries, since the reduction in the proportion of income spent on imports was offset by the increase in the volume of income. In many cases, however, it did stimulate employment at home at the expense of international trade and of employment in other countries. Wherever restrictive measures were not necessitated by an adverse balance of payments, policies designed to improve a country's balance of trade were undoubtedly a most objectionable method of relieving domestic depression and unemployment, though one for which Governments unfortunately often found it easier to secure political support than for alternative policies. When, as in the case of the U.S.A., a large export surplus was maintained as a supplement to an inadequate public works policy, the effects were doubly disastrous because such a policy virtually ruled out the restoration of international equilibrium and the working of any international monetary system.

2. Four of the five countries which we have studied, and most others in which the gold standard did not make this impossible, tried during the nineteen-thirties to combat the depression by a policy of 'cheap money'. Most Governments had little difficulty during the depression in reducing interest rates to unprecedentedly low levels and making abundant credit on easy terms available to investors. The result was that in none of these countries was a revival of private investment hampered by credit stringency—in itself a major achievement. Where building played an important part in the recovery, the reduction of interest rates also helped to increase effective demand. But on the whole, 'cheap

money', while wholly beneficial, could not decisively counteract deflation or produce a recovery. So long as entrepreneurs expected to make losses rather than profits on any new investment, interest rates could never be reduced sufficiently to make new investment appear worth while.

The relative inefficiency of these first two methods was due to the fact that they did not go to the heart of the problem of deflation, the deficiency of internal effective demand. It was to raise one or the other of the two components of total effective demand, the effective demand for consumption goods and the effective demand for capital goods, that became the chief object of 'recovery' policies during the nineteen-thirties. So long as 'recovery' and in particular the reduction of unemployment, was the most important objective of Government economic policy, it was a matter of indifference on which of these two forms of demand these efforts were concentrated—the more so as the one naturally helped to stimulate the other—and the choice between them was determined largely by their relative efficacy in reducing unemployment quickly, by the general social complexion of the Government's policy, and by the part which rearmament played in it.

3. Methods of increasing effective consumers' demand directly were at first forced on Governments, without a very clear conception of their economic import, by the exigencies of the depression, the urgent need to relieve destitution; and they tended to be given preference by Governments with a progressive social policy. President Roosevelt's New Deal in particular was largely based on the conception of stimulating recovery by increasing consumers' purchasing power and effective demand directly. The general conception—until then generally condemned as economic heresy—was perfectly sound. A general deficiency of effective consumers' demand was an essential aspect of deflation, and any policy which served to increase that demand in a depression was *pro tanto* beneficial to recovery. Broadly speaking, two methods were used for this purpose. Efforts were made to redistribute income in favour of the poorer classes with a higher propensity to consume, and public money was distributed directly to consumers in the form of relief or otherwise. The substantial success which the New Deal achieved in promoting recovery was largely due to these two policies, particularly the latter. That success, however, was far from complete, and the reason was that the increase in consumers' demand did not lead to a corresponding revival of demand for capital goods. The experience of the New Deal has shown that in the advanced industrial countries in which capital goods industries represent a large proportion of total productive capacity and are responsible for a large proportion of employment, methods of increasing effective consumers'

demand cannot be relied upon to produce a recovery, once a depression has been allowed to gather momentum.

4. In order to ensure a quick recovery of employment not only in the consumption but also in the investment goods industries, it proved necessary at least to supplement these methods of stimulating effective consumers' demand by methods specifically directed towards reviving the demand for investment goods. The fact that it is the demand for investment goods which is most liable to fluctuate in an unregulated private enterprise economy, and that it was in the capital goods industries that the depression and unemployment were most severe in all the advanced industrial countries, led Governments sooner or later to concentrate on the latter methods. In a broad sense, all recovery policies, including protectionist policies, 'cheap money', and the methods of increasing consumers' demand just mentioned, aimed indirectly at stimulating private investment activity; and in several countries investment subsidies were used with considerable success for the same object. But the two main methods used during the nineteen-thirties were the use of public capital expenditure to offset fluctuations in private investment activity and the subjection of private investment to direct State control. Several countries, especially Sweden, Germany and the U.S.A., attempted the former policy in the shape of more or less clearly conceived public works policies; and Germany and other countries pursued it in practice by rearmament. The latter method was used in peace-time only in Nazi Germany, although, for a different purpose, it has become a universal instrument of war economy.

While the evidence of the nineteen-thirties is not quite conclusive, it can hardly be doubted that public capital expenditure—even when it does not take the form of rearmament—can bring about a complete recovery, provided certain conditions are fulfilled. In the first place, it is essential that the public works should be planned and prepared well in advance. During the great depression their efficacy was greatly reduced by the time-lag which ensued before public works schemes could be put into effect and, as the experience of both the U.S.A. and Great Britain showed, by the difficulty of co-ordinating the capital expenditure of local as well as central authorities. Secondly, it is equally essential that capital flight should be prevented. The experience of the Blum experiment in France has shown that a public works policy can be rendered completely nugatory if capital flight is allowed to develop, and that a persistent tendency towards capital flight can be effectively checked only by exchange control of capital transactions. Thirdly, to be effective capital expenditure must be on an adequate scale (assuming for the moment that unlimited capital expenditure is desirable in the interest of recovery, a question to which we shall return presently). It is here that the chief difficulty lay during the nineteen-thirties.

That difficulty was not one of finance. During the nineteen-thirties several countries, and particularly the U.S.A., considerably increased their national debt in their efforts to combat the depression. Fears of 'unsound' finance among the general public and among business men in particular greatly hampered the application of public works policies and deterred Governments in some countries from resorting to them. But it was this psychological and political reaction rather than the intrinsic disadvantages which made deficit expenditures a problem. At the bottom of these fears was the failure to recognize that the finance of the State must differ in essential respects from the finance of a private firm, and that the principles governing public finance which are sound in a state of full employment are not necessarily sound in a state of depression. By contrast to the private firm, the primary object of State finance is not to show a regular profit year by year, or even to avoid at all costs an occasional financial loss, but to maintain the real national income at the highest possible level; and that object may justify in certain circumstances what appears as a temporary loss in the budget accounts.

The most frequent but least justified objection to deficit expenditure in a depression was the fear of inflation. For it is clear on theoretical grounds, and has been amply confirmed by the experience of the U.S.A. and other countries during the nineteen-thirties, that in deflationary conditions in which the volume of purchasing power is inadequate to secure the employment of all productive resources, an increase in total purchasing power will not produce any inflationary increase in prices.

A somewhat weightier objection was the fear that deficit expenditure financed by borrowing would permanently increase the tax burden of the national debt service. The objection, however, overlooked two points. In the first place, it was clearly inapplicable to any productive capital expenditure which, directly or indirectly, yielded income sufficient to cover interest charges. It is true that in practice such public capital expenditure had always largely been financed by borrowing in most countries. But this had by no means been the universal practice; little attempt had been made to vary the volume of such expenditure in accordance with the needs of the general economy, and where such borrowing and expenditure figured in the ordinary budget it gave the appearance of a budget deficit and hence of 'unsound finance'. For these reasons, the adoption of the Swedish system of an entirely separate capital budget would not only be logical but might have psychological advantages.

Secondly, the objection ignored the fact that a growing national debt does not impose any additional tax burden at all, so long as the national income—and with it the revenue yield of existing taxation—increases sufficiently to meet the increase in interest charges on the national debt.[1] It is true that, in the long run, this principle sets fairly narrow limits to the rate of growth of the national debt which is possible without higher taxation, the more so as it is clearly undesirable to squander all the automatic increase in State revenue on the national debt service. In a depression, however, when the national income has fallen far below its normal 'full employment' level, public deficit expenditure can be expected to raise the national income, directly or indirectly (by 'pump-priming'), at a rate exceeding the normal long-term rate of growth. Thus—even if it is borne in mind that the rapid increase in income continues only for a few years, while the increase in the national debt service is permanent—a substantial volume of public deficit expenditure may be possible in deflationary conditions without resulting in any permanent increase in the tax burden of the national debt.

Finally, there is of course no reason why an increase in the rates of taxation (once the depression has been overcome) should be ruled out altogether. Even in a private enterprise economy there are no rigid upper limits to the level of taxation. Provided the system of taxation is sufficiently progressive, such redistributory taxation need not aggravate the maldistribution of income; and it may be possible to devise methods of taxation which will minimize the discouraging effects on private investment activity even of very high rates of taxation.

It is clearly undesirable to use public work policies of an unproductive character where existing resources could be more advantageously employed on productive work or where other equally effective methods of preventing depressions are available. And the preceding analysis has shown that there are limits beyond which deficit expenditure cannot go without raising new problems—limits which the current reaction against former orthodox ideas may be thought to treat too lightly. But our analysis has also shown that the scope for financially sound deficit expenditure is much greater than was generally thought during the years of the great depression.

Far more real than the financial difficulty of a recovery policy based on public capital expenditure proved during the nineteen-thirties to be the adverse reaction of public on private investment activity and the limitations which this imposed on the scope for public works. In all the countries studied, public capital expenditure was designed to supplement not to supplant private invest-

---

[1] For a more detailed discussion of the problems of budget policy and the burden of the national debt, see above, ch. ii, p. 54 ff.

ment. On this assumption there was always the danger that an extension of public investment would further discourage private investment activity. It was the great advantage of rearmament as a public works policy that it completely avoided this dilemma: the State's demand for armaments was an entirely additional, non-competitive demand.[1] Any other public works schemes not confined to 'non-competitive' investment were liable to lead private investors to react to an intrusion by the State into the spheres traditionally reserved for private enterprise by 'loss of confidence'. This not only greatly narrowed the scope and efficacy of public works as an instrument of recovery; but it also resulted in the employment of labour and capital on projects which, while not useless, were certainly not the most urgent and beneficial additions to the nation's capital equipment. 'It is possible to imagine a point beyond which road building and the like might become an even less advantageous method of curing unemployment than the famous expedient of digging holes in the ground and filling them up again. This method at least leaves no traces behind, while unnecessary roads occupy space that might be better used.'[2]

(b.) The Maintenance of Full Employment

The various policies discussed in the preceding paragraphs aim at counteracting the large deflationary processes which were the characteristic feature of the severe depressions of the inter-war period. If successful, they would undoubtedly reduce the problem of general unemployment to relatively manageable proportions. But they do not go to the root of the problem of instability. They are directed primarily towards the recovery *rather* than the *maintenance* of full employment. The latter problem is bound up with the liability of the unregulated private enterprise economy to 'shocks' which, as we have seen, constitute the second and hardly less important aspect of the problem of the trade cycle.

The threats to stability proved to be of three main kinds: (1) over-expansion of the investment industries; (2) inflation; and (3) external shocks. All three raise problems of great difficulty.

1. Several of the major depressions of the inter-war period, in particular the immediate post-war depressions in the belligerent countries and, to some extent, also the American depression of 1929, were probably set going by a sudden fall in the demand for investment goods following a period during which the investment goods industries had been expanded beyond the normal long-run requirements of the various economies. In the case of the post-war depressions the over-expansion of the investment industries

---

[1] See on this point above, ch. vi, p. 173.
[2] *The Times*, 22 January 1943.

had been brought about by the war-time production of armaments (most of which resemble capital goods in the type of
machines and factories required to produce them). In the case of
the American depression of 1929, the over-expansion was in the
main due to the exceptional investment boom in a number of new
industries such as the motor-car industry, coupled with a large
boom in residential building and a very large volume of foreign
investment. This over-expansion was by no means an isolated
phenomenon. On the contrary, there are reasons to believe that
the process of capital formation in the capitalist economy has
always proceeded in leaps: booms stimulated by the appearance
of promising new investment opportunities led to a larger construction of capital equipment than was required in the long run,
with the result that sooner or later the demand for new capital
equipment was satiated, and a period of slack investment activity,
excess capacity in the capital goods industries, and depression
supervened.

The fact that several of the major depressions of the inter-war
period hit economies in which the capital goods sector had grown
too large, and were in fact largely the consequence of this type of
maladjustment, has an important bearing on the problem of trade
cycle control. On the one hand, it underlines a point already
stressed, namely, the need to prevent (or at least reduce) the
apparently natural tendency in an unregulated economy towards
fluctuations in the volume of investment; the need, in other words,
to ensure that the process of capital construction proceeds
smoothly, instead of in leaps. On the other hand, however, it
suggests that the choice between the various recovery policies
outlined above must be guided, to a larger extent than was the
case during the nineteen-thirties, by the requirements of a
soundly adjusted industrial structure; and in particular, that in
the circumstances most likely to prevail at the onset of a depression public capital expenditure may, from this point of view, be
a second-best choice.

The point is of special significance at the present time, because
it is quite certain that on the next occasion on which a slump will
threaten the Western industrial countries, their economies will,
owing to the war and the period of reconstruction, have experienced an abnormal expansion of their investment goods industries. The danger of a slump will arise when private reconstruction demand for capital goods is satisfied and threatens to fall off
—say, two or three years after the war. In the circumstances, it
would clearly not do to attempt to offset any decline in production and employment in the capital goods industries automatically
by a corresponding increase in public capital expenditure. What
will be wanted may be, on the contrary, a reduction in the pro-

portion of national output devoted to the production of capital goods, and an increase in the production of consumption goods (and services or leisure). The problem with which Governments will be faced will, therefore, not be merely to maintain aggregate effective demand and employment, but the twofold problem of ensuring a shift in effective demand from capital goods to consumption goods and a shift in resources from the capital to the consumption goods industries; and since, in relation to any given national income the proportion of income that is spent rather than saved must be adjusted to the proportion of national output that takes the form of consumption goods, the former of these two problems involves also the need for some further redistribution of the national income in favour of the lower income groups with a higher propensity to consume. The twofold, or even threefold, problem is a formidable one, although methods can undoubtedly be devised to meet it. To outline these methods here would take us too far afield. Nor is it possible to dogmatize on the magnitude of the shift that would be required in varying national conditions. The long-run requirements of a country for new capital equipment are highly elastic, varying with the most desirable rate of economic progress, the movements of population trends, and the nature of foreign demand, and are, even within these limits, adjustable by Government policy. What it is important to bear in mind, however, is that the two problems of trade cycle control (in the narrow sense) and structural adjustment of national economies must be treated together, and that in the immediate post-war situation the latter aspect will bulk larger than ever.

2. The second, equally difficult aspect of the problem of maintaining, as opposed to the problem of reaching, full employment was the danger of inflation, and closely connected with it the subsidiary problem of speculation. After the spectacular stock exchange boom and crash in the U.S.A. in 1929 growing attention was devoted to the problem of controlling the boom, of preventing speculative excesses and inflationary cost and price increases from setting in before unemployment was anything like fully absorbed. But the repetition of some of the same features in the 1936–7 boom and the subsequent collapse in 1937–8 showed that little progress had been made in that direction. It is true that the banking system was more secure and speculation had been somewhat curbed by legislation. But, as we have seen, there was speculation, and the tendency of a chase between wages and prices became increasingly apparent both in 1937, and again after 1940 until the war emergency made it possible to introduce stricter measures of control. Nor should we assume that the danger of internal shocks due to inflationary developments was confined to the American economy. In an unregulated economy

the scarcity of resources which, by definition, characterizes a
state of full employment is bound to give rise to the danger of
inflation, the more surely if the boom leads to speculative excesses.

The peculiar difficulty of preventing full employment from
leading to a runaway inflation lies largely in the fact that it is a
political almost as much as an economic problem. It was solved
in Nazi Germany and in Soviet Russia by the imposition of complete control of wages, prices and credit, on the one hand, and
labour supply, raw materials and consumption, on the other; and
it has been solved again in the capitalist countries in war-time by
the same methods. But rigid control of wages, profits and occupation imposed sacrifices on workers and employers which were
accepted only in special conditions. In Germany control was
supplemented by the destruction of the trade unions, by the
Gestapo and the concentration camp, and by appeals to nationalist sentiment. In Soviet Russia similar methods of ensuring
strict discipline were reinforced by a general conviction on the
part of the workers that any sacrifices they made were solely in
the interest of the community, and would not benefit private
employers. In war-time Britain and the U.S.A. patriotic motives
have induced workers and employers alike to make sacrifices
which they might not so readily concede in times of peace. The
political aspect of this problem requires as much attention as the
purely economic aspects.[1]

3. Security against both these main types of internal shocks
would still leave national economies exposed to the danger of
shocks from without. This again is partly an international economic problem which, however, requires a few words of comment here.

In the first place, it is clear that the international monetary
system of the nineteen-thirties, the gold standard, needlessly
aggravated the danger of external shocks to national economies.
Under the orthodox gold standard which linked the domestic
credit structure rigidly to inflows and outflows of gold, the level
of economic activity and employment of every country was
largely dependent on the state of its balance of international payments. The vagaries of international capital movements and the
obligation to meet a deficit on the balance of payments by deli-

---

[1] One possible approach to the political problem in Great Britain was recently
outlined in *The Times* (23 January 1943): 'Price control, limitation of profits,
and full publicity in respect of costs (as advocated by the 120 industrialists in
'A National Policy for Industry'), combined with a social security programme
at least as generous as that proposed by Sir William Beveridge, and with an
extension of works councils which would give the workers a voice in the day-to-
day affairs of the factory, might produce a situation in which the workers would
be prepared to accept discipline to the necessary and reasonable extent, and to
accept an overall wage treaty which would prevent the vicious spiral from setting
in.'

berate internal deflation presented a constant menace to the internal economic stability of the country. The desire to insulate national economies against this menace, both before and even more after the experience of the world financial crisis of 1931, was the chief motive for the universal abandonment of the gold standard. As we shall elaborate more fully below, this special aspect of the problem could be met by the adoption of some such international monetary system as that outlined in the 'Keynes Plan' which would permit countries to prevent capital flight by capital exchange control, and would substitute other methods, including in the last resort internationally agreed adjustments of exchange rates, for adjustments by deflation and inflation.

But such a system would clearly not provide a complete guarantee against such external shocks. It would, for instance, have in no way diminished the impact on the British economy of the sudden fall in world demand for British exports which took place in 1929–31. This danger is inherent in the dependence of employment in export industries on the demand of other countries for their products; it is the price which countries pay for the advantages of international trade. There is indeed no reason why a sudden fall in foreign demand should inevitably lead to widespread and prolonged unemployment. On the one hand, Germany, as we have seen, managed to insulate her economy almost completely against this danger by means of her system of foreign trade control which enabled her, through the use of appropriate export subsidies, to substitute a decline in her terms of trade for the decline in the volume of her exports and domestic employment which would otherwise have resulted from a fall in foreign demand. While this possibility should not be altogether excluded, it would clearly not work beyond a certain point if all countries resorted to it. On the other hand, steps should be taken, if necessary, to ensure the transfer of resources from the export industries which have been hit to other employment; although the fact that such changes in foreign demand are liable to happen suddenly and may be only temporary presents a special difficulty. But in the last resort the only way of safeguarding national economies against external shocks is to diminish international economic instability, on the one hand, by the maintenance of internal economic stability and full employment in the main world import markets, and on the other, by internationally co-ordinated regulation or planning of international trade and investment.

4. EFFICIENCY OF INDUSTRY

Obviously, 'full employment' cannot be the sole criterion of economic policy. It is not enough not to leave our resources idle;

beyond that it is necessary that we should use them efficiently. From a strictly economic point of view, indeed, unemployment was probably a less important obstacle to prosperity than inefficiency.[1] In the case of Great Britain, for instance, if all the unemployed had been brought into employment during the inter-war period, this would hardly have increased national output by more than 5—6 per cent *per annum*; if all inefficiency had been got rid of, the increase in national output would undoubtedly have been far greater.

One major obstacle to the most efficient use of the world's resources during the inter-war years was an international economic system which made it difficult if not impossible for countries to take full advantage of the opportunities for increasing productivity by international division of labour. With that problem we shall deal in the following section. At least as important, however, were the brakes on efficiency which resulted from the internal organization of industry in the advanced capitalist countries. Except in connection with commodity controls and up to a point with tariffs, the problems of industrial structure, competition and monopoly, were not so conspicuous in international economic relations and have, therefore, concerned us only in passing in the earlier chapters of this report. But they cannot possibly be ignored in a study of the economic lessons of the nineteen-thirties.

Classical economic theory which showed how an economic system of private enterprise, governed by the profit motive, assured the most efficient use of resources rested on the assumption of a competititive individualist economy. That assumption was very largely justified during the nineteenth century. During the inter-war period it had lost much of its justification. Even in the non-totalitarian countries, the atomistic *laisser-faire* basis of industry had largely disappeared and industry was approaching organization along corporative lines. The reasons for this change are partly to be found in technical progress, in particular the development of mass production, which had greatly increased the optimum scale of production; and partly in the fact that large sections of private industry were coming to rely less on price competition than on competition by advertising, deliberate product differentiation, and competitive distribution services. The result was an industrial system which in many respects combined the disadvantages of competition with those of monopoly. On the one hand, competition by advertising and other marketing costs

---

[1] The problems of inefficiency and unemployment were, of course, interconnected: large-scale unemployment tended to reduce the incentive to the most efficient use of resources, and obstacles to the most advantageous international division of labour as well as monopoly both aggravated the unemployment problem.

i*

constituted an immense waste of resources and an obstacle to the most efficient organization of production and distribution; on the other hand, the growth of monopolies, cartels and other monopolistic forms of economic organization, reduced the stimulus to efficiency which price competition had normally provided, led to restriction of output and maldistribution of resources, and aggravated the existing inequalities of income.

The benefits which economic theory and popular belief associated with competition presupposed that competition took the form of price competition (or, what comes to the same thing, competition in quality). It was only where firms competed by continually trying to underbid each other (or offer the better product or service) that competition provided a stimulus to maximum efficiency and ensured that the benefits of increased productivity accrued to the community at large. In many spheres of production and distribution, modern technical development, with its opportunities for mass production and economies of scale, has rendered competition of any kind between small units wasteful. But this had become a relatively minor source of inefficiency during the inter-war period. With certain exceptions private enterprise had been quick enough to seize the advantages of large-scale production. Far more important was the fact that most competition no longer took the form of price competition. In many industries in all the advanced industrial countries, and internationally among all the most important raw material producers, cartel agreements prevented firms from undercutting each other; and even where no such explicit agreements existed, the fear that price-cutting, once started, would not stop until profits were completely wiped out, was often enough to deter producers from engaging in a price war. Instead, firms tended to compete at home by advertising, packings, armies of salesmen, competitive distribution services and other methods which, while making at best a very small contribution to the national welfare, wasted valuable resources in unproductive activities—the money costs being borne by the consumers in the form of higher prices. Not the least harmful of these methods was deliberate product differentiation, the production of innumerable types and brands of the same product (and frequent changes in these types) solely for purposes of competition, which prevented anything like full use of the potentialities of mass production.

This was one aspect of the problem. The other, no less important, aspect was the growth of monopoly and the monopolistic price and production policies which this type of competition involved. The natural tendency of monopoly is to maintain prices at a higher and output at a lower level than the level which would obtain under the, admittedly theoretical, conditions of 'perfect' competition and which would be the most beneficial to the community. Monopolies in the narrowest sense of the word, that is to say, single firms controlling the output of a whole industry, were rare and in any case not the worst evil. For while they tended to keep up prices and restrict output, thus securing monopoly profits and preventing the most advantageous allocation of resources, they had generally secured their monopoly position by realizing to the full the advantages of large-scale production; their greater efficiency often more than compensated the community for these disadvantages.[1] The most harmful development lay in the far more widespread conclusion of price agreements (or allocation of restrictive production quotas) between all or most of the firms in one industry, grouped together in cartels or trade associations. Although such trade associations occasionally made possible economies in such matters as research and marketing, they too often in effect, by preventing beneficial price competition between the existing firms and, as far as possible, excluding outside competition by concerted action against new firms or restrictions on entry into the industry,[2] had all the disadvantages of monopolies without realizing the economies of large-scale production. By keeping prices much higher than the costs of production with the most efficient methods, they allowed inefficient firms to exist side by side with efficient ones; with the result that for one really efficient firm in an industry there were several 'parasites'—inefficient firms with obsolete methods which could not have survived at all if the efficient firms had reduced their prices to the level of costs. In the absence of effective price com-

[1] Strictly speaking, this applies only to monopolies based on 'internal economies', that is to say, on conditions in which the same output can be produced more cheaply by one than by two or more firms, however efficient the latter may be. It does not apply to 'natural' monopolies. Nor does it necessarily apply, except to a limited degree, to purely financial combinations (trusts or mergers) or to 'oligopolies', i.e. a small number of firms controlling an industry in concert, although in most cases of large financial combines and oligopolies, the units of production may well be of an economic size. Moreover, while it is true that the possibility of earning monopoly profits provides a powerful incentive to increased efficiency by concentration and large-scale production, monopolies, once securely established, have little incentive to maintain maximum efficiency: on the contrary, the interest of the monopoly concern or group may lie in suppressing new methods or buying up patents which, while ultimately cheapening production, would necessitate the scrapping of existing plant. In the long run, monopoly can exact a high price in terms of inefficiency and maldistribution of income for the service it has originally rendered to the community by organizing production on an efficient scale.

[2] The major obstacle to new entry, and the foundation of most modern monopoly, was of course the growing initial amounts of capital required in modern industry, and the growing risks which threatened potential competitors in case of concerted retaliation by the existing firms. One of the effects (and objects) of advertising and high selling costs was to increase the difficulties of entry, since high selling costs are as effective a deterrent as high fixed costs. It was only in industries or trades with a large number of small independent firms, where these factors were not sufficient to deter outside competition, that there was an urgent demand for compulsory powers of restriction on new entry.

petition, the incentive to adopt new and more efficient methods of production was much reduced; and such improvements as were made augmented profits rather than lowered prices to consumers.

These problems of the relative inefficiency of the system of private enterprise as it had developed before the present war are often ignored or dismissed by a reference to the fact that, in Great Britain, for instance, productivity throughout the inter-war period increased at an average rate of $1\frac{1}{2}$ per cent *per annum*. The obvious answer is that, while considerable advances were undoubtedly made, they fell far short of what would have been possible but for the facts just discussed.

Another cause of misunderstanding has been the effect of financial organization on the fortunes and efficiency of enterprises. The ease with which a firm could obtain credit depended on its balance sheets and the volume of its profits rather than on its real efficiency.[1] Firms earning large monopolistic profits, therefore, were in a better position to obtain credit for extensions of business than financially weaker firms which quite possibly were in fact more efficient; the accumulation of capital resources out of profits naturally worked in the same direction. The result was a vicious circle by which financially strong and well organized, that is to say, primarily monopolistic but not necessarily efficient, firms were able to expand, while financially weaker but often more efficient firms were squeezed out. It is clear that in such circumstances the fortunes of different firms and industries provided no reliable guide to their relative efficiency.

The experience of the inter-war period affords little guidance on the problem of eliminating these grave defects of a private enterprise economy. In most countries, Governments during the nineteen-thirties actively encouraged monopolization, as we found in the case of the American N.R.A., and in our discussion of British policy. Political factors apart, the motive was either a misdirected attempt to counteract price deflation or the desire to reduce outstanding inefficiencies of the first type discussed above, those connected with an excessive number of small firms and wasteful marketing. But the result was only too often the promotion of industrial groups more conspicuous for monopolistic price and output policies than for exemplary efficiency. In this connection, the effects of mass unemployment in damping down the incentive towards greater efficiency should not be forgotten: there was little point in releasing labour by encouraging the adoption of technical improvements (which in most cases meant

---

[1] Here, as elsewhere in this section, the term 'efficiency' is used in the sense of the degree to which a unit of production contributes to the 'social marginal net product', as defined by Professor Pigou.

labour-saving devices) if that labour would merely have swelled the ranks of the unemployed. In this respect, as in so many others, the exigencies of war have forced upon our attention the need for maximum efficiency and have stimulated the development of new methods of tackling that problem.

As far as the first group of problems, those connected with wasteful competition are concerned, the need is, in the first place, for the prevention of the immense waste of resources involved in excessive selling costs, and in the second place, for greater concentration of production and even more of distribution. The war-time device of utility goods may show the way towards economy of resources by greater standardization, which would do away not only with the evil of deliberate product differentiation but also with production of an excessive and unnecessary variety of types of the same commodity where it is simply a relic of small-scale production. By compulsory utility specifications or the production of standard types in Government-operated plants, sold at or near cost price, the state can reintroduce the element of price competition and thus force private firms to reduce selling costs; and there may be other ways of achieving the same object. Secondly, although concentration has already gone far in most industries and would clearly not be desirable in all, war-time experience suggests that in various spheres there is still ample scope, in peace conditions, for improvements of efficiency by concentration and rationalization. But the experience of the inter-war period has shown that rationalization and concentration by private enterprise inevitably raise the problem of price maintenance and monopoly.

It need hardly be said that the solution to that problem cannot lie in a return to the individualist competitive economy of the nineteenth century, the breaking up of industry into small independent units, which would not only be impracticable, but would fly in the face of that rationalization and concentration which, we have just agreed, is an equally desirable objective. Something might be done by legislation prohibiting monopolistic practices, especially the fixing of minimum prices, maximum production quotas, restrictions on entry, and combination to reduce capacity, and by such measures as reform of the patent law and curtailment of legal trade mark protection. Legislation, to be effective and to cover not only monopolistic agreements between several firms but also monopolies proper, might have to be supplemented by suitable adaptation of some of the methods of public control which have proved valuable in war-time, including powers to fix maximum prices, based on inspection of accounts, more uniform cost-accounting, and standards of efficiency set by Government-operated plants and utility specifications. War-time experience also suggests, however, that public control would not necessarily solve the problem. It might be worse than useless if the controlling authorities were merely the old monopoly interests in a new disguise. And even if the power of control were really public, there would remain the problem of finding in peace-time adequate substitutes for the incentive to efficiency which the profit motive provided in a competitive *laisser-faire* economy.

II. INTERNATIONAL ECONOMIC PROBLEMS

1. INTERNATIONAL TRADE

IN considering the lessons of the inter-war period in the sphere of international economics, many would subscribe to the view expressed in the following recent statement by a prominent American official:

'Our experience of the 1930's has made certain facts indisputably clear. We have learned that no industrial nation to-day can possibly carry on without a very large volume of exports and imports. No serious statesman in this day and generation advocates the complete elimination of all tariff walls. But responsible statesmen do advocate . . . the elimination after the war of those unconscionable trade barriers which inescapably choke the flow of international trade, and as a result substantially depress the standard of living of entire peoples. The pre-war system of mounting and excessive tariffs, of quota restrictions and artificial exchange controls, of Governmental monopolies, of bilateralistic trade arrangements—the whole economic panoply of fighting devices to enforce some form or other of special privilege or unfair discrimination—all these must go if our criterion is to be not the private profit of small pressure groups buttressed with political power but the welfare and advancement of humanity.'[1]

Now, if our analysis in the preceding chapters is at all sound, the view expressed in this statement provides a most inadequate theoretical basis for international economic reconstruction after this war. In view of the widespread popularity which it has enjoyed and still enjoys, however, it serves as a useful starting point for a summary of the lessons which in our opinion should be drawn from those two decades.

There is no dispute about the fact that, by contrast with the rapid growth of international trade, investment, and migration during the century preceding the first world war, the inter-war period witnessed a relative decline of international division of

---

[1] U.S. Department of Commerce, *Foreign Commerce Weekly*, vol. x, No. 5. 30 January 1943, p. 13; (from a recent address by Francis B. Sayre, Special Assistant to the Secretary of State of the United States).

labour and trade, and, at any rate during the second decade, an almost complete breakdown of international migration and international investment. Nor is there any doubt that the stagnation of international trade during the past twenty-five years has meant a substantial loss of potential wealth and prosperity to the world; nor even that this development may in a sense be said to have been 'caused' by the growth of trade barriers. What is questionable and even dangerous in the view illustrated by the passage quoted above is the implicit assumption that a removal of those 'trade barriers' could have solved the problem during the inter-war years or would do so at the end of this war.

Our analysis of the economic events and policies of the nineteen-thirties has shown that the 'growth of trade barriers' cannot be considered as an independent factor in the course of economic events of those years; it was a reflection of underlying defects in the economic organization of the different countries and of the world as a whole. So long as these defects persisted, the 'trade barriers' were not only unavoidable but in many cases even alleviated conditions, at any rate for particular countries; conversely, there is little hope of a better world economic order unless we go beyond the symptoms to the causes of the disease.

Before we turn to these causes, however, a word or two must be said on the relative importance of the problem presented by the growth of trade barriers and the stagnation of international trade itself. There has been a tendency, partly in justified reaction against the narrow nationalist outlook which prevailed in most countries during the inter-war period, vastly to exaggerate the relative importance of this as compared with other factors, as a source of poverty and obstacle to social welfare. If we are to consider the problem in its proper perspective, three points should be borne in mind.

In the first place, a distinction must be made between the changes in the *methods* and the changes in the *volume and direction* of international trade of the past decades. During the nineteenth century trade had overwhelmingly been carried on by private enterprise with a minimum of State control and, apart from tariffs, State intervention. The first world war and again the great depression resulted in the adoption in most countries of varying degrees of State intervention in foreign trade, ranging from relatively isolated measures in the U.S.A. and Great Britain to complete State control of foreign trade in the totalitarian countries. Many of these measures were, in the circumstances, designed to curtail the international movements of goods and services, capital and persons. But it is clearly wrong to lump together tariffs, quotas, exchange controls, bilateral arrangements and Government monopolies indiscriminately under the heading of 'barriers to international trade'. We have seen that, in the conditions which obtained at the time, the development of bilateral trading arrangements served to increase rather than restrict the volume of international trade of Germany, Great Britain and other countries. There is even less prima facie reason to assume that Government monopolies in foreign trade necessarily meant a smaller volume of foreign trade than would have been carried on by private enterprise.

The inter-war period witnessed a 'disintegration' of the formerly integrated world market economy in the sense that national economies increasingly ceased to be linked in international markets and co-ordinated by market forces. It can also be said that the world 'disintegrated' in the quite different sense of a diminution in the volume of economic intercourse between different nations. But there is no necessary connection between these two. It must be proved, not assumed, that the replacement of free private enterprise and market forces by Government control and planning in international economic relations—defective as that control and planning were on their national basis—was the cause of the relative decline of international trade during the inter-war period.

Secondly, it is wrong to think of the relative decline of international trade during those years as an unrelieved evil. Up to a point, it was the natural corollary of economic progress. As national incomes rose, a growing proportion of output and income took the form of services which were in their nature localized and could not enter into international trade, such as retail trade, professional services, catering, public utilities, public administration and so on. Moreover, while it is not true, as is sometimes asserted, that industrialization diminishes the opportunities for mutually advantageous international division of labour, one effect of technical progress is on balance to reduce the margin of comparative cost advantage between different countries in the production of different commodities. The comparative advantage of Malaya over Germany in the production of rubber was infinite thirty years ago. Even now it is substantial, because natural rubber is produced relatively more cheaply in Malaya than synthetic rubber in Germany. But the time may not be far off when this difference will have disappeared. Similarly, the immense comparative advantage which Great Britain enjoyed over Japan in industrial production during the nineteenth century has already been greatly reduced and, until the war, seemed likely to diminish further. That does not mean that international division of labour and trade are ceasing to be economically advantageous, or that the absolute volume of international trade must be expected to decline. What it does mean is that there has been a tendency to underestimate the speed with which, in modern conditions, comparative cost advantages can be wiped out by improvements of productive methods and training of labour, and that part of the decline in the proportion of world income which was derived from international trade was a natural and in no way undesirable symptom of increasing world prosperity.

In practice, the relative decline of international trade undoubtedly went much further than could be accounted for by this explanation. But, and this is the third point, even to the extent to which that decline involved a loss of potential world income that loss can easily be exaggerated. It is worth remembering that the maximization of international trade is not an end in itself. International division of labour and trade are merely one, though a very important, method of increasing the productivity of the world's resources. If this fact had been more clearly kept in mind, it would have been obvious that in the conditions of large-scale unemployment which prevailed in most of the capitalist countries throughout a large part of the nineteen-thirties, Governments could not be expected to pay much attention to comparative cost considerations in their commercial policies. Whatever the money costs, the 'opportunity costs' (in the sense of the alternative output forgone by the withdrawal of resources from other employment) of producing at home goods formerly imported from abroad was *nil*, provided that the resources thus employed would otherwise have remained idle. Another point which is often ignored is the fact that the advantage in terms of comparative costs of an international division of labour clearly varies greatly between different commodities. It is infinite for that part, usually a very small part, of a country's foreign trade which it cannot produce at home at all, and it is likely to be very great for a further broad range of goods which it can produce at home only at much greater cost than the cost of the exports with which it can purchase them abroad. But as the range of goods widens the margin of advantage diminishes, and for a very large proportion —possibly as much as one-third—of the goods which traditionally entered into international trade the margin of difference was probably very small. Thus, the economic loss which a country incurred by a reduction in the volume of its foreign trade was, if not negligible, at least a factor which could reasonably be weighed against such other factors as the need to reduce unemployment, economic stability, military security and so forth. Taken as a whole, it is very doubtful whether the economic loss which the world and individual countries suffered owing to the failure to take full advantage of the opportunities for international division of labour during the inter-war period was comparable to the loss due to the failure of the wealthy industrial countries to ensure the full employment of their productive resources, or to the impediments to economic progress and productive efficiency due to monopoly—although it is true that monopolization was often facilitated and encouraged by the growth of trade barriers. If we interpret the term 'standard of living' sufficiently broadly, so as to take into account the 'psychic income' of social security, the effects of the reduction in the international division of labour in lowering the standards of living of the peoples of the world were almost certainly negligible as compared with those of the catastrophic economic instability of the world during those twenty years.

These considerations are not intended to explain away the loss of potential income which the world incurred during the inter-war period owing to the growth of obstacles to international trade. But they must be borne in mind if we are to avoid a wholly disproportionate emphasis on this aspect of the problem of world economic organization.

What then were the causes of the growth of 'trade barriers'? Broadly speaking, they may be reduced to three, (a) international political insecurity; (b) the 'trade cycle'; and (c) the inadequacy and breakdown of the international gold standard system.

a. The failure of the world to solve the problem of international political security was a factor of fundamental importance throughout the inter-war period. Even during the nineteen-twenties the feeling in all the major countries that it was essential to ensure the supplies of essential foodstuffs and raw materials in case of another war played a part in their economic policies. It was responsible for much of the agricultural protectionism of the Western European countries during these years, for the special protection of 'key industries' even in relatively free trade countries like Great Britain, and for much of the, for the most part, uneconomic concentration on heavy industry in the policies of industrialization of the new countries of South-Eastern and Central Europe. During the nineteen-thirties, preparation for war entirely dominated the economic policies of Germany, Italy, and Japan and played a growing part in that of most other powers. The history of those two decades shows that, so long as countries have reason to fear the recurrence of war, no emphasis on the economic benefits of international trade will induce them to forgo such·a measure of economic self-sufficiency as their Governments consider feasible and desirable for their military security. At the same time, while we should not ignore the extent to which economic causes contributed to international hostility and political insecurity, this is essentially a political problem to the solution of which economists cannot make any direct contribution.

There is little point in debating which of the other two factors —the internal instability of the major capitalist economies and the defects and final breakdown of the world monetary system— was the more important. Both together, the one aggravating the disastrous consequences of the other, were responsible for the world depression of 1929–33 and were thus the direct cause of the process of international economic disintegration which characterized the second inter-war decade. Both must be solved before we can hope to avoid a repetition of the experience of the nineteen-thirties and to enlist to the full the opportunities of international division of labour for the improvement of living standards.

b. There is no need to emphasize the connection between the problem of the trade cycle and the 'growth of trade barriers'. It was the American slump of 1929 which, by upsetting the precarious equilibrium in the balances of international payments, thrust upon a large number of other countries balance of payments difficulties that could often only be met by measures restricting the flow of international trade. It was the internal instability of all the other major economies, with the single exception of Russia, which made the depression cumulative the world over, and magnified the balance of payments chaos and its restrictive effect on world trade. Moreover, in their efforts to meet their domestic unemployment problems all countries did their utmost to shift unemployment on to other countries by shutting out imports and pushing exports. Although the U.S.A. was the only country in which this policy of using an export surplus as a 'public works policy' stood in flagrant contradiction to the requirements of equilibrium in its balance of international payments, the 'recovery' motive played a dominant part in the commercial policies of most countries during the nineteen-thirties and, coupled with the fact that it was far easier for any one country to curtail its imports than to increase its exports, it was one of the major causes of the stagnation of international trade.

The experience of the nineteen-thirties has shown that there are at least three reasons why the solution of the problem of the trade cycle is an essential precondition of a reintegration of the world economy. In the first place, it is doubtful whether an international monetary system can withstand the impact of the internal collapse of one of the three or four large import markets, the U.S.A., Great Britain, and to a lesser extent Germany or France. Secondly, unless these countries learn to maintain full employment at home by other methods, the temptation to shift the burden on to other countries by striving for the most favourable possible balances of trade is bound to prove irresistible. Thirdly, even if most countries manage to make their own economies immune to internal cyclical fluctuations, the mere existence of the danger that one of the largest markets, and the U.S.A. in particular, may suddenly collapse, will inevitably act as a powerful incentive to all countries to reduce to a minimum their dependence on foreign markets.

c. We have seen that the catastrophe of the world depression of 1929–33 cannot be attributed to the internal instability of the advanced industrial countries alone. It was not merely a phase in the 'trade cycle'. The world depression would not have been nearly as severe and disastrous in its consequences if it had not been for the fact that ever since the first world war the economic structure of the world and of individual countries had been in a state of acute disequilibrium which the existing world economic system proved quite incapable of correcting and the consequences of which it aggravated. These disequilibria, most of which appeared as maladjustments in the balances of payments of different countries but which in reality represented fundamental maladjustments in the economic structure of the countries concerned and of the world as a whole, were too large to be corrected by market forces operating within the framework of an automatic international monetary system, such as the gold standard. At the same time, they prevented the gold standard from functioning smoothly and with the American slump of 1929 led to its complete breakdown. Their persistence was primarily responsible for the restrictive commercial policies pursued during the nineteen-thirties, at any rate by the debtor countries. Both Great Britain and Germany were, as we have seen, virtually forced by their balance of payments difficulties (which were aggravated but not caused by the depression) into import restrictions, the former choosing depreciation and tariffs, the latter exchange control. With the breakdown of the system of multilateral settlement of international payments after 1931, moreover, bilateral trading arrangements, whatever their disadvantages from the point of view of an optimum international division of labour, inevitably followed as the best method of carrying on international trade available in the circumstances. Most important of all, with the collapse of the gold standard disappeared the only existing system for the co-ordination of national economic policies; in the absence of any such co-ordinating mechanism during the nineteen-thirties, the existence of some fifty-odd sovereign States, acting independently of each other, and with small regard to the external repercussions of their policies, inevitably meant international economic chaos.

It may be objected that this classification of the causes of the growth of trade barriers leaves out the two which have generally been considered the most important of all (and which are also implicitly made the scapegoats in the above quotation), economic nationalism and the pressure of vested interests. A word must, therefore, be said here about both.

It may be true that, in the last analysis, an ideal world economic order is impossible unless the nations of the world cease to give preference to their own interests over those of other nations. It is certainly not very helpful. A more useful question is how much economic nationalism would have mattered during the inter-war period had it not been for the two outstanding economic problems just mentioned. Many of the actions of national Governments during the years of the world depression, such as the British depreciation of the pound and adoption of a general tariff, the imposition of exchange control by Germany and the similar measures taken in other countries, which were condemned at the time and have often been held up since as conspicuous manifestations of economic nationalism, have on closer inspection turned out to have been the inescapable consequences of a defective international monetary and economic system. Similarly, it is both more helpful and more correct to trace the disastrous American tariff policy to the failure of the U.S.A. to pursue an effective policy of trade cycle control than to American economic nationalism. This is not to assert that with a solution of those two problems of economic organization all economic conflicts of interest between nations would disappear. There would remain situations in which the economic interests of nations would clash and political sanctions, if such can be devised, would be needed to enforce international good behaviour. On the other hand, it is plain that but for ignorance, which sometimes led to actions that would never have been taken on a sounder interpretation of national self-interest and which often suggested a conflict of national interests where there was none, and but for the defects of the existing international economic institutions and the domestic economic systems of most countries, the evil effects of economic nationalism, in the sense of the precept that 'charity begins at home', would have been negligible by comparison with its actual effects during the inter-war period.

Much the same applies to the problem of 'vested interests'. While the extent to which the pressure of sectional groups was responsible for the growth and maintenance of barriers to international trade has sometimes been exaggerated, it certainly played a significant part in the commercial policies of most countries. Reductions in the American tariff would have been far easier, some British tariffs or quotas might have been dispensed with, had national rather than sectional interests determined policy. But, quite apart from the fact that such cases were probably insignificant by comparison with the magnitude of the international economic problem as a whole, the question may again be asked how insistent the pressure of sectional interests would have been in expanding rather than stagnating economies and if more had been done to relieve sectional groups of the costs of adjustments which were in the interest of the whole community. As in the case of economic nationalism, and indeed most of our major economic problems, even the most perfect economic organization would not solve the problem of 'vested interests'. It would leave a residual political problem. The fact remains that but for the failure to solve what were essentially technical economic problems—though undoubtedly they raised great social and political issues—both economic nationalism and 'vested interests' might have been relatively innocuous. To put the blame for the growth of trade barriers, or for any of the other economic evils of the inter-war period on the prevalence of economic nationalism and the pressure of vested interests is to blind our eyes to these economic problems and may indeed be a counsel of despair.

To sum up, we have seen that the 'growth of trade barriers' constitutes a most inadequate explanation of the relative decline of international trade during the inter-war period—itself but one and not perhaps the gravest economic problem of those years. The growth of trade barriers was itself the result of three main factors, international political insecurity, the internal instability of the capitalist economies, and the inadequacy of the existing world monetary and economic system in the face of the profound maladjustments which were the aftermath of the first world war. A discussion of the first of these problems lies outside the scope of this report. Enough has been said already about the vital necessity of solving the problem of the trade cycle. That leaves the third, and in many respects the most important, cause of the international economic chaos of the nineteen-thirties. Before we turn to a summary of the lessons on this problem, however, it may be worth while to consider how far these conclusions are confirmed by inspecting the causes that led to the other major development detrimental to the most efficient organization of the world economy, the breakdown of international migration and investment.

2. INTERNATIONAL MIGRATION AND INVESTMENT

If there has been a tendency to exaggerate the seriousness of the relative decline of international trade as a factor retarding the improvement of world standards of life, the seriousness of the breakdown of international migration and long-term investment during the nineteen-thirties has generally been underestimated.

Both had played an essential part in the unprecedented economic progress of the world during the nineteenth century. The large and continuous flow of people from Europe and the Far East to the new countries of the Western and Southern Hemisphere, by bringing labour from parts of the world where it was over-abundant to others where it was scarce, had not only raised the standards of life of the migrants, but also indirectly those of the peoples already in the new countries and of those who remained in the old.

Similarly, the large sums annually invested by the advanced industrial countries in poorer parts of the world had utilized the abundant capital resources of the former to raise productivity in the latter, by the application of capital primarily to the development of virgin land and the exploitation of mineral resources, but partly also to large manpower resources by industrialization. It is worth restating these facts, because the political and social disadvantages which attended the actual processes of international migration and investment have tended to overshadow their solid economic advantages. Both international migration and international long-term investment largely broke down during the inter-war period. None of the former immigration countries restored the pre-war freedom of immigration when the war ended, and with the virtual closing of the doors to the U.S.A. in 1924 international migration was reduced to a mere trickle. The volume of international long-term investment during the years of prosperity of the late nineteen-twenties was probably not much below the peak pre-war years; but it rested on far less stable foundations and failed almost completely to revive after the collapse during the world depression. Here again, it is not enough to point to the restrictive measures taken by various countries as the causes of breakdown. In so far as such measures played a decisive part, the question is still why these measures were adopted. Although we have not dealt specifically with the problem of migration in the historical chapters of this report, it is not difficult to list the chief reasons for both those developments.

The reason why all the new countries of the Western and Southern Hemisphere, almost without exception, virtually closed their doors to immigrants was clearly not that their natural resources set limits to any further population increase. Even if it is true that in most of them opportunities for new land settlement were beginning to disappear with the end of the 'Frontier', that did not mean that henceforth further immigration could not increase the wealth of these countries; much less was it bound to lower the standard of living of their existing populations. The latter's standards of life were, after all, rising because more efficient agricultural production enabled an increasing proportion of them to earn higher incomes in industry, trade and 'services'. The reason for the opposition to immigration among labour was partly that, in the economic and social systems of these countries in which the share of labour in the national income depended ultimately on its bargaining power *vis-à-vis* the employers, the immigrants who were difficult to organize and accustomed to lower standards of living tended to undermine that bargaining power and thus constituted a threat to wages and working conditions; while on the other hand, the danger of political radicalism being imported by the immigrants began to outweigh their advantages as cheap labour in the eyes of the employers. But the importance of these factors was immeasurably increased during the inter-war period by the inability of these countries to ensure full employment for their own workers. There can be no doubt that the domestic unemployment problem of all these countries, and particularly of the U.S.A., was the chief economic reason for their exclusion of immigrants.

On the other hand, the decline of international migration cannot be attributed entirely or even mainly to economic factors. The restrictions imposed on immigration were, in part at least, motivated by the social problems of assimilation and social integration involved in large-scale immigration, particularly since the potential immigrants from the most overpopulated countries of the world, Eastern Europe and the Far East, differed widely in their social and cultural background, and in the case of the Far Eastern immigrants also in race, from the populations of the new countries. In this connection the disappearance of the 'Frontier' was far more relevant than to the strictly economic aspects of the problem; for it meant that the old inhabitants and the immigrants could no longer evade each other by 'going West'; the old and the new population *had* to learn to live together. Moreover, it should not be assumed too readily that the migrants themselves would willingly have left their homelands if alternative means of escaping poverty and raising the standards of life of their overpopulated countries had been available. In theory, international investment could have provided such an alternative. In view of the social disadvantages of international migration, therefore, its cessation might have been welcomed if international investment had taken its place. The failure of international investment to fulfil that function and its breakdown certainly constituted the more serious of the two problems.

It is doubtful whether even in its heyday private international investment ever adequately fulfilled that function. We shall return to that question later. We are here concerned with the reasons for the almost complete breakdown of international long-term investment during the nineteen-thirties.

Now, it is clear that direct restrictions on foreign lending played a negligible part in this breakdown. Although such restrictions were in force during the nineteen-thirties in the three wealthiest and as such the most important potential lending countries, the U.S.A., Great Britain, and Germany, we have seen that they probably did little to prevent foreign long-term investment that would otherwise have taken place. Even so it is worth while to glance briefly at the motives for these restrictions. The motive was obviously not lack of capital. In all three countries the outstanding problem of those years was to find means of employing idle capital, both money capital (idle deposits) and real capital (idle factories and machines). Except in the case of the American restrictions, where political considerations played the dominant part, two motives led to the imposition of such restrictions: the (largely erroneous) view that they were necessary in order to canalize all available funds into home investment to promote domestic recovery, and the need to protect the balance of payments. Now, it is patent that the first motive was directly bound up with the problem of the trade cycle; while both would have fallen to the ground if it had not been for the failure of the international monetary system to function properly. For if Governments could have been sure, as they very largely could have been sure during the nineteenth century, that foreign lending would lead to a corresponding increase in the lending country's exports, neither balance of payments nor 'recovery' considerations would have stood in the way of foreign investment. So much for the reasons for the restrictions on foreign lending. But, as has been pointed out, private international investment had broken down before any such restrictions were imposed. Why were persons with investable funds in the potential lender countries, and particularly in the U.S.A., not inclined to invest abroad during the nineteen-thirties?

Briefly the answer is that the risks of foreign investment were considered too high. The private American investors were in the position of the 'burnt child' after the experience of the nineteen-twenties. If we inquire into the causes of the 'fire', the mass defaults on American investments during the years of the world depression, we find, apart from the depression itself, two factors both of which were in a sense merely aspects of the problem of the international monetary system. One was that the vast American lending of the nineteen-twenties had been undertaken with little regard to the extent to which the loans, by increasing productivity in the borrowing countries, would automatically ensure the ability of the debtor countries to pay interest and amortization. The other, which was in practice even more important, was that all this lending had taken place without any assurance that the U.S.A. would be prepared to accept interest and amortization payments in the form of goods and services; it had served to postpone and aggravate, rather than to facilitate, the adjustment of the balance of payments and economic structure of the U.S.A. to her creditor position.

In addition, there were two other factors which, by increasing the risk of foreign investment, frightened off potential investors during the nineteen-thirties. One was the prevailing economic instability, and in particular the unprecedented instability of exchange rates. While the importance of this factor as an obstacle to international trade has often been exaggerated, it undoubtedly constituted a major obstacle to a revival of international lending. There is no need to labour once again the causes of this exchange instability. At the same time, it is worth noting the desirability of reasonably stable exchange rates for international investment.

The other deterrent to international investment was the prevailing political instability. In so far as this was part of the problem of international political security it need not detain us again. In part, however, the deterrent was undoubtedly fear of internal social and political upheavals in the debtor countries, the decline in respect for the sanctity of private property in many parts of the world. This was conspicuously the reason for the disinclination of Western capitalists to risk their money in Soviet Russia. The need to ensure respect for the obligations to foreign creditors, whether private or public, is clearly an important aspect of the problem of organizing international investment.

The mention of Soviet Russia, at the same time, draws attention to another political aspect of the problem of the breakdown of international investment which must not be ignored. The decision of the Soviet Government to carry out its staggering programme of industrialization entirely out of Russia's own capital resources, without foreign aid, that is to say, at considerable cost to her peoples in terms of the postponement of consumption in favour of capital construction, was not solely or even mainly due to the unwillingness of foreigners to invest in Russia. It was a decision, deliberately and voluntarily taken, in order to safeguard Russia against the real or presumed danger of becoming economically and politically dependent on her foreign capitalist creditors. Nor was that phenomenon confined to Russia. Many other undeveloped countries which could have benefited economically from the aid of foreign capital were reluctant to admit foreign capital for the same reason. The economic methods and political implications which international investment assumed in the age of imperialism have brought this technique of economic progress into disrepute in the eyes of many peoples and countries. It is doubtful whether in future any undeveloped country (if it has the power to decide the matter) will take advantage of foreign capital assistance, unless the system of international investment safeguards the debtor country against economic exploitation and political domination.

This rapid survey of the causes which led to the breakdown of international migration and investment has thus led us back to the three main factors which we found underlying the growth of trade barriers. The decline of international migration must be attributed, in so far as it was due to economic factors, primarily to the failure of the immigration countries to ensure domestic full employment. At the root of the breakdown of international investment were, apart from political factors, again the problem of the trade cycle, and the inadequacy of the world monetary and economic system of the post-war decade. As regards international investment, the latter of these two problems was undoubtedly the more important, not only because it was the more decisive cause of breakdown, but because international capital movements constituted a vital link in the smooth operation of the gold standard, and must play an important part in the operation of any international monetary system. The problem of international investment and of the organization of a sound international monetary system are closely intertwined.

It is now time to turn to the latter problem, which together with the problem of full employment, has turned out to have been at the root of all the international economic troubles of the inter-war period.

3. THE INTERNATIONAL MONETARY SYSTEM

When the first world war ended, the world, under the leadership of the victorious Powers, returned unquestioningly to the pre-war international monetary system, the gold standard; and all efforts towards international economic co-operation during the first post-war decade aimed, directly or indirectly, at making this system work. We know that these efforts failed.

The term 'international monetary system' is really a misnomer for the international gold standard. The gold standard, it is true, was primarily a method of relating national currencies to each other; it was in fact the 'world money' dreamed of by many latter-day monetary reformers. But it was far more than that. It was a system for the almost automatic co-ordination of the multitude of national economies and national economic policies, the framework of an integrated world economy. The problems raised by its breakdown consequently cannot be solved by monetary reforms alone.

The system had two distinct features. One was that it provided a world currency standard. The value of all national currencies was kept stable in terms of gold, and therefore in terms of each other. This meant that any disequilibria in the balances of international payments that might arise could not, normally, be corrected by adjustments in exchange rates, but had to be corrected by the adjustment of national price/income levels to the fixed exchange rates. The various subtle techniques of the gold standard, the right to exchange national currencies freely for gold, reserve ratios, gold points, discount policy, etc., were all incidental to this objective.

The other, even more essential, feature of the gold standard system was that it rested on the foundations of a competitive market economy. The instrument of every adjustment to economic change under the gold standard was the price mechanism. The gold standard could perform its function as a world economic system and co-ordinating mechanism only because, and so long as, market forces were strong enough, and were permitted, to enforce the myriad necessary adjustments—not only adjustments of the flow of exports and imports to changes in world demand and supply; of balances of payments to every change in the volume and flow of international trade and international capital movements; and of national price, income, and employment levels to the requirements of equilibrium in the balance of payments; but also of the volume of production of particular goods and services, and of the amounts of capital invested and the number of persons employed in particular industries, to all these pulls and pushes of the system.

The 'automatic' character of the gold standard system was merely a reflection of its reliance on market forces. Under the gold standard national economies were 'automatically' co-ordinated because the necessary adjustments occurred as the result of millions of decisions by individuals taken, not at all with any conscious view to these adjustments, but in response to market forces whose methods of operation varied from allurements of higher profits to the harsh threat of unemployment and starvation.

Nor should the degree to which the gold standard functioned 'automatically' be exaggerated. Not only is there much to be said for the view that the gold standard could never have functioned as it did during its nineteenth-century heyday if it had not been for the unrivalled supremacy of the City of London in the field of international finance and the unrivalled knowledge and experience of the London banks and acceptance houses. But the operation of the gold standard itself required even during the nineteenth century, and still more after the widespread adoption of the gold exchange standard during the nineteen-twenties, the conscious intervention of the central bank authorities responsible for the control of the volume of credit in the different countries.

Through the obligation which the gold standard imposed on the national monetary authorities to observe the 'rules of the game', it in effect imposed a far-reaching limitation of national sovereignty with regard to what we now recognize to be one of the key points of national economic policy. As long as the gold standard functioned, the countries accepting it were in fact voluntarily surrendering a substantial part of their freedom of economic policy. Conversely, when, after the war, countries increasingly ceased to observe the 'rules of the game' the system could not function, though we should hasten to add that it is not enough to attribute this failure to observe the rules to the ill-will or 'economic nationalism' of national monetary authorities.

The failure of the gold standard system should not blind us to the great advantages which it possessed, at least in theory. We have already had occasion to note the advantages, other things being equal, of exchange stability. There can be no doubt that the 'automatic' character of the system was in itself an immense advantage. Provided it worked, the instrument of the price mechanism and of market forces—the 'invisible hand'—represented a very large saving in manpower and effort as compared with a system working by conscious administrative planning and control; it also ensured the psychological satisfaction of the feeling of freedom which, up to a point, people have when they are forced to do things by the impersonal forces of the 'market' and which they lack when they are told to do the same things by administrative authorities. Finally, a more technical but none the less important point, the gold standard, owing to the free convertibility of national currencies into each other (which in turn depended on its ability to maintain equilibrium in the balances of international payments) made possible the multilateral settlement of international payments and thereby enabled countries to take full advantage of opportunities of multilateral international trade. There is no doubt that an ideal international monetary system should, as far as possible, embody some or all of these three features.

Why did the gold standard system fail to function properly during the nineteen-twenties and break down during the world depression?

We have seen that a number of factors combined to impede the smooth functioning of the system during the first post-war decade. One was the problem of 'hot money'. The rapid and unpredictable movements of huge volumes of capital from one country to another which played a large part in the breakdown of the gold standard during the years 1931-3 and which were largely responsible for the unprecedented instability of exchange rates during the nineteen-thirties, were an altogether new phenomenon of the inter-war period. They fulfilled no useful economic function whatever, while at the same time rendering any international currency system unworkable and, in the form of 'capital flight', representing a constant menace to the internal economic stability of the 'flight' countries. Up to a point their disturbing effects on exchange rates and, via the gold reserve, on the internal credit structure of the countries involved, could be counteracted by the technique of Exchange Equalization Accounts which was developed by Great Britain and other countries during the nineteen-thirties. But exchange equalization operations, even when they were conducted by international co-operation between several national accounts, as under the Tripartite Monetary Agreement, could not maintain exchange rates against persistent attacks by capital flight; and they could do nothing to prevent the disastrous effects of capital flight on the volume of home investment and employment in the 'flight' country. The only effective answer to any serious capital flight proved to be the imposition of exchange control. The experience of Germany and many other countries with exchange control shows that it presents considerable administrative problems. Assuming for the moment that it is desirable to leave foreign trade uncontrolled, it has the further disadvantage that it is difficult (though, as the experiment which Austria successfully conducted during the years from 1934 to 1938 showed, not impossible) to prevent undesirable capital exports without interfering with *bona fide* commercial and other transactions. These problems must be recognized. But, after the experience of the nineteen-thirties, it is most unlikely that any Government will ever again allow complete freedom to private individuals to menace the economic stability of their (and other) countries and to sabotage their economic policies by sending their money abroad.

Another accidental obstacle to the smooth functioning of the gold standard during the nineteen-twenties—accidental in the sense that it was not an essential aspect of the system itself—was the fact that, partly owing to the inherent difficulty of knowing what the correct exchange rate would be but partly also for prestige and other reasons, several countries in returning to the gold standard after the war realigned their currencies to gold at wrong rates of exchange, i.e. rates which did not assure equilibrium in their balances of payments. The outstanding and warning example of this was, of course, the overvaluation of the British pound in 1925. There is no doubt that it contributed considerably to the depressed condition of the British economy during the years 1925-9 and to the calamitous events of 1931. At the same time, we have seen that the British balance of payments problem and the depressed state of the British export industries of the nineteen-twenties cannot be completely explained in terms of the overvaluation of the pound. The faulty choice of the exchange rate merely aggravated the existing maladjustment of the British economic structure and balance of payments. Moreover, it is most unlikely that any exchange rate, however correctly chosen, could by itself have corrected that maladjustment. The experience of the inter-war period has shown the importance of the 'correct' choice of exchange rates within the framework of an automatic international monetary system. But we have also seen that, on balance, this was not the decisive factor in the failure of the gold standard.

More important was the failure of most countries at one time or another to observe, in their internal monetary policies, the rules of the gold standard game. Under a system of fixed exchange rates such as the gold standard the maintenance of equilibrium in the balances of international payments required each country, through its internal credit policy, to adjust its domestic price/income level to the state of its balance of payments. A 'surplus' country had to inflate, a 'deficit' country to deflate its domestic credit structure. Thus, according to the rules of the game, the U.S.A. in 1927–9 should, in view of her large surplus, have inflated at the risk of stimulating still further the runaway boom. Great Britain, according to these rules, should during the same years have deflated still further in order to reduce costs, and so stimulate exports and curtail imports. The fact that both countries, in common with most others, refused to adhere rigidly to these rules automatically rendered the gold standard system of adjustment inoperative; the market forces on which the system relied to maintain and restore international equilibrium were not released. What really matters, however, is that these countries had good reasons for their refusal to observe these rules, and, furthermore, that it is very doubtful whether even the most rigid adherence to them could by itself have maintained and restored international equilibrium. The failure of various countries to observe the rules of the gold standard game, while undoubtedly an important factor in the final breakdown of the system, was not an independent factor. It was merely the reflection of inherent defects in the system itself.

The root cause of the failure and final breakdown of the gold standard system was the combination of two factors, the large maladjustments in the balances of payments and productive structure of most countries and the world economy as a whole which the war had left behind, and rigidities in the economic systems of all countries which made the correction of these maladjustments by market forces alone impossible. Neither of these factors *by itself* would have mattered a great deal. If every particle of the economic system had responded as smoothly and speedily to the pressure of market forces as classical economic theory had tended to assume, the largest maladjustments would quickly have been corrected. Conversely, the system might conceivably have worked with all its rigidities, if the initial maladjustments had not been so large. Together they rendered the whole mechanism inoperative.

There is no need to analyse here the various major maladjustments which have forced themselves on our attention at every point of our historical analysis. It is enough to mention only the most outstanding: the failure of the U.S.A. to adapt her balance of trade to her new creditor position, the reparations obligation imposed on Germany, the British export problem, the tendency towards relative overproduction in world agriculture, and—in rather a different category—the persistence of large international 'depressed areas' in South-Eastern Europe, the Caribbean and the Far East.

Two points about these maladjustments have to be noticed. First, not all of them were due to the war (and the peace treaties) alone. Of those just mentioned, only the German reparations problem can be entirely attributed to the war. All the others were the result of accumulated failures of adjustment to long-term economic changes. The war merely hastened these changes and for five years and more prevented the forces from working which might otherwise have made for adjustment. That fact in many cases made all the difference to the magnitude and intractability of the problem. But it would be wrong to dismiss the whole issue of the world economic system by reference to the 'exceptional shock' of the war.

This is an academic point, worth bearing in mind, but of little relevance at a time when a new and even greater war is once again creating immense maladjustments in the world and in every national economy. The second point is of far greater practical significance. All these maladjustments, with the exception of the last (and to some extent the last but one), appeared primarily as disequilibria in the balances of payments of different countries. The U.S.A. was not *importing* as much as the surplus on her *balance of payments* on current account required. Germany was unable to make her reparations payments because she could not increase her *exports* or curtail her *imports* sufficiently. Great Britain found it difficult to maintain the *exchange value* of the pound. Most of the overseas primary producing countries found themselves in *balance of payments* difficulties, at any rate after the slump in agricultural prices in 1928-9. Actually, as we have pointed out several times before, the maladjustments in the balances of payments merely reflected maladjustments in the economic structure of the countries concerned. This applies even to such apparently pure balance of payments problems as that of the German reparations. In order to make these large transfers possible, both Germany and her creditors would have had to bring about substantial adjustments in their internal economies. Not only would German prices and costs of production (or the exchange rate of the mark) probably have had to be lower than they were, but this adjustment in turn would have been effective only if it had resulted in all sorts of changes in the productive structure of the German economy—for instance, shifts of German labour and capital hitherto employed in production for the home market to the production of export goods, and out of industries which were dependent on raw materials which could no longer be imported. What was even more important in the circumstances, similar adjustments, *mutatis mutandis*, would have had to take place in the U.S.A. and the other creditor countries.

As the last example shows, the adjustments required—and the 'rigidities' which made them difficult if not impossible—were of two types: (a) adjustments in cost and price levels and (b) adjustments in the productive structure of the various national economies. To a large extent, the failure during the inter-war period to appreciate the nature of the problem was due to the fact that attention was concentrated on the first and in practice less serious of these, while the second was generally ignored.

a. The gold standard system was thought to provide an 'automatic' mechanism for the correction of any disequilibria in the balances of payments because, in its simplest form, any disequilibrium would lead to gold movements which, in turn, would either automatically lead to contractions or expansions in the volume of credit in the country concerned or would at least function as danger signals to that country's monetary authorities that a process of deflation or inflation, as the case might be, was required. Deflation would reduce costs and prices, discourage imports and stimulate exports and thus readjust the balance of payments. Inflation would work in the opposite direction. Now, whether this process of adjustment had ever worked as smoothly as the text-books suggested or not, it certainly ceased to work during the inter-war period, or, rather, its costs in social and economic terms had become prohibitive. The reason was largely the greatly increased rigidity in the price and cost structure of the advanced industrial countries, due on the one hand to the growth of monopoly and monopolistic price determination and, on the other, to the growth of trade union organization and collective bargaining. Monopoly not only kept up prices by maintaining excessive profit margins, but also by reducing the incentive to improvements in efficiency and cost reductions. Large wage

K

reductions, on the other hand, were possible, if at all, only at the price of internal social and political conflict; and, with an inflexible cost and price structure, deflation spelled unemployment and depression. The disadvantages of inflation, though more indirect, were equally obvious. The evidence of the inter-war period is overwhelming that any international economic system which relies on adjustments in price/income levels to maintain international equilibrium is unsuited to modern economic conditions.

b. But adjustments in price/income levels were not the only type of adjustments required. In fact, they were merely the instruments employed under the gold standard system for effecting the adjustments that really mattered—changes in the allocation of productive resources, labour, capital and land, changes in the kinds and amounts of commodities produced in one country, and in the kinds and volumes of services provided in another. What was required in Great Britain owing to the decline in world demand for her coal and cotton goods, for example, was that some of the workers and capital hitherto employed in producing coal and cheap textiles should turn to the production either of other goods which foreign countries were prepared to buy from Great Britain or, if necessary, to the production of goods which Great Britain had hitherto imported from abroad. The whole monetary process of deflation was merely the means by which this shift in resources was to be brought about. Similarly, reflation in the U.S.A. would merely have served the purpose of inducing those shifts of capital and labour out of the protected import-competing industries which were needed for an adjustment of the American economic structure. Under the gold standard system, these adjustments in the productive structures of different economies were left to the pressure of market forces. And the basic reason for the failure of the system was that adjustments of this kind and of the magnitude required after the world war could either not be effected by market forces at all or only at prohibitive social and economic costs.

This judgment would be challenged by many. They would argue that market forces could have done the job very well if only they had been allowed to take their course, if Governments had not constantly interfered by tariffs, quotas, subsidies, and other forms of 'planning' and 'control'. A moment's reflection will show that this argument, though undoubtedly valid in particular instances, does not meet the point. We need merely ask ourselves why Governments intervened in this way. The answer may be that Governments were induced to intervene by vested interests which would have suffered if, in the prevailing conditions of disequilibrium, market forces had been allowed free rein. In many cases, however, these 'vested interests' undoubtedly represented so large a proportion of the population that to protect them was obviously in the national interest. In either case, the real reason for intervention was the costs of adjustment which, in turn, were due to the immobility of resources. If, as classical economic theory generally assumed, labour had been perfectly mobile, if any fall in their income had induced workers, farmers and entrepreneurs to move into different occupations, industries, or parts of the country, the costs of adjustment would have been negligible. In fact, psychological resistance to change (including the hope that the fall in income might be merely temporary), specialization and the costs of retraining, lack of knowledge of openings elsewhere and, last but not least, the fact that in the conditions of depression and economic stagnation which prevailed in many countries throughout much of the inter-war period, jobs elsewhere were not in fact available, meant that labour responded only slowly if at all to the pressure of the 'market'; even substantial reductions in income, acute poverty, and years of unemployment moved but few of the farmers of the Middle West, the miners of South Wales and the peasants of the Balkans into more profitable occupations. The same applies to capital and land, though in the case of the former some costs of change to its owners (but not to the community as a whole), due to the loss of invested capital, could never be wholly avoided.[1]

So far we have only considered the cases where the operation

[1] This also provides at least a partial answer to a question which readily comes to mind. It may be asked why the gold standard system, and the market mechanism on which it depended, should have functioned adequately during most of the nineteenth century and should have ceased to function in the twentieth. It is possible to exaggerate the smoothness with which market forces operated during the nineteenth century, and there were cases even before 1914 when the gold standard broke down. But the contrast is sufficiently striking to demand an explanation. That explanation lies partly in the fact that during the nineteenth century the operation of market forces was immensely facilitated by the exceptional rate of world economic expansion—due to rapid population growth, geographical expansion into new and undeveloped territories, and revolutionary improvements in technique—which characterized that period. Just as cyclical depressions temporarily reduce mobility, so the decline in the long-term rate of expansion of the world economy during the past fifty years has tended to diminish the mobility of resources. An equally important factor, however, has been the persistent increase during the past hundred years and more in the optimum scale of economic enterprise. This has had the effect of reducing the mobility of resources in various ways. In the first place it has greatly increased the amount of capital required to start production on an economic and profitable basis. Correspondingly, it has increased the amount of fixed capital that is lost when one unit of production ceases, for one reason or another, to be able to compete with more efficient rivals, and consequently the insistence with which its owners demand protection. Indirectly it has also rendered labour, whose employment is bound up with the scale of production, less mobile. Finally, it has been the most important single economic factor in the development of monopoly. Together, the decline in the rate of world economic expansion and the increase in the optimum scale of production account for most of the apparent decline in the mobility of resources and in the efficiency of the market mechanism.

of market forces was prevented by Government action of one kind or another. But the problem clearly extends much further. Owing to the immobility of resources, market forces could not in fact be relied upon to effect the necessary adjustments. If the pressure of market forces was small, resources either did not move at all—workers if necessary accepted lower wages, farmers lower incomes, entrepreneurs losses, capital failed to move into industries or countries where it could earn higher returns—or even moved in the wrong directions, as when farmers responded to a fall in prices by increasing production, or when 'hot money' flowed 'uphill'. If the pressure was large, the costs in terms of losses of capital, poverty and unemployment threatened to be such as to force Governments to intervene.

One aspect of this problem which needs a special word of comment is its significance in connection with international capital movements. In essence, the problem here was the same as in the case of other resources. Market forces for one reason or another failed to move capital in the volumes and directions which would have been desirable. This, for instance, was at bottom the cause of the persistent poverty of the international 'depressed areas' in Eastern Europe, the Far East, and elsewhere. The special significance of the problem in the case of international capital movements is due to the fact that, in theory, international lending and borrowing might have greatly facilitated the correction of the large maladjustments in the balances of international payments and economic structure of different countries at the end of the last war. Countries which, for one reason or another, were faced with deficits in their balances of payments on current account could have borrowed from countries which, for one reason or another, found themselves with surpluses. Such international lending could clearly not by itself have solved the problem of these maladjustments. But, *provided it fulfilled certain conditions*, it could have granted a breathing space during which the necessary adjustments might have been effected.

As we know, international capital movements did take place on the largest scale during the nineteen-twenties. What is more, broadly speaking, these capital movements followed the direction just indicated, i.e. most of the capital flowed from the countries with the largest credit balances, particularly the U.S.A., to the countries with the largest deficits, particularly Germany. But these capital movements completely failed to fulfil those essential conditions. Capital was poured into Europe by American investment banks with a totally inadequate regard to the extent to which that capital raised the productivity and capacity to export of the debtor countries and thereby automatically enabled them to service the loans. Some of the 'political' loans, such as the

Dawes, Young, and League of Nations loans, as we have seen, had the disadvantage that they did not automatically lead to corresponding increases in the imports of the borrowing countries and thus represented a danger to the balances of payments of some of the lending countries, particularly Great Britain. In both respects, these post-war investments were no longer self-liquidating, as most of the international investments of the nineteenth century had been. This fact was of course not the only or even the main reason for the subsequent collapse of international investment, for which the depression and the failure of the U.S.A. to accept repayment in the form of goods and services were chiefly responsible. But it played a substantial part in this collapse and as such represented a particularly serious aspect of the failure of market forces to operate smoothly during the inter-war period.

We have now come to the roots of the failure of the gold standard system. The gold standard system failed to function and finally broke down because, given the large maladjustments in the balances of payments and economic structure of different countries which the war had left behind, (a) the correction of maladjustments in the balances of payments by means of adjustments in price/income levels had become impracticable or intolerable as a result of the greatly increased rigidity in the cost and price structure of the advanced capitalist economies, and (b) because, ultimately owing to the immobility of resources, market forces either could not or—for good reasons—were not allowed to effect the necessary adjustments in the productive structure of the various national economies.

It is to these two facts that, in the last resort, most of the international economic problems of the inter-war period can be traced. The failure of the process of adjustment of national price/income levels *ipso facto* deprived the gold standard system of its character as an automatic mechanism for the co-ordination of national economies. That function of the gold standard had, as we have seen, rested in part on the willingness of national monetary authorities to follow the 'rules of the game' in their domestic credit policies. With their failure to adhere rigidly to these rules during the nineteen-twenties and the complete abandonment of the whole principle during the nineteen-thirties this automatic mechanism of co-ordination disappeared. We have frequently had occasion to point to the consequences of the fact that no other machinery of co-ordination was put in its place. In particular, much of the tariff and currency 'warfare' of the nineteen-thirties was directly due to the impossibility of correcting maladjustments in the balances of payments by the orthodox gold standard method.

The inability of market forces to effect the necessary adjustments in the industrial and general economic structure of national economies (except at prohibitive social costs) coupled with the fact that Governments in most countries continued to rely on their corrective power, was largely responsible for the persistence of these maladjustments, either directly, or because it led Governments to protect sections of their national economies against the pressure of market forces by tariffs, subsidies, quota restrictions and other methods. The breakdown of the gold standard system of multilateral settlement of international payments forced Germany and other countries to find a way out of their foreign exchange difficulties by means of the clearing system which, in the circumstances, necessarily confined international trade into bilateral channels. More generally, given the persistence of large maladjustments in the economic structure and balances of payments of different countries, many of the economic principles which had been accepted as a matter of course on the assumption of international equilibrium and a smoothly functioning automatic system ceased to be true.

In particular, it ceased to be true that each country (and the world as a whole) would benefit by adhering to the principle of buying in the cheapest and selling in the dearest market. The fact that, quality for quality, American cotton was cheaper than Egyptian or Brazilian cotton was quite irrelevant to Germany when she did not possess the dollars (or gold or foreign exchange freely convertible into dollars) with which to buy American cotton. Nor was it a matter of indifference to Great Britain whether she bought her wheat from a country of the sterling area or from a country outside the sterling area, even though the *price* of wheat in both countries may have been the same. The fact that the German or British shortage of foreign exchange was in the last resort due to maladjustments in their economic structure which, *in the long run*, could have been corrected by suitable changes, made no difference to the short-run position. We have seen the difficulties which the U.S.A. experienced in trying to get other countries to accept the principle of 'non-discrimination' in their commercial policies. To a large extent these difficulties were due to the fact that the principle of 'non-discrimination' completely ignored these problems. Even when all allowance is made for the political considerations which largely determined Nazi commercial policy, Germany obviously could not help 'discriminating' against American exports. Much of the international trade that did take place during the nineteen-thirties could not have taken place if the principle of 'non-discrimination' had been rigidly adhered to. In the last resort, the principle of 'non-discrimination' assumed equilibrium conditions and virtually lost all meaning in the actual conditions of acute dis-

equilibrium which obtained all over the world during the
nineteen-thirties. Judged by the only criterion which gave the
principle any *economic* content—the criterion of long-term
equilibrium—export subsidies, bilateral and barter trade arrangements, price discrimination, 'tied' loans, and quantitative controls
were no more 'discriminatory' than the fact that entrepreneurs
are prepared at times to produce at a loss or that workers are
prepared at times to work for wages below those corresponding
to their productivity. Economic policies which were sound in
theoretical conditions of equilibrium were not necessarily sound
in the actual conditions in which equilibrium neither obtained
nor could easily or quickly be restored.

We might content ourselves with this analysis of the factors
which were primarily responsible for the international economic
chaos of the inter-war period. But it may be worth while, without
going deeply into questions of future practical policies, to follow
up some of the implications of the conclusions which we have
reached. This will be the object of the final section of this
chapter and report.

4. SOME ECONOMIC AND POLITICAL IMPLICATIONS

The first conclusion which has emerged inescapably from this
analysis is that we can no longer let the co-ordination of national
economic policies look after itself or rely for it on an 'automatic'
international system. It is generally recognized that the gold
standard mechanism of violent changes in national price/income
levels is no longer possible, and that its place must be taken by
adjustments in exchange rates. What is not so generally recognized is that it was through that mechanism that the gold standard
system ensured at least a minimum of international co-ordination.
If that mechanism is abandoned its place must be taken by some
system of direct co-ordination of national economic policies,
whether by means of international co-operation or supranational
control. What is needed, in fact, is that countries should—at the
very least—again submit their economic affairs to that degree of
international discipline to which, often admittedly without
realizing it, they submitted them voluntarily by obeying the rules
of the gold standard game.

But this is clearly not enough. An international monetary
system which makes provision for the periodic adjustment of
exchange rates by international agreement would overcome the
first of the two major defects of the gold standard system which
we noted above. But it would clearly contribute nothing whatever
to the solution of the second, more fundamental, problem.
Adjustments of exchange rates rely just as much as deflation and
inflation on market forces to effect the basic changes in the alloca-

tion of productive resources which a restoration of equilibrium may require; and they may be equally ineffective.[1]

To meet this second problem, the inefficacy of market forces in the face of major maladjustments in the balances of payments and productive structure of different countries, the choice would prima facie seem to lie between two methods of approach. One would be to attempt to render market forces more effective by endeavouring in various ways to reduce the obstacles which have obstructed their operation. The other is to supplement and in part replace the market mechanism by direct control and planning.

Proceeding along the first line of approach, steps might be taken to heighten the mobility of labour by the provision of retraining facilities, improved labour exchanges, travelling assistance, and other social services. Subsidies and compensation for losses of invested capital might be used to heighten the mobility of capital. A variety of measures might be attempted to reduce the effects of monopolization and trade union organization on price and cost rigidities, though here formidable political difficulties would have to be overcome. Finally, it is clear that a sound general economic policy which maintains an atmosphere of economic expansion, both domestically and internationally, would enormously reduce the existing obstacles and resistance to adjustment.

Now there is no doubt whatever that all these measures would be eminently desirable. But equally our analysis has made it appear most unlikely that, however vigorously they might be

[1] It is important to note that most of the proposals for reform of the international monetary system at present under discussion go no further than this. Both the British 'Keynes Plan' for the establishment of an international clearing union and the American 'White Plan' for the establishment of an international exchange stabilization fund have the advantage over the traditional gold standard system that they would give an initial expansionary 'push' to international trade, the former by the grant of overdrafts to individual countries, the latter (rather less effectively) by the provision of foreign exchange on certain conditions to countries requiring it. This alone would help to get international trade going in the period of acute disequilibrium at the end of the war. In so far as both in the last resort provide, among other measures, for adjustments of exchange rates by international agreement, they would make unnecessary the costly processes of adjustments in price/income levels, while exchange stabilization operations would ensure reasonable exchange stability. A multilateral clearing system, moreover, would have the advantage over the American plan that, in theory at least, there is no reason why under such a system exchange rates should still be tied to the value of gold and the vagaries of world gold production; it would thus overcome another technical defect of the gold standard not specifically mentioned in the text. But this is where the difference between either of these proposals and the pre-war gold standard system ends. On the most fundamental non-monetary question, the extent to which the world economic system as a whole can continue to rely on the operation of market forces, the currency proposals so far published constitute no advance on the gold standard system (although we have been promised proposals for the reconstruction of international investment and international economic planning which may fill this gap). Their adequacy to the post-war situation, therefore, stands and falls with the urgency of that problem.

pursued, they would suffice to meet the problem. Not only is it hard to believe that it should be possible to reverse the long trends of social and economic development which have, during the past century, greatly reduced the flexibility of most of the large industrial economies; but it must not be forgotten that even in the far more flexible economies of the nineteenth century market forces were able to correct maladjustments of a similar order of magnitude only at the cost of social suffering on a scale which the combined social conscience and political power of the masses in the twentieth-century Western world would no longer tolerate.

Failing this remedy, the only alternative would be to supplement or replace the operation of market forces by deliberate Government policy and action. This would in fact appear to be our second major conclusion: The correction of maladjustments in the world economy of the magnitude of those which confronted the world after the last war and will again confront it at the end of this war cannot be left to market forces. The necessary adjustments will have to be carefully planned if we are to avoid a repetition of the international economic chaos of the inter-war period. It is important to see what this implies.

It implies in the first place a conscious policy designed to ensure the requisite changes in the productive structure of the various national economies. Instead of merely increasing the mobility of resources and leaving their movements to be directed by the pressure of market forces, it implies advance planning of the types of changes required—changes in the amounts of labour and capital employed in particular industries, in the types and volumes of commodities produced and the methods of production —and the planned execution of these changes. While in the last resort that planned execution may have to employ the instruments of direct orders and compulsory powers, there is no reason why it should not make use of—in fact, it is highly desirable that it should rely as far as possible on—all the indirect (economical and impersonal) methods of control of the market, the price mechanism, and other monetary and also non-monetary incentives, always provided that these controls are subordinated to, and operate within the framework of, the general plan.

It implies, in the second place, a measure of control of the volume and directions of international trade and investment. Such control will be essential in the immediate post-war years when most countries will be faced with acute disequilibria in their balances of payments, unless they are provided with adequate international credits of the type proposed by the 'Keynes plan'. Without such credits, countries with large deficits in their balances of payments on current account will have to adjust the volume of their imports to what they can pay for by means of exports, which may involve selective import restrictions (so as to ensure that priority is given to essential over unessential imports), export subsidies, and bilateral trade arrangements. Surplus countries will have to increase their imports which, though a much simpler process, may also have to be carefully timed and controlled. In addition to short-term credits, long-term international lending would greatly facilitate both these processes. But this lending, in turn, will have to follow some definite plan if it is not merely to aggravate the existing maladjustments. The planning of international investment will be particularly necessary if, as appears desirable, the advantages of international lending as a means of temporarily overcoming maladjustments in the balances of international payments are combined with the need for international investment as a method of solving the problem of the international 'depressed areas'; for the essence of the latter problem in the past has been, as we have seen, that market forces failed to canalize international investment into these areas.

The third and inescapable implication of the need for planned adjustment is the need for international co-operation if not supranational economic authorities.

Many readers will be reluctant to accept the conditions of the last three paragraphs. They may claim that our advice for the future appears to be to re-enact the international economic chaos of the past. The argument cannot be lightly dismissed.

There are indeed a good many things to be said against accepting it uncritically. In the first place, it may be worth repeating what was said at the beginning of this chapter and what should have become even more obvious in the course of the discussion: A planned foreign trade policy does not *ipso facto* involve a decline in international trade; on the contrary, we have given good reasons to suppose that it is the *sine qua non* of the full use by the world of the advantages of international division of labour and trade in modern economic conditions. In the second place, we have seen that, from the purely economic point of view, there is no inherent merit in those particular methods of carrying on international trade which are the 'natural' methods of free private enterprise in a market economy. Much of the horror and suspicion with which such methods as export subsidies, differential prices, bilateral trade arrangements, Government trade monopolies and quantitative controls have been regarded has been due to the unconscious assumption that anything which departs from the natural laws of the 'market' is bad; on a more intellectual level, it has been due to the failure to recognize that the laws of the market, such as the principle of comparative costs and of 'non-discrimination', were not necessarily beneficial if the fundamental assumption of long-term equilibrium on which they rested

was not realized. Finally, it would generally be admitted that the
international economic chaos of the nineteen-thirties was due
primarily to the lack of any co-ordination of national economic
policies rather than to the particular methods of commercial
policy that were employed; although, as we have tried to show in
the chapter on international action, the failure to recognize that
the old automatic system of co-ordination could no longer be
relied upon played a not inconsiderable part in diverting the
attention of statesmen from the imperative need for a new system
of conscious co-ordination.

When all this is said, however, there remains a solid core of
truth in the suspicion with which many of those least blind to the
need for an international economic order view the advocacy of
State control of foreign trade in general and so-called 'discriminatory' practices in particular. State control of foreign trade, the
argument runs, would turn every commercial transaction into a
subject for diplomatic negotiations backed on each side with the
full political power of the modern nation State; in the end the
politically and militarily stronger Power would be bound to get
the best of every bargain; the upshot would be perpetual international conflict and war.

The argument should not be accepted blindly. The contrast
between the perpetual warfare of a world of trading States and
the blissful peace of international economic intercourse carried
on by the peaceful merchant according to the laws of supply and
demand can be overdone. It ignores the countless occasions
during the heyday of capitalism when the flag followed trade
with fire and sword. It also ignores the extent to which the intensity of international economic conflict, at any rate during the
inter-war period, was directly due to the failure of the capitalist
countries to solve their domestic economic problems, in particular the problem of unemployment. There is no doubt whatever
that sane domestic economic policies and a sounder organization
of the national economies would immeasurably reduce the
pressure behind economic nationalism and the scope for international economic conflict. At the same time, it would be dangerous to close one's eyes to the element of truth in the argument.
Similarly, while most of the purely economic objections to
'discriminatory' practices are found on closer analysis to be
groundless, there are undoubtedly political advantages in the
subjection of national commercial policies to some 'objective'
criterion such as the principle of 'non-discrimination' provides.

There are some who are so impressed with these political
dangers that they would oppose State control of foreign trade and
'discriminatory' methods even though they might be prepared to
concede the economic arguments in their favour. We feel that

this is a dangerous attitude. Dangerous not so much because it may not be legitimate to weigh political against economic considerations, but because this opposition is bound to fail. It is conceivable that some, though almost certainly not all, countries after this war could be induced to renounce State control of foreign trade and discriminatory practices. But, if our analysis has been correct, the result of leaving international economic relations to market forces at the end of this war would inevitably be a new collapse which, equally inevitably, would force Governments to intervene and assume control—after much unnecessary suffering and in conditions of panic and chaos.

Surely the obvious, and the only, answer to the dilemma is that there must indeed be planning of international trade and investment, and that there may even be 'discrimination', but that planning must be international wherever possible. In some respects international control may confine itself to agreement on rules of international good behaviour in economic matters. Such rules will have to make provision for such methods of commercial policy as countries cannot reasonably be expected to forego; 'non-discrimination' will not do. Such rules could undoubtedly be devised. In many spheres, however, international co-operation will have to go beyond agreement on 'don'ts'. There will have to be direct planning of international economic intercourse. How far this will have to take the form of international co-operation, how far it will be possible to get countries to submit to supranational authorities—these are important but secondary questions, provided the imperative need for planned international action is recognized and acknowledged. In the last resort, international good behaviour in the economic as in the political field will still require the sanction and backing of power—and the will to use that power effectively in the general interest.

One final question arises. It will be recognized that the preceding argument showing the need for a measure of planning in the sphere of international economic relations relates solely to conditions in which large disequilibria obtain. All that has been insisted upon so far is that in such conditions of disequilibrium as we shall have to expect at the end of this war, it will be impossible to rely on market forces to restore equilibrium. Nothing in this argument, therefore, as such precludes the possibility that, once international equilibrium has been restored, the world may return to some sort of automatic system based on the operation of market forces. In favour of this possibility might be cited the fact, to which we have drawn attention before, that the efficacy of market forces is largely a function of the magnitude of the disequilibria that have to be corrected.

But it would be disingenuous to present the prospect as probable. There are at least three reasons why it is unlikely in the extreme. In the first place, it may be doubted whether in practice that ideal condition of 'approximate equilibrium' is ever likely to be reached. The world does not stand still. As one maladjustment is on the way to being corrected, political if not economic forces will have given rise to others.

In the second place, and this is a very important consideration, we must reckon with the fact that the tendency towards planning and State control in the domestic economies of most countries, which was already pronounced during the inter-war period, will continue at an accelerated pace after the war. We have shown before that a substantial measure of internal economic planning will be desirable and essential in all countries. But even if all these arguments were rejected, it is quite obvious that one, at least, of the most important countries will in fact have a planned economy, whether we like it or not. In the circumstances, an international economic system which was based on the assumption of free private enterprise in *all* countries and the free operation of market forces the world over, which laid down rules that lose virtually all their meaning if applied to planned economies, and which explicitly banned methods of economic control that are essential instruments of planned economies, would clearly stand little chance of universal acceptance. Internal planning obviously requires that the planning authority should have a minimum of certainty as to the nature, volume and directions of exports, and can rely with some assurance, and over a minimum period, on obtaining the necessary supplies of raw material and other imports; it is hardly possible if foreign trade and international capital movements are left to be determined by the unpredictable influences of world market forces.

This leads us to the third and more general point. Economists in the past have tended to concentrate attention on the problem of the optimum allocation of the world's productive resources for the maximization of world output: they have paid far too little attention to the advantages of stability and certainty. They have been fascinated by the uncanny way in which market forces—the invisible hand'—tend, with certain qualifications which have been more or less freely admitted, to readjust the allocation of resources to any changes in the framework of demand and supply so as to reproduce optimum conditions; they have tended to ignore the costs in terms of instability which this process involved. These costs were not only social costs—the disruption of established communities, the uprooting of people, personal insecurity—but measureable economic costs—losses due to uncertainty, high risks, and transitional unemployment or underemployment of resources. To give but one example, the gain which the peasants of Rumania derived from the long-term contracts which the Nazis concluded with Rumania cannot be measured in terms of the prices they received for their produce alone. These prices may have been higher or lower than the prices ruling at any moment in the world market. But they were stable. They enabled the peasants to grow their crops with the assurance that what they sowed in the spring they would be able to sell in the autumn. The Nazis, in turn, benefited from being able to rely on an assured supply of the commodities they needed. We are far from underestimating the importance of ensuring the most efficient use of the world's resources. Changes in methods and forms of production will constantly have to take the place. What we do plead for is that the economic advantages of the optimum allocation of resources at any one moment should be weighed against the social and economic disadvantages of instability. The significance of this for our problem is obvious. It means that, quite apart from any other considerations, there is much to be said for superseding the free rule of market forces, by commodity controls, by long-term contracts in international trade, and in other ways, so as to effect a compromise between the need for change and adjustment and the desirability of reducing to a minimum that instability which is inherent in the operation of the market mechanism and which exacted a terrible price in terms of social insecurity and economic loss during the inter-war period.

APPENDIX

THIS study in economics consists of an analysis of the inter-war period and of conclusions based on the analysis as to the future economic structure of the world. The analysis, often brilliant, is as objective as the writer's sincere efforts could make it, but to many people it will appear to be unconsciously tendentious. The conclusions do not always appear to be based very firmly on the analysis, and would not be accepted by those who place a different interpretation on the events of the last twenty years. It seems to me important, therefore, that there should be a note of dissent from someone who, having participated in most of the discussions of the group for which this report was made, takes a different view of the causes which operated to produce economic chaos and of the policy which will be required for national and international well-being after this war is ended.

I believe that the general impression which would be left on the mind of any reader of this study not equipped by experience for its critical examination would be that, to use Bradley's famous definition of optimism, the world between 1919 and 1939 'was the best of all possible worlds and everything in it was a necessary evil.' He is given a picture of Governments 'not altogether unjustifiably' pursuing policies which were a hair of the dog that had bitten them; they were 'reluctantly forced' to behave internationally in ways which were open to grave objection. He is incited to believe that the root trouble was that an international *laisser-faire* system broke down finally in 1931, having struggled to maintain itself for the previous ten years against long-term trends which had been accelerated by the last war, but not set in motion by it. The world had ceased to require the same degree of international specialization, the capital requirements of the world were no longer expanding, and international trade, no longer so necessary for national well-being, yielded precedence to the necessity of providing internal employment by the full use of all resources.

The reader who accepts this broad outline is invited to conclude that the proper policy after this war will be much more extensive planning (a term not sufficiently defined and somewhat ambiguously used); if the mistakes of the inter-war period are to be corrected we must not try to free trade from the fetters which have been put upon it but intensify controls. This thought is developed in a way which may be illustrated by three passages, the last of which is the conclusion of the work. 'A planned foreign trade . . . is the *sine qua non* of the full use by the world of the advantages of international division of labour and trade in modern economic conditions.' In this context 'a planned foreign trade' might be so loose a term as to cover merely the kind of orderly restoration of private enterprise, based on an international currency, as has long been the subject of public discussion here and in the U.S.A. But the later passages show that something much more drastic is contemplated. 'It is conceivable that some, though certainly not all, countries after this war could be induced to renounce State control of foreign trade and discriminatory practices. But if our analysis has been correct the result of leaving international economic relations to market forces at the end of this war would inevitably be a new collapse, which equally inevitably would force Governments to intervene and assume control.' Here again the passage is open to more than one interpretation; it might refer to the transition period during which we shall have to pass from a war to a peace economy, but further reading makes it clear that the writer is commending a fundamental and lasting economic change. 'There will have to be direct planning of international economic intercourse . . . there is much to be said for superseding the free rule of market forces by commodity controls, by long-term contracts in international trade and in other ways, so as to effect a compromise between the need for change and adjustment and the desirability of reducing to a minimum that instability which is inherent in the operation of the market mechanism and which exacted a terrible price in time of social insecurity and economic loss during the inter-war period.'

I am aware that there are various qualifications to the above statements scattered about the work; it would, indeed, be possible by another selection of isolated passages to build up a different picture, but I maintain that those which I have quoted would be accepted by the ordinary reader as the basic theme. There is another view, based on a different interpretation (or selection) of facts leading to a different conclusion, and it is desirable that it should be presented to the reader of a work on such a subject issuing from the Royal Institute of International Affairs.

It may be agreed that there were profound maladjustments in the world in 1920 and subsequent years; it may be agreed that the failure to readjust was the inevitable cause of utter breakdown later. But it is quite gratuitous to represent that failure as the weakness of *laisser-faire* or of free enterprise and market forces. The war and the peace settlements injected into the world intractable elements for which market forces were not responsible, which they could not digest, and which they could not be expected to remove. The profound maladjustments, which are mentioned but in my opinion minimized, were a debt structure which was radically different from any which could have resulted from market forces, the multiplications of frontiers and of fiscal barriers, and the distortion of trade channels by the operation of war and the temporary dislocation of international trade; these were all purely economic factors, but their harmful effects were greatly enhanced by political insecurity. This is not to deny that there were other maladjustments of a long-term character which had been accelerated by war, but which the economic system could have digested in the absence of profounder derangements.

No attempt was made to avoid the economic effects of the political disintegration of Europe following upon the defeat of Germany and, even more importantly, the break-up of the Austro-Hungarian Empire. A comprehensive settlement of debts arising out of the war was rejected, and for more than ten sterile years thereafter the reparation debt and inter-allied debts were regarded by the principal creditor as independent and disconnected problems. American insistence resulted in the demobilization of all organs which could co-ordinate international economic policy and 'plan' the transition from war to peace. Market forces were expected, therefore, to work under conditions which made their failure almost a foregone conclusion.

The lesson for the immediate future would appear to be this: unless there is continued direction and substantial control of an international character during the period when the world should be making the major adjustments which will be required after more than four years of concentration on military production and the organization of civilian scarcity, market forces will again exhibit their inability to cope with structural maladjustments for which they were not responsible.

The necessity for such control for a period would be almost universally accepted by thinking citizens of all schools of political and economic thought. There is a grave danger that a revolt against it will be fostered precisely by those who desire control and regimentation for its own sake.

After the initial failure to prepare the field for the revival of enterprise, market forces had no chance. They were so progressively weakened by tariffs, which are clearly an interference with market forces, and by the growth of monopoly, which may be a natural tendency of large-scale industrial enterprise but is not uncontrollable or inherent in the capitalist system, that it is a distortion of the truth to represent the breakdown of the nineteen-thirties as due to the failure of a system which was not allowed to operate.

Nor can it be accepted without question that international

K

trade tended to decline because it had lost part of its beneficence, or that the need of capital expansion had disappeared. It may be true that internal trade will naturally become a larger proportion of a larger aggregate of total trade, but there is little to suggest that an absolute decrease in external trade is compatible with a larger return of overall activity. The direction and character of international investment will doubtless change, but in a world which is almost everywhere underfed, in which half the population is living on a deplorably low standard, and in which numerous territories are undeveloped it is perverse to think in terms of restriction rather than of expansion.

Theoretically it is conceivable that expansion can take place as rapidly under controlled national economies as under a régime of private enterprise tempered by such measures of over-riding public control as shall generally direct economic activity. But there is nothing in the facts narrated in this work to enforce the conclusion that when we are faced with a choice between more economic freedom than we enjoyed in the twenty years between 1919 and 1939 and a continuance and intensification of the totalitarian economy of war we shall do well to vote for the latter.

It is admitted that 'planned foreign trade', which means the control of exports and imports and exchange control, must be the basis of the planned economic structure which we are invited to adopt in the post-war world. The uninformed reader will be led to think that this kind of planning has worked, in Germany before the war and throughout the world during the war, and therefore been tested by experience. If he reads carefully he will find in the work itself reason for doubting whether it can claim any success in Germany which had the promise of permanence. He will find it stated that 'any attempt, if such had ever been contemplated, to switch the Nazi war economy to the needs of peace, would have faced the Nazis with so gigantic a social and economic problem that war would in any case have appeared as the line of least resistance', and that 'the substitution of State control for private enterprise in Germany's foreign trade, which meant the substitution of administrative decisions by exchange control authorities and economic experts for the profit incentive and experience of private business men, often led to the unnecessary loss of former German markets.' The kind of nightmare economy in which Nazi Germany lived may be a *pis aller* in a world in which international trade has broken down and no concerted efforts are made to revive it, but it is not evidence of the comparative unimportance of international trade or of the impossibility of freeing it for the future.

The reader will also find it stated that war-time experience suggests that public control will not necessarily solve our problem. His attention, however, is not directed to the fact that it cannot be expected to solve the problem because it is a different one. The problem of every country in war (and in Russia and Germany in peace) has been to organize scarcity; there is nothing in experience to prove that it can organize plenty and much in experience to cast doubt upon its power to do so. There is so much popular misconception on this subject that it is perhaps justifiable to point out in a few words what are the salient differences between our present economy and a peace-time régime. Firstly, as said above, we are now busy organizing scarcity of goods available for civilian consumption and their equitable distribution. Secondly, we are all united on the object, which can be simply stated and is a short-term problem. Thirdly, we are substantially united on the means by which that object is to be achieved, and content to leave executive decisions and the solution of executive problems to the Government. Fourthly, we are prepared to accumulate a large internal debt for economically unproductive purposes. Fifthly, we are enabled to concentrate on our task and to neglect international trade because our alliance ensures us the minimum necessary for our food and clothing; we need not pay for our necessary imports.

Only one of these factors will be operative in peace-time; we shall be agreed only on one object, and that only if it is stated in the most general terms as the banishment of fear and want and the progressive improvement of standards of living everywhere. There will be plenty of disagreement as to the means, and there will be nothing like general agreement that the means are to be found in the concluding chapter of this study or that their employment is shown to be desirable by the earlier historical review.

I have attempted to confine this note to a broad statement of policy, and must overlook numerous passages which challenge comment. I shall instance only one. It is stated that, in France, 'the destruction of the *Front Populaire* at the hands of the Conservatives left the industrial working class resentful and embittered and left the direction of French industry and finance in the hands of men who, while able for a time to run the economy successfully on their own terms, were prepared to deliver themselves up to Hitler rather than risk the danger of another attempt from below to oust them from their position of privilege.' A summary judgment of this character on a very complex political and social situation is, to say the least, out of place in an economic study, and calculated to offend even Frenchmen and friends of France who find much to deplore in the events of the last four years preceding the war.

Professor A. G. B. Fisher has read the above Dissenting Note and is in substantial agreement with it.

к*

INDEX